Mastering PostgreSQL 17

Elevate your database skills with advanced deployment, optimization, and security strategies

Hans-Jürgen Schönig

Mastering PostgreSQL 17

Group Product Manager: Apeksha Shetty

Publishing Product Manager: Chayan Majumdar

Book Project Manager: Aparna Nair

Senior Editor: Rohit Singh

Technical Editor: Rahul Limbachiya

Copy Editor: Safis Editing

Proofreader: Rohit Singh

Indexer: Tejal Soni

Production Designer: Gokul Raj S.T

DevRel Marketing Executive: Nivedita Singh

First published: January 2018

Second edition: October 2018

Third edition: November 2019

Fourth edition: November 2020

Fifth edition: January 2023

Sixth edition: December 2024

Production reference: 1061224

Published by Packt Publishing Ltd.

Grosvenor House

11 St Paul's Square

Birmingham

B3 1RB, UK.

ISBN 978-1-83620-597-5

www.packtpub.com

Contributors

About the author

Hans-Jürgen Schönig has 25 years of experience with PostgreSQL. He is the CEO of a PostgreSQL consulting and support company called CYBERTEC PostgreSQL International GmbH, which has successfully served countless customers around the globe. Before founding CYBERTEC PostgreSQL International GmbH in 2000, he worked as a database developer at a private research company that focused on the Austrian labor market, where he primarily worked on data mining and forecast models. He has also written several books about PostgreSQL.

About the reviewer

Rajneesh Verma is a seasoned technology leader with over 18 years of experience, currently heading IT and security at CYBERTEC PostgreSQL Services. Specializing in enterprise design and architecture, he is passionate about building reliable platforms, including database-as-a-service solutions and innovative setups for cloud and on-premises environments, IAAS, PAAS, and security. His technical stack includes PostgreSQL, SQL Server, Python, Flask, HTML, and CSS. Curious by nature, Rajneesh loves figuring out "how things work" and shares this enthusiasm through book reviews, exploring tech, leadership, and innovation with technical depth and approachable storytelling.

Table of Contents

3

Making Use of Indexes   49

4

Handling Advanced SQL   97

5

Log Files and System Statistics   153

6

Optimizing Queries for Good Performance   185

7

Writing Stored Procedures   245

8

Managing PostgreSQL Security   293

9

Handling Backup and Recovery   327

10

Making Sense of Backups and Replication   337

11

Deciding on Useful Extensions   381

12

Troubleshooting PostgreSQL   407

13

Migrating to PostgreSQL   423

Preface

Welcome to *Mastering PostgreSQL 17*, the ultimate guide to unlocking the full potential of one of the world's most popular open source relational databases – PostgreSQL. With decades of history and a community-driven development process, PostgreSQL has become the go-to choice for organizations seeking a robust, scalable, and reliable database solution. This has been true for many years and this will be the case for many years to come.

In this book, we'll take you on a comprehensive journey through the latest features and enhancements in PostgreSQL 17, the newest major release of the database system. Whether you're a seasoned DBA looking to expand your skillset or a developer seeking to improve your application's performance and scalability, this book is designed to help you master the art of working with PostgreSQL and it will hopefully be an enjoyable thing to read that helps you to understand things better, be more productive, and simply have a better time.

Mastering the art of handling data is an ever more important skill that is important to have. In a digital world, "data" is more or less the "new oil" – an important asset that drives the world and the importance of data is growing as we speak. Every sector of IT is data-driven. It does not matter whether you are at the forefront of machine learning or whether you are working on bookkeeping software – at the end of the day, IT is all about data.

PostgreSQL has become a hot technology in the area of open source, and it is an excellent technology to store and process data in the most efficient way possible. This book will teach you how to use PostgreSQL in the most professional way and explain how to operate, optimize, and monitor this core technology, which has become so popular over the years.

By the end of the book, you will be able to use PostgreSQL to its utmost capacity by applying advanced technology and cutting-edge features.

Who this book is for

This book is tailored for database administrators, PostgreSQL developers, and IT professionals aiming to implement advanced functionalities and tackle complex administrative tasks using PostgreSQL 17. A foundational understanding of PostgreSQL and core database concepts is essential, along with familiarity with SQL. Prior experience in database administration will enhance your ability to leverage the advanced techniques discussed throughout the book.

What this book covers

Chapter 1, What is New in PostgreSQL 17, guides you through the most important features that have made it into the new release of PostgreSQL and explains how those features can be used.

Chapter 2, Understanding Transactions and Locking, explains the fundamental concepts of transactions and locking. Both topics are key requirements to understand storage management in PostgreSQL.

Chapter 3, Making Use of Indexes, introduces the concept of indexes, which are the key ingredient when dealing with performance in general. You will learn about simple indexes as well as more sophisticated concepts.

Chapter 4, Handling Advanced SQL, unleashes the full power of SQL and outlines the most advanced functionality a query language has to offer. You will learn about windowing functions, ordered sets, hypothetical aggregates, and a lot more. All those techniques will open a totally new world of functionality.

Chapter 5, Log Files and System Statistics, explains how you can use runtime statistics collected by PostgreSQL to make operations easier and to debug the database. You will be guided through the internal information-gathering infrastructure.

Chapter 6, Optimizing Queries for Good Performance, is all about good query performance and outlines optimization techniques that are essential to bringing your database up to speed to handle even bigger workloads.

Chapter 7, Writing Stored Procedures, introduces you to the concept of server-side code such as functions, stored procedures, and a lot more. You will learn how to write triggers and dive into server-side logic.

Chapter 8, Managing PostgreSQL Security, helps you to make your database more secure and explains what can be done to ensure safety and data protection at all levels.

Chapter 9, Handling Backup and Recovery, helps you to make copies of your database to protect yourself against crashes and database failure.

Chapter 10, Making Sense of Backups and Replication, follows up on backups and recovery and explains additional techniques, such as streaming replication, redundancy, and a lot more. It covers the most advanced topics.

Chapter 11, Deciding on Useful Extensions, explores extensions and additional useful features that can be added to PostgreSQL.

Chapter 12, Troubleshooting PostgreSQL, completes the circle of topics and explains what can be done if things don't work as expected. You will learn how to find the most common issues and understand how problems can be fixed.

Chapter 13, Migrating to PostgreSQL, teaches you how to move your databases to PostgreSQL efficiently and quickly. It covers the most common database systems people will migrate from.

To get the most out of this book

This book has been written for a broad audience. However, some basic knowledge of SQL is necessary to follow along and make full use of the examples presented. In general, it is also a good idea to familiarize yourself with basic Unix commands as most of the book has been produced on Linux and macOS.

Software/hardware covered in the book	Operating system requirements
pgAdmin4	Windows, macOS, or Linux
PostgreSQL 17	
SQL Shell (psql)	

> **Note**
> Some parts of chapters, that is, 8, 9, 10, 11, 12, and 13 are mostly dedicated to Unix/Linux and macOS users, and the rest run fine on Windows.

Conventions used

There are a number of text conventions used throughout this book.

`Code in text`: Indicates code words in text, database table names, folder names, filenames, file extensions, pathnames, dummy URLs, user input, and Twitter handles. Here is an example: "The community has removed this feature and introduced a new variable called `transaction_timeout`, which can be set per session."

A block of code is set as follows:

```
CREATE OR REPLACE FUNCTION on_login_proc()
RETURNS event_trigger AS
$$
BEGIN
    INSERT INTO user_lo (w) VALUES (SESSION_USER);
    RAISE NOTICE 'You are welcome!';
END;
$$ LANGUAGE plpgsql;
```

When we wish to draw your attention to a particular part of a code block, the relevant lines or items are set in bold:

```
test=# SHOW event_triggers;
 event_triggers
```

Any command-line input or output is written as follows:

```
test=# CREATE TABLE t_data (
    id      int,
    data    text
);
```

Bold: Indicates a new term, an important word, or words that you see onscreen. For instance, words in menus or dialog boxes appear in **bold**. Here is an example: "A new process called **summarizer** was added to PostgreSQL."

> **Tips or important notes**
> Appear like this.

Get in touch

Feedback from our readers is always welcome.

General feedback: If you have questions about any aspect of this book, email us at customercare@packtpub.com and mention the book title in the subject of your message.

Errata: Although we have taken every care to ensure the accuracy of our content, mistakes do happen. If you have found a mistake in this book, we would be grateful if you would report this to us. Please visit www.packtpub.com/support/errata and fill in the form.

Piracy: If you come across any illegal copies of our works in any form on the internet, we would be grateful if you would provide us with the location address or website name. Please contact us at copyright@packt.com with a link to the material.

If you are interested in becoming an author: If there is a topic that you have expertise in and you are interested in either writing or contributing to a book, please visit authors.packtpub.com.

Share Your Thoughts

Once you've read *Mastering PostgreSQL 17 – Sixth Edition*, we'd love to hear your thoughts! Scan the QR code below to go straight to the Amazon review page for this book and share your feedback.

https://packt.link/r/1-836-20597-X

Your review is important to us and the tech community and will help us make sure we're delivering excellent quality content.

Download a free PDF copy of this book

Thanks for purchasing this book!

Do you like to read on the go but are unable to carry your print books everywhere?

Is your eBook purchase not compatible with the device of your choice?

Don't worry, now with every Packt book you get a DRM-free PDF version of that book at no cost.

Read anywhere, any place, on any device. Search, copy, and paste code from your favorite technical books directly into your application.

The perks don't stop there, you can get exclusive access to discounts, newsletters, and great free content in your inbox daily

Follow these simple steps to get the benefits:

1. Scan the QR code or visit the link below

https://packt.link/free-ebook/978-1-83620-597-5

2. Submit your proof of purchase
3. That's it! We'll send your free PDF and other benefits to your email directly

What is New in PostgreSQL 17

PostgreSQL has come a long way since its first release in 1986. Today, it's one of the most widely used open source databases in the world. In this chapter, you will be introduced to all the most important and shiny features of PostgreSQL 17. Of course, the list of new stuff is almost infinite; therefore, this chapter will focus on those things that are expected to be most relevant to the majority of users.

We will cover the following topics in this chapter:

- Understanding DBA and administration features
- Using SQL and developer features
- Making use of new replication and backup add-ons
- Considering breaking changes in PostgreSQL 17

By the end of this chapter, you will know all about these shiny new features and you will understand how to use the new functionality in more detail.

Understanding DBA and administration features

In every release, a comprehensive set of features is added to make the lives of **database administrators (DBAs)** easier and more effective. The same is true for PostgreSQL. So, let us take a look and dive into the new features of PostgreSQL 17.

Terminating long transactions

PostgreSQL supports various features to limit the duration of statements, the maximum time a query will wait for locks, and a lot more. However, there is one feature that has been requested by customers for some time and has finally made it into the next release of PostgreSQL – the ability to limit the duration of a transaction. In the past, PostgreSQL supported an instance-wide configuration variable called `old_snapshot_threshold`. The idea of this variable was to limit the maximum length of a transaction to avoid table bloat as well as some other issues that are dangerous for the server. However, the `old_snapshot_threshold` variable could only be set per instance and not in a more fine-grained way. Thus, the community has removed this feature and introduced a new variable called `transaction_timeout`, which can be set per session.

The default value of this new setting is "unlimited" (0):

```
test=# SHOW transaction_timeout ;
 transaction_timeout
---------------------
 0
(1 row)
```

However, if you want to limit the duration of your transaction, you can simply set a value inside your session. The following command sets the configuration variable to 5 seconds (5000 milliseconds):

```
test=# SET transaction_timeout TO 5000;
SET
test=# BEGIN;
BEGIN
test=*# SELECT now();
              now
-------------------------------
 2024-06-21 19:37:35.81715+00
(1 row)


test=*# SELECT now();
              now
-------------------------------
 2024-06-21 19:37:35.81715+00
(1 row)


test=*# SELECT now();
FATAL:  terminating connection due to transaction timeout
server closed the connection unexpectedly
	This probably means the server terminated abnormally
	before or while processing the request.
The connection to the server was lost. Attempting reset: Succeeded.
test=#
```

After 5 seconds, our transaction will terminate and PostgreSQL closes the connection entirely. It is the easiest way to eliminate unnecessarily long transactions and prevent table bloat.

However, PostgreSQL 17 has more to offer.

Improved event triggers

Event triggers are an important feature and were introduced in PostgreSQL many years ago. What is the main idea behind an event trigger? Imagine somebody changes your data structure by creating a table, an index, or some other kind of object. An event trigger allows us to react to those events and execute code as needed.

In PostgreSQL, some functionality has been added. First of all, we now have a configuration variable that looks as follows:

```
test=# SHOW event_triggers;
 event_triggers
----------------
 on
(1 row)
```

When this one is enabled, event triggers will fire for all applicable statements. The important part here is that only superusers can change this value to a different setting.

In PostgreSQL, there is also the possibility to create an event trigger on REINDEX. However, this is not as critical as the next new feature that has to be discussed – the ability to trigger LOGIN. Now, what is a LOGIN trigger? It basically calls a function (or fires) when a new connection to the database is established. Needless to say, this is an incredibly powerful footgun and can cause serious issues because many things can go wrong.

But before we discuss running a trigger during LOGIN, it makes sense to take a look at a simple example and understand how things work in general. The most basic example is to write a trigger that is supposed to track login attempts in a table. To do that, we can create a simple table:

```
login_trigger=# CREATE TABLE user_logins (
    id serial,
    who text
);
CREATE TABLE
```

In PostgreSQL, a trigger will always launch a function. Therefore, the first step is to come up with the function we want to run:

```
CREATE FUNCTION on_login_proc()
RETURNS event_trigger AS
$$
BEGIN
    INSERT INTO user_logins (who)
    VALUES (SESSION_USER);
```

```
    RAISE NOTICE 'You are welcome!';
END;
$$ LANGUAGE plpgsql;
```

What we see here is that the return value of this function is `event_trigger` – it is a special data type specifically designed for this purpose. The rest is plain and simple PL/pgSQL code that does not require a return value.

Finally, we can define the trigger itself:

```
CREATE EVENT TRIGGER on_login_event
ON ddl_command_start
EXECUTE FUNCTION on_login_proc();
```

Note that the event we are interested in is `login`. The rest is like a normal event trigger that calls a function of our choice. In the next step, we can already enable the trigger:

```
login_trigger=# ALTER EVENT TRIGGER on_login_trigger ENABLE ALWAYS;
ALTER EVENT TRIGGER
```

Congratulations, the trigger has been deployed successfully. Let us log out and reconnect to the database. After we have reestablished the new connection, we can already see the content of our audit table:

```
login_trigger=# SELECT * FROM user_logins;
 id | who
----+-----
  1 | hs
(1 row)
```

This looks pretty successful but why did we just call this type of trigger a footgun? Let us modify the function and see what happens:

```
CREATE OR REPLACE FUNCTION on_login_proc()
RETURNS event_trigger AS
$$
BEGIN
    INSERT INTO user_lo (w) VALUES (SESSION_USER);
    RAISE NOTICE 'You are welcome!';
END;
$$ LANGUAGE plpgsql;
```

The function is essentially buggy. The consequences are nothing short of a total failure:

```
linux$ psql login_trigger
psql: error: connection to server
  on socket "/tmp/.s.PGSQL.5432"
```

```
  failed: FATAL:   relation "user_lo" does not exist
 LINE 1: INSERT INTO user_lo (w) VALUES (SESSION_USER)

 QUERY:   INSERT INTO user_lo (w) VALUES (SESSION_USER)
 CONTEXT:   PL/pgSQL function on_login_proc() line 3 at SQL statement
```

The entire authentication process will fail. That is important because small mistakes can lead to large-scale outages. It is therefore highly recommended to think twice before deploying event triggers to handle login attempts. What is important to understand is that PostgreSQL does exactly what it has been designed to do – it just does so in a sensitive area that can cause a lot of trouble.

The problem is that when you have installed a broken event trigger and you want to get rid of it, you have a hard time ahead. First of all, you have to shut down the database and then you have to start it in single-user mode (https://www.postgresql.org/docs/17/app-postgres.html). In single-user mode, you can then drop the event trigger because, in single-user mode, event triggers are actually disabled – you can therefore log in without those functions being fired.

Inspecting wait events in PostgreSQL

PostgreSQL provides a shiny new system view called pg_wait_events. For many years, wait events have been an integral feature of PostgreSQL, and allowed us to monitor and inspect all kinds of performance problems. However, in real life, DBAs often had to switch between the database and the documentation to figure out which type of wait events actually do exist.

pg_wait_events puts an end to this type of problem and provides an easy way to understand which events are there and what they mean. Here is an example:

```
test=# \x
Expanded display is on.

test=# SELECT *
FROM pg_wait_events
WHERE name = 'DataFileFlush';
-[ RECORD1 ]-----------------------------------------
type        | IO
name        | DataFileFlush
description | Waiting for a relation data file to
              reach durable storage
```

What we can see here is that DataFileFlush means that we are waiting for the operating system to write the data to your physical storage device.

The beauty is that this new view provides a comprehensive overview that might surprise many people:

```
test=# SELECT  type, count(*)
FROM     pg_wait_events
GROUP BY ROLLUP (1)
ORDER BY 1;
   type     | count
------------+-------
 Activity   |    16
 BufferPin  |     1
 Client     |     9
 Extension  |     1
 IO         |    77
 IPC        |    57
 LWLock     |    81
 Lock       |    12
 Timeout    |    10
            |   264
(10 rows)
```

Yes, this is true: PostgreSQL knows a grand total of 264 different types of events, which is a huge number.

Digging into checkpoints and background writing

The background writer and the checkpoint process have been around for many years. In the latest release of PostgreSQL, the system statistics related to those processes have been changed. First of all, a couple of fields have been removed from the pg_stat_bgwriter system view:

```
test=# \d pg_stat_bgwriter
    View "pg_catalog.pg_stat_bgwriter"
     Column         |          Type    ...
--------------------+-------------------------
 buffers_clean      | bigint
 maxwritten_clean   | bigint
 buffers_alloc      | bigint
 stats_reset        | timestamp with time zone
```

The view is way more compact now because a great deal of this information has been moved to a new system view that is defined as follows:

```
test=# \d pg_stat_checkpointer
                  View "pg_catalog.pg_stat_checkpointer"
         Column           |          Type ...
--------------------------+-------------------------
```

```
num_timed              | bigint
num_requested          | bigint
restartpoints_timed    | bigint
restartpoints_req      | bigint
restartpoints_done     | bigint
write_time             | double precision
sync_time              | double precision
buffers_written        | bigint
stats_reset            | timestamp with time zone
```

The `pg_stat_checkpointer` view contains most of the information previously found in `pg_stat_bgwriter`. Therefore, it is necessary to adjust your monitoring queries to reflect those changes.

Improving pg_stat_statements

The `pg_stat_statements` module is an extension for PostgreSQL that is shipped as part of the `contrib` package. To me, it has always been the gold standard for performance analysis; therefore, I am happy to see even more changes made to improve the data provided by this view. There are various interesting ones worth mentioning:

- `CALL` statements now support parameters as placeholders

- Allows placeholders for savepoint and 2PC-related commands

- Tracks `DEALLOCATE` statements

- Adds support for local block I/O statistics

- Adds more details to JIT statistics

- Adds an optional argument to `pg_stat_statements_reset()`

Overall, these improvements will make `pg_stat_statements` more compact and thus make it easier to find relevant information.

Adding permissions for maintenance tasks

In the past, maintenance was often done by the superuser. The goal is to avoid this. Therefore, more and more permissions and roles have been added over the years to reduce the need for the superuser.

PostgreSQL 17 has added the `MAINTAIN` permission to a couple of commands, which allows us to execute various important tasks such as the following:

- `VACUUM` and `ANALYZE`

- `CLUSTER`

- REINDEX

- REFRESH MATERIALIZED VIEW

- LOCK TABLE

The feature works as follows:

```
test=# CREATE USER joe;
CREATE ROLE
test=# GRANT MAINTAIN ON …
```

The tab completion will reveal the full power of this new feature. The number of options you have are quite numerous:

- ALL FUNCTIONS IN SCHEMA DATABASE

- TABLE

- ALL PROCEDURES IN SCHEMA

- DOMAIN

- LANGUAGE

- ROUTINE

- TABLESPACE

- ALL ROUTINES IN SCHEMA

- FOREIGN DATA WRAPPER

- LARGE OBJECT

- SCHEMA

- TYPE

- ALL SEQUENCES IN SCHEMA

- FOREIGN SERVER

- PARAMETER

- SEQUENCE

- ALL TABLES IN SCHEMA

- FUNCTION

- PROCEDURE

After dealing with DBA-related functionalities, we can now turn our attention to some more developer-oriented functionalities.

Using SQL and developer features

In this section, we will discuss some of the most desired developer and SQL features that have made it into PostgreSQL 17.

Teaching COPY error handling

Let us start with my personal favorite: COPY is finally able to handle errors in a reasonably good way. Many people were frustrated by the error-handling behavior. Standard PostgreSQL will stop COPY when it hits an error. It is good to see that this vital functionality has made it into the official release of PostgreSQL.

The main question arising is: how can we make use of this feature? Here is a simple command to create a sample table:

```
test=# CREATE TABLE t_data (
    id     int,
    data   text
);
CREATE TABLE
```

The goal is to import the following dataset into the table and make sure those errors are handled properly:

```
1   hans
2   paul
abc joe
4   jane
def james
5   laura
```

What we see here is that the data is definitely wrong. The following listing proves this beyond doubt:

```
test=# COPY t_data FROM '/tmp/file.txt';
ERROR:  invalid input syntax for type integer: "abc"
CONTEXT:  COPY t_data, line 3, column id: "abc"
```

Fortunately, we can handle this kind of problem in PostgreSQL 17 and simply ignore the error:

```
test=# COPY t_data FROM '/tmp/file.txt'
WITH (ON_ERROR 'ignore');
NOTICE:  2 rows were skipped due to data type incompatibility
COPY 4
test=# SELECT * FROM t_data ;
 id | data
----+-------
```

```
1 | hans
2 | paul
4 | jane
5 | laura
(4 rows)
```

PostgreSQL will import the data and simply skip over invalid data. A NOTICE label will indicate how many rows have been skipped. As of version 17, two types of ON_ERROR settings are supported: stop and ignore. In the future, it is likely that more options will be available.

Splitting and merging partitions

In the previous years, there has not been a single version of PostgreSQL that has not provided relevant improvements to partitioning as a whole. The same holds true for the new release. This time, the development team has been working on splitting and merging partitions, which has been a frequent requirement over the years.

The following listing shows how a simple table including a partition can be created:

```
CREATE TABLE t_timeseries (
    id serial,
    d date,
    payload text
) PARTITION BY RANGE (d);


CREATE TABLE t_timeseries_2024
PARTITION OF t_timeseries
FOR VALUES FROM ('2024-01-01')
TO ('2025-01-01');
```

Here is a typical example one would encounter in real life. We have some kind of time series and we are using range partitions to split the data into smaller chunks for various reasons (faster cleanup, scalability, and so on). However, tables are often too large and we have to break them up into smaller chunks. This is when PostgreSQL can do some of the heavy lifting for us:

```
ALTER TABLE t_timeseries
   SPLIT PARTITION t_timeseries_2024
   INTO (
     PARTITION t_timeseries_2024_h1
    FOR VALUES FROM ('2024-01-01') TO ('2024-07-01'),
   PARTITION t_timeseries_2024_h2
     FOR VALUES FROM ('2024-07-01') TO ('2025-01-01')
 );
```

What we do here is take our partition and split it into two new chunks that contain roughly half of the data. Note that this is a single command that takes care of this operation.

While splitting partitions into various pieces might be by far the most common new operation, it is also possible to reverse this decision and unify various partitions into a single entity. The way to do that is by using the ALTER TABLE ... MERGE PARTITIONS ... command, which is equally as easy to use as the SPLIT command that we have observed and tested before:

```
ALTER TABLE t_timeseries
MERGE PARTITIONS (
    t_timeseries_2024_h1,
    t_timeseries_2024_h2
)
INTO t_timeseries_2024;
```

All we have to do here is to tell PostgreSQL which partitions are supposed to form the new entity and let the database engine do its magic.

Tuning numbers into binary and octal values

One of the lesser-known features that made it into PostgreSQL is the ability to convert numbers to a binary and, respectively, octal representation. Two overloaded functions have been added – to_bin and to_oct:

```
test=# \df *to_bin*
   List of functions
   Schema    |  Name  | Result data type | Argument data types | Type
-------------+--------+------------------+---------------------+------
 pg_catalog  | to_bin | text             | bigint              | func
 pg_catalog  | to_bin | text             | integer             | func
(2 rows)


test=# \df *to_oct*
   List of functions
   Schema    |  Name  | Result data type | Argument data types | Type
-------------+--------+------------------+---------------------+------
 pg_catalog  | to_oct | text             | bigint              | func
 pg_catalog  | to_oct | text             | integer             | func
(2 rows)
```

Both functions can be called with 32- or 64-bit integer values. The following listing shows an example of those functions in action:

```
test=# SELECT to_bin(4711), to_oct(4711);
    to_bin    | to_oct
```

```
---------------+--------
 1001001100111 | 11147
(1 row)
```

Improving MERGE even more

MERGE has been around for various releases. In SQL, the MERGE command is used to merge data from two tables into one table. This command is useful when you need to update or insert rows based on a common column between the two tables.

The new release of PostgreSQL has also introduced another feature, namely, WHEN NOT MATCHED BY SOURCE THEN. This additional syntax allows us to define the behavior even better and adds some flexibility.

Here is how it works:

```
CREATE TABLE t_demo (
    a int PRIMARY KEY,
    b int
);

INSERT INTO t_demo
VALUES (1, 4711),
       (2, 5822),
       (3, 6933);

CREATE TABLE t_source (
    a int PRIMARY KEY,
    b int
);

INSERT INTO t_source
VALUES (2, 6822),
       (3, 6933),
       (4, 1252);

MERGE INTO t_demo AS t1
USING t_source AS t2
ON t1.a = t2.a
WHEN MATCHED THEN
    UPDATE SET b = t1.b * 100
WHEN NOT MATCHED THEN
```

```
    INSERT (a, b) VALUES (t2.a, t2.b)
WHEN NOT MATCHED BY SOURCE THEN
    DELETE
RETURNING t1.*, t2.*;
```

This MERGE statement will return the following data:

```
a |    b     | a |  b
--+---------+---+------
1 |    4711 |   |
2 |  582200 | 2 | 6822
3 |  693300 | 3 | 6933
4 |    1252 | 4 | 1252
(4 rows)
```

RETURNING * can be really useful to debug the statement as a whole. The same is true in my example: a = 1 is available in the original table but not in the source table and the row is therefore deleted. In the case of a = 2 and a = 3, we got a full match and, therefore, the UPDATE statement will execute. a = 4 is only present in the t_source table and is therefore inserted into the t_demo table.

The following table shows what we can expect to find after the MERGE operation:

```
a |    b
--+---------
2 |  582200
3 |  693300
4 |    1252
(3 rows)
```

As you can see, all three cases defined in the MERGE statement have been executed successfully. The question is: which row was touched by which rule? We can modify the RETURNING clause a bit:

```
RETURNING merge_action(), t1.*, t2.*
```

In this case, PostgreSQL will provide us with even more information, as we can see in the following listing:

```
merge_action | a |    b     | a |  b
-------------+---+---------+---+------
DELETE       | 1 |    4711 |   |
UPDATE       | 2 |  582200 | 2 | 6822
UPDATE       | 3 |  693300 | 3 | 6933
INSERT       | 4 |    1252 | 4 | 1252
(4 rows)
```

Additional JSON functionality

The number of JSON-related functionalities has skyrocketed over the years. The same is true for version 17, which provides many more features that will make JSON easier to use and more powerful overall. The first thing that caught my attention was the fact that more standard compliant functions have been added – namely, JSON_EXISTS(), JSON_QUERY(), and JSON_VALUE().

What is also noteworthy is JSON_TABLE, which allows us to turn a JSON document into a tabular format in one go. This is pretty similar to what XMLTABLE does.

The syntax might look as follows:

```
SELECT jt.*
FROM customers,
    JSON_TABLE (
        js, '$.favorites[*]' COLUMNS (
            id FOR ORDINALITY,
            country text PATH '$.country',
            branch text PATH '$.industry[*].branch' WITH WRAPPER,
            ceo text PATH '$.company[*].ceo' WITH WRAPPER
        )
    ) AS jt;
```

What this does is to address various elements in the JSON document and return it in a format we can actually and safely read.

Creating BRIN indexes in parallel

Technically, this is not a developer feature, but given the fact that performance topics are often hard to categorize, I decided to include this here. BRIN indexes are often used in data warehouses to quickly filter data without carrying the overhead of full-blown B-tree indexes. Creating B-trees has long been possible using more than one CPU. However, in PostgreSQL 17, it is now possible to create BRIN indexes in parallel, which can greatly speed up the process

Making use of new replication and backup add-ons

As you've worked your way through some of the new developer-related features, you're now ready to address the new version's powerful set of advanced features related to database administration. In this section, we'll delve into the more complex world of database management, exploring topics that are new to PostgreSQL 17.

More powerful pg_dump, again

pg_dump is the single most well-known tool to run a basic backup in PostgreSQL. It is a command-line utility that comes with PostgreSQL, used for backing up a PostgreSQL database or extracting its schema and data in a format suitable for loading into another PostgreSQL database. The main question is: after 38 years of development, what might have been added to this tool that is not already there? Well, the answer is that you can now define a file that configures what you want to dump and what you want to ignore. By adding the --filter option, we can feed a file containing all our desired rules.

Handling incremental base backups

Talking about backups in general, pg_basebackup has also been extended. PostgreSQL 17 supports the idea of incremental base backups. Why is that important? Often, we might want to use a simple backup policy such as "Take a base backup every night and keep it for 7 days." The problem is that if your database is large (say, 50 TB) but static (virtually no changes), you will waste a lot of space just to store the backup, which can, of course, lead to serious cost considerations. Incremental base backup addresses this issue:

```
summarize_wal = on
wal_summary_keep_time = '7d'
```

A new process called **summarizer** was added to PostgreSQL. It will keep track of all those blocks that have been changed and help pg_basebackup to only copy those blocks that have indeed been touched, which reduces the amount of space needed for the backups to drop significantly.

Here is how it works:

```
pg_basebackup -h source_server.com \
  -D /data/full --checkpoint=fast
...
pg_basebackup -h source_server.com \
  --checkpoint=fast \
  --incremental=/data/full/backup_manifest \
    -D /backup/incremental
```

The secret to success is the backup manifest that is needed to run the incremental backup. It contains all the necessary information to tell the tooling what has to be done.

After running those two commands, we have a full backup as well as an incremental one. The question now is: how can we combine those things together and turn them into something usable? The following command shows how this works:

```
$ pg_combinebackup --help
pg_combinebackup reconstructs full backups from incrementals.
```

```
Usage:
  pg_combinebackup [OPTION]... DIRECTORY...

Options:
  -d, --debug                generate lots of debugging output
  -n, --dry-run              do not actually do anything
  -N, --no-sync              do not wait for changes to be written
                             safely to disk
  -o, --output               output directory
  -T, --tablespace-mapping=OLDDIR=NEWDIR
                             relocate tablespace in OLDDIR to NEWDIR
      --clone                clone (reflink) instead of copying files
      --copy-file-range      copy using copy_file_range() syscall
      --manifest-checksums=SHA{224,256,384,512}|CRC32C|NONE
                             use algorithm for manifest checksums
      --no-manifest          suppress generation of backup manifest
      --sync-method=METHOD   set method for syncing files to disk
  -V, --version              output version information, then exit
  -?, --help                 show this help, then exit
```

pg_combinebackup does exactly what we want. It creates the desired set of files that are then needed for recovery. Given our example, we could use the following instruction to combine our full backup with our incremental backup:

```
pg_combinebackup -o /data/combined \
  /data/full \
  /backup/incremental
```

What is noteworthy here is that this process works for one base backup and exactly one incremental backup. However, in real life, we might have to apply a set of incremental backups to reach the desired state. In this case, we can simply list all those incremental ones one after the other, as shown in the next listing:

```
pg_combinebackup -o /data/combined \
  /data/full \
  /backup/incremental \
  /backup/incremental2 \
  /backup/incremental3
```

Simply list all the incremental backups to produce the desired state.

Logical replication upgraded

In PostgreSQL, there are two types of replication: physical (binary) and logical (text) replication. While binary replication is ideal for all kinds of backup, logical replication has become more and more widespread in heterogeneous environments to achieve cross-cloud portability.

The trouble is that publications and subscriptions (the backbone of logical replication) were lost during `pg_upgrades` prior to PostgreSQL 17. This has now changed and has significantly eased the burden.

Adding pg_createsubscriber

In the new release, we can all enjoy a new command-line tool called `pg_createsubscriber`. What is the purpose of this new tool? When people decide to use logical replication, the initial sync phase can take quite a while – especially when the database instance is large. `pg_createsubscriber` has been designed to help solve this problem. It converts a physical standby (binary replication) and turns it into a logical standby by wiring all the publications, subscriptions, and so on for you. For each database, a replication set will be created and automatically configured. The command has to be executed on the target system.

Considering breaking changes in PostgreSQL 17

PostgreSQL tries to keep the user interface as constant as possible. However, once in a while, breaking changes are necessary. This is, of course, also true for the current release.

Let us take a look at some of those changes. The first thing that has happened is the fact that support for AIX has dropped. This somehow makes sense because nobody here at CYBERTEC nor any other fellow PostgreSQL consultant I know has seen deployment on AIX in years.

The next thing is that `--disable-thread-safety` and MSVC builds have been dropped. All those things won't hurt users at all.

What is more important is that some toolings have been removed from the `contrib` section. The one module I am referring to is `adminpack`, which has not been widely used anyway. The same is true for `snapshot too old`, which has been replaced with a way better implementation (`transaction_timeout`).

Finally, `search_path` is now fully secured during maintenance operations, which means that maintenance scripts should use fully qualified object names.

Summary

The new release has countless new features and it is close to impossible to mention them all. During the development cycle, well over 2,000 commits have happened and thousands of things have been improved.

Some of the key features, such as fault-tolerant `COPY` and improved partitioning, have long been awaited and finally made it into the core. Things such as incremental base backups will significantly reduce the cost of large-scale PostgreSQL deployments. And other features simply lead to a way better user experience.

Therefore, relax, lean back, and enjoy the brand-new release of PostgreSQL, which will be covered in this book in great detail.

In *Chapter 2, Understanding Transactions and Locking*, we will discuss important concepts such as transactions and locking, which form a core component of every relational database system.

2

Understanding Transactions and Locking

Now that we've been introduced to PostgreSQL 17 and all the new shiny features it brings to the table, we want to focus our attention on the next important topic. **Locking** is a vital concept for any kind of database. It is not enough to understand how locking works just to write proper or better applications – it is also essential from a performance point of view and, therefore, proper locking behavior will directly translate to an excellent user experience. Without handling locks properly, your applications might not only be slow – they might also behave in very unexpected ways (for example, timeouts, unpredictable results, and a lot more). In my opinion, locking is the key to performance. Why is that the case? There is no slower form of execution than waiting on something. Even more CPUs will not speed up waiting. Therefore, understanding locking and transactions is important for administrators and developers alike.

In this chapter, you will learn about the following topics:

- Working with PostgreSQL transactions
- Understanding basic locking
- Making use of FOR SHARE and FOR UPDATE
- Understanding transaction isolation levels
- Observing deadlocks and similar issues
- Utilizing advisory locks
- Optimizing storage and managing cleanup

By the end of this chapter, you will be able to understand and utilize PostgreSQL transactions in the most efficient way possible. You will see that many applications can benefit from improved performance.

Working with PostgreSQL transactions

PostgreSQL provides you with highly advanced transaction machinery that offers countless features to developers and administrators alike. In this section, we will look at the basic concept of transactions. The first important thing to know is that, in PostgreSQL, everything is a transaction. If you send a simple query to the server, it is already a transaction. Here is an example:

```
test=# SELECT now(), now();
               now             |              now
-------------------------------+-------------------------------
 2024-05-24 12:59:33.594603+02 | 2024-05-24 12:59:33.594603+02
(1 row)
```

In this case, the SELECT statement will be a separate transaction. If the same command is executed again, different timestamps will be returned.

> **Tip**
>
> Keep in mind that the now() function will return the transaction time. The SELECT statement will, therefore, always return two identical timestamps. If you want the *real time*, consider using clock_timestamp() instead of now().

If more than one statement has to be a part of the same transaction, the BEGIN statement must be used, as follows:

```
test=# \h BEGIN
Command: BEGIN
Description: start a transaction block
Syntax:
 BEGIN [ WORK | TRANSACTION ] [ transaction_mode [, ...] ]
where transaction_mode is one of:
   ISOLATION LEVEL { SERIALIZABLE | REPEATABLE READ | READ COMMITTED |
READ UNCOMMITTED }
     READ WRITE | READ ONLY
     [ NOT ] DEFERRABLE
URL: https://www.postgresql.org/docs/17/sql-begin.html
```

The BEGIN statement will ensure that more than one command is packed into a transaction. Here is how it works:

```
test=# BEGIN;
BEGIN
test=*# SELECT now();
               now
-------------------------------
```

```
 2024-05-24 13:00:39.864604+02
(1 row)
```

```
test=*# SELECT now();
                now
-------------------------------
 2024-05-24 13:00:39.864604+02
(1 row)
```

```
test=*# COMMIT;
COMMIT
```

The important point here is that both timestamps will be identical. As we mentioned earlier, we are talking about transaction time.

To end the transaction, COMMIT can be used:

```
test=# \h COMMIT
Command: COMMIT
Description: commit the current transaction
Syntax:
 COMMIT [ WORK | TRANSACTION ] [ AND [ NO ] CHAIN ]
 URL: https://www.postgresql.org/docs/17/sql-commit.html
```

There are a few syntax elements here. You can just use COMMIT, COMMIT WORK, or COMMIT TRANSACTION. All three commands have the same meaning. If this is not enough, there's more – the END command is identical to COMMIT and can be used interchangeably:

```
test=# \h END
Command: END
Description: commit the current transaction
Syntax:
 END [ WORK | TRANSACTION ] [ AND [ NO ] CHAIN ]
 URL: https://www.postgresql.org/docs/17/sql-end.html
```

As you can see, the END clause is the same as the COMMIT clause from a feature point of view.

ROLLBACK is the counterpart of COMMIT. Instead of successfully ending a transaction, it will simply stop the transaction without ever making things visible to other transactions, as shown in the following code:

```
test=# \h ROLLBACK
Command: ROLLBACK
Description: abort the current transaction
```

```
Syntax:
 ROLLBACK [ WORK | TRANSACTION ] [ AND [ NO ] CHAIN ]
 URL: https://www.postgresql.org/docs/17/sql-rollback.html
```

Some applications use ABORT instead of ROLLBACK (those two commands are interchangeable in PostgreSQL). The meaning is the same. What is really useful in PostgreSQL is the idea of transaction chains. COMMIT AND CHAIN will help you to achieve exactly that:

```
test=# SHOW transaction_read_only;
 transaction_read_only
-----------------------
 Off
 (1 row)
test=# BEGIN TRANSACTION READ ONLY ;
 BEGIN
test=*# SELECT 1;
 ?column?
----------
        1
 (1 row)
test=*# COMMIT AND CHAIN;
 COMMIT
test=*# SHOW transaction_read_only;
 transaction_read_only
-----------------------
 On
 (1 row)
test=*# SELECT 1;
 ?column?
----------
        1
 (1 row)
test=*# COMMIT AND NO CHAIN;
 COMMIT
test=# SHOW transaction_read_only;
 transaction_read_only
-----------------------
 Off
 (1 row)
test=# COMMIT;
 WARNING: there is no transaction in progress
 COMMIT
```

Let's go through this example step by step:

1. Display the content of the `transaction_read_only` setting. It is `Off` because, by default, we are in read/write mode.

2. Start a read-only transaction using `BEGIN`. This will automatically adjust the `transaction_read_only` variable.

3. Commit the transaction using `AND CHAIN`, and then PostgreSQL will automatically start a new transaction featuring the same properties as the previous transaction.

In our example, we will also be in read-only mode, just like the transaction before. There is no need to explicitly open a new transaction and set whatever values again, which can dramatically reduce the number of round trips between the application and the server. In the case of high latency systems, saving on commands can really make a difference. If a transaction is committed normally (= `NO CHAIN`), the read-only attribute of the transaction will be gone.

Handling errors inside a transaction

In this section, we will dig deeper into error handling and learn how to handle problems inside a database transaction. It is not always the case that transactions are correct from beginning to end. Things might just go wrong for whatever reason. However, in PostgreSQL, only error-free transactions can be committed. The following listing shows a failing transaction, which errors out due to a `division by zero` error:

```
test=# BEGIN;
 BEGIN
test=*# SELECT 1;
 ?column?
----------
        1
(1 row)
test=*# SELECT 1 / 0;
 ERROR: division by zero
test=!# SELECT 1;
 ERROR: current transaction is aborted, commands ignored until end of
transaction block
test=!# SELECT 1;
 ERROR: current transaction is aborted, commands ignored until end of
transaction block
test=!# COMMIT;
 ROLLBACK
```

Note that `division by zero` did not work out.

> **Note**
>
> In any proper database, an instruction similar to this will instantly error out and make the statement fail.

It is important to point out that PostgreSQL will error out. After an error has occurred, no more instructions will be accepted, even if those instructions are semantically and syntactically correct. It is still possible to issue COMMIT. However, PostgreSQL will roll back the transaction because it is the only correct thing to be done at that point.

Making use of SAVEPOINT

In professional applications, it can be pretty hard to write reasonably long transactions without ever encountering a single error. To solve this problem, users can utilize something called SAVEPOINT, as follows:

```
test=# \h SAVEPOINT
Command:     SAVEPOINT
Description: define a new savepoint within the current transaction
Syntax:
SAVEPOINT savepoint_name

URL: https://www.postgresql.org/docs/17/sql-savepoint.html
```

As the name indicates, a savepoint is a safe place inside a transaction that the application can return to if things go terribly wrong. Here is an example:

```
test=# BEGIN;
BEGIN
test=*# SELECT 1;
 ?column?
----------
        1
 (1 row)
test=*# SAVEPOINT a;
SAVEPOINT
test=*# SELECT 2 / 0;
ERROR: division by zero
test=!# SELECT 2;
ERROR: current transaction is aborted, commands ignored until end of
transaction block
test=!# ROLLBACK TO SAVEPOINT a;
ROLLBACK
```

```
test=*# SELECT 3;
 ?column?
----------
        3
(1 row)
test=*# COMMIT;
COMMIT
```

After the first SELECT clause, I decided to create a savepoint to make sure that the application can always return to this point inside the transaction. As you can see, the savepoint has a name, which is referred to later.

After returning to the savepoint called a, the transaction can proceed normally. The code has jumped back to before the error, so everything is fine.

The number of savepoints inside a transaction is practically unlimited. We have seen customers with over 250,000 savepoints in a single operation. PostgreSQL can easily handle this.

If you want to remove a savepoint from inside a transaction, there's the RELEASE SAVEPOINT command:

```
test=# \h RELEASE
Command: RELEASE SAVEPOINT
Description: destroy a previously defined savepoint
Syntax:
 RELEASE [ SAVEPOINT ] savepoint_name
URL: https://www.postgresql.org/docs/17/sql-release-savepoint.html
```

Many people ask what will happen if you try to reach a savepoint after a transaction has ended. The answer is that the life of a savepoint ends as soon as the transaction ends. In other words, there is no way to return to a certain point in time after the transactions have been completed.

Transactional DDLs

PostgreSQL has a very nice feature that is unfortunately not present in many commercial database systems. In PostgreSQL, it is possible to run DDLs (commands that change the data structure) inside a transaction block. In a typical commercial system, a DDL will implicitly commit the current transaction by default. This does not occur in PostgreSQL.

Apart from some minor exceptions (DROP DATABASE, CREATE TABLESPACE, DROP TABLESPACE, and so on), all DDLs in PostgreSQL are transactional, which is a huge advantage and a real benefit to end users.

Here is an example:

```
test=# BEGIN;
BEGIN
```

```
test=*# CREATE TABLE t_test (id int);
CREATE TABLE
test=*# ALTER TABLE t_test ALTER COLUMN id TYPE int8;
ALTER TABLE
test=*# \d t_test
              Table "public.t_test"
 Column |  Type   | Collation | Nullable | Default
--------+---------+-----------+----------+---------
 id     | bigint  |           |          |
test=*# ROLLBACK;
ROLLBACK
test=# \d t_test
Did not find any relation named "t_test".
```

In this example, a table has been created and modified, and the entire transaction has been aborted. As you can see, there is no implicit COMMIT command or any other strange behavior. PostgreSQL simply acts as expected.

Transactional DDLs are especially important if you want to deploy software. Just imagine running a **content management system** (CMS). If a new version is released, you'll want to upgrade. Running the old version would still be okay; running the new version would also be okay, but you really don't want a mixture of old and new. Therefore, deploying an upgrade in a single transaction is highly beneficial, as it upgrades an atomic operation.

> **Note**
>
> To facilitate good software practices, we can include several separately coded modules from our source control system into a single deployment transaction.

After dealing with transaction and error handling in general, it is important to focus our attention more on locking and concurrency.

Understanding basic locking

In this section, you will learn about basic locking mechanisms. The goal is to understand how locking works in general and how to get simple applications right.

To show you how things work, we will create a simple table. For demonstrative purposes, I will add one row to the table using a simple INSERT command:

```
test=# CREATE TABLE  t_test (id int);
CREATE TABLE
```

```
test=# INSERT INTO t_test VALUES (0);
INSERT 0 1
```

The first important thing is that tables can be read concurrently. Many users reading the same data at the same time won't block each other. This allows PostgreSQL to handle thousands of users without any problems.

The question now is what happens if reads and writes occur at the same time? Here is an example. Let's assume that the table contains one row and `id = 0`:

Transaction 1	Transaction 2
`BEGIN;`	`BEGIN;`
`UPDATE t_test SET id = id + 1 RETURNING *;`	
User will see 1	`SELECT * FROM t_test`
	User will see 0
	`COMMIT;`
`COMMIT;`	

Table 2.1 – Transaction isolation

Two transactions are opened. The first one will change a row. However, this is not a problem, as the second transaction can proceed. It will return to the old row as it was before `UPDATE`. This behavior is called **multi-version concurrency control (MVCC)**.

> **Note**
>
> A transaction will only see data if it has been committed by the write transaction before the initiation of the read transaction. One transaction cannot inspect the changes that have been made by another active connection. A transaction can see only those changes that have already been committed.

There is also a second important aspect – many commercial or open source databases are still unable to handle concurrent reads and writes. In PostgreSQL, this is absolutely not a problem – reads and writes can coexist.

> **Note**
>
> Write transactions won't block read transactions.

What will happen when two people try to change the same row at the same time? Can we actually end up with data loss or does PostgreSQL handle the operation properly? Let us give it a try:

Transaction 1	Transaction 2
BEGIN;	BEGIN;
UPDATE t_test SET id = id + 1 RETURNING *;	
It will return 2	UPDATE t_test SET id = id + 1 RETURNING *;
	It will wait for transaction 1
COMMIT;	It will wait for transaction 1
	It will reread the row, find 2, and return 3
	COMMIT;

Table 2.2 – Handling concurrent updates

Suppose you want to count the number of hits on a website. If you run the preceding code, no hits will be lost because PostgreSQL guarantees that one UPDATE statement is performed after another.

> **Note**
>
> PostgreSQL will only lock rows affected by UPDATE. So, if you have 1,000 rows, you can theoretically run 1,000 concurrent changes on the same table.

It is also worth noting that you can always run concurrent reads. Our two writes will not block reads.

Avoiding typical mistakes and explicit locking

In my life as a professional PostgreSQL consultant (https://www.cybertec-postgresql.com), I have seen a couple of mistakes that are repeated frequently. If there are constants in life, these typical mistakes are definitely among them. The following listing shows one of the most common problems:

Transaction 1	Transaction 2
BEGIN;	BEGIN;
SELECT max(id) FROM product;	SELECT max(id) FROM product;
User will see 17	User will see 17
User decides to set to 18	User decides to set to 18

Transaction 1	**Transaction 2**
`INSERT INTO product … VALUES (18, ...)`	`INSERT INTO product … VALUES (18, ...)`
`COMMIT;`	`COMMIT;`

Table 2.3 – Potential locking-related problems

In this case, there will be either a duplicate key violation or two identical entries. Neither variation of the problem is all that appealing.

One way to fix this problem is to use explicit table locking. The following code shows us the syntax definition of LOCK:

```
test=# \h LOCK
Command: LOCK
Description: lock a table
Syntax:
 LOCK [ TABLE ] [ ONLY ] name [ * ] [, ...] [ IN lockmode MODE ] [
NOWAIT ]
 where lockmode is one of:
     ACCESS SHARE | ROW SHARE | ROW EXCLUSIVE | SHARE UPDATE EXCLUSIVE
     | SHARE | SHARE ROW EXCLUSIVE | EXCLUSIVE | ACCESS EXCLUSIVE
URL: https://www.postgresql.org/docs/17/sql-lock.html
```

As you can see, PostgreSQL offers eight types of locks to lock an entire table. In PostgreSQL, a lock can be as light as an ACCESS SHARE lock or as heavy as an ACCESS EXCLUSIVE lock. The following list shows what these locks do:

- ACCESS SHARE: This type of lock is taken by reads and conflicts only with ACCESS EXCLUSIVE, which is set by DROP TABLE, and so on. Practically, this means that SELECT cannot start if a table is about to be dropped. This also implies that DROP TABLE has to wait until a reading transaction is complete.

- ROW SHARE: PostgreSQL takes this kind of lock in the case of SELECT FOR UPDATE or SELECT FOR SHARE. It conflicts with EXCLUSIVE and ACCESS EXCLUSIVE.

- ROW EXCLUSIVE: This lock is taken by INSERT, UPDATE, and DELETE. It conflicts with SHARE, SHARE ROW EXCLUSIVE, EXCLUSIVE, and ACCESS EXCLUSIVE.

- SHARE UPDATE EXCLUSIVE: This kind of lock is taken by CREATE INDEX CONCURRENTLY, ANALYZE, ALTER TABLE, VALIDATE, and some other flavors of ALTER TABLE, as well as by VACUUM (not VACUUM FULL). It conflicts with the SHARE UPDATE EXCLUSIVE, SHARE, SHARE ROW EXCLUSIVE, EXCLUSIVE, and ACCESS EXCLUSIVE lock modes.

- **SHARE**: When an index is created, SHARE locks will be set. These conflict with ROW EXCLUSIVE, SHARE UPDATE EXCLUSIVE, SHARE ROW EXCLUSIVE, EXCLUSIVE, and ACCESS EXCLUSIVE.

- **SHARE ROW EXCLUSIVE**: This one is set by CREATE TRIGGER and some forms of ALTER TABLE and conflicts with everything except ACCESS SHARE.

- **EXCLUSIVE**: This type of lock is by far the most restrictive one. It protects against reads and writes alike. If this lock is taken by a transaction, nobody else can read or write to the table that's been affected.

- **ACCESS EXCLUSIVE**: This lock prevents concurrent transactions from reading and writing.

Given the PostgreSQL locking infrastructure, one solution to the max problem we outlined previously would be as follows. The example in the following code shows how to lock a table:

```
BEGIN;
LOCK  TABLE  product IN ACCESS EXCLUSIVE MODE;
INSERT INTO  product SELECT max(id) + 1, ... FROM product;
COMMIT;
```

Keep in mind that this is a pretty nasty way of doing this kind of operation because nobody else can read or write to the table during your operation. Therefore, ACCESS EXCLUSIVE should be avoided at all costs.

Checking for locks

Checking for locks is not a trivial matter. There are various options. The first one is to see whether a lock is causing an issue at all. Note that to simulate this, you have to open various command lines. Remember, each session will create an entry in pg_stat_activity:

```
test=# SELECT pid, wait_event_type, wait_event, query
FROM   pg_stat_activity
WHERE  datname = 'test';
...
-[ RECORD 3 ]---+---------------------------------------------
pid             | 23068
wait_event_type | Client
wait_event      | ClientRead
query           | lock table t_test in access exclusive mode ;
-[ RECORD 4 ]---+---------------------------------------------
pid             | 23071
wait_event_type | Lock
wait_event      | relation
query           | SELECT count(*) FROM t_test;
```

What we can see here is the query causing the lock, as well as the query waiting on the lock (as shown in the `wait` event).

Considering alternative solutions

There is an alternative solution to this problem. Consider an example where you are asked to write an application to generate invoice numbers. The tax office might require you to create invoice numbers without gaps and without duplicates. How would you do this? Of course, one solution would be a table lock. However, you can really do better. Here is what you can do to handle the numbering problem we are trying to solve:

```
test=# CREATE TABLE t_invoice (id int PRIMARY KEY);
CREATE TABLE
test=# CREATE TABLE  t_watermark (id int);
CREATE TABLE
test=# INSERT INTO  t_watermark VALUES (0);
INSERT 0
test=# WITH  x AS (UPDATE t_watermark
           SET id = id + 1 RETURNING *)
INSERT INTO  t_invoice
SELECT * FROM x RETURNING *;
 id
----
  1
 (1 row)
```

In this case, we introduced a table called `t_watermark`. It contains just one row. The `WITH` command will be executed first. The row will be locked and incremented, and the new value will be returned. Only one person can do this at a time. The value returned by the CTE is then used in the `invoice` table. It is guaranteed to be unique. The beauty is that there is only a simple row lock on the `watermark` table, which leads to no reads being blocked in the `invoice` table. Overall, this way is more scalable.

Making use of FOR SHARE and FOR UPDATE

Sometimes, data is selected from the database, then some processing happens in the application, and finally, some changes are made back on the database side. This is a classic example of `SELECT  FOR UPDATE`.

Here is an example that shows the way `SELECT` is often executed in the wrong way:

```
BEGIN;
SELECT * FROM  invoice WHERE  processed = false;
** application magic  will  happen here  **
UPDATE invoice SET processed = true  ...
COMMIT;
```

The problem here is that two people might select the same unprocessed data. Changes that are made to these processed rows will then be overwritten. In short, a race condition will occur.

To solve this problem, developers can make use of SELECT FOR UPDATE. Here's how it can be used. The following example will show a typical scenario:

```
BEGIN;
SELECT * FROM invoice WHERE processed = false FOR UPDATE;
** application magic  will  happen here  **
UPDATE invoice SET processed = true ...
COMMIT;
```

SELECT FOR UPDATE will lock rows just like UPDATE would. This means that no changes can happen concurrently. All locks will be released on COMMIT as usual.

If one SELECT FOR UPDATE command is waiting for another SELECT FOR UPDATE command, you will have to wait until the other one completes (COMMIT or ROLLBACK). If the first transaction doesn't want to end for whatever reason, the second transaction possibly waits forever. To avoid this, we can use SELECT FOR UPDATE NOWAIT. Consider the following scenario:

Transaction 1	Transaction 2
BEGIN;	BEGIN;
SELECT ... FROM tab ... WHERE FOR UPDATE NOWAIT;	
Some processing	
Some processing	SELECT ... FROM tab ... WHERE FOR UPDATE NOWAIT;
Some processing	ERROR: could not obtain lock on row in relation tab

Table 2.4 – Managing NOWAIT

If NOWAIT is not flexible enough for you, consider using lock_timeout. It will contain the amount of time you want to wait on locks. You can set this on a per-session level:

```
test=# SET lock_timeout TO 5000;
SET
```

In this case, the value is set to 5 seconds.

While SELECT does basically no locking, SELECT FOR UPDATE can be pretty harsh. Just imagine the following business process – we want to fill up an airplane that has 200 seats. Many people want to book seats concurrently. In this case, the following might happen:

Transaction 1	Transaction 2
BEGIN;	BEGIN;
SELECT ... FROM flight LIMIT 1 FOR UPDATE;	
Waiting on user input	SELECT ... FROM flight LIMIT 1 FOR UPDATE;
Waiting on user input	It has to wait

Table 2.5 – Concurrent FOR UPDATE operations

The trouble is that only one seat can be booked at a time. There are potentially 200 seats available, but everybody has to wait for the first person. While the first seat is blocked, nobody else can book a seat, even if people don't care which seat they get in the end.

SELECT FOR UPDATE SKIP LOCKED will fix the problem. Let's create some sample data first:

```
test=# CREATE TABLE t_flight AS
SELECT * FROM generate_series(1, 200) AS id;
SELECT 200
```

Transaction 1	Transaction 2
BEGIN;	BEGIN;
SELECT * FROM t_flight LIMIT 2 FOR UPDATE SKIP LOCKED;	SELECT * FROM t_flight LIMIT 2 FOR UPDATE SKIP LOCKED;
Returns 1 and 2	Returns 3 and 4

Table 2.6 – Concurrent SKIP LOCKED operations

If everybody wants to fetch two rows, we can serve 100 concurrent transactions at a time without having to worry about blocking transactions.

> **Note**
>
> Keep in mind that waiting is the slowest form of execution. If only one transaction can be active at a time, it is pointless to buy ever more expensive servers if your real problems are caused by locking and conflicting transactions in general.

However, there's more. In some cases, FOR UPDATE can have unintended consequences. Most people are not aware of the fact that FOR UPDATE will have an impact on foreign keys. Let's assume that we have two tables – one to store currencies and the other to store accounts. The following code shows an example of this:

```
CREATE TABLE t_currency (
      id      int,
      name    text,
      PRIMARY KEY (id)
);
INSERT INTO t_currency VALUES (1, 'EUR');
INSERT INTO t_currency VALUES (2, 'USD');

CREATE TABLE t_account (
      id            int,
      currency_id   int REFERENCES t_currency (id)
                        ON UPDATE CASCADE
                        ON DELETE CASCADE,
      balance       numeric
);

INSERT INTO t_account VALUES (1, 1, 100);
INSERT INTO t_account VALUES (2, 1, 200);
```

Now, we want to run SELECT FOR UPDATE on the account table:

Transaction 1	Transaction 2
BEGIN;	
SELECT * FROM t_account FOR UPDATE;	BEGIN;
Waiting for the user to proceed	UPDATE t_currency SET id = id * 10;
Waiting for the user to proceed	It will wait on transaction 1

Table 2.7 – Handling FOR UPDATE

Although there is a SELECT FOR UPDATE command on accounts, the UPDATE command on the currency table will be blocked. This is necessary because, otherwise, there is a chance of breaking the foreign key constraint altogether. In a fairly complex data structure, you can therefore easily end up with contentions in an area where they are least expected (some highly important lookup tables).

As well as FOR UPDATE, there's also FOR SHARE, FOR NO KEY UPDATE, and FOR KEY SHARE. The following list describes what these modes actually mean:

- FOR NO KEY UPDATE: This one is pretty similar to FOR UPDATE. However, the lock is weaker, and therefore, it can coexist with SELECT FOR SHARE.

- FOR SHARE: FOR UPDATE is pretty strong and works on the assumption that you are definitely going to change rows. FOR SHARE is different because more than one transaction can hold a FOR SHARE lock at the same time.

- FOR KEY SHARE: This behaves similarly to FOR SHARE, except that the lock is weaker. It will block FOR UPDATE but will not block FOR NO KEY UPDATE.

The important thing here is to simply try things out and observe what happens. Improving locking behavior is really important, as it can dramatically improve the scalability of your application.

Understanding transaction isolation levels

Up until now, you have seen how to handle locking, as well as some basic concurrency. In this section, you will learn about transaction isolation. To me, this is one of the most neglected topics in modern software development. Only a small fraction of software developers are actually aware of this issue, which, in turn, leads to mind-boggling bugs.

Here is an example of what can happen:

Transaction 1	Transaction 2
BEGIN;	
SELECT sum(balance) FROM t_account;	BEGIN;
User will see 300	INSERT INTO t_account (balance) VALUES (100);
	COMMIT;
SELECT sum(balance) FROM t_account;	
User will see 400	
COMMIT;	

Table 2.8 – Transactional visibility

Most users would actually expect the first transaction to always return 300, regardless of the second transaction. However, this isn't true. By default, PostgreSQL runs in the READ COMMITTED transaction isolation mode. This means that every statement inside a transaction will get a new snapshot of the data, which will be constant throughout the query.

> **Note**
>
> A SQL statement will operate on the same snapshot and will ignore changes by concurrent transactions while it is running.

If you want to avoid this, you can use TRANSACTION ISOLATION LEVEL REPEATABLE READ. In this transaction isolation level, a transaction will use the same snapshot throughout the entire transaction. Here's what will happen:

Transaction 1	Transaction 2
BEGIN TRANSACTION ISOLATION LEVEL REPEATABLE READ;	
SELECT sum(balance) FROM t_account;	BEGIN TRANSACTION ISOLATION LEVEL REPEATABLE READ;
User will see 300	INSERT INTO t_account (balance) VALUES (100);
	COMMIT;
SELECT sum(balance) FROM t_account;	SELECT sum(balance) FROM t_account;
User will see 300	User will see 400
COMMIT;	

Table 2.9 – Managing REPEATABLE READ transactions

As we've outlined, the first transaction will freeze its snapshot of the data and provide us with constant results throughout the entire transaction. This feature is especially important if you want to run reports. The first and last pages of a report should always be consistent and operate on the same data. Therefore, the repeatable read is key to consistent reports.

Note that isolation-related errors won't always pop up instantly. Sometimes, trouble is noticed years after an application has been moved to production.

> **Note**
>
> Repeatable read is not more expensive than read committed. There is no need to worry about performance penalties. For normal **online transaction processing (OLTP)**, read committed has various advantages because changes can be seen much earlier and the odds of unexpected errors are usually lower.

Considering serializable snapshot isolation transactions

On top of read committed and repeatable read, PostgreSQL offers **serializable snapshot isolation (SSI)** transactions. So, overall, PostgreSQL supports three isolation levels (read committed, repeatable read, and serializable). Note that `Read Uncommitted` (which still happens to be the default in some commercial databases) is not supported; if you try to start a read uncommitted transaction, PostgreSQL will silently map to read committed. Let's get back to the serializable isolation level.

> **Note**
>
> If you want to know more about this isolation level, consider checking out `https://wiki.postgresql.org/wiki/Serializable`.

The idea behind serializable isolation is simple; if a transaction is known to work correctly when there is only a single user, it will also work in the case of concurrency when this isolation level is chosen. However, users have to be prepared; transactions may fail (by design) and error out. In addition to this, a performance penalty has to be paid.

> **Note**
>
> Consider using serializable isolation only when you have a decent understanding of what is going on inside the database engine.

Observing deadlocks and similar issues

Deadlocks are an important issue and can happen in every database. Basically, a deadlock will happen if two transactions have to wait on each other.

In this section, you will see how this can happen. Let's suppose we have a table containing two rows:

```
CREATE TABLE t_deadlock (id int);
INSERT INTO t_deadlock VALUES (1), (2);
```

The following example shows what can happen:

Transaction 1	Transaction 2
BEGIN;	BEGIN;
UPDATE t_deadlock SET id = id * 10 WHERE id = 1;	UPDATE t_deadlock SET id = id * 10 WHERE id = 2;
UPDATE t_deadlock SET id = id * 10 WHERE id = 2;	

Transaction 1	Transaction 2
BEGIN;	BEGIN;
Waiting on transaction 2	UPDATE t_deadlock SET id = id * 10 WHERE id = 1;
Waiting on transaction 2	Waiting on transaction 1
	Deadlock will be resolved after 1 second (deadlock_timeout)
COMMIT;	ROLLBACK;

Table 2.10 – Understanding deadlocks

As soon as the deadlock is detected, the following error message will show up:

```
psql: ERROR: deadlock detected
DETAIL: Process 91521 waits for ShareLock on transaction 903;
    blocked by process 77185.
 Process 77185 waits for ShareLock on transaction 905;
 blocked by process 91521.
 HINT: See server log for query details.
 CONTEXT: while updating tuple (0,1) in relation "t_deadlock"
```

PostgreSQL is even kind enough to tell us which row has caused the conflict. In my example, the root of all evil is a tuple, (0, 1). What you can see here is ctid, which is a unique identifier of a row in a table. It tells us about the physical position of a row inside a table. In this example, it is the first row in the first block (0).

It is even possible to query this row if it is still visible in your transaction. Here's how it works:

```
test=# SELECT ctid, *
FROM    t_deadlock
WHERE   ctid = '(0, 1)';
ctid   | id
-------+-----
(0,1)  |  10
 (1 row)
```

Keep in mind that this query might not return a row if it has already been deleted or modified.

However, this isn't the only case where deadlocks can lead to potentially failing transactions. Transactions also cannot be serialized for various reasons. The following example shows what can happen. To make this example work, I assume that you've still got the two rows, `id = 1` and `id = 2`:

Transaction 1	Transaction 2
`BEGIN TRANSACTION ISOLATION LEVEL REPEATABLE READ;`	
`SELECT * FROM t_deadlock;`	
Two rows will be returned	
	`DELETE FROM t_deadlock;`
`SELECT * FROM t_deadlock:`	
Two rows will be returned	
`DELETE FROM t_deadlock;`	
The transaction will error out	
`ROLLBACK;` – we cannot COMMIT anymore (`ERROR: could not serialize access due to concurrent delete`)	

Table 2.11 – Transaction isolation and DELETE

In this example, two concurrent transactions are at work. As long as the first transaction is just selecting data, everything is fine because PostgreSQL can easily preserve the illusion of static data. But what happens if the second transaction commits a `DELETE` command? As long as there are only reads, there is still no problem. The trouble begins when the first transaction tries to delete or modify data that is already dead at this point. The only solution for PostgreSQL is to error out due to a conflict caused by our transactions:

```
test=# DELETE FROM t_deadlock;
psql: ERROR: could not serialize access due to concurrent update
```

Practically, this means that end users have to be prepared to handle erroneous transactions. If something goes wrong, properly written applications must be able to try again.

Utilizing advisory locks

PostgreSQL has highly efficient and sophisticated transaction machinery that is capable of handling locks in a really fine-grained and efficient way. A few years ago, people came up with the idea of using this code to synchronize applications with each other. Thus, advisory locks were born.

When using advisory locks, it is important to mention that they won't go away on COMMIT as normal locks do. Therefore, it is really important to make sure that unlocking is done properly and in a totally reliable way.

If you decide to use an advisory lock, what you really lock is a number. So, this isn't about rows or data; it is really just a number. Here's how it works:

Transaction 1	Transaction 2
BEGIN;	
SELECT pg_advisory_lock(15);	
	SELECT pg_advisory_lock(15);
	It has to wait
COMMIT;	It still has to wait
SELECT pg_advisory_unlock(15);	It still has to wait
	Lock is taken

Table 2.12 – Sessions 1 and 2 on an advisory lock

The first transaction will lock 15. The second transaction has to wait until this number has been unlocked again. The second session will even wait until after the first one has committed. This is highly important, as you cannot rely on the fact that the end of the transaction is nicely and miraculously solving things for you.

If you want to unlock all locked numbers, PostgreSQL offers the pg_advisory_unlock_all() function to do exactly this:

```
test=# SELECT pg_advisory_unlock_all();
pg_advisory_unlock_all
----------------------
 
(1 row)
```

Sometimes, you might want to see whether you can get a lock and error out if this isn't possible. To achieve this, PostgreSQL offers a couple of functions; to see a list of all such available functions, enter \df *try*advisory* at the command line.

Optimizing storage and managing cleanup

Transactions are an integral part of the PostgreSQL system. However, transactions come with a small price tag attached. As we've already shown in this chapter, sometimes, concurrent users will be presented with different data. Not everybody will get the same data returned by a query. In addition to this, DELETE and UPDATE are not allowed to actually overwrite data, since ROLLBACK would not work. If you happen to be in the middle of a large DELETE operation, you cannot be sure whether you will be able to use COMMIT or not. In addition to this, data is still visible while you perform the DELETE operation, and sometimes, data is even visible once your modification has long since finished.

Consequently, this means that cleanup has to happen asynchronously. A transaction cannot clean up its own mess, and any COMMIT/ROLLBACK operation might be too early to take care of dead rows.

The solution to this problem is VACUUM. The following code block provides you with a syntax overview (https://www.postgresql.org/docs/17/sql-vacuum.html):

```
test=# \h VACUUM
Command:       VACUUM
Description: garbage-collect and optionally analyze a database
Syntax:
VACUUM [ ( option [, ...] ) ] [ table_and_columns [, ...] ]

where option can be one of:

    FULL [ boolean ]
    FREEZE [ boolean ]
    VERBOSE [ boolean ]
    ANALYZE [ boolean ]
    DISABLE_PAGE_SKIPPING [ boolean ]
    SKIP_LOCKED [ boolean ]
    INDEX_CLEANUP { AUTO | ON | OFF }
    PROCESS_MAIN [ boolean ]
    PROCESS_TOAST [ boolean ]
    TRUNCATE [ boolean ]
    PARALLEL integer
    SKIP_DATABASE_STATS [ boolean ]
    ONLY_DATABASE_STATS [ boolean ]
    BUFFER_USAGE_LIMIT size

  and table_and_columns is:

    table_name [ ( column_name [, ...] ) ]
```

VACUUM will visit all of the pages that potentially contain modifications and find all the dead space. The free space that's found is then tracked by the **free space map** (FSM) of the relation.

Note that VACUUM will, in most cases, not shrink the size of a table. Instead, it will track and find free space inside existing storage files.

> **Note**
> Tables will usually have the same size after VACUUM. If there are no valid rows at the end of a table, file sizes can go down, although this is rare. This is not the rule, but rather the exception.

What this means to end users will be outlined in the *Watching VACUUM at work* subsection of this chapter.

Configuring VACUUM and autovacuum

Back in the early days of PostgreSQL projects, people had to run VACUUM manually. Fortunately, those days are long gone. Nowadays, administrators can rely on a tool called autovacuum, which is part of the PostgreSQL server infrastructure. It automatically takes care of cleanup and works in the background. It wakes up once per minute (see autovacuum_naptime = 1 in postgresql. conf) and checks whether there is work to do. If there is work, autovacuum will fork up to three worker processes (see autovacuum_max_workers in postgresql.conf).

The main question is, when does autovacuum trigger the creation of a worker process?

> **Note**
> Actually, the autovacuum process doesn't fork processes itself. Instead, it tells the main process to do so. This is done to avoid zombie processes in the event of failure and to improve robustness.

The answer to this question can, again, be found in postgresql.conf, as shown in the following code:

```
autovacuum_vacuum_threshold = 50
autovacuum_analyze_threshold = 50
autovacuum_vacuum_scale_factor = 0.2
autovacuum_analyze_scale_factor = 0.1
autovacuum_vacuum_insert_threshold = 1000
```

The autovacuum_vacuum_scale_factor command tells PostgreSQL that a table is worth vacuuming if 20% of its data has been changed. The trouble is that if a table consists of one row, one change is already 100%. It makes absolutely no sense to fork a complete process to clean up just one row. Therefore, autovacuum_vacuum_threshold says that we need 20% plus at least 50 rows. Otherwise, VACUUM won't kick in. The same mechanism is used when it comes to the creation of optimizer statistics. We need 10% plus at least 50 rows to justify new optimizer statistics. Ideally, autovacuum creates new statistics during a normal VACUUM to avoid unnecessary trips to the table.

However, there is more – in the past, autovacuum was not triggered by workloads consisting of only INSERT statements, which could be a major issue. The new autovacuum_vacuum_insert_threshold parameter was added to fix exactly this kind of problem. From PostgreSQL 13 onward, the autovacuum activity will happen even if only INSERT statements are occurring in the database.

Digging into transaction wraparound-related issues

There are two more settings in `postgresql.conf` that are quite important to understand to really make use of PostgreSQL. As we have stated already, understanding VACUUM is key to performance:

```
autovacuum_freeze_max_age = 200000000
autovacuum_multixact_freeze_max_age = 400000000
```

To understand the overall problem, it is important to understand how PostgreSQL handles concurrency. The PostgreSQL transaction machinery is based on the comparison of transaction IDs and the states that transactions are in.

Let's look at an example. If I am transaction ID `4711` and you happen to be `4712`, I won't see you because you are still running. If I am transaction ID `4711` but you are transaction ID `3900`, I will see you. If your transaction has failed, I can safely ignore all of the rows that are produced by your failing transaction.

The trouble is as follows – transaction IDs are finite, not unlimited. At some point, they will start to wrap around. In reality, this means that transaction number 5 might actually be after transaction number `800,000,000`. How does PostgreSQL know what was first? It does so by storing a watermark. At some point, those watermarks will be adjusted, and this is exactly when VACUUM starts to be relevant. By running VACUUM (or `autovacuum`), you can ensure that the watermark is adjusted in such a way that there are always enough future transaction IDs left to work with.

> **Note**
>
> Not every transaction will increase the transaction ID counter. As long as a transaction is still reading, it will only have a virtual transaction ID. This ensures that transaction IDs are not burned too quickly.

The `autovacuum_freeze_max_age` command defines the maximum number of transactions (age) that a table's `pg_class.relfrozenxid` field can attain before a VACUUM operation is forced to prevent transaction ID wraparound within the table. This value is fairly low because it also has an impact on clog cleanup (the **clog** or **commit log** is a data structure that stores two bits per transaction, which indicates whether a transaction is running, aborted, committed, or still in a subtransaction).

The `autovacuum_multixact_freeze_max_age` command configures the maximum age that a table's `pg_class.relminmxid` field can attain before a VACUUM operation is forced to prevent the `multixact` ID wraparound within the table. Freezing tuples is an important performance issue, and there will be more on this process in *Chapter 6, Optimizing Queries for Good Performance*, where we will discuss query optimization.

In general, trying to reduce the VACUUM load while maintaining operational security is a good idea. A VACUUM operation on large tables can be expensive, and therefore, keeping an eye on these settings makes perfect sense.

A word on VACUUM FULL

Instead of the normal VACUUM, you can also use VACUUM FULL. However, I really want to point out that VACUUM FULL actually locks the table and rewrites the entire relationship. In the case of a small table, this might not be an issue. However, if your tables are large, the table lock can really kill you in minutes! VACUUM FULL blocks upcoming writes, and therefore, some people talking to your database might get the impression that it is down. Hence, a lot of caution is advised.

> **Note**
>
> To get rid of VACUUM FULL, I recommend that you check out pg_squeeze (https://www.cybertec-postgresql.com/en/introducing-pg_squeeze-a-postgresql-extension-to-auto-rebuild-bloated-tables/), which can rewrite a table without blocking writes.

Watching VACUUM at work

Now, it is time to see VACUUM in action. I have included this section here because my practical work as a PostgreSQL consultant and supporter (https://www.postgresql.org/support/) indicates that most people only have a very vague understanding of what happens on the storage side.

To stress this point again, in most cases, VACUUM will not shrink your tables; space is usually not returned to the filesystem.

Here is my example, which shows you how to create a small table with customized autovacuum settings. The table is filled with 100000 rows:

```
CREATE TABLE t_test (id int)
WITH (autovacuum_enabled = off);
INSERT INTO t_test
SELECT * FROM generate_series(1, 100000);
```

The idea is to create a simple table containing 100000 rows. Note that it is possible to turn autovacuum off for specific tables. Usually, this is not a good idea for most applications. However, there is a corner case, where autovacuum_enabled = off makes sense. Just consider a table whose life cycle is very short. It doesn't make sense to clean out tuples if the developer already knows that the entire table will be dropped within seconds. In data warehousing, this can be the case if you use tables as staging areas. VACUUM is turned off in this example to ensure that nothing happens in the background. Everything you see is triggered by me and not by some process.

First of all, consider checking the size of the table by using the following command:

```
test=# SELECT pg_size_pretty(pg_relation_size('t_test'));
 pg_size_pretty
---------------
```

```
3544 kB
(1 row)
```

The `pg_relation_size` command returns the size of a table in bytes. The `pg_size_pretty` command will take this number and turn it into something human-readable.

Then, all of the rows in the table will be updated using a simple UPDATE statement, as shown in the following code:

```
test=# UPDATE t_test SET id = id + 1;
UPDATE 100000
```

What happens is highly important to understand PostgreSQL. The database engine has to copy all the rows. Why? First of all, we don't know whether the transaction will be successful, so the data cannot be overwritten. The second important aspect is that a concurrent transaction might still be seeing the old version of the data.

The UPDATE operation will copy rows.

Logically, the size of the table will be larger after the change has been made:

```
test=# SELECT pg_size_pretty(pg_relation_size('t_test'));
 pg_size_pretty
----------------
 7080 kB
(1 row)
```

After UPDATE, people might try to return space to the filesystem:

```
test=# VACUUM t_test;
VACUUM
```

As we stated previously, VACUUM does not return space to the filesystem in most cases. Instead, it will allow space to be reused. The table, therefore, doesn't shrink at all:

```
test=# SELECT pg_size_pretty(pg_relation_size('t_test'));
pg_size_pretty
----------------
 7080 kB
(1 row)
```

However, the next UPDATE will not make the table grow because it will eat the free space inside the table. Only a second UPDATE would make the table grow again because all the space is gone, so additional storage is needed:

```
test=# UPDATE t_test SET id = id + 1;
UPDATE 100000
```

```
test=# SELECT pg_size_pretty(pg_relation_size('t_test'));
pg_size_pretty
----------------
 7080 kB
 (1 row)
test=# UPDATE t_test SET id = id + 1;
UPDATE 100000
test=# SELECT pg_size_pretty(pg_relation_size('t_test'));
 pg_size_pretty
----------------
 10 MB
 (1 row)
```

If I had to decide on a single thing you should remember after reading this book, this is it. Understanding storage is the key to performance and administration in general.

Let's run some more queries:

```
VACUUM t_test;
UPDATE t_test SET id = id + 1;
VACUUM t_test;
```

Again, the size is unchanged (pg_relation_size will yield the same). Let's see what's inside the table:

```
test=# SELECT ctid, * FROM t_test ORDER BY ctid DESC;
  ctid       | id
-------------+--------
 . . .
 (1327, 46)  | 112
 (1327, 45)  | 111
 (1327, 44)  | 110
 . . .
 (884, 20)   | 99798
 (884, 19)   | 99797
 . . .
```

The ctid command is the physical position of a row on a disk. By using ORDER BY ctid DESC, you will basically read the table backward in physical order. Why should you care? Because there are some very small values and some very big values at the end of the table. The following code shows how the size of the table changes when data is deleted:

```
test=# DELETE FROM t_test
WHERE id > 99000
OR id < 1000;
```

```
DELETE 1999
test=# VACUUM t_test;
VACUUM
test=# SELECT pg_size_pretty(pg_relation_size('t_test'));
 pg_size_pretty
----------------
 3504 kB
 (1 row)
```

Although only 2% of the data has been deleted, the size of the table has gone down by two-thirds. The reason for this is that if VACUUM only finds dead rows after a certain position in the table, it can return space to the filesystem. This is the only case in which you will actually see the table size go down. Of course, normal users have no control over the physical position of data on the disk. Therefore, storage consumption will most likely stay somewhat the same unless all rows are deleted.

> **Important note**
>
> Why are there so many small and big values at the end of the table anyway? After the table is initially populated with 100,000 rows, the last block is not completely full, so the first UPDATE will fill up the last block with changes. This shuffles the end of the table a bit. In this carefully crafted example, this is the reason for the strange layout at the end of the table.

In real-world applications, the impact of this observation cannot be stressed enough. There is no performance tuning without really understanding storage.

Making use of more VACUUM features

VACUUM has steadily improved over the years. In this section, you will learn about some of the most important features.

In many cases, VACUUM can skip pages. This is especially true when the visibility map suggests that a block is visible to everyone. VACUUM may also skip a page that is heavily used by some other transaction. DISABLE_PAGE_SKIPPING disables this kind of behavior and ensures that all pages are cleaned during this run.

One more way to improve on VACUUM is to use SKIP_LOCKED; the idea here is to make sure that VACUUM does not harm concurrency. If SKIP_LOCKED is used, VACUUM will automatically skip over relations, which cannot instantly be locked, thus avoiding conflict resolution. This kind of feature can be very useful in the event of heavy concurrency. One of the important and sometimes overlooked aspects of VACUUM is the need to clean up indexes. After VACUUM has successfully processed a heap, indexes are taken care of. If you want to prevent this from happening, you can make use of INDEX_CLEANUP. By default, INDEX_CLEANUP is true, but depending on your workload, you might decide to skip index cleanup in some rare cases. So, what are those rare cases? Why might anybody not want to clean up indexes? The answer is simple – if your database may potentially soon shut down due to transaction wraparound, it makes sense to run VACUUM as quickly as possible. If you've got a choice between downtime and some kind of postponed cleanup, you should opt for VACUUM quickly to keep your database alive.

In recent versions of PostgreSQL, the PROCESS_TOAST option has been added. The idea is to give users a chance to skip TOAST altogether. In real life, there are not too many cases when this is actually desirable.

The next option that has been added is TRUNCATE, either true or false. As we have mentioned already, it can happen that VACUUM cuts off a file at the end if only dead tuples are found. This behavior can now be controlled. The default value is, of course, true. However, you can disable file truncation if it is necessary.

VACUUM used to work using a single CPU core for a long time. However, those times have changed for good. It is now possible for VACUUM to make full use of your system and utilize more than one CPU core. Usually, the number of cores is determined by the size of the table, similar to how it is with normal SELECT statements. By using the PARALLEL option, you can decide how many cores VACUUM is supposed to use.

Summary

In this chapter, you learned about transactions, locking and its logical implications, and the general architecture the PostgreSQL transaction machinery can have for storage, concurrency, and administration. You saw how rows are locked, and some of the features (such as advisory locks, concurrency, and a lot more) that are available in PostgreSQL.

In *Chapter 3, Making Use of Indexes*, you will learn about one of the most important topics in database work – indexing. You will also learn about the PostgreSQL query optimizer, as well as various types of indexes and their behavior.

3

Making Use of Indexes

In *Chapter 2, Understanding Transactions and Locking*, you learned about concurrency and locking. In this chapter, it's time to attack indexing and therefore the very core of performance head-on. The importance of this topic cannot be stressed enough – indexing is (and will most likely remain) one of the most important topics in the work of every database engineer.

Having over 25 years of professional, full-time PostgreSQL consulting and PostgreSQL 24/7 support experience (www.cybertec-postgresql.com), I can say one thing for sure: bad indexing is the main source of bad performance. Of course, it's important to adjust memory parameters and all that. However, this is all in vain if indexes aren't used properly. There is simply no replacement for a missing index. To make my point clear, there's no way to achieve good performance without proper indexing, so always make it a point to check the indexing if performance is bad. My recommendation is that if performance is bad, always check for missing indexes before anything else.

What's often misunderstood here is a simple thing – let's assume the following scenario:

- 1000 queries x 1 ms = 1 second
- 1 query x 1000 ms = 1 second

Note that each line represents 50% of the total time spent. In other words, 1 out of 1,001 queries causes half the load. If we could just remove this single slow query, we could double the speed. Proper indexing might just be the secret to getting rid of this slow operation.

This is the reason behind dedicating an entire chapter to indexing alone. This will give you as many insights as possible.

In this chapter, we'll cover the following topics:

- Understanding simple queries and the cost model
- Improving speed using clustered tables
- Understanding additional B-tree features
- Introducing operator classes

- Understanding PostgreSQL index types
- Achieving better answers with fuzzy searching
- Understanding full-text searches

By the end of this chapter, you'll understand how indexes can be used beneficially in PostgreSQL.

Understanding simple queries and the cost model

In this section, we'll get started with indexes. To understand how things work, some test data is needed. The following code snippet shows how data can easily be created:

```
test=# DROP TABLE IF EXISTS t_test;
DROP TABLE
test=# CREATE TABLE t_test (id serial, name text);
CREATE TABLE
test=# INSERT INTO t_test (name) SELECT 'hans'
FROM generate_series(1, 2000000);
INSERT 0 2000000
test=# INSERT INTO t_test (name) SELECT 'paul'
FROM generate_series(1, 2000000);
INSERT 0 2000000
```

In the first line, a simple table is created. Two columns are used; the first is an auto-increment column that continually creates numbers, and the second is a column that will be filled with static values.

The generate_series function will generate numbers from 1 to 2 million. So, in this example, 2 million static values for hans and 2 million static values for paul are created.

All in all, 4 million rows have been added:

```
test=# SELECT name, count(*) FROM t_test GROUP BY 1;
 name | count
------+---------
 hans | 2000000
 paul | 2000000
(2 rows)
```

These 4 million rows have some nice properties that we'll be using throughout this chapter. The IDs are numbers in ascending order, and there are only two distinct names.

Let's run a simple query:

```
test=# \timing
Timing is on.
```

```
SELECT * FROM t_test WHERE id = 432332;
   id   | name
--------+------
 432332 | hans
(1 row)
Time: 87.967 ms
```

In this case, the `timing` command will tell `psql` to show the runtime of a query.

This isn't the real execution time on the server, but the time measured by `psql`. In the event of very short queries, network latency can be a substantial part of the total time, so this has to be taken into account.

Making use of EXPLAIN

In this example, reading 4 million rows has taken around 100 milliseconds. From a performance point of view, this is a total disaster. To figure out what went wrong, PostgreSQL offers the EXPLAIN command, which is defined as follows:

```
test=# \h explain
Command:     EXPLAIN
Description: show the execution plan of a statement
Syntax:
EXPLAIN [ ( option [, ...] ) ] statement

where option can be one of:

    ANALYZE [ boolean ]
    VERBOSE [ boolean ]
    COSTS [ boolean ]
    SETTINGS [ boolean ]
    GENERIC_PLAN [ boolean ]
    BUFFERS [ boolean ]
    SERIALIZE [ { NONE | TEXT | BINARY } ]
    WAL [ boolean ]
    TIMING [ boolean ]
    SUMMARY [ boolean ]
    MEMORY [ boolean ]
    FORMAT { TEXT | XML | JSON | YAML }

 URL: https://www.postgresql.org/docs/17/sql-explain.html
```

When you have a feeling that a query isn't performing well, EXPLAIN will help you reveal the real cause of the performance problem.

Here's how it works:

```
test=# EXPLAIN SELECT * FROM t_test WHERE id = 432332;
        QUERY PLAN
-----------------------------------------------------------------
 Gather (cost=1000.00..43455.43 rows=1 width=9)
   Workers Planned: 2
   -> Parallel Seq Scan on t_test
        (cost=0.00..42455.33   rows=1 width=9)
          Filter: (id = 432332)
 (4 rows)
```

What you can see here is an execution plan. In PostgreSQL, a SQL statement will be executed in four stages. The following components are at work:

- The **parser** will check for syntax errors and obvious problems
- The **rewrite** system takes care of rules (views and other things)
- The **optimizer** will figure out how to execute a query most efficiently and work out a plan
- The **plan** provided by the optimizer will be used by the executor to create the result

The purpose of EXPLAIN is to see what the planner has come up with to run the query efficiently. In my example, PostgreSQL will use a parallel sequential scan. This means that two workers will cooperate and work on the filter condition together. The partial results are then united through something called a gather node, which was introduced in PostgreSQL 9.6 (it's part of the parallel query infrastructure). If you look at the plan more closely, you'll see how many rows PostgreSQL expects at each stage of the plan (in this example, we have rows=1, so one row will be returned).

The number of parallel workers will be determined by the size of the table. The larger the operation is, the more parallel workers PostgreSQL will fire up. For a very small table, parallelism isn't used as it would create too much overhead.

Parallelism is not a must. It's always possible to reduce the number of parallel workers to mimic pre-PostgreSQL 9.6 behavior by setting the following variable to 0:

```
test=# SET max_parallel_workers_per_gather TO 0;
SET
```

> **Note**
>
> This change has no side effects as it's only in your session. Of course, you can also make this change in the postgresql.conf file, but I would advise against doing this as you might lose quite a lot of the performance optimization that's provided by the parallel queries.

Digging into the PostgreSQL cost model

If only one CPU is used, the execution plan will look like this:

```
test=# EXPLAIN SELECT * FROM t_test WHERE id = 432332;
                          QUERY PLAN
---------------------------------------------------------
 Seq Scan on t_test (cost=0.00..71622.00 rows=1 width=9)
    Filter: (id = 432332)
(2 rows)
```

PostgreSQL will sequentially read (that is, sequentially scan) the entire table and apply the filter. It expects the operation to cost 71622 penalty points. Now, what does this mean? Penalty points (or costs) are mostly an abstract concept. They are needed to compare the different ways to execute a query. If a query can be executed by the executor in many different ways, PostgreSQL will decide on the execution plan by promising the lowest cost possible. The question now is how PostgreSQL ended up with 71622 points.

Here's how it works:

```
test=# SELECT pg_relation_size('t_test') / 8192.0;
       ?column?
--------------------
 21622.000000
(1 row)
```

The pg_relation_size function will return the size of the table in bytes. Given this example, you can see that the relation consists of 21622 blocks (8,192 bytes each). According to the cost model, PostgreSQL will add a cost of 1 for each block it has to read sequentially.

The configuration parameter to influence this is as follows:

```
test=# SHOW seq_page_cost;
 seq_page_cost
---------------
 1
(1 row)
```

However, reading a couple of blocks from a disk isn't everything we need to do. It's also necessary to apply the filter and send these rows through a CPU. The two parameters shown in the following code block account for these costs:

```
test=# SHOW cpu_tuple_cost;
 cpu_tuple_cost
----------------
 0.01
```

```
 (1 row)
test=# SHOW cpu_operator_cost;
 cpu_operator_cost
--------------------
 0.0025
 (1 row)
```

This leads to the following calculation:

```
test=# SELECT 21622*1 + 4000000*0.01 + 4000000*0.0025;
    ?column?
 ------------
 71622.0000
 (1 row)
```

As you can see, this is exactly the number that's shown in the plan. Costs will consist of a CPU part and an I/O part, which will all be turned into a single number. The important thing here is that costs have nothing to do with real execution, so it's impossible to translate costs into milliseconds. The number the planner comes up with is just an estimate.

Of course, some more parameters have been outlined in this brief example. PostgreSQL also has special parameters for index-related operations, as follows:

- `random_page_cost = 4`: If PostgreSQL uses an index, there's usually a lot of random I/O involved. On traditional spinning disks, random reads are much more important than sequential reads, so PostgreSQL will account for them accordingly. Note that on SSDs or NVMe, the difference between random and sequential reads no longer applies, so it can make sense to set `random_page_cost = 1` in the `postgresql.conf` file.

- `cpu_index_tuple_cost = 0.005`: If indexes are used, PostgreSQL will also consider a CPU cost. The default value is `0.005`. Usually, it isn't recommended to change that.

If you're utilizing parallel queries, there are even more cost parameters:

- `parallel_tuple_cost = 0.1`: This defines the cost of transferring one tuple from a parallel worker process to another process. It accounts for the overhead of moving rows around inside the infrastructure. Usually, the default value (that is, `0.1`) isn't changed.

- `parallel_setup_cost = 1000.0`: This adjusts the costs of firing up a worker process. Of course, starting processes to run queries in parallel isn't free, so this parameter tries to model the costs associated with process management.

- `min_parallel_tables_scan_size = 8 MB`: This defines the minimum size of a table that's considered for parallel queries. The larger a table grows, the more CPUs PostgreSQL will use. The size of the table has to triple to accommodate another worker process.

- `min_parallel_index_scan_size = 512kB`: This defines the size of an index, which is necessary to consider a parallel scan.

Deploying simple indexes

Firing up additional worker processes to scan ever larger tables is sometimes not the solution. Reading entire tables just to find a single row is usually not a good idea.

Therefore, it makes sense to create indexes:

```
test=# CREATE INDEX idx_id ON t_test (id);
CREATE INDEX

test=# SELECT * FROM t_test WHERE id = 43242;
  id   | name
-------+------
 43242 | hans
(1 row)
Time: 0.259 ms
```

PostgreSQL uses Lehman-Yao's high-concurrency B-tree for standard indexes (`https://www.csd.uoc.gr/~hy460/pdf/p650-lehman.pdf`). Along with some PostgreSQL-specific optimizations, these trees provide end users with excellent performance. The most important thing is that Lehman-Yao allows you to run many operations (reading and writing) on the very same index at the same time, which helps to improve throughput dramatically.

However, indexes aren't free. The following code shows how much space an index will occupy on disk. We can see that this isn't an irrelevant amount of storage:

```
test=# \x
Expanded display is on.

test=# \di+ idx_id
List of relations
-[ RECORD 1 ]-+----------
Schema        | public
Name          | idx_id
Type          | index
Owner         | hs
Table         | t_test
Persistence   | permanent
Access method | btree
Size          | 86 MB
Description   |
```

As you can see, our index, which contains 4 million rows, will eat up 86 MB of disk space. In addition to this, the writes to the table will be slower because the index has to be kept in sync at all times.

In other words, if you use INSERT on a table that has 20 indexes, you also have to keep in mind that you have to write to all those indexes on INSERT, which seriously slows down the process.

Since the introduction of version 11, PostgreSQL now supports parallel index creation for B-tree indexes. In version 17, we can even build BRIN indexes in parallel – more on those later in this chapter. What this means is that it's possible to utilize more than one CPU core to build an index, thereby speeding up the process considerably. For now, this is only possible if you want to build a normal B-tree – there's no support for other index types yet. However, this will most likely change in the future. The parameter to control the level of parallelism is max_parallel_maintenance_workers. This tells PostgreSQL how many processes it can use as an upper limit.

Making use of sorted output

B-tree indexes aren't just used to find rows; they're also used to feed sorted data to the next stage in a process:

```
test=# EXPLAIN SELECT *
FROM   t_test
ORDER BY id DESC
LIMIT 10;
                     QUERY PLAN
-----------------------------------------------------------
 Limit (cost=0.43..0.74 rows=10 width=9)
   -> Index Scan Backward using idx_id on t_test
        (cost=0.43..125505.43 rows=4000000 width=9)
(2 rows)
```

In this case, the index already returns data in the right sort order, so there's no need to sort the entire set of data. Reading the last 10 rows of the index will be enough to answer this query. Practically, this means that it's possible to find the top N rows of a table in a fraction of a millisecond.

However, ORDER BY isn't the only operation that requires sorted output. The min and max functions are also all about sorted output, so an index can be used to speed up these two operations as well. Here's an example:

```
test=# explain SELECT min(id), max(id) FROM t_test;
                        QUERY PLAN
-----------------------------------------------------------
 Result  (cost=0.91..0.92 rows=1 width=8)
    InitPlan 1
      -> Limit  (cost=0.43..0.46 rows=1 width=4)
          -> Index Only Scan using idx_id on t_test
```

```
                    (cost=0.43..103880.43 rows=4000000 width=4)
   InitPlan 2
     ->  Limit  (cost=0.43..0.46 rows=1 width=4)
          ->  Index Only Scan Backward using idx_id
                on t_test t_test_1  (cost=0.43..103880.43
                    rows=4000000 width=4)
(7 rows)
```

In PostgreSQL, an index (a B-tree, to be more precise) can be read in normal order or backward. A B-tree can be seen as a sorted list, so naturally, the lowest value is at the beginning and the highest value is at the end. Therefore, min and max are perfect candidates for a speed-up. What's also worth noting is that the main table doesn't need to be referenced at all in this case.

In SQL, many operations rely on sorted input; therefore, understanding these operations is essential because there are serious implications on the indexing side.

Using more than one index at a time

So far, you've seen that one index at a time has been used. However, in many real-world situations, this is nowhere near sufficient. Certain cases demand more logic in the database.

PostgreSQL permits the use of multiple indexes in a single query. Of course, this makes sense if many columns are queried at the same time. However, that's not always the case. It can also be that a single index is used multiple times to process the very same column.

Here's an example:

```
test=# explain SELECT * FROM t_test WHERE id = 30 OR id = 50;
                          QUERY PLAN
-----------------------------------------------------------
 Bitmap Heap Scan on t_test
   (cost=8.88..16.85 rows=2 width=9)
   Recheck Cond: ((id = 30) OR (id = 50))
   -> BitmapOr (cost=8.88..8.88 rows=2 width=0)
         -> Bitmap Index Scan on idx_idv
               (cost=0.00..4.44 rows=1 width=0)
               Index Cond: (id = 30)
         -> Bitmap Index Scan on idx_id
               (cost=0.00..4.44 rows=1 width=0)
               Index Cond: (id = 50)
(7 rows)
```

The point here is that the id column is needed twice. First, the query looks for 30, and then for 50. As you can see, PostgreSQL will go for a bitmap scan.

> **Note**
>
> A bitmap scan isn't the same as a bitmap index, which people who have a good Oracle background might know of. They are two distinct things and have nothing in common. Bitmap indexes are an index type in Oracle while bitmap scans are a scan method.

The idea behind a bitmap scan is that PostgreSQL will scan the first index, collecting a list of blocks (pages of a table) containing the data. Then, the next index will be scanned to – again – compile a list of blocks. This is done for as many indexes as desired. In the case of OR, these lists will then be unified, leaving us with a long list of blocks containing the data. Using this list, the table will be scanned to retrieve these blocks.

The trouble now is that PostgreSQL has retrieved a lot more data than needed. In our case, the query will look for two rows; however, a couple of blocks might have been returned by the bitmap scan. Therefore, the executor will do a recheck to filter out these rows – that is, the ones that don't satisfy our conditions.

Bitmap scans will also work for AND conditions or a mixture of AND and OR. However, if PostgreSQL sees an AND condition, it doesn't necessarily force itself into a bitmap scan. Let's suppose that we have a query looking for everybody living in Austria and a person with a certain ID. It makes no sense to use two indexes here because, after searching for the ID, there isn't much data left. Scanning both indexes would be much more expensive because there are over 8 million people (including me) living in Austria and reading so many rows to find just one person is pretty pointless from a performance standpoint. The good news is that the PostgreSQL optimizer will make all these decisions for you by comparing the costs of different options and potential indexes, so there's no need to worry.

In general, OR can be a pretty expensive operation. If you have the feeling that a query containing OR is too expensive, consider trying out UNION to see whether it runs faster. In many cases, this can produce a relevant performance boost.

Using bitmap scans effectively

The question naturally arising now is when a bitmap scan is most beneficial and when it is chosen by the optimizer. From my point of view, there are only two use cases:

- To avoid fetching the same block over and over again
- To combine relatively bad conditions

The first case is quite common. Suppose you're looking for everybody who speaks a certain language. For the sake of this example, we can assume that 10% of all people stored in the index speak the required language. Scanning the index would mean that a block in the table has to be scanned all over again since many skilled speakers might be stored in the same block. Applying a bitmap scan ensures that a specific block is only used once, which, of course, leads to better performance.

The second common use case is to use relatively weak criteria together. Let's suppose we're looking for everybody between 20 and 30 years of age who owns a yellow shirt. Now, maybe 15% of all people are between 20 and 30, and maybe 15% of all people own a yellow shirt. Scanning a table sequentially is expensive, so PostgreSQL might decide to choose two indexes because the final result might consist of just 1% of the data. Scanning both indexes might be cheaper than reading all of the data.

Since PostgreSQL 10.0, parallel bitmap heap scans are supported. Usually, bitmap scans are used for comparatively expensive queries. Added parallelism in this area is, therefore, a huge step forward and beneficial.

Using indexes intelligently

So far, applying an index feels like the Holy Grail, always improving performance magically. However, this is not the case. Indexes can also be pretty pointless in some cases.

Before digging into things more deeply, here's the data structure we've used for this example. Remember that there are only two distinct names and unique IDs:

```
test=# \d t_test
                    Table "public.t_test"
 Column |  Type   | Collation | Nullable |  Default
--------+---------+-----------+----------+----------------
 id     | integer |           | not null | nextval(
't_test_id_seq'::regclass)
 name   | text    |           |          |
Indexes:
    "idx_id" btree (id)
```

At this point, one index has been defined, which covers the id column. In the next step, the name column will be queried. Before doing this, an index on the name will be created:

```
test=# CREATE INDEX idx_name ON t_test (name);
CREATE INDEX
```

Now, it's time to see whether the index is used correctly; consider the following code block:

```
test=# EXPLAIN SELECT * FROM t_test WHERE name = 'hans2';
                    QUERY PLAN
---------------------------------------------------
 Index Scan using idx_name on t_test
    (cost=0.43..4.45 rows=1 width=9)
    Index Cond: (name = 'hans2'::text)
(2 rows)
```

As expected, PostgreSQL will decide on using the index. Most users would expect this. However, note that my query says hans2. Remember, hans2 doesn't exist in the table and the query plan perfectly reflects this. Here, rows=1 indicates that the planner only expects a very small subset of data to be returned by the query.

There isn't a single row in the table, but PostgreSQL will never estimate zero rows because it would make subsequent estimations a lot harder. This is because having useful cost calculations of other nodes in the plan would be close to impossible.

Let's see what happens if we look for more data:

```
test=# EXPLAIN SELECT *
FROM t_test
WHERE name = 'hans'
OR name = 'paul';
                        QUERY PLAN
------------------------------------------------------------------
 Seq Scan on t_test (cost=0.00..81622.00 rows=3000005 width=9)
    Filter: ((name = <hans'::text) OR (name = 'paul'::text))
(2 rows)
```

In this case, PostgreSQL will go for a straight sequential scan. Why's that? Why is the system ignoring all indexes? The reason is simple: hans and paul make up the entire dataset because there are no other values (PostgreSQL knows that by checking the system's statistics). Therefore, PostgreSQL figures that the entire table must be read anyway. There's no reason to read all of the indexes and the full table if reading the table is sufficient.

In other words, PostgreSQL won't use an index just because there is one. PostgreSQL will use indexes when they make sense. If the number of rows is smaller, PostgreSQL will, again, consider bitmap scans and normal index scans:

```
test=# EXPLAIN SELECT *
FROM t_test
WHERE name = 'hans2'
OR name = 'paul2';
                        QUERY PLAN
------------------------------------------------------------------
 Bitmap Heap Scan on t_test (cost=8.88..12.89 rows=1 width=9)
    Recheck Cond: ((name = <hans2'::text) OR (name = 'paul2'::text))
    -> BitmapOr (cost=8.88..8.88 rows=1 width=0)
          -> Bitmap Index Scan on idx_name
             (cost=0.00..4.44 rows=1 width=0)
                Index Cond: (name = <hans2'::text)
```

```
        -> Bitmap Index Scan on idx_name
           (cost=0.00..4.44 rows=1 width=0)
              Index Cond: (name = ‹paul2'::text)
```

The most important point to learn here is that execution plans depend on input values.

They aren't static and not independent of the data inside the table. This is a very important observation that must be kept in mind at all times. In real-world examples, the fact that plans change can often be the reason for unpredictable runtimes.

Understanding index de-duplication

What's important to mention regarding PostgreSQL 13 and beyond is that not all indexes are created equal. With the introduction of version 13, PostgreSQL is now able to de-duplicate index entries. In other words, an index that stores many identical values will be a lot smaller than a "normal" index:

```
test=# \di+
 List of relations
 Schema |    Name    |  Type  | Owner |  Table  | Persistence | Size ...
--------+------------+--------+-------+---------+-------------+----
 public | idx_id     | index  | hs    | t_test  | permanent   | 86 MB |
 public | idx_name   | index  | hs    | t_test  | permanent   | 26 MB |
```

Smaller indexes greatly improve efficiency by ensuring higher cache hit rates and better access times.

Improving speed using clustered tables

In this section, you'll learn about the power of correlation and clustered tables. What's this about? Imagine that you want to read a whole area of data. This might be a certain time range, a block, some IDs, and so on.

The runtime of these queries will vary depending on the amount of data and the physical arrangement of data on the disk, so even if you're running queries that return the same number of rows, two systems might not provide the answer within the same period as the physical disk layout might make a difference.

Here's an example:

```
test=# EXPLAIN (analyze true, buffers true, timing true)
SELECT *
FROM   t_test
WHERE id < 10000;
                        QUERY PLAN
-------------------------------------------------------------
 Index Scan using t_test_id_idx on t_test
     (cost=0.43..341.96 rows=9859 width=9)
```

```
      (actual time=0.043..3.132 rows=9999 loops=1)
   Index Cond: (id < 10000)
   Buffers: shared hit=85
 Planning:
   Buffers: shared hit=10
 Planning Time: 0.443 ms
 Execution Time: 4.307 ms
(7 rows)
```

As you can see, the data has been loaded in an organized and sequential way. Data has been added ID after ID, so it can be expected that the data will be on the disk in sequential order. This holds if data is loaded into an empty table using an auto-increment column.

You've already seen EXPLAIN in action. In this example, EXPLAIN (analyze true, buffers true, and timing true) has been utilized. The idea is that analyze will not just show the plan but also execute the query and show us what's happened.

The EXPLAIN analyze parameter is perfect for comparing planner estimates with what happened. It's the best way to figure out whether the planner was correct or way off. The buffers true parameter will tell us how many of the 8k blocks were touched by the query. In this example, a total of 85 blocks were touched. A shared hit means that data was coming from the PostgreSQL I/O cache (shared buffers). Altogether, it took PostgreSQL around 3.3 milliseconds to retrieve the data.

What happens if the data in your table is somewhat random? Will things change?

To create a table containing the same data but in a random order, you can simply use ORDER BY random(). It will ensure that the data is indeed shuffled on disk:

```
test=# CREATE TABLE t_random AS
SELECT * FROM t_test ORDER BY random();
SELECT 4000000
```

To ensure a fair comparison, the same column is indexed:

```
test=# CREATE INDEX idx_random ON t_random (id);
CREATE INDEX
```

To function properly, PostgreSQL will need optimizer statistics. These statistics will tell PostgreSQL how much data there is, how the values are distributed, and whether the data is correlated on disk. To speed things up even more, I've added a VACUUM call:

```
test=# VACUUM ANALYZE t_random;
VACUUM
```

Now, let's run the same query that we ran previously:

```
test=# EXPLAIN (analyze true, buffers true, timing true)
SELECT * FROM t_random WHERE id < 10000;
                                QUERY PLAN
------------------------------------------------------------
 Bitmap Heap Scan on t_random
   (cost=175.71..17153.27 rows=9198 width=9)
   (actual time=5.337..27.991 rows=9999 loops=1)
   Recheck Cond: (id < 10000)
   Heap Blocks: exact=8034
   Buffers: shared hit=4677 read=3387 written=975
   I/O Timings: shared/local read=9.640 write=5.664
   -> Bitmap Index Scan on idx_random
       (cost=0.00..173.42 rows=9198 width=0)
       (actual time=3.434..3.434 rows=9999 loops=1)
         Index Cond: (id < 10000)
         Buffers: shared hit=3 read=27
         I/O Timings: shared/local read=0.253
 Planning:
   Buffers: shared hit=10 read=3
   I/O Timings: shared/local read=0.081
 Planning Time: 0.471 ms
 Execution Time: 28.578 ms
(14 rows)
```

I've executed the same query twice to show the impact of caching, but let's go through things one after the other.

There are a couple of things to observe here. First of all, a staggering total of 8034 blocks were needed during the first execution, and the runtime has skyrocketed to over 28 milliseconds. This is a major loss compared to organizing the data using some kind of key.

However, there's more to see. First, even the plan has changed. PostgreSQL now uses a bitmap scan instead of a normal index scan. This is to reduce the number of blocks needed in the query to prevent even worse behavior.

How does the planner know how data is stored on the disk? The pg_stats system view contains all the statistics about the content of the columns. The following query reveals the relevant content:

```
test=# SELECT tablename, attname, correlation
FROM   pg_stats
WHERE tablename IN ('t_test', 't_random')
ORDER BY 1, 2;
 tablename | attname | correlation
-----------+---------+-------------
```

```
t_random  | id      | -0.005975342
t_random  | name    | 0.49059877
t_test    | id      | 1
t_test    | name    | 1
(4 rows)
```

Here, you can see that PostgreSQL takes care of every single column. The content of the view is created by ANALYZE, which is defined as follows, and is vital to performance:

```
test=# \h ANALYZE
Command:     ANALYZE
Description: collect statistics about a database
Syntax:
ANALYZE [ ( option [, ...] ) ] [ table_and_columns [, ...] ]

where option can be one of:

    VERBOSE [ boolean ]
    SKIP_LOCKED [ boolean ]
    BUFFER_USAGE_LIMIT size

and table_and_columns is:

    table_name [ ( column_name [, ...] ) ]

URL: https://www.postgresql.org/docs/17/sql-analyze.html
```

Usually, ANALYZE is automatically executed in the background using the autovacuum daemon, which will be covered later in this book.

Back to our query. As you can see, both tables have two columns (id and name). In the case of t_test.id, the correlation is 1, which means that the next value somewhat depends on the previous one. In my example, the numbers are simply ascending. The same applies to t_test.name. First, we have entries containing hans, and then we have entries containing paul. All identical names are therefore stored together.

In t_random, the situation is quite different; a negative correlation means that data is shuffled. You can also see that the correlation for the name column is around 0.5. In reality, this means that there's usually no straight sequence of identical names in the table, but that names keep switching all the time when the table is read in physical order.

Why does this lead to so many blocks being hit by the query? The answer is relatively simple. If the data we need isn't packed together tightly and spread out through the table evenly, more blocks are needed to extract the same amount of information, which, in turn, leads to worse performance.

Clustering tables

In PostgreSQL, the CLUSTER command allows us to rewrite a table in the desired order. It's possible to point to an index and store data in the same order as the index:

```
test=# \h CLUSTER
Command:     CLUSTER
Description: cluster a table according to an index
Syntax:
CLUSTER [ ( option [, ...] ) ] [ table_name [ USING index_name ] ]

where option can be one of:

    VERBOSE [ boolean ]

URL: https://www.postgresql.org/docs/17/sql-cluster.html
```

The CLUSTER command has been around for many years and serves its purpose well. However, there are some things to consider before blindly running it on a production system:

- The CLUSTER command will lock the table while it's running. You can't insert or modify data while CLUSTER is running. This might not be acceptable in a production system.

- Data can only be organized according to one index. You cannot order a table by ZIP code, name, ID, birthday, and so on at the same time. This means that CLUSTER only makes sense if there's one search criterion that's used most of the time.

- Keep in mind that the example outlined in this book is more of a worst-case scenario. In reality, the performance difference between a clustered and a non-clustered table will depend on the workload, the amount of data retrieved, cache hit rates, and a lot more.

- The clustered state of a table will not be maintained as changes are made to a table during normal operations. The correlation will usually deteriorate as time goes on.

Here's an example of how to run the CLUSTER command:

```
test=# CLUSTER t_random USING idx_random;
CLUSTER
```

Depending on the size of the table, the time needed to cluster will vary.

Making use of index-only scans

So far, you've seen when an index is used and when it isn't. In addition to this, bitmap scans have been discussed.

However, there's more to indexing. The following two examples only differ slightly, although the performance difference might be fairly large. Here's the first query:

```
test=# EXPLAIN SELECT * FROM t_test WHERE id = 34234;
                        QUERY PLAN
-------------------------------------------------------------
 Index Scan using idx_id on t_test
   (cost=0.43..8.45 rows=1 width=9)
   Index Cond: (id = 34234)
```

There's nothing unusual here. PostgreSQL uses an index to find a single row. What happens if only a single column is selected?

```
test=# EXPLAIN SELECT id FROM t_test WHERE id = 34234;
                        QUERY PLAN
-------------------------------------------------------------
 Index Only Scan using idx_id on t_test
   (cost=0.43..8.45 rows=1 width=4)
   Index Cond: (id = 34234)
(2 rows)
```

As you can see, the plan has changed from an index scan to an index-only scan. In our example, the id column has been indexed, so its content is naturally in the index. There's no need to go to the table in most cases if all the data can already be taken out of the index. Going to the table is (almost) only required if additional fields are queried, which isn't the case here. Therefore, the index-only scan will promise significantly better performance than a normal index scan.

Practically, it can even make sense to include an additional column in an index here and there to enjoy the benefits of this feature. In SQL, adding additional columns is known as **covering indexes**. Since PostgreSQL 11, we have the same functionality, which uses the INCLUDE keyword in CREATE INDEX.

Understanding additional B-tree features

In PostgreSQL, indexing is a large field and covers many aspects of database work. As I've outlined in this book already, indexing is the key to performance. There's no good performance without proper indexing. Therefore, it's worth inspecting the indexing-related features that we will cover in the following subsections in detail.

Combined indexes

In my job as a professional PostgreSQL support vendor, I'm often asked about the difference between combined and individual indexes. In this section, I'll try to shed some light on this question.

The general rule is that if a single index can answer your question, it's usually the best choice. However, you can't index all of the possible combinations of fields people are filtering with. What you can do instead is use the properties of combined indexes to achieve as much as possible.

Let's suppose we have a table containing three columns: `postal_code`, `last_name`, and `first_name`. A telephone book would make use of a combined index such as this. You'll see that data is ordered by location. Within the same location, data will be sorted by last name and first name.

The following table shows which operations are possible given the three-column index:

Query	Possible?	Remarks

`postal_code = 2700`
 	
`AND last_name = 'Schönig'`
 	
`AND first_name = 'Hans'`
	Yes	This is the ideal use case for this index.

`postal_code = 2700`
 	
`AND last_name = 'Schönig'`
	Yes	No restrictions.

`last_name = 'Schönig '`
 	
`AND postal_code = 2700`
	Yes	PostgreSQL will simply swap conditions.

`postal_code = 2700`	Yes	This is just like an index on `postal_code`; the combined index just needs more space on the disk.
`first_name = 'Hans'`	Yes, but a different use case	PostgreSQL cannot use the sorted property of the index anymore. However, in some rare cases (usually very broad tables with countless columns), PostgreSQL will scan the entire index if it's as cheap as reading the very broad table.

Table 3.1 – Operations given in the three-column index

If columns are indexed separately, you'll most likely end up seeing bitmap scans. Of course, a single hand-tailored index is better.

Adding functional indexes

So far, you've seen how to index the content of a column as-is. However, this might not always be what you want. Therefore, PostgreSQL allows you to create functional indexes. The idea is very simple: instead of indexing a value, the output of a function is stored in the index.

The following example shows how the cosine of the id column can be indexed:

```
test=# CREATE INDEX idx_cos ON t_random (cos(id));
CREATE INDEX
test=# ANALYZE;
ANALYZE
```

All you have to do is apply the function to the list of columns, and you're done. Of course, this won't work for all kinds of functions. Functions can only be used if their output is immutable, as shown in the following example:

```
test=# SELECT age('2010-01-01 10:00:00'::timestamptz);
               age
----------------------------------
 14 years 5 mons 4 days 14:00:00
(1 row)
```

Functions such as age aren't suitable for indexing because their output isn't constant. Time goes on and, consequently, the output of age will change too. PostgreSQL will explicitly prohibit functions that have the potential to change their result given the same input. The cos function is fine in this respect because the cosine of a value will still be the same 1,000 years from now.

To test the index, I've written a simple query to show what will happen:

```
test=# EXPLAIN SELECT * FROM t_random WHERE cos(id) = 10;
                      QUERY PLAN
----------------------------------------------------------------
 Index Scan using idx_cos on t_random
   (cost=0.43..8.45 rows=1 width=9)
   Index Cond: (cos((id)::double precision) = '10'::double precision)
(2 rows)
```

As expected, the functional index will be used just like any other index.

Reducing space consumption

Indexing is nice, and its main purpose is to speed things up as much as possible. As with all good stuff, indexing comes with a price tag: space consumption. To work its magic, an index must store values in an organized fashion. If your table contains 10 million integer values, the index belonging to the table will logically contain these 10 million integer values, plus additional overhead.

A B-tree will contain a pointer to each row in the table, so it's certainly not free of charge. To figure out how much space an index will need, you can ask `psql` using the `\di+` command:

```
test=# \di+
                        List of relations
 Schema |    Name     | Type  | Owner |  Table   | Persistence | Size
--------+-------------+-------+-------+----------+-------------+---  ...
 public | idx_cos     | index | hs    | t_random | permanent   | 86 MB
 public | idx_id      | index | hs    | t_test   | permanent   | 86 MB
 public | idx_name    | index | hs    | t_test   | permanent   | 26 MB
 public | idx_random  | index | hs    | t_random | permanent   | 86 MB
(4 rows)
```

In my database, a staggering amount of 284 MB has been burned to store these indexes. Now, compare this to the amount of storage that's burned by the underlying tables:

```
test=# \d+
                        List of relations
 Schema |     Name      |   Type   | Owner | Persistence |   Size
--------+---------------+----------+-------+-------------+-------  ...
 public | t_random      | table    | hs    | permanent   | 169 MB
 public | t_test        | table    | hs    | permanent   | 169 MB
 public | t_test_id_seq | sequence | hs    | permanent   | 8192 bytes
(3 rows)
```

The size of both tables combined is just 338 MB. In other words, our indexing needs more space than the actual data. In the real world, this is common and pretty likely. Recently, I visited a CYBERTEC customer in Germany and I saw a database in which 64% of the database size was made up of indexes that were never used (not a single time for months). Therefore, over-indexing can be an issue, just like under-indexing. Remember, these indexes don't just consume space. Every INSERT or UPDATE function must maintain the values in the indexes as well. In extreme cases, such as our example, this vastly decreases the write throughput.

If there are just a handful of different values in a table, partial indexes are a solution:

```
test=# DROP INDEX idx_name;
DROP INDEX
test=# CREATE INDEX idx_name ON t_test (name)
WHERE name NOT IN ('hans', 'paul');
CREATE INDEX
```

In the following case, the majority has been excluded from the index and a small, efficient index can be enjoyed:

```
test=# \di+ idx_name
                            List of relations
 Schema |   Name   | Type  | Owner | Table  | Persistence |   Size ...
--------+----------+-------+-------+--------+-------------+---------
 public | idx_name | index | hs    | t_test | permanent   | 8192 bytes
(1 row)
```

Note that it only makes sense to exclude very frequent values that make up a large part of the table (at least 25% or so). Ideal candidates for partial indexes are gender (we assume that most people are male or female), nationality (assuming that most people in your country are of the same nationality), and so on. Of course, applying this kind of trickery requires some deep knowledge of your data, but it certainly pays off.

Adding data while indexing

Creating an index is easy. However, keep in mind that you can't modify a table while an index is being built. The CREATE INDEX command will lock the table using a SHARE lock to ensure that no changes occur. While this isn't a problem for small tables, it will cause issues for large ones in production systems. Indexing 1 TB of data or so will take some time, and therefore blocking a table for too long can become an issue.

The solution to this problem is the CREATE INDEX CONCURRENTLY command. Building the index will take a lot longer (usually, at least twice as long), but you can use the table normally during index creation.

Here's how it works:

```
test=# CREATE INDEX CONCURRENTLY idx_name2 ON t_test (name);
CREATE INDEX
```

Note that PostgreSQL doesn't guarantee success if you're using the CREATE INDEX CONCURRENTLY command. An index can end up being marked as invalid if the operations running on your system somehow conflict with the creation of the index. If you want to figure out whether your indexes are invalid, use \d on the relation.

Introducing operator classes

So far, the goal has been to figure out what to index and whether to indiscriminately apply an index to a column or a group of columns. There is one assumption, however, that we've silently accepted to make this work. Up until now, we've worked under the assumption that the order in which the data has to be sorted is a somewhat fixed constant. In reality, this assumption might not hold. Sure, numbers will always be in the same order, but other kinds of data will most likely not have a predefined, fixed sort order.

To prove my point, I've compiled a real-world example. Take a look at the following two records:

```
1118 09 08 78
2345 01 05 77
```

My question now is whether these two rows are ordered properly. They might be because one comes before another. However, this is wrong because these two rows have some hidden semantics. What you're looking at here are two Austrian Social Security numbers. Here, 09 08 78 refers to August 9, 1978, and 01 05 77 refers to May 1, 1977. The first four numbers consist of a checksum and some sort of auto-incremented three-digit number. Therefore, in reality, 1977 comes before 1978, and we might consider swapping those two lines to achieve the desired sort order.

The problem is that PostgreSQL has no idea what these two rows mean. If a column is marked as text, PostgreSQL will apply the standard rules to sort the text. If the column is marked as a number, PostgreSQL will apply the standard rules to sort numbers. Under no circumstances will it ever use something as odd as I've described. If you think that the facts I outlined previously are the only things to consider when processing those numbers, you're wrong. How many months does a year have? 12? Far from true, in this case. In the Austrian social security system, these numbers can hold up to 14 months. Why? Remember that . . ., being three digits, is simply an auto-increment value. The trouble is that if an immigrant or a refugee has no valid paperwork and their birthday isn't known, they will be assigned an artificial birthday in the 13th month.

During the Balkan wars in 1990, Austria offered asylum to over 115,000 refugees. Naturally, this three-digit number wasn't enough, and a 14th month was added. Now, which standard data type can handle this kind of COBOL leftover from the early 1970s (which was when the layout of the Social Security number was introduced)? The answer is none of them.

To handle special-purpose fields logically, PostgreSQL offers operator classes:

```
test=# \h CREATE OPERATOR CLASS
Command:     CREATE OPERATOR CLASS
Description: define a new operator class
Syntax:
CREATE OPERATOR CLASS name [ DEFAULT ] FOR TYPE data_type
  USING index_method [ FAMILY family_name ] AS
  {  OPERATOR strategy_number operator_name
 [ ( op_type, op_type ) ] [ FOR SEARCH |
 FOR ORDER BY sort_family_name ]
   | FUNCTION support_number
  [ ( op_type [ , op_type ] ) ] function_name
```

```
( argument_type [, ...] )
  | STORAGE storage_type
} [, ... ]
URL: https://www.postgresql.org/docs/17/sql-createopclass.html
```

An `operator` class will tell an index how to behave. Let's take a look at a standard binary tree. It can perform five operations:

Strategy	Operator	Description
1	<	Less than
2	<=	Less than or equal to
3	=	Equals
4	>=	Greater than or equal to
5	>	Greater than

Table 3.2 – Presentation of five operations in a standard binary tree

The standard `operator` classes support the standard data types and standard operators we've used throughout this book. If you want to handle Social Security numbers, it's necessary to come up with operators that are capable of providing you with the logic you need. Those custom operators can then be used to form an `operator` class, which is nothing more than a strategy that's passed to the index to configure how it should behave.

Creating an operator class for a B-tree

To give you a practical example of what an `operator` class looks like, I've put together some code to handle Social Security numbers. To keep it simple, I've paid no attention to details such as checksums.

Creating new operators

The first thing we must do is come up with the desired operators. Note that five operators are needed. There's one operator for each strategy. A strategy of an index is like a plugin that allows you to put in code.

Before getting started, I've compiled some test data:

```
CREATE TABLE t_sva (sva text);
INSERT INTO t_sva VALUES ('1118090878');
INSERT INTO t_sva VALUES ('2345010477');
```

Now that the test data is there, it's time to create an operator. For this purpose, PostgreSQL offers the CREATE OPERATOR command:

```
test=# \h CREATE OPERATOR
Command:     CREATE OPERATOR
Description: define a new operator
Syntax:
CREATE OPERATOR name (
    {FUNCTION|PROCEDURE} = function_name
    [, LEFTARG = left_type ] [, RIGHTARG = right_type ]
    [, COMMUTATOR = com_op ] [, NEGATOR = neg_op ]
    [, RESTRICT = res_proc ] [, JOIN = join_proc ]
    [, HASHES ] [, MERGES ]
)
URL: https://www.postgresql.org/docs/17/sql-createoperator.html
```

The concept here is that operator calls a function, which gets one or two parameters – one for the left argument and one for the right argument of operator.

As you can see, an operator is nothing more than a function call, so it's necessary to implement the logic needed in those functions that are hidden by the operators. To fix the sort order, I've written a function called normalize_si:

```
CREATE OR REPLACE FUNCTION public.normalize_si(text) RETURNS text AS
$$
    BEGIN
      RETURN substring($1, 9, 2) ||
            substring($1, 7, 2) ||
            substring($1, 5, 2) ||
            substring($1, 1, 4);
    END; $$
LANGUAGE 'plpgsql' IMMUTABLE;
```

Calling this function will return the following result:

```
test=# SELECT normalize_si('1118090878');
 normalize_si
--------------
 7808091118
(1 row)
```

As you can see, all we did was swap some digits. It's now possible to just use the normal string sort order. In the next step, this function can already be used to compare Social Security numbers directly.

The first function that's needed is the less than (_lt) function, which is needed by the first strategy:

```
CREATE OR REPLACE FUNCTION public.si_lt(text, text)
      RETURNS boolean AS $$
  BEGIN
    RETURN normalize_si($1) < normalize_si($2);
  END; $$
LANGUAGE 'plpgsql' IMMUTABLE;
```

There are two important things to note here:

- The function must not be written in SQL. It only works in a procedural or compiled language. The reason for this is that SQL functions can be inlined under some circumstances, and this would thwart the entire endeavor.

- The second issue is that you should stick to the naming convention used in this chapter – it's widely accepted by the community. Less than functions should be called _lt, less than or equal to functions should be called _le, and so on.

Given this knowledge, the next set of functions that are needed by our future operators can be defined as follows:

```
-- lower equals
CREATE OR REPLACE FUNCTION public.si_le(text, text)
    RETURNS boolean AS
$$
  BEGIN
    RETURN public.normalize_si($1) <= public.normalize_si($2);
  END;
$$
LANGUAGE 'plpgsql' IMMUTABLE;

-- greater equal
CREATE OR REPLACE FUNCTION public.si_ge(text, text)
    RETURNS boolean AS
$$
BEGIN
    RETURN public.normalize_si($1) >= public.normalize_si($2);
END;
$$
LANGUAGE 'plpgsql' IMMUTABLE;

-- greater
CREATE OR REPLACE FUNCTION public.si_gt(text, text)
    RETURNS boolean AS
```

```
$$
BEGIN
    RETURN public.normalize_si($1) > public.normalize_si($2);
END;
$$
LANGUAGE 'plpgsql' IMMUTABLE;
```

So far, four functions have been defined. A fifth function for the `equals` operator isn't necessary. We can simply take the existing operator because `equals` doesn't depend on sort order anyway.

Now that all the functions are in place, it's time to define these operators:

```
-- define operators
CREATE OPERATOR <# ( PROCEDURE=public.si_lt,
                     LEFTARG=text,
                     RIGHTARG=text);
```

The design of the operator is very simple. The operator needs a name (in my case, `<#`), a procedure that's supposed to be called, and the data type of the left and right arguments. When the operator is called, the left argument will be the first parameter of `si_lt`, and the right argument will be the second parameter.

The remaining three operators follow the same principle:

```
CREATE OPERATOR <=# ( PROCEDURE=public.si_le,
                      LEFTARG=text,
                      RIGHTARG=text);


CREATE OPERATOR >=# ( PROCEDURE=public.si_ge,
                      LEFTARG=text,
                      RIGHTARG=text);


CREATE OPERATOR ># ( PROCEDURE=public.si_gt,
                     LEFTARG=text,
                     RIGHTARG=text);
```

Depending on the type of index you're using, a couple of support functions are needed. In the case of standard B-trees, only one support function is needed, and this is used to speed things up internally:

```
CREATE OR REPLACE FUNCTION public.si_same(text, text)
RETURNS int AS $$
BEGIN
    IF public.normalize_si($1) < public.normalize_si($2) THEN
        RETURN -1;
    ELSIF public.normalize_si($1) > public.normalize_si($2) THEN
```

```
        RETURN +1;
    ELSE
        RETURN 0;
    END IF;
END;
$$ LANGUAGE 'plpgsql' IMMUTABLE;
```

The si_same function will return -1 if the first parameter is smaller, 0 if both parameters are equal, or 1 if the first parameter is greater. Internally, the _same function is the workhorse, so you should make sure that your code is optimized.

Creating operator classes

Finally, all the components are in place, and it's possible to create the operator class that's needed by the index:

```
CREATE OPERATOR CLASS sva_special_ops
FOR TYPE text USING btree
AS
    OPERATOR 1 <# ,
    OPERATOR 2 <=# ,
    OPERATOR 3 = ,
    OPERATOR 4 >=# ,
    OPERATOR 5 ># ,
    FUNCTION 1 public.si_same(text, text);
```

The CREATE OPERATOR CLASS command connects strategies and operators to OPERATOR 1. Here, <# means that the strategy of 1 will use the <# operator. Finally, the _same function is connected to the operator class.

Note that the operator class has a name and that it has been explicitly defined to work with B-trees. The operator class can already be used during index creation:

```
CREATE INDEX idx_special ON t_sva (sva sva_special_ops);
```

Creating an index works in a slightly different way than before: sva sva_special_ops means that the sva column is indexed using the sva_special_ops operator class. If sva_special_ops isn't explicitly used, then PostgreSQL will not go for our special sort order, and will instead decide on the default operator class.

Testing custom operator classes

In our example, the test data consists of just two rows. Therefore, PostgreSQL will never use an index because the table is just too small to justify the overhead of even opening the index. To still be able to test without having to load too much data, you can advise the optimizer to make sequential scans more expensive.

You can make operations more expensive in your session by using the following command:

```
SET enable_seqscan TO off;
```

The index works as expected:

```
test=# explain SELECT *
FROM   t_sva
WHERE sva = '0000112273';
                            QUERY PLAN
---------------------------------------------------------------
 Index Only Scan using idx_special on t_sva
    (cost=0.13..8.14 rows=1 width=32)
    Index Cond: (sva = '0000112273'::text)
(2 rows)
test=# SELECT * FROM t_sva;
    sva
------------
 2345010477
 1118090878
(2 rows)
```

Without the `operator` class, we would see a normal sequential scan and not the index representing our special logic. Therefore, the `operator` class is an important contribution to facilitating advanced indexing that isn't covered by "standard means."

Understanding PostgreSQL index types

So far, only binary trees have been discussed. However, in many cases, B-trees are just not enough. Why's that? As we've already discussed in this chapter, B-trees are based on sorting. The <, <=, =, >=, and > operators can be handled using B-trees. The trouble is that not every data type can be sorted in a useful way. Just imagine a polygon. How would you sort these objects in a useful way? Sure, you can sort by the area covered, its length, and so on, but doing this won't allow you to find them using a geometric search.

The solution to this problem is to provide more than just one index type. Each index will serve a special purpose and do exactly what's needed. The following six index types are available (as of PostgreSQL 17.0):

```
test=# SELECT * FROM pg_am;
 oid  | amname  |       amhandler       | amtype
------+---------+-----------------------+--------
    2 | heap    | heap_tableam_handler  | t
  403 | btree   | bthandler             | i
  405 | hash    | hashhandler           | i
  783 | gist    | gisthandler           | i
 2742 | gin     | ginhandler            | i
```

```
 4000 | spgist | spghandler           | i
 3580 | brin   | brinhandler          | i
(7 rows)
```

B-trees have already been discussed in great detail, but what are the other index types useful for? The following sections will outline the purpose of each index type that's available in PostgreSQL.

Note that there are some extensions out there that can be used on top of what you can see here. Some additional index types that are available on the web are `rum`, `vodka`, and, in the future, `cognac`.

Hash indexes

Hash indexes have been around for many years. While B-trees are sorted lists, hash indexes store the hash of the value we want to index. A hash index is a large hash map stored on disk. The idea is to hash the input value and store it for later lookups. Having hash indexes makes sense. However, before PostgreSQL 10.0, it wasn't advisable to use hash indexes because PostgreSQL had no WAL support for them. In PostgreSQL 10.0 and beyond, this has changed. Hash indexes are now fully logged and are therefore ready for replication and considered to be 100% crash-safe.

Hash indexes are generally a bit larger than B-tree indexes. Suppose you want to index 4 million integer values. A B-tree will need around 90 MB of storage to do this. A hash index will need around 125 MB on disk. The assumption that's made by many people is that a hash is super small on disk and in many cases, that assumption is wrong.

GiST indexes

Generalized Search Tree (GiST) indexes are a highly important index type because they're used for a variety of different things. GiST indexes can be used to implement R-tree behavior, and it's even possible for them to act as B-trees. However, abusing GiST for B-tree indexes isn't recommended.

Let's consider some typical use cases for GiST:

- Range types
- Geometric indexes (for example, ones that are used by the highly popular PostGIS extension)
- Fuzzy searching

Understanding how GiST works

To many people, GiST is still a black box. Therefore, I've decided to add a section to this chapter that outlines how GiST works internally.

Consider the following diagram:

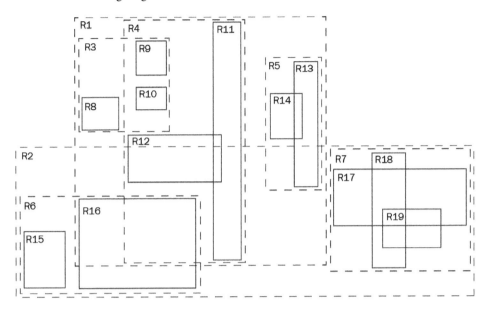

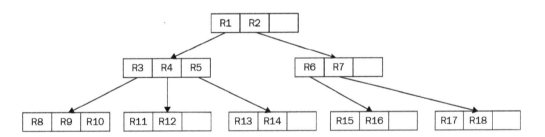

Figure 3.1 – A GiST tree

Take a look at the tree. You can see that **R1** and **R2** are at the top. **R1** and **R2** are the bounding boxes that contain everything else. **R3**, **R4**, and **R5** are contained by **R1**. **R8**, **R9**, and **R10** are contained by **R3**, and so on. Therefore, a GiST index is hierarchically organized. What you can see in the preceding diagram is that some operations that aren't available in B-trees are supported. Some of those operations are overlaps, left-of, right-of, and so on. The layout of a GiST tree is ideal for geometric indexing.

Extending GiST

Of course, it's also possible to come up with your own operator classes. The following strategies are supported:

Operation	Strategy
1	Strictly left of
2	Does not extend to right of
3	Overlaps
4	Does not extend to left of
5	Strictly right of
6	Same
7	Contains
8	Contained by
9	Does not extend above
10	Strictly below
11	Strictly above
12	Does not extend below

Table 3.3 – Strategies of operator classes

If you want to write operator classes for GiST, a couple of support functions have to be provided. In the case of a B-tree, there's only one function – GiST indexes provide a lot more:

Function	Description	Support Function Number
consistent	This determines whether a key satisfies the query qualifier. Internally, strategies are looked up and checked.	1
union	This calculates the union of a set of keys. In the case of numeric values, the upper and lower values or a range are computed. This is especially important to geometries.	2
compress	This computes a compressed representation of a key or value.	3
decompress	This is the counterpart of the compress function.	4

Function	Description	Support Function Number
penalty	During insertion, the cost of inserting into the tree will be calculated. The cost determines where the new entry will go inside the tree. Therefore, a good penalty function is key to getting good overall performance from the index.	5
picksplit	This determines where to move entries in the case of a page split. Some entries have to stay on the old page while others will go to the new page being created. Having a good picksplit function is essential to delivering good index performance.	6
equal	The equal function is similar to the same function you saw in B-trees.	7
distance	This calculates the distance between two keys, which is important for **K-nearest neighbors** (**KNN**) search.	8
fetch	This determines the original representation of a compressed key. It's needed to handle index-only scans, as supported by the most recent version of PostgreSQL.	9

Table 3.4 – Function – GiST indexes

Implementing operator classes for GiST indexes is usually done in C. If you're interested in a good example, I recommend checking out the btree_GiST module in the contrib directory. It shows how to index standard data types using GiST and is a good source of information, as well as inspiration.

GIN indexes

Generalized Inverted (**GIN**) indexes are a good way to index text. Suppose you want to index 1 million text documents. A certain word may occur millions of times. In a normal B-tree, this would mean that the key is stored millions of times. This isn't the case with GIN indexes. Each key (or word) is stored once and assigned to a document list. Keys are organized in a standard B-tree. Each entry will have a document list pointing to all the entries in the table that have the same key. A GIN index is very small and compact. However, it lacks an important feature that's found in B-trees – sorted data. In GIN, the list of item pointers associated with a certain key is sorted by the position of the row in the table, and not by some arbitrary criteria.

Extending GIN

Just like any other index, GIN can be extended. The following strategies are available:

Operator	Strategy Number
Overlap	1
Contains	2
Is contained by	3
Equal	4

Table 3.5 – GIN strategies

On top of this, the following support functions are available:

Function	Description	Support Function Number
Compare	This function is similar to the same function you saw regarding B-trees. If two keys are compared, it returns -1 (lower), 0 (equal), or 1 (higher).	1
extractValue	This extracts keys from a value to be indexed. A value can have many keys. For example, a text value might consist of more than one word.	2
extractQuery	This extracts keys from a query condition.	3
consistent	This checks whether a value matches a query condition.	4
comparePartial	This compares a partial key from a query and a key from the index. It returns -1, 0, or 1 (similar to the same function supported by B-trees).	5
triConsistent	This determines whether a value matches a query condition (ternary variant). It's optional if the consistent function is present.	6

Table 3.6 – Support functions

If you're looking for a good example of how to extend GIN, consider looking at the btree_gin module in the PostgreSQL contrib directory. It's a valuable source of information and a good way for you to start an implementation.

If you're interested in a full-text search, more information will be provided in the *Understanding full-text searches* section of this chapter.

SP-GiST indexes

Space-Partitioned GiST (SP-GiST) is mainly designed for in-memory use. The reason for this is that an SP-GiST stored on disk needs a fairly high number of disk hits to function. Disk hits are far more expensive than just following a couple of pointers in the RAM.

The beauty is that SP-GiST can be used to implement various types of trees, such as quadtrees, k-d trees, and radix trees (tries).

The following strategies are provided:

Operation	Strategy
Strictly left of	1
Strictly right of	5
Same	6
Contained by	8
Strictly below	10
Strictly above	11

Table 3.7 – Operation strategies

To write your own `operator` classes for SP-GiST, a couple of functions must be provided:

Function	Description	Support Function Number
Config	Provides information about the operator class in use	1
Choose	Figures out how to insert a new value into an inner tuple	2
picksplit	Figures out how to partition or split a set of values	3
inner_consistent	Determines which subpartitions need to be searched for a query	4
leaf_consistent	Determines whether the key satisfies the query qualifier	5

Table 3.8 – Functions for SP-GiST

BRINs

Block Range Indexes (**BRINs**) are of great practical use. All of the indexes we've discussed so far now need quite a lot of disk space. Although a lot of work has gone into shrinking GIN indexes and the like, they still need quite a lot of disk space because an index pointer is needed for each entry. So, if there are 10 million entries, there will be 10 million index pointers. Space is the main concern that's addressed by BRINs. A BRIN doesn't keep an index entry for each tuple and instead stores the minimum and maximum values of 128 (default) blocks of data (1 MB). Therefore, the index is very small but involves losses. Scanning the index will return more data than we asked for. PostgreSQL has to filter out these additional rows in a later step.

The following example demonstrates how small a BRIN is:

```
test=# CREATE INDEX idx_brin ON t_test USING brin(id);
CREATE INDEX
test=# \di+ idx_brin
                              List of relations
 Schema |    Name   |  Type  | Owner | Table  | Persistence | Size ...
--------+-----------+--------+-------+--------+-------------+-------
 public | idx_brin  | index  | hs    | t_test | permanent   | 48 kB
(1 row)
```

In my example, the BRIN is 2,000 times smaller than a standard B-tree. The question that naturally arises is why we don't always use BRINs. To answer this kind of question, it's important to reflect on the layout of a BRIN; the minimum and maximum values for 1 MB are stored. If the data is sorted (highly correlated), a BRIN is pretty efficient because we can fetch 1 MB of data and scan it, and we're done. However, what if the data is shuffled? In this case, a BRIN won't be able to exclude chunks of data anymore because it's very likely that something close to the overall high and the overall low is within that 1 MB of data. Therefore, BRINs are mostly made for highly correlated data. In reality, correlated data is quite likely in data warehousing applications. Often, data is loaded every day, and therefore dates can be highly correlated.

Extending BRINs

A BRIN supports the same strategies as a B-tree and therefore needs the same set of operators. The code can be reused nicely:

Operation	Strategy Number
Less than	1
Less than or equal	2
Equal	3

Operation	Strategy Number
Greater than or equal	4
Greater than	5

Table 3.9 – BRINs

The following support functions are required by BRINs:

Function	Description	Support Function Number
opcInfo	Provides internal information about the indexed columns	1
add_value	Adds an entry to an existing summary tuple	2
consistent	Checks whether a value matches a condition	3
Union	Calculates the union of two summary entries (minimum/maximum values)	4

Table 3.10 – Support functions required by BRINs

Adding additional indexes

Since PostgreSQL 9.6, there's been an easy way to deploy entirely new index types as extensions. This is pretty cool because if those index types provided by PostgreSQL aren't enough, it's possible to add additional ones that serve your purpose. The instruction to do this is CREATE ACCESS METHOD:

```
test=# \h CREATE ACCESS METHOD
Command:     CREATE ACCESS METHOD
Description: define a new access method
Syntax:
CREATE ACCESS METHOD name
    TYPE access_method_type
    HANDLER handler_function
URL: https://www.postgresql.org/docs/17/sql-create-access-method.html/
```

Don't worry too much about this command – if you ever deploy your own index type, it will come as a ready-to-use extension.

One of these extensions implements bloom filters, which are probabilistic data structures. They sometimes return too many rows, but never too few. Therefore, a bloom filter is a good way to pre-filter data.

How does it work? A `bloom` filter is defined on a couple of columns. A bitmask is calculated based on the input values, which is then compared to your query. The upside of a `bloom` filter is that you can index as many columns as you want. The downside is that the entire `bloom` filter has to be read. Of course, the `bloom` filter is smaller than the underlying data, so in many cases, it's very beneficial.

To use `bloom` filters, just activate the extension, which is a part of the PostgreSQL `contrib` package:

```
test=# CREATE EXTENSION bloom;
CREATE EXTENSION
```

As we stated previously, the idea behind a `bloom` filter is that it allows you to index as many columns as you want. In many real-world applications, the challenge is indexing many columns without knowing which combinations the user will need at runtime. In the case of a large table, it's impossible to create standard B-tree indexes on, say, 80 fields or more. A `bloom` filter might be an alternative in this case:

```
test=# CREATE TABLE t_bloom (x1 int, x2 int, x3 int,
                        x4 int, x5 int, x6 int, x7 int);
CREATE TABLE
```

Creating the index is easy:

```
test=# CREATE INDEX idx_bloom ON t_bloom
USING bloom(x1, x2, x3, x4, x5, x6, x7);
CREATE INDEX
```

If sequential scans are turned off, the index can be seen in action:

```
test=# SET enable_seqscan TO off;
SET
test=# explain SELECT *
FROM    t_bloom
WHERE   x5 = 9 AND x3 = 7;
                          QUERY PLAN
-----------------------------------------------------------------
 Bitmap Heap Scan on t_bloom
    (cost=18.50..22.52 rows=1 width=28)
    Recheck Cond: ((x3 = 7) AND (x5 = 9))
    -> Bitmap Index Scan on idx_bloom
        (cost=0.00..18.50 rows=1 width=0)
          Index Cond: ((x3 = 7) AND (x5 = 9))
```

Note that I've queried a combination of random columns; they aren't related to the actual order in the index. The `bloom` filter will still be beneficial.

Achieving better answers with fuzzy searching

Performing precise searching isn't the only thing expected by users these days. Modern websites have taught users to always expect a result, regardless of their input. If you search on Google, there will always be an answer, even if the user input is wrong, full of typos, or simply pointless. People expect good results, regardless of the input data. This section will cover even more fuzzy string search techniques.

Taking advantage of pg_trgm

To do fuzzy searching with PostgreSQL, you can add the pg_trgm extension. To activate the extension, just run the following command:

```
test=# CREATE EXTENSION pg_trgm;
CREATE EXTENSION
```

The pg_trgm extension is pretty powerful. To show you what it's capable of, I've compiled some sample data consisting of 2,354 names of villages and cities here in Austria.

Our sample data can be stored in a simple table:

```
test=# CREATE TABLE t_location (name text);
CREATE TABLE
```

My company website has all the data available, and PostgreSQL allows you to load the data directly:

```
test=# COPY t_location FROM PROGRAM
'curl https://www.cybertec-postgresql.com/secret/orte.txt';
COPY 2354
```

> **Note**
>
> curl (a command-line tool for fetching data) has to be installed. If you don't have this tool, download the file normally and import it from your local filesystem.

Once the data has been loaded, it's possible to check out the contents of the table:

```
test=# SELECT * FROM t_location LIMIT 4;
              name
--------------------------------
 Eisenstadt
 Rust
 Breitenbrunn am Neusiedler See
 Donnerskirchen
(4 rows)
```

If German isn't your mother tongue, it may be difficult to spell the names of some of those locations without severe mistakes.

Here, pg_trgm provides us with a distance operator that computes the distance between two strings:

```
test=# SELECT 'abcde' <-> 'abdeacb';
 ?column?
----------
 0.833333
(1 row)
```

The distance is a number between 0 and 1. The lower the number, the more similar the two strings are.

How does this work? Trigrams take a string and dissect it into sequences of three characters each:

```
test=# SELECT show_trgm('abcdef');
               show_trgm
-------------------------------------
 {" a"," ab",abc,bcd,cde,def,"ef "} (1 row)
```

These sequences will then be used to come up with the distance you've just seen. Of course, the distance operator can be used inside a query to find the closest match:

```
test=# SELECT *
FROM t_location
ORDER BY name <-> 'Kramertneusiedel'
LIMIT 3;
      name
-----------------
 Gramatneusiedl
 Klein-Neusiedl
 Potzneusiedl
(3 rows)
```

As we can see, Gramatneusiedl is pretty close to Kramertneusiedel. It sounds similar and using K instead of G is a pretty common mistake. On Google, you will sometimes see *Did you mean...?* It's quite likely that Google is using n-grams here to do that.

In PostgreSQL, it's possible to use GiST to index text using trigrams:

```
test=# CREATE INDEX idx_trgm ON t_location
USING GiST(name GiST_trgm_ops);
CREATE INDEX
```

The pg_trgm extension provides us with the GiST_trgm_ops operator class, which is designed to do similarity searches. The following code shows that the index is used as expected:

```
test=# explain SELECT *
FROM t_location
ORDER BY name <-> 'Kramertneusiedel'
LIMIT 5;
                              QUERY PLAN
-----------------------------------------------------------
 Limit (cost=0.14..0.58 rows=5 width=17)
   -> Index Scan using idx_trgm on t_location
        (cost=0.14..207.22 rows=2354 width=17)
        Order By: (name <-> <Kramertneusiedel'::text)
(3 rows)
```

In this example, I've used a GiST index to index the trigram. However, for large datasets, it's a lot better to use GIN instead. I've written a blog post that shows the difference. You can find it on my website at https://www.cybertec-postgresql.com/en/postgresql-more-performance-for-like-and-ilike-statements/.

Speeding up LIKE queries

LIKE queries definitely cause some of the worst performance problems faced by users around the globe these days. In most database systems, LIKE is pretty slow and requires a sequential scan. In addition to this, end users quickly figure out that a fuzzy search will, in many cases, return better results than precise queries. A single type of a LIKE query on a large table can, therefore, often diminish the performance of an entire database server if it's called often enough.

Fortunately, PostgreSQL offers a solution to this problem, and the solution happens to be installed already:

```
test=# explain SELECT *
FROM    t_location
WHERE   name LIKE '%neusi%';
                            QUERY PLAN
-----------------------------------------------------------
 Bitmap Heap Scan on t_location
   (cost=4.33..19.05 rows=24 width=13)
   Recheck Cond: (name ~~ <%neusi%'::text)
   -> Bitmap Index Scan on idx_trgm
      (cost=0.00..4.32 rows=24 width=0)
        Index Cond: (name ~~ <%neusi%'::text)
(4 rows)
```

The trigram index that we deployed in the previous section is also suitable for speeding up `LIKE`. Note that the `%` symbols can be used at any point in the search string. This is a major advantage over standard B-trees, which just happen to speed up wildcards at the end of a query.

Handling regular expressions

However, this is still not everything. Trigram indexes are even capable of speeding up simple regular expressions. The following example shows how this can be done:

```
test=# SELECT *
FROM    t_location
WHERE   name ~ '[A-C].*neu.*';
     name
- - - - - - - - - - - - - -
 Bruckneudorf
(1 row)
test=# explain SELECT *
FROM    t_location
WHERE name ~ '[A-C].*neu.*';
                         QUERY PLAN
- - - - - - - - - - - - - - - - - - - - - - - - - - - - - - - - - - - - - - - - - - - - - - - - -
 Index Scan using idx_trgm on t_location (cost=0.14..8.16
   rows=1 width=13)
   Index Cond: (name ~ <[A-C].*neu.*'::text)
(2 rows)
```

PostgreSQL will inspect the regular expression and use the index to answer the question.

> **Note**
> Internally, PostgreSQL can transform the regular expression into a graph and traverse the index accordingly.

Understanding full-text searches

If you're looking up names or looking for simple strings, you're usually querying the entire content of a field. With a full-text search, this is different. The purpose of the full-text search is to look for words or groups of words that can be found in a text. Therefore, a full-text search is more of a `contains` operation as you're never looking for an exact string.

In PostgreSQL, a full-text search can be done using GIN indexes. The idea is to dissect a piece of text, extract valuable lexeme (preprocessed tokens of words) strings, and index those elements rather than the underlying text. To make your search even more successful, those words are preprocessed.

Here's an example:

```
test=# SELECT to_tsvector('english','A car,
    I want a car. I would not even mind having many cars');
                            to_tsvector
---------------------------------------------------------------
 'car':2,6,14 'even':10 'mani':13 'mind':11 'want':4 'would':8
(1 row)
```

This example shows a simple sentence. The `to_tsvector` function will take the string, apply English language rules, and perform a stemming process. Based on the configuration (`english`), PostgreSQL will parse the string, throw away stop words, and stem individual words. For example, `car` and `cars` will be transformed into `car`. Note that this isn't just about finding the word stem. In the case of `many`, PostgreSQL will simply transform the string into `mani` by applying standard rules that work nicely with the English language.

Note that the output of the `to_tsvector` function is highly language-dependent. If you tell PostgreSQL to treat the string as `dutch`, the result will be different:

```
test=# SELECT to_tsvector('dutch', 'A car,
    I want a car. I would not even mind having many cars');
                            to_tsvector
--------------------------------------------------------------
 'a':1,5 'car':2,6,14 'even':10 'having':12 'i':3,7 'many':13
    <mind>:11 <not>:9 <would>:8
(1 row)
```

To figure out which configurations are supported, consider running the following query:

```
SELECT cfgname FROM pg_ts_config;
```

Now, let's learn how to compare strings.

Comparing strings

After taking a brief look at the stemming process, it's time to figure out how a stemmed text can be compared to a user query. The following code snippet looks for `wanted`:

```
test=# SELECT to_tsvector(
'english', 'A car, I want a car. I would not even mind having many
cars') @@ to_tsquery('english', 'wanted');
?column?
----------
 t
(1 row)
```

Note that wanted doesn't show up in the original text. Still, PostgreSQL will return true. The reason is that want and wanted are both transformed into the same lexeme, so the result is true. Practically, this makes a lot of sense. Imagine that you're looking for a car on Google. If you find pages selling cars, this is fine. Finding common lexemes is, therefore, an intelligent idea.

Sometimes, people want to find a set of words rather than a single word. With to_tsquery, this is made possible, as shown in the following example:

```
test=# SELECT to_tsvector('english', 'A car, I want a car. I would not
even mind having many cars') @@ to_tsquery('english', 'wanted & bmw');
?column?
----------
 f
(1 row)
```

In this case, false is returned because bmw can't be found in our input string. In the to_tsquery function, & means and, and | means or. So, it's easy to build complex search strings.

Defining GIN indexes

If you want to apply text search to a column or a group of columns, there are two choices:

- Create a functional index using GIN

- Add a column containing ready-to-use tsvector objects and a trigger to keep them in sync

In this section, both options will be outlined. To show you how things work, I've created some sample data:

```
test=# CREATE TABLE t_fts AS SELECT comment
FROM pg_available_extensions;
 SELECT 43
```

Indexing the column directly with a functional index is a slower but more space-efficient way to get things done:

```
test=# CREATE INDEX idx_fts_func ON t_fts
USING gin(to_tsvector('english', comment));
 CREATE INDEX
```

Deploying an index on the function is easy, but it can lead to some overhead. Adding a materialized column needs more space, but this will lead to better runtime behavior:

```
test=# ALTER TABLE t_fts ADD COLUMN ts tsvector;
 ALTER TABLE
```

The only trouble is, how do you keep this column in sync? The answer is by using a trigger:

```
test=# CREATE TRIGGER tsvectorupdate
BEFORE INSERT OR UPDATE ON t_fts
FOR EACH ROW
EXECUTE PROCEDURE
tsvector_update_trigger(somename, 'pg_catalog.english', 'comment');
```

Fortunately, PostgreSQL already provides a C function that can be used by a trigger to sync the `tsvector` column. Just pass a name, the desired language, and a couple of columns to the function, and you're already done. The `trigger` function will take care of all that's needed. Note that a trigger will always operate within the same transaction as the statement that is making a modification. Therefore, there's no risk of being inconsistent.

Debugging your search

Sometimes, it isn't quite clear why a query matches a given search string. To debug your query, PostgreSQL offers the `ts_debug` function. From a user's point of view, it can be used just like `to_tsvector`. It reveals a lot about the inner workings of the full-text search infrastructure:

```
test=# \x
Expanded display is on.
test=# SELECT *
FROM ts_debug('english', 'go to www.cybertec-postgresql.com');
-[ RECORD 1 ]+-----------------------------
alias        | asciiword
description  | Word, all ASCII
token        | go
dictionaries | {english_stem}
dictionary   | english_stem
lexemes      | {go}
-[ RECORD 2 ]+-----------------------------
alias        | blank
description  | Space symbols
token        |
dictionaries | {}
dictionary   |
lexemes      |
-[ RECORD 3 ]+-----------------------------
alias        | asciiword
description  | Word, all ASCII
token        | to
dictionaries | {english_stem}
dictionary   | english_stem
```

```
lexemes       | {}
-[ RECORD 4 ]+-----------------------------
alias         | blank
description   | Space symbols
token         |
dictionaries  | {}
dictionary    |
lexemes       |
-[ RECORD 5 ]+-----------------------------
alias         | host
description   | Host
token         | www.cybertec-postgresql.com
dictionaries  | {simple}
dictionary    | simple
lexemes       | {www.cybertec-postgresql.com}
```

The `ts_debug` function will list every token found and display information about the token. You will see which token the parser found, the dictionary used, and the type of object. In my example, blanks, words, and hosts have been found. You might also see numbers, email addresses, and a lot more. Depending on the type of string, PostgreSQL will handle things differently. For example, it makes absolutely no sense to stem hostnames and email addresses.

Gathering word statistics

A full-text search can handle a lot of data. To give end users more insight into their texts, PostgreSQL offers the `ts_stat` function, which returns a list of words:

```
SELECT * FROM  ts_stat('SELECT to_tsvector(''english'', comment)
    FROM  pg_available_extensions')
ORDER BY 2 DESC
LIMIT 3;
  word     | ndoc | nentry
----------+------+--------
function  | 10   | 10
data      | 10   | 10
type      | 7    | 7
(3 rows)
```

The `word` column contains the stemmed words; `ndoc` tells us about the number of documents a certain word occurs in. Finally, `nentry` indicates how often a word was found altogether.

Taking advantage of exclusion operators

So far, indexes have been used to speed things up and to ensure uniqueness. However, a couple of years ago, somebody came up with the idea of using indexes for even more. As you've seen in this chapter, GiST supports operations such as intersects, overlaps, contains, and many others, so why not use those operations to manage data integrity?

Here's an example:

```
test=# CREATE EXTENSION btree_gist;

test=# CREATE TABLE t_reservation (
    room int,
    from_to tsrange,
    EXCLUDE USING GiST (room with =, from_to with &&)
);
CREATE TABLE
```

The EXCLUDE USING GiST clause defines additional constraints. If you're selling rooms, you might want to allow different rooms to be booked at the same time. However, you don't want to sell the same room twice during the same period. What the EXCLUDE clause says in my example is that if a room is booked twice at the same time, an error should occur (the data in from_to must not overlap with && if it's related to the same room).

The following two rows will not violate the constraints:

```
test=# INSERT INTO t_reservation
VALUES (10, '["2017-01-01", "2017-03-03"]');
 INSERT 0 1
test=# INSERT INTO t_reservation
VALUES (13, '["2017-01-01", "2017-03-03"]');
INSERT 0 1
```

However, the next INSERT will cause a violation because the data overlaps:

```
test=# INSERT INTO t_reservation
VALUES (13, '["2017-02-02", "2017-08-14"]');
 psql: ERROR:  conflicting key value violates exclusion constraint "t_
reservation_room_from_to_excl"
DETAIL:  Key (room, from_to)=(13, ["2017-02-02 00:00:00","2017-08-14
00:00:00"]) conflicts with existing key (room, from_to)=(13, ["2017-
01-01 00:00:00","2017-03-03 00:00:00"]).
```

The use of exclusion operators is very useful and can provide you with highly advanced means to handle integrity.

Summary

This chapter was all about indexes. We learned about when PostgreSQL will decide on an index and which types of indexes exist. On top of just using indexes, it's also possible to implement strategies to speed up your applications with custom operators and indexing strategies.

If you want to push its capabilities to the limit, PostgreSQL offers custom access methods.

In *Chapter 4, Handling Advanced SQL*, we'll talk about advanced SQL. Many people aren't aware of what SQL is capable of, so I'm going to show you some efficient, more advanced SQL techniques.

Handling Advanced SQL

4

In *Chapter 3*, *Making Use of Indexes*, you learned about indexing, as well as about PostgreSQL's ability to run custom indexing code to speed up queries. In this chapter, you will learn about advanced SQL. Most of the people who read this book will have some experience in using SQL. However, my experience has shown that the advanced features outlined in this book are not widely known, and therefore, it makes sense to cover them in this context to help people achieve their goals faster and more efficiently. There has been a long discussion about whether a database is just a simple data store or whether the business logic should be in the database. This chapter will shed some light on this and show how capable a modern relational database really is. SQL is not what it used to be back when SQL-92 was around. Over the years, the language has grown and become more and more powerful.

This chapter is about modern SQL and its features. A variety of different and sophisticated SQL features are covered and presented in detail. We will cover the following topics in this chapter:

- Supporting range types
- Introducing grouping sets
- Making use of ordered sets
- Understanding hypothetical aggregates
- Utilizing windowing functions and analytics
- Writing your own aggregates
- Handling recursions
- Working with JSON and JSONB

By the end of this chapter, you will understand and be able to use advanced SQL. I highly recommend studying this chapter in great detail. A couple of lines of SQL can help you to reduce the amount of client code by a significant amount.

Supporting range types

One of the most powerful features of PostgreSQL is the ability to make use of range types. Why is that important? When dealing with all kinds of data, we will often see that information is only valid for a certain period. Maybe we want to store prices that change over time, or we want to handle measurement data that is only valid for a certain period.

Normally, what you would do is use two columns, as shown in the next example:

```
test=# CREATE TABLE t_price (
    id              SERIAL,
    product_name    TEXT,
    price           NUMERIC,
    price_from      DATE,
    price_until     DATE,
    CHECK (price_until >= price_from)
);
CREATE TABLE
```

In this case, the price is valid for a certain period. If we want to query whether price periods overlap or if we want to do other more complicated calculations, we can easily end up with a fairly hard-to-read AND/OR program that is hard to debug.

The solution to the problem is to use ranges. Consider the following example:

```
test=# CREATE TABLE t_price_range (
    id              serial,
    product_name    text,
    price           numeric,
    price_range     daterange
);
```

Two columns have been replaced by a single column. The beauty is that we can even skip the CHECK constraint ensuring that the validity of the data has to end before it starts.

However, the way we interface with this data is not the same as in the case of two separate columns. Range types must be formed. The next code block shows how this can be done:

```
test=# SELECT int4range(10, 20);
 int4range
-----------
 [10,20)
(1 row)
test=# SELECT daterange('2025-10-04', '2027-05-01');
```

```
      daterange
-------------------------
 [2025-10-04,2027-05-01)
(1 row)
```

The first example shows how to form an integer range. `int4range(10, 20)` means that `10` is included in the range, while `20` is not. The brackets and parentheses indicate exactly that. Therefore, these two ranges are identical:

```
test=# SELECT '[10, 19]'::int4range, '[10,20)'::int4range;
 int4range | int4range
-----------+-----------
 [10,20)   | [10,20)
(1 row)
```

Many different data types can be ranges: numbers, dates, timestamps, and the like. In other words, every representation of a number (and dates are just strange numbers) that can be sorted can also be a range.

Armed with this new knowledge, we can start to insert some data into our table:

```
test=# INSERT INTO t_price_range
    (product_name, price, price_range)
VALUES
    ('Apple', 1.5, '[2022-01-01, 2022-03-03]');INSERT 0 1
test=# INSERT INTO t_price_range
    (product_name, price, price_range)
VALUES
    ('Peach', 2.67, '[2055-01-01, 2022-03-03]');
ERROR:   range lower bound must be less than or equal to
    range upper bound
LINE 1: ..._name, price, price_range)
    VALUES ('Peach', 2.67, '[2055-01-...
```

The most important observation here is that range types come with implicit quality checks. PostgreSQL ensures that the boundaries make sense. Otherwise, an error is issued.

Querying ranges efficiently

However, it is not only about validating data. Once data has been added to a table, we want to query this information. To make this really easy, PostgreSQL provides a rich set of operators, allowing us to quickly get a handle on the data. One of the most commonly used operators is the `contains` operator. Suppose we want to figure out whether `17` is part of our range:

```
test=# SELECT 17 <@ '[10, 19]'::int4range;
 ?column?
```

```
----------
 t
(1 row)
```

The <@ operator tells us that 17 is indeed part of the range.

PostgreSQL offers many operators to process ranges. The following table contains an overview of what is available. Note that this list is straight from the PostgreSQL documentation (https://www.postgresql.org/docs/12/functions-range.html), which contains this information in table form. Later versions of the docs don't have the data in this format anymore:

Operator	Description	Example	Result
=	equal	`int4range(1,5) = '[1,4]'::int4range`	t
<>	not equal	`numrange(1.1,2.2) <> numrange(1.1,2.3)`	t
<	less than	`int4range(1,10) < int4range(2,3)`	t
>	greater than	`int4range(1,10) > int4range(1,5)`	t
<=	less than or equal	`numrange(1.1,2.2) <= numrange(1.1,2.2)`	t
>=	greater than or equal	`numrange(1.1,2.2) >= numrange(1.1,2.0)`	t
@>	contains range	`int4range(2,4) @> int4range(2,3)`	t
@>	contains element	`'[2011-01-01,2011-03-01)'::tsrange @> '2011-01-10'::timestamp`	t
<@	range is contained by	`int4range(2,4) <@ int4range(1,7)`	t
<@	element is contained by	`42 <@ int4range(1,7)`	f
&&	overlap (have points in common)	`int8range(3,7) && int8range(4,12)`	t
<<	strictly left of	`int8range(1,10) << int8range(100,110)`	t
>>	strictly right of	`int8range(50,60) >> int8range(20,30)`	t
&<	does not extend to the right of	`int8range(1,20) &< int8range(18,20)`	t

Operator	Description	Example	Result
&>	does not extend to the left of	`int8range(7,20) &> int8range(5,10)`	t
-|-	is adjacent to	`numrange(1.1,2.2) -|- numrange(2.2,3.3)`	t
+	union	`numrange(5,15) + numrange(10,20)`	`[5,20)`
*	intersection	`int8range(5,15) * int8range(10,20)`	`[10,15)`
-	difference	`int8range(5,15) - int8range(10,20)`	`[5,10)`

Table 4.1 – PostgreSQL documentation representation

After taking a look at basic ranges, we can dive deeper and see what has been added after PostgreSQL 14: multirange types.

Handling multirange types

So far, you have learned about simple ranges. However, there is more. A **multirange** consists of one or more ranges packed together in a single column. This is super useful for various reasons. In the case of our product prices, we could have reduced the content of our table dramatically because all we need now is a single row for each product containing all periods where the same price is valid.

That being said, let us see how multirange types can be used in the first place:

```
test=# SELECT int4multirange('{(10, 20), (30, 40)}');
   int4multirange
-------------------
 {[11,20),[31,40)}
(1 row)
test=# SELECT 33 <@ int4multirange('{(10, 20), (30, 40)}');
 ?column?
----------
 t
(1 row)
test=# SELECT 25 <@ int4multirange('{(10, 20), (30, 40)}');
 ?column?
----------
 f
(1 row)
```

The `contains` operator (`<@`) works normally. We can also see that those ranges are simply passed to PostgreSQL as an ordinary array.

Of course, we can also check whether ranges overlap with multiranges:

```
test=# SELECT
    int4multirange('{(10, 20), (30, 40)}')
    && int4range(18, 32);
 ?column?
----------
 t
(1 row)
```

The important point when looking at this example is that the range we are checking against basically touches two parts of our multirange. If one of those ranges matches, the operator will return `true`.

PostgreSQL is even more clever. Check out the following example:

```
test=# SELECT int4multirange('{(10, 20), (15, 30)}');
 int4multirange
----------------
 {[11,30)}
(1 row)
```

The database engine has figured out that those ranges are actually one. It folded those ranges into one big range.

When to use range types

Range types can add a lot of efficiency to your data structures. However, the downside is definitely portability. If PostgreSQL is the only database your application has to support, range types are ideal. If your goal is portability, you have to keep in mind that we are talking about a PostgreSQL-specific feature here.

However, there is a compromise that can be beneficial to many people. You can mix the "traditional representation" of data with range types, as shown in the following listing:

```
test=# CREATE VIEW v AS
    SELECT
        id,
        product_name,
        price,
        lower(price_range),
        upper(price_range)
    FROM
```

```
        t_price_range;
CREATE VIEW
test=# \x
Expanded display is on.
test=# SELECT * FROM v;
-[ RECORD 1 ]+-----------
id           | 1       .
product_name | Apple
price        | 1.5
lower        | 2022-01-01
upper        | 2022-03-04
```

By exposing views, it is often possible to hide what is really going on behind the scenes while still harnessing the full power of PostgreSQL. Most client applications will be able to handle views just like tables and, therefore, operate smoothly.

After dealing with range types, we can focus on another important topic that many people are not aware of: grouping sets.

Introducing grouping sets

Every advanced user of SQL should be familiar with the GROUP BY and HAVING clauses. But are they also aware of CUBE, ROLLUP, and GROUPING SETS? If not, this chapter is a must-read. What is the basic idea behind a grouping set? Basically, the concept is simple: by using a grouping set, you can combine various aggregations into a single query. The main advantage is that you have to read data only once while producing many different aggregation sets at the same time.

Loading some sample data

To make this chapter a pleasant experience for you, we will compile some sample data that has been taken from the BP energy report, which can be found at https://www.bp.com/en/global/corporate/energy-economics.html.

Here is the data structure that will be used:

```
test=# CREATE TABLE t_oil (
    region          TEXT,
    country         TEXT,
    year            INT,
    production      INT,
    consumption     INT
);
CREATE TABLE
```

The test data can be downloaded from our website using `curl` directly:

```
test=# COPY t_oil
FROM PROGRAM
'curl https://www.cybertec-postgresql.com/secret/oil_ext.txt';
COPY 644
```

As we did in the previous chapter, we can download the file before importing it. On some operating systems, `curl` is not present by default or has not been installed, so downloading the file before importing it might be an easier option for many people.

We have some data on oil production and consumption from 1965 to 2010 from 14 nations in 2 regions of the world:

```
test=# SELECT
    region,
    AVG(production)
FROM
    t_oil
GROUP BY
    region
ORDER BY
    1;
    region    |         avg
--------------+---------------------
 Middle East  | 1992.6036866359447005
 North America | 4541.3623188405797101
(2 rows)
```

The result is exactly what we would expect: two rows containing the average production.

Applying grouping sets

The `GROUP BY` clause will turn many rows into one row per group. However, if you do reporting in real life, users might also be interested in the overall average. One additional line might be needed.

This is how this can be achieved:

```
test=# SELECT
    region,
    AVG(production)
```

```
FROM
    t_oil
GROUP BY
    ROLLUP (region)
ORDER BY
    1;
    region     |          avg
---------------+------------------------
 Middle East   | 1992.6036866359447005
 North America | 4541.3623188405797101
               | 2607.5139860139860140
(3 rows)
```

The ROLLUP keyword will inject an additional line, which will contain the overall average. Note that this is *not* the average of the averages—it represents the real overall average, as defined by the underlying data. If you do reporting, it is very likely that a summary line will be needed. Instead of running two queries, PostgreSQL can provide the data by running just a single query. There is also a second thing you might notice here: different versions of PostgreSQL might return data in a different order. The reason for this is that in PostgreSQL 10.0, the way those grouping sets are implemented has improved significantly. Back in version 9.6 and before, PostgreSQL had to do a lot of sorting. Starting with version 10.0, it is possible to use hashing for those operations, which will speed things up dramatically in many cases, as shown in the following code block:

```
test=# SELECT
    region, AVG(production)
FROM
    t_oil
GROUP BY
    ROLLUP (region)
ORDER BY
    1;
                      QUERY PLAN
---------------------------------------------------------------
 Sort  (cost=17.33..17.34 rows=3 width=44)
   Sort Key: region
   ->  MixedAggregate  (cost=0.00..17.31 rows=3 width=44)
         Hash Key: region
         Group Key: ()
         ->  Seq Scan on t_oil  (cost=0.00..12.44 rows=644 width=16)
(6 rows)
```

If we want the data to be sorted and ensure that all of the versions return the data in exactly the same order, it is necessary to add an ORDER BY clause to the query.

Of course, this kind of operation can also be used if you are grouping by more than just one column:

```
test=# SELECT
    region, country, AVG(production)
FROM
    t_oil
WHERE
    country IN ('USA', 'Canada', 'Iran', 'Oman')
GROUP BY
    ROLLUP (region, country)
ORDER BY
    1, 2;
    region      | country |          avg
---------------+---------+-----------------------
 Middle East   | Iran    | 3631.6956521739130435
 Middle East   | Oman    |  586.4545454545454545
 Middle East   |         | 2142.9111111111111111
 North America | Canada  | 2123.2173913043478261
 North America | USA     | 9141.3478260869565217
 North America |         | 5632.2826086956521739
               |         | 3906.7692307692307692
(7 rows)
```

In the preceding example, PostgreSQL will inject three lines into the result set. One line will be injected for the Middle East, and one line will be injected for North America. On top of that, we will get a line for the overall averages. If we are building a web application, the current result is ideal because you can easily build a GUI to drill into the result set by filtering out the null values.

ROLLUP is suitable when you instantly want to display a result. Personally, I have always used it to display final results to end users. However, if you are doing reporting, then you might want to precalculate more data to ensure more flexibility. The CUBE keyword will help you with this:

```
test=# SELECT region, country, avg(production)
FROM    t_oil
WHERE   country IN ('USA', 'Canada', 'Iran', 'Oman')
GROUP BY CUBE (region, country)
ORDER BY 1, 2;
    region      | country |          avg
---------------+---------+-----------------------
 Middle East   | Iran    | 3631.6956521739130435
 Middle East   | Oman    |  586.4545454545454545
 Middle East   |         | 2142.9111111111111111
 North America | Canada  | 2123.2173913043478261
 North America | USA     | 9141.3478260869565217
```

```
North America |             | 5632.2826086956521739
              | Canada      | 2123.2173913043478261
              | Iran        | 3631.6956521739130435
              | Oman        |  586.4545454545454545
              | USA         | 9141.3478260869565217
              |             | 3906.7692307692307692
(11 rows)
```

Note that even more rows have been added to the result. CUBE will create the same data as GROUP BY region, country + GROUP BY region + GROUP BY country + the overall average. So, the whole idea is to extract many results and various levels of aggregation at once. The resultant cube contains all possible combinations of groups.

ROLLUP and CUBE are really just convenience features on top of the GROUPING SETS clause. With the GROUPING SETS clause, you can explicitly list the aggregates you want:

```
test=# SELECT   region, country, avg(production)
FROM    t_oil
WHERE   country IN ('USA', 'Canada',
        'Iran', 'Oman')
GROUP BY GROUPING SETS ( (), region, country)
ORDER BY 1, 2;
    region     | country |          avg
---------------+---------+------------------------
 Middle East   |         | 2142.9111111111111111
 North America |         | 5632.2826086956521739
               | Canada  | 2123.2173913043478261
               | Iran    | 3631.6956521739130435
               | Oman    |  586.4545454545454545
               | USA     | 9141.3478260869565217
               |         | 3906.7692307692307692
(7 rows)
```

In this section, I went for three grouping sets: the overall average, group by region, and group by country. If you want regions and countries combined, use (region, country).

Investigating performance

Grouping sets are a powerful feature; they help to reduce the number of expensive queries. Internally, PostgreSQL will basically use MixedAggregate to perform the aggregation. It can perform many operations at once, which ensures efficiency, as shown in the following example:

```
test=# explain SELECT region, country, avg(production)
FROM    t_oil
WHERE   country IN ('USA', 'Canada',
```

```
                    'Iran', 'Oman')
GROUP BY GROUPING SETS ( (), region, country)
ORDER BY 1, 2;
                            QUERYPLAN
-------------------------------------------------------------
Sort   (cost=18.52..18.56 rows=17 width=52)
    Sort Key: region, country
    -> MixedAggregate  (cost=0.00..18.17 rows=17 width=52)
          Hash Key: region
          Hash Key: country
          Group Key: ()
          -> Seq Scan on t_oil
              (cost=0.00..15.66 rows=184 width=24)
              Filter: (country = ANY
('{USA,Canada,Iran,Oman}'::text[]))
(8 rows)
```

In older versions of PostgreSQL, the system used GroupAggregate to perform this operation in all cases. In more modern versions, MixedAggregate has been added. However, you can still force the optimizer to use the old strategy using the enable_hashagg setting. MixedAggregate is essentially HashAggregate and therefore, the same setting applies, as shown in the next example:

```
test=# SET enable_hashagg TO off;
SET
test=# explain SELECT region, country, avg(production)
FROM   t_oil
WHERE   country IN ('USA', 'Canada',
        'Iran', 'Oman')
GROUP BY GROUPING SETS ( (), region, country)
ORDER BY 1, 2;
                            QUERY PLAN
-------------------------------------------------------------
Sort   (cost=32.82..32.87 rows=17 width=52)
    Sort Key: region, country
    -> GroupAggregate  (cost=22.58..32.48 rows=17 width=52)
          Group Key: region
          Group Key: ()
          Sort Key: country
            Group Key: country
          -> Sort  (cost=22.58..23.04 rows=184 width=24)
              Sort Key: region
              -> Seq Scan on t_oil
                  (cost=0.00..15.66 rows=184 width=24)
                  Filter: (country = ANY
('{USA,Canada,Iran,Oman}'::text[]))
```

```
(11 rows)
test=# SET enable_hashagg TO on;
SET
```

In general, the hash-based version (`MixedAggregate`) is faster and is favored by the optimizer if there is enough memory to keep the hash needed for `MixedAggregate` in memory.

Combining grouping sets with the FILTER clause

In real-world applications, grouping sets can often be combined with `FILTER` clauses. The idea behind the `FILTER` clause is to be able to run partial aggregates. Here is an example:

```
test=# SELECT region,
    avg(production) AS all,
    avg(production) FILTER (WHERE year  < 1990) AS old,
    avg(production) FILTER (WHERE year  >= 1990) AS new
FROM t_oil
GROUP BY ROLLUP (region)
ORDER BY 1;
    region     | all            | old            | new
---------------+----------------+----------------+---------
 Middle East   | 1992.603686635 | 1747.325892857 | 2254.233333333
 North America | 4541.362318840 | 4471.653333333 | 4624.349206349
               | 2607.513986013 | 2430.685618729 | 2801.183150183
(3 rows)
```

The idea here is that not all columns will use the same data for aggregation. The `FILTER` clause allows you to selectively pass data to those aggregates. In this example, the second aggregate will only consider data before 1990, the third aggregate will take care of more recent data, and the first one will get all the data.

> **Tip**
> If it is possible to move conditions to a `WHERE` clause, it is always more desirable because less data has to be fetched from the table. `FILTER` is only useful if the data left by the `WHERE` clause is not needed by each aggregate.

`FILTER` works for all kinds of aggregates and offers a simple way to pivot your data. Also, `FILTER` is faster than mimicking the same behavior with `CASE WHEN ... THEN NULL ... ELSE END`. You can find some real performance comparisons here: `https://www.cybertec-postgresql.com/en/postgresql-9-4-aggregation-filters-they-do-pay-off/`.

After this important topic, we have to look at an SQL feature that is often underappreciated. We are of course talking about ordered sets.

Making use of ordered sets

Ordered sets are powerful features but are not widely regarded as such and are not widely known in the developer community. The idea is actually quite simple: data is grouped normally, and then the data inside each group is ordered given a certain condition. The calculation is then performed on this sorted data.

A classic example is the calculation of the median.

> **Important note**
>
> The median is the middle value. For example, if you are earning the median income, the numbers of people earning less and more than you are identical: 50% of people are earning more, and 50% of people are earning less.

One way to get the median is to take sorted data and move 50% into the dataset. This is an example of what the WITHIN GROUP clause will ask PostgreSQL to do:

```
test=# SELECT
    region,
    percentile_disc(0.5) WITHIN GROUP (ORDER BY production)
FROM t_oil
GROUP BY 1
ORDER BY 1;
    region     | percentile_disc
---------------+-----------------
 Middle East   |            1082
 North America |            3054
(2 rows)
```

The percentile_disc function will skip 50% of the group and return the desired value.

> **Important note**
>
> Note that the median can significantly deviate from the mean.

In economics, the deviation between the median and the average income can even be used as an indicator of social equality or inequality. The higher the median is compared to the average, the greater the income inequality. To provide more flexibility, the ANSI standard does not just propose a median function. Instead, percentile_disc allows you to use any value between 0 and 1.

The beauty is that you can even use ordered sets along with grouping sets, as shown in the following code:

```
test=# SELECT
    region,
```

```
    percentile_disc(0.5) WITHIN GROUP (ORDER BY production)
FROM t_oil
GROUP BY ROLLUP (1)
ORDER BY 1;
    region      | percentile_disc
---------------+-----------------
 Middle East   |            1082
 North America |            3054
               |            1696
(3 rows)
```

In this case, PostgreSQL will again inject additional lines into the result set.

As proposed by the ANSI SQL standard, PostgreSQL provides you with two percentile_ functions. The percentile_disc function will return a value that is contained by the dataset, while the percentile_cont function will interpolate a value if no exact match is found. The following example shows how this works:

```
test=# SELECT
    percentile_disc(0.62) WITHIN GROUP (ORDER BY id),
    percentile_cont(0.62) WITHIN GROUP (ORDER BY id)
FROM
    generate_series(1, 5) AS id;
 percentile_disc | percentile_cont
-----------------+-----------------
 4               |            3.48
(1 row)
```

4 is a value that really exists—3.48 has been interpolated. The percentile_ functions are not the only ones provided by PostgreSQL. To find the most frequent value within a group, the mode function is available. Before showing an example of how to use the mode function, I have compiled a query telling us a bit more about the contents of the table:

```
test=# SELECT production, count(*)
FROM    t_oil
WHERE   country = 'Other Middle East'
GROUP   BY production
ORDER   BY 2 DESC
LIMIT   4;
 production | count
------------+-------
 50         |     5
 48         |     5
 52         |     5
```

```
    53              |     4
    (4 rows)
```

Three different values occur exactly five times. Of course, the mode function can only give us one of them:

```
test=# SELECT
    country,
    mode() WITHIN GROUP (ORDER BY production)
FROM   t_oil
WHERE country = 'Other Middle East'
GROUP BY 1;
 country            | mode
--------------------+------
 Other  Middle East | 48
(1 row)
```

The most frequent value is returned, but SQL won't tell us how often the number actually occurs. It might be that the number only occurs once.

Understanding hypothetical aggregates

Hypothetical aggregates are pretty similar to standard ordered sets. However, they help to answer a different kind of question: what would be the result if a value was in the data? As you can see, this is not about values inside the database but about the result if a certain value was actually there.

The only hypothetical function that's provided by PostgreSQL is rank, as shown in the following code:

```
test=# SELECT
    region,
    rank(9000) WITHIN GROUP (ORDER BY production DESC NULLS LAST)
FROM t_oil
GROUP BY ROLLUP (1)
ORDER BY 1;
    region     | rank
---------------+------
 Middle East   |   21
 North America |   27
               |   47
(3 rows)
```

The preceding code tells us this: if somebody produced 9,000 barrels of oil per day, it would be ranked the 27th-best year in North America and the 21st-best year in Middle East.

> **Tip**
>
> In this example, I used NULLS LAST. When data is sorted, nulls are usually at the end. However, if the sort order is reversed, nulls should still be at the end of the list. NULLS LAST ensures exactly that.

Utilizing windowing functions and analytics

Now that we have discussed ordered sets, it is time to take a look at windowing functions. Aggregates follow a fairly simple principle: take many rows and turn them into fewer aggregated rows. A windowing function is different. It compares the current row with all rows in the group. The number of rows returned does not change. Here is an example:

```
test=# SELECT avg(production) FROM t_oil;
    avg
-----------
 2607.5139
(1 row)
test=# SELECT
    country,
    year,
    production,
    consumption,
    avg(production) OVER ()
FROM t_oil
LIMIT 4;

 country | year | production | consumption |    avg
---------+------+------------+-------------+-----------
 USA     | 1965 |       9014 |       11522 | 2607.5139
 USA     | 1966 |       9579 |       12100 | 2607.5139
 USA     | 1967 |      10219 |       12567 | 2607.5139
 USA     | 1968 |      10600 |       13405 | 2607.5139
(4 rows)
```

The average production of oil in our dataset is around 2.6 million barrels per day. The goal of this query is to add this value as a column. It is now easy to compare the current row to the overall average.

Keep in mind that the OVER clause is essential. PostgreSQL is unable to process the query without it:

```
test=# SELECT
    country,
    year,
    production,
```

```
        consumption,
        avg(production) OVER (PARTITION BY country, year)
FROM
        t_oil;
psql: ERROR: column "t_oil.country" must  appear in the GROUP BY
clause or be used
        in an aggregate function
LINE  1: SELECT country, year,  production, consumption,
avg(productio...
```

This makes sense because the average has to be defined precisely. The database engine cannot just guess any value.

> **Important note**
>
> Other database engines can accept aggregate functions without an OVER or even a GROUP BY clause. However, from a logical point of view, this is wrong, and, on top of that, a violation of SQL.

Partitioning data

So far, the same result can also easily be achieved using sub-select. However, if you want more than just the overall average, sub-select will turn your queries into nightmares due to complexity. Suppose you don't just want the overall average but the average of the country you are dealing with. A PARTITION BY clause is what you need:

```
test=# SELECT
    country,
    year,
    production,
    consumption,
    avg(production) OVER (PARTITION BY country)
FROM
    t_oil;
 country  | year | production | consumption |    avg
----------+------+------------+-------------+-----------
 Canada   | 1965 |    920     |    1108     | 2123.2173
 Canada   | 2010 |    3332    |    2316     | 2123.2173
 Canada   | 2009 |    3202    |    2190     | 2123.2173
 ...
 Iran     | 1966 |    2132    |    148      | 3631.6956
 Iran     | 2010 |    4352    |    1874     | 3631.6956
 Iran     | 2009 |    4249    |    2012     | 3631.6956
 ...
```

The OVER clause defines the window we are looking at. In this case, the window is the country the row belongs to. In other words, the query returns the rows according to the rest of the rows in this country.

> **Important note**
> The year column is not sorted. The query does not contain an explicit sort order, so it might be that data is returned in random order. Remember, SQL does not promise sorted output unless you explicitly state what you want.

Basically, a PARTITION BY clause takes any expression. Usually, most people will use a column to partition the data. Here is an example:

```
test=# SELECT year, production,
    avg(production) OVER (PARTITION BY year < 1990)
FROM   t_oil
WHERE   country = 'Canada'
ORDER  BY year;
 year  | production |          avg
-------+------------+-----------------------
 1965  |        920 | 1631.6000000000000000
 1966  |       1012 | 1631.6000000000000000
 ...
 1990  |       1967 | 2708.4761904761904762
 1991  |       1983| 2708.4761904761904762
 1992  |       2065| 2708.4761904761904762
 ...
```

The point is that data is split using an expression. year < 1990 can return two values: true or false. Depending on the group a year is in, it will be assigned to the pre-1990 average or the post-1990 average. PostgreSQL is really flexible here. Using functions to determine group membership is not uncommon in real-life applications.

Ordering data inside a window

A PARTITION BY clause is not the only possible thing you can put into an OVER clause. Sometimes, it is necessary to sort data inside a window. ORDER BY will provide data to your aggregate functions in a certain way. Here is an example:

```
test=# SELECT country, year, production,
    min(production)OVER (PARTITION BY country ORDER BY year)
FROM   t_oil
WHERE   year BETWEEN 1978 AND 1983
        AND country IN ('Iran', 'Oman');
 country | year | production | min
```

```
--------+------+------------+------
Iran    | 1978 |       5302 | 5302
Iran    | 1979 |       3218 | 3218
Iran    | 1980 |       1479 | 1479
Iran    | 1981 |       1321 | 1321
Iran    | 1982 |       2397 | 1321
Iran    | 1983 |       2454 | 1321
Oman    | 1978 |        314 |  314
Oman    | 1979 |        295 |  295
Oman    | 1980 |        285 |  285
Oman    | 1981 |        330 |  285
 . . .
```

Two countries (Iran and Oman) are chosen from our dataset for the period of 1978 to 1983. Keep in mind that there was a revolution going on in Iran in 1979, so this had some impact on the production of oil. The data reflects this.

What the query does is calculate the minimum production up to a certain point in our time series. At this point, it is a good idea for SQL students to remember what an ORDER BY clause does inside an OVER clause. In this example, the PARTITION BY clause will create one group for each country and order data inside the group. The min function will loop over the sorted data and provide the required minimums.

If you are new to windowing functions, there is something you should be aware of. It really does make a difference, irrespective of whether you use an ORDER BY clause or not:

```
test=# SELECT country, year, production,
    min(production) OVER (),
    min(production) OVER (ORDER BY year)
FROM   t_oil
WHERE year BETWEEN 1978 AND 1983
    AND country = 'Iran';
 country | year | production  | min  | min
---------+------+-------------+------+------
 Iran    | 1978 |        5302 | 1321 | 5302
 Iran    | 1979 |        3218 | 1321 | 3218
 Iran    | 1980 |        1479 | 1321 | 1479
 Iran    | 1981 |        1321 | 1321 | 1321
 Iran    | 1982 |        2397 | 1321 | 1321
 Iran    | 1983 |        2454 | 1321 | 1321
(6 rows)
```

If the aggregate is used without ORDER BY, it will automatically take the minimum of the entire dataset inside your windows. This doesn't happen if there is an ORDER BY clause. In this case, it will always be the minimum up to this point, given the order that you have defined.

Using sliding windows

So far, the window we have used inside our query has been static. However, for calculations such as a moving average, this is not enough. A moving average needs a sliding window that moves along as data is processed.

Here is an example of how a moving average can be achieved:

```
test=# SELECT
    country,
    year,
    production,
    min(production) OVER (
        PARTITION BY country
        ORDER BY year
        ROWS BETWEEN 1 PRECEDING AND 1 FOLLOWING
    )
FROM
    t_oil
WHERE
    year BETWEEN 1978 AND 1983
    AND country IN ('Iran', 'Oman');
 country | year | production | min
---------+------+------------+------
 Iran    | 1978 |       5302 | 3218
 Iran    | 1979 |       3218 | 1479
 Iran    | 1980 |       1479 | 1321
 Iran    | 1981 |       1321 | 1321
 Iran    | 1982 |       2397 | 1321
 Iran    | 1983 |       2454 | 2397
 Oman    | 1978 |        314 | 295
 Oman    | 1979 |        295 | 285
 Oman    | 1980 |        285 | 285
 Oman    | 1981 |        330 | 285
 Oman    | 1982 |        338 | 330
 Oman    | 1983 |        391 | 338
(12 rows)
```

The most important thing is that a moving window should be used with an ORDER BY clause. Otherwise, there will be major problems. PostgreSQL would actually accept the query, but the result would be totally wrong. Remember, feeding data to a sliding window without ordering it first will simply lead to random data.

`ROWS BETWEEN 1 PRECEDING AND 1 FOLLOWING` defines the window. In this example, up to three rows will be in use: the current row, the one before it, and the one after the current row. To illustrate how the sliding window works, check out the following example:

```
test=# SELECT *,
    array_agg(id)OVER (
        ORDER BY id
        ROWS BETWEEN 1 PRECEDING AND 1 FOLLOWING)
FROM  generate_series(1, 5) AS id;
id | array_agg
----+-----------
  1 | {1,2}
  2 | {1,2,3}
  3 | {2,3,4}
  4 | {3,4,5}
  5 | {4,5}
(5 rows)
```

The `array_agg` function will turn a list of values into a PostgreSQL array. It will help to explain how the sliding window operates.

Actually, this trivial query has some very important aspects. What you can see is that the first array contains only two values. There is no entry before `1`, and therefore, the array is not full. PostgreSQL does not add null entries because they would be ignored by aggregates anyway. The same happens at the end of the data.

However, sliding windows offer more. There are a couple of keywords that can be used to specify the sliding window. Consider the following code:

```
test=# SELECT *,
        array_agg(id) OVER (
            ORDER BY id
            ROWS BETWEEN UNBOUNDED PRECEDING AND 0 FOLLOWING
        )
FROM generate_series(1, 5) AS id;
 id | array_agg
----+-------------
  1 | {1}
  2 | {1,2}
  3 | {1,2,3}
  4 | {1,2,3,4}
  5 | {1,2,3,4,5}
(5 rows)
```

The UNBOUNDED PRECEDING keyword means that everything before the current line will be in the window. The counterpart to UNBOUNDED PRECEDING is UNBOUNDED FOLLOWING. Let's look at the following example:

```
test=# SELECT *,
    array_agg(id) OVER (
        ORDER BY id
        ROWS BETWEEN 2 FOLLOWING AND UNBOUNDED FOLLOWING
    )
FROM generate_series(1, 5) AS id;
 id | array_agg
----+-----------
  1 | {3,4,5}
  2 | {4,5}
  3 | {5}
  4 |
  5 |
(5 rows)
```

But there is more: in some cases, you might want to exclude the current row from your calculation. To do that, SQL offers some syntactic sugar, as shown in the next example:

```
test=# SELECT   year,
    production,
    array_agg(production) OVER (ORDER BY year
        ROWS BETWEEN 1 PRECEDING AND 1 FOLLOWING
        EXCLUDE CURRENT ROW)
FROM      t_oil
WHERE     country = 'USA' AND year < 1970;
 year | production |    array_agg
------+------------+---------------
 1965 |       9014 | {9579}
 1966 |       9579 | {9014,10219}
 1967 |      10219 | {9579,10600}
 1968 |      10600 | {10219,10828}
 1969 |      10828 | {10600}
(5 rows)
```

As you can see, it is also possible to use a window that is in the future. PostgreSQL is very flexible here.

Understanding the subtle difference between ROWS and RANGE

So far, you have seen sliding windows using OVER ... ROWS. However, there is more. Let's take a look at the SQL specification taken directly from the PostgreSQL documentation:

```
{ RANGE | ROWS | GROUPS } frame_start [ frame_exclusion ]
{ RANGE | ROWS | GROUPS } BETWEEN frame_start AND frame_end [ frame_
exclusion ]
```

There is more than just ROWS. In real life, we have seen that many people struggle to understand the difference between RANGE and ROWS. In many cases, the result is the same, which adds even more to the confusion. To understand the problem, let's first create some simple data:

```
test=# SELECT *, x / 3 AS y
FROM    generate_series(1, 15) AS x;
  x | y
----+---
  1 | 0
  2 | 0
  3 | 1
  4 | 1
  5 | 1
  6 | 2
  7 | 2
  8 | 2
  9 | 3
 10 | 3
 11 | 3
 12 | 4
 13 | 4
 14 | 4
 15 | 5
(15 rows)
```

This is a simple dataset. Be particularly aware of the second column, which contains a couple of duplicates; they will be relevant in a minute:

```
test=# SELECT *, x / 3 AS y,
    array_agg(x) OVER (ORDER BY x
        ROWS BETWEEN 1 PRECEDING AND 1 FOLLOWING) AS rows_1,
    array_agg(x) OVER (ORDER BY x
        RANGE BETWEEN 1 PRECEDING AND 1 FOLLOWING) AS range_1,
    array_agg(x/3) OVER (ORDER BY (x/3)
        ROWS BETWEEN 1
            PRECEDING AND 1 FOLLOWING) AS rows_2,
    array_agg(x/3) OVER (ORDER BY (x/3)
```

```
        RANGE BETWEEN 1
            PRECEDING AND 1 FOLLOWING) AS range_2
FROM    generate_series(1, 15) AS x;
 x | y |   rows_1    |   range_1    |  rows_2 | range_2
---+---+-------------+--------------+---------+-------------
 1 | 0 |    {1,2}    |    {1,2}     |  {0,0}  | {0,0,1,1,1}
 2 | 0 |   {1,2,3}   |   {1,2,3}    | {0,0,1} | {0,0,1,1,1}
 3 | 1 |   {2,3,4}   |   {2,3,4}    | {0,1,1} | {0,0,1,1,1,2,2,2}
 4 | 1 |   {3,4,5}   |   {3,4,5}    | {1,1,1} | {0,0,1,1,1,2,2,2}
 5 | 1 |   {4,5,6}   |   {4,5,6}    | {1,1,2} | {0,0,1,1,1,2,2,2}
 6 | 2 |   {5,6,7}   |   {5,6,7}    | {1,2,2} | {1,1,1,2,2,2,3,3,3}
 7 | 2 |   {6,7,8}   |   {6,7,8}    | {2,2,2} | {1,1,1,2,2,2,3,3,3}
 8 | 2 |   {7,8,9}   |   {7,8,9}    | {2,2,3} | {1,1,1,2,2,2,3,3,3}
 9 | 3 |  {8,9,10}   |  {8,9,10}    | {2,3,3} | {2,2,2,3,3,3,4,4,4}
10 | 3 |  {9,10,11}  |  {9,10,11}   | {3,3,3} | {2,2,2,3,3,3,4,4,4}
11 | 3 | {10,11,12}  | {10,11,12}   | {3,3,4} | {2,2,2,3,3,3,4,4,4}
12 | 4 | {11,12,13}  | {11,12,13}   | {3,4,4} | {3,3,3,4,4,4,5}
13 | 4 | {12,13,14}  | {12,13,14}   | {4,4,4} | {3,3,3,4,4,4,5}
14 | 4 | {13,14,15}  | {13,14,15}   | {4,4,5} | {3,3,3,4,4,4,5}
15 | 5 |   {14,15}   |   {14,15}    |  {4,5}  | {4,4,4,5}
(15 rows)
```

After listing the x and y columns, I applied windowing functions on x. As you can see, the results are the same for both columns. rows_1 and range_1 are absolutely identical. The situation changes if we start to use the column containing those duplicates. In the case of ROWS, PostgreSQL simply takes the previous and the next rows. In the case of RANGE, it takes the entire group of duplicates. Hence, the array is a lot longer. The entire group of identical values is taken.

Removing duplicates using EXCLUDE TIES and EXCLUDE GROUP

Sometimes, you want to make sure that duplicates don't make it into the result of your windowing function. The EXCLUDE TIES clause helps you to achieve exactly that. If a value shows up in a window twice, it will be removed. This is a neat way to avoid complicated workarounds, which can be costly and slow. The following listing contains a simple example:

```
SELECT *,
    x / 3 AS y,
    array_agg(x/3) OVER (ORDER BY x/3
        ROWS BETWEEN 1 PRECEDING AND 1 FOLLOWING) AS rows_1,
    array_agg(x/3) OVER (ORDER BY x/3
        ROWS BETWEEN 1 PRECEDING AND 1 FOLLOWING EXCLUDE TIES) AS
        rows_2
FROM generate_series(1, 10) AS x;
 x | y |  rows_1  | rows_2
---+---+----------+--------
```

```
 1 | 0 |   {0,0} | {0}
 2 | 0 | {0,0,1} | {0,1}
 3 | 1 | {0,1,1} | {0,1}
 4 | 1 | {1,1,1} | {1}
 5 | 1 | {1,1,2} | {1,2}
 6 | 2 | {1,2,2} | {1,2}
 7 | 2 | {2,2,2} | {2}
 8 | 2 | {2,2,3} | {2,3}
 9 | 3 | {2,3,3} | {2,3}
10 | 3 |   {3,3} | {3}
(10 rows)
```

I have again used the `generate_series` function to create data. Using a simple time series is a lot easier than digging through some more complicated real-life data. `array_agg` will turn all values added to the window into an array. As you can see in the last column, however, the array is a lot shorter. Duplicates have been removed automatically.

In addition to the EXCLUDE TIES clause, PostgreSQL also supports EXCLUDE GROUP. The idea here is that you want to remove an entire set of rows from the dataset before it makes it to the aggregation function. Let's take a look at the following example. We have four windowing functions here.

The first one is the classic ROWS BETWEEN example you have already seen. I have included this column so that it is easier to spot the differences between the standard and the EXCLUDE GROUP version. What is also important to note here is that the `array_agg` function is not the only one you can use here—avg or any other window or aggregation function works just fine. I simply used `array_agg` to make it easier to see what PostgreSQL does. In the following example, you can see that EXCLUDE GROUP removes the entire set of rows:

```
SELECT *,
    x / 3 AS y,
    array_agg(x/3) OVER (ORDER BY x/3
        ROWS BETWEEN 1 PRECEDING AND 1 FOLLOWING) AS rows_1,
    avg(x/3) OVER (ORDER BY x/3
        ROWS BETWEEN 1 PRECEDING AND 1 FOLLOWING) AS avg_1,
    array_agg(x/3) OVER (ORDER BY x/3
        ROWS BETWEEN 1 PRECEDING AND 1 FOLLOWING EXCLUDE GROUP) AS
        rows_2,
    avg(x/3) OVER (ORDER BY x/3
        ROWS BETWEEN 1 PRECEDING AND 1 FOLLOWING EXCLUDE GROUP) AS
          avg_2
FROM generate_series(1, 10) AS x;
 x | y |  rows_1 |   avg_1  | rows_2 |  avg_2
---+---+---------+----------+--------+----------
 1 | 0 |   {0,0} | 0.000000 |        |
```

```
 2 | 0 | {0,0,1} | 0.333333 |   {1} | 1.000000
 3 | 1 | {0,1,1} | 0.666666 |   {0} | 0.000000
 4 | 1 | {1,1,1} | 1.000000 |       |
 5 | 1 | {1,1,2} | 1.333333 |   {2} | 2.000000
 6 | 2 | {1,2,2} | 1.666666 |   {1} | 1.000000
 7 | 2 | {2,2,2} | 2.000000 |       |
 8 | 2 | {2,2,3} | 2.333333 |   {3} | 3.000000
 9 | 3 | {2,3,3} | 2.666666 |   {2} | 2.000000
10 | 3 |  {3,3}  | 3.000000 |       |
(10 rows)
```

The entire group containing the same value is removed. That, of course, also impacts the average calculated on top of this result.

Abstracting window clauses

A windowing function allows us to add columns to the result set that has been calculated on the fly. However, it is a frequent phenomenon that many columns are based on the same window. Putting the same clauses into your queries over and over again is definitely not a good idea, because your queries will be hard to read and, therefore, hard to maintain.

The WINDOW clause allows developers to predefine a window and use it in various places in the query. This is how it works:

```
SELECT country, year, production,
    min(production) OVER (w),
    max(production) OVER (w)
FROM t_oil
WHERE country = 'Canada'
    AND year BETWEEN 1980
    AND 1985
WINDOW w AS (ORDER BY year);
 country | year  | production | min  | max
---------+-------+------------+------+------
 Canada  | 1980  |       1764 | 1764 | 1764
 Canada  | 1981  |       1610 | 1610 | 1764
 Canada  | 1982  |       1590 | 1590 | 1764
 Canada  | 1983  |       1661 | 1590 | 1764
 Canada  | 1984  |       1775 | 1590 | 1775
 Canada  | 1985  |       1812 | 1590 | 1812
(6 rows)
```

The preceding example shows that min and max will use the same clause.

Of course, it is possible to have more than just one `WINDOW` clause—PostgreSQL does not impose serious restrictions on users here.

Using on-board windowing functions

Having introduced you to the basic concepts, it is time to take a look at which windowing functions PostgreSQL supports out of the box. You have already seen that windowing works with all standard aggregate functions. On top of those functions, PostgreSQL offers some additional functions that are exclusive to windowing and analytics.

In this section, some highly important functions will be explained and discussed.

The rank() and dense_rank() functions

The `rank()` and `dense_rank()` functions are, in my judgment, the most prominent functions in SQL. The `rank()` function returns the number of the current row within its window. The counting starts at 1.

Here is an example:

```
test=# SELECT
    year,
    production,
    rank() OVER (ORDER BY production)
FROM    t_oil
WHERE   country = 'Other Middle East'
ORDER BY rank
LIMIT 7;
 year  | production | rank
-------+------------+------
 2001  |    47      |   1
 2004  |    48      |   2
 2002  |    48      |   2
 1999  |    48      |   2
 2000  |    48      |   2
 2003  |    48      |   2
 1998  |    49      |   7
(7 rows)
```

The `rank` column will number those tuples in your dataset. Note that many rows in my sample are equal. Therefore, the rank will jump from 2 to 7 directly, because many production values are identical. If you want to avoid that, the `dense_rank()` function is the way to go about this:

```
test=# SELECT year, production,
    dense_rank() OVER (ORDER BY production)
FROM   t_oil
```

```
WHERE country = 'Other Middle East'
ORDER BY dense_rank
LIMIT 7;
 year  | production | dense_rank
-------+------------+-----------
 2001  |         47 |          1
 2004  |         48 |          2
 ...
 2003  |         48 |          2
 1998  |         49 |          3
(7 rows)
```

PostgreSQL will pack the numbers more tightly. There will be no more gaps.

The ntile() function

Some applications require data to be split into ideally equal groups. The `ntile()` function will do exactly that for you.

The following example shows how data can be split into groups:

```
test=# SELECT year, production,
    ntile(4) OVER (ORDER BY production)
FROM   t_oil
WHERE  country = 'Iraq' AND year BETWEEN 2000 AND 2006;
 year  | production | ntile
-------+------------+-------
 2003  |       1344 |     1
 2005  |       1833 |     1
 2006  |       1999 |     2
 2004  |       2030 |     2
 2002  |       2116 |     3
 2001  |       2522 |     3
 2000  |       2613 |     4
(7 rows)
```

The query splits the data into four groups. The trouble is that only seven rows are selected, which makes it impossible to create four even groups. As you can see, PostgreSQL will fill up the first three groups and make the last one a bit smaller. You can rely on the fact that the groups at the end will always tend to be a bit smaller than the rest.

> **Important note**
>
> In this example, only a handful of rows are used. In real-life applications, millions of rows will be involved, and therefore, it is no problem if groups are not perfectly equal.

The ntile() function is usually not used alone. Sure, it helps to assign a group ID to a row. However, in real-life applications, people want to perform calculations on top of those groups. Suppose you want to create a quartile distribution for your data. This is how it works:

```
test=# SELECT grp, min(production),
    max(production),
    count(*)
FROM   (
    SELECT year, production,
        ntile(4) OVER (ORDER BY production) AS grp
    FROM    t_oil
    WHERE   country = 'Iraq'
  ) AS x
GROUP  BY ROLLUP (1);
 grp | min  | max  | count
-----+------+------+-------
  1  | 285  | 1228 |   12
  2  | 1313 | 1977 |   12
  3  | 1999 | 2422 |   11
  4  | 2428 | 3489 |   11
     | 285  | 3489 |   46
(5 rows)
```

The most important thing is that the calculation cannot be done in one step. When I do SQL training courses at Cybertec (https://www.cybertec-postgresql.com), I try to explain to students that whenever they don't know how to do it all at once, they should consider using sub-select. In analytics, this is usually a good idea. In this example, the first thing that's done in sub-select is attaching a group label to each group. Then, those groups are taken and processed in the main query.

The result is already something that could be used in a real-life application (maybe as a legend located next to a graph, for example).

The lead() and lag() functions

While the ntile() function is essential for splitting a dataset into groups, the lead() and lag() functions are here to move lines within the result set. A typical use case is to calculate the difference in production from one year to the next, as shown in the following example:

```
test=# SELECT year, production,
    lag(production, 1) OVER (ORDER BY year)
FROM   t_oil
WHERE country = 'Mexico'
LIMIT 5;
 year | production | lag
------+------------+-----
```

```
1965  |          362  |
1966  |          370  | 362
1967  |          411  | 370
1968  |          439  | 411
1969  |          461  | 439
(5 rows)
```

Before actually calculating the change in production, it makes sense to sit back and see what the `lag()` function actually does. You can see that the column is moved by one row. The data moved as defined in the ORDER BY clause. In my example, this means down. An ORDER BY DESC clause would, of course, have moved the data up.

From this point on, the query is easy:

```
test=# SELECT
    year,
    production,
    production - lag(production, 1) OVER (ORDER BY year)
FROM   t_oil
WHERE country = 'Mexico'
LIMIT 3;
 year | production | ?column?
------+------------+----------
 1965 |        362 |
 1966 |        370 |        8
 1967 |        411 |       41
(3 rows)
```

All you have to do is to calculate the difference like you would with any other column. Note that the `lag()` function has two parameters. The first one indicates which column is to be displayed. The second column tells PostgreSQL how many rows you want to move. Putting in 7, then, means that everything is off by seven rows.

Note that the first value is `null` (as are all of the other lagged rows without a preceding value).

The `lead()` function is the counterpart of the `lag()` function; it will move rows up instead of down:

```
test=# SELECT year, production,
    production - lead(production, 1) OVER (ORDER BY year)
FROM   t_oil
WHERE country = 'Mexico'
LIMIT 3;
 year  | production | ?column?
-------+------------+----------
 1965  |        362 |       -8
```

```
   1966  |          370  |      -41
   1967  |          411  |      -28
(3 rows)
```

Basically, PostgreSQL will also accept negative values for the `lead` and `lag` columns.
`lag(production, -1)` is therefore a replacement for `lead(production, 1)`. However, it
is definitely cleaner to use the right function to move data in the direction you want.

So far, you have seen how to lag a single column. In most applications, lagging a single value will be
the standard case used by most developers. The point is that PostgreSQL can do a lot more than that.
It is possible to lag entire lines:

```
test=# \x
Expanded display is on.
test=# SELECT
    year,
    production,
    lag(t_oil, 1) OVER (ORDER BY year)
FROM  t_oil
WHERE country = 'USA'
LIMIT 3;
-[ RECORD 1 ]---------------------------------------
year         | 1965
production   | 9014
lag          |
-[ RECORD 2 ]---------------------------------------
year         | 1966
production   | 9579
lag          | ("North America",USA,1965,9014,11522)
-[ RECORD 3 ]---------------------------------------
year         | 1967
production   | 10219
lag          | ("North America",USA,1966,9579,12100)
```

The beauty here is that more than just a single value can be compared to the previous row. The trouble,
though, is that PostgreSQL will return the entire row as a composite type and therefore it is hard to
work with. To dissect a composite type, you can use parentheses and a star (*):

```
test=# SELECT
    year,
    production,
    (lag(t_oil, 1) OVER (ORDER BY year)).*
FROM  t_oil
WHERE country = 'USA'
```

```
LIMIT 3;
 year | prod  | region      | country | year | prod  | consumption
------+-------+-------------+---------+------+-------+-------
 1965 | 9014  |             |         |      |       |
 1966 | 9579  | N. America  |     USA | 1965 | 9014  | 11522
 1967 | 10219 | N. America  |     USA | 1966 | 9579  | 12100
(3 rows)
```

Why is that useful? Lagging an entire row will make it possible to see whether the data has been inserted more than once. It is pretty simple to detect duplicate rows (or close-to-duplicate rows) in your time series data.

Check out the following example:

```
test=# SELECT *
FROM (SELECT t_oil, lag(t_oil) OVER (ORDER BY year)
    FROM   t_oil
    WHERE country = 'USA'
    ) AS x
WHERE t_oil = lag;
 t_oil  | lag
--------+-----
(0 rows)
```

Of course, the sample data doesn't contain duplicates. However, in real-life examples, duplicates can easily happen, and it is easy to detect them, even if there is no primary key.

> **Important note**
>
> The t_oil row is really the entire row. The lag returned by sub-select is also a complete row. In PostgreSQL, composite types can be compared directly in case the fields are identical. PostgreSQL will simply compare one field after the other.

The first_value(), nth_value(), and last_value() functions

Sometimes, it is necessary to calculate data based on the first value of a data window. Unsurprisingly, the function to do that is first_value():

```
test=# SELECT
    year,
    production,
    first_value(production) OVER (ORDER BY year)
FROM   t_oil
WHERE  country = 'Canada'
LIMIT  4;
```

```
year  | production | first_value
------+------------+-------------
1965  |        920 |         920
1966  |       1012 |         920
1967  |       1106 |         920
1968  |       1194 |         920
(4 rows)
```

Again, a sorting order is needed to tell the system where the first value actually is. PostgreSQL will then put the same value into the last column. If you want to find the last value in the window, simply use the `last_value()` function instead of the `first_value()` function.

If you are not interested in the first or last value but are looking for something in the middle, PostgreSQL provides the `nth_value()` function:

```
test=# SELECT
    year,
    production,
    nth_value(production, 3) OVER (ORDER BY year)
FROM   t_oil
WHERE  country = 'Canada';
 year  | production | nth_value
-------+------------+-----------
 1965  |        920 |
 1966  |       1012 |
 1967  |       1106 |      1106
 1968  |       1194 |      1106
 . . .
```

In this case, the third value will be put into the last column. However, note that the first two rows are empty. The trouble is that when PostgreSQL starts going through the data, the third value is not known yet. Therefore, null is added. The question now is, how can we make the time series more complete and replace those two `null` values with the data to come? Here is one way to do this:

```
test=# SELECT *, min(nth_value) OVER ()
FROM   (
    SELECT year, production,
        nth_value(production, 3) OVER (ORDER BY year)
    FROM   t_oil
    WHERE  country = 'Canada'
    ) AS x
LIMIT  4;
 year  | production | nth_value | min
-------+------------+-----------+------
```

```
1965  |          920 |              | 1106
1966  |         1012 |              | 1106
1967  |         1106 |       1106 | 1106
1968  |         1194 |       1106 | 1106
(4 rows)
```

`sub-select` will create an incomplete time series. The `SELECT` clause on top of that will complete the data. The clue here is that completing the data might be more complex, and therefore, `sub-select` might create a couple of opportunities to add more complex logic than just doing it in one step.

The row_number() function

The last function we will discuss in this section is the `row_number()` function, which can simply be used to return a virtual ID. Sounds simple, doesn't it? Here it is:

```
test=# SELECT
    country,
    production,
    row_number() OVER (ORDER BY production)
FROM   t_oil
LIMIT 3;
 country | production | row_number
---------+------------+------------
 Yemen   |         10 |          1
 Syria   |         21 |          2
 Yemen   |         26 |          3
(3 rows)
```

The `row_number()` function simply assigns a number to the row. There are definitely no duplicates. The interesting point here is that this can be done even without an order (in case it is not relevant to you):

```
test=# SELECT country, production,
    row_number() OVER ()
FROM   t_oil
LIMIT 3;
 country | production | row_number
---------+------------+------------
 USA     |       9014 |          1
 USA     |       9579 |          2
 USA     |      10219 |          3
(3 rows)
```

The result is exactly what we would expect.

Writing your own aggregates

In this book, you will learn about most of the built-in functions provided by PostgreSQL. However, what SQL provides might not be enough for you. The good news is that it is possible to add your own aggregates to the database engine. In this section, you will learn how that can be done.

Creating simple aggregates

For this example, the goal is to solve a very simple problem. If a customer takes a taxi, they usually have to pay for getting in the taxi—for example, €2.50. Now, let's assume that for each kilometer, the customer has to pay €2.20. The question now is, what is the total price of a trip?

Of course, this example is simple enough to solve without a custom aggregate; however, let's see how it works. First, some test data needs to be created:

```
test=# CREATE TABLE t_taxi (trip_id int, km numeric);
CREATE TABLE
test=# INSERT INTO t_taxi
VALUES (1, 4.0), (1, 3.2), (1, 4.5),
       (2, 1.9), (2, 4.5);
INSERT 0 5
```

To create aggregates, PostgreSQL offers the CREATE AGGREGATE command. The syntax of this command has become so powerful and long over time that it doesn't make sense anymore to include its output here in this book. Instead, I recommend going to the PostgreSQL documentation, which can be found at https://www.postgresql.org/docs/devel/static/sql-createaggregate.html.

The first thing that's needed when writing an aggregate is a function, which is called for every line. It will take an intermediate value and data that's taken from the line that was processed. Here is an example:

```
test=# CREATE FUNCTION taxi_per_line (numeric, numeric)
RETURNS numeric AS
$$
  BEGIN
      RAISE NOTICE 'intermediate: %, per row:  %', $1, $2;
      RETURN $1 + $2*2.2;
  END;
$$
LANGUAGE 'plpgsql';
```

Now, it is already possible to create a simple aggregate:

```
test=# CREATE AGGREGATE taxi_price (numeric)
(
```

```
        INITCOND = 2.5,
        SFUNC = taxi_per_line,
        STYPE = numeric
);
CREATE AGGREGATE
```

As we stated previously, every trip starts at €2.50 for getting in the taxi, which is defined by INITCOND (the init condition). It represents the starting value for each group. Then, a function is called for each line in the group. In my example, this function is taxi_per_line and has already been defined. As you can see, it needs two parameters. The first parameter is an intermediate value. Those additional parameters are the parameters that are passed to the function by the user.

The following statement shows what data is passed, when it is passed, and how it is passed:

```
test=# SELECT trip_id, taxi_price(km)
FROM t_taxi
GROUP  BY 1;
psql: NOTICE:    intermediate: 2.5, per row:   4.0
psql: NOTICE:    intermediate: 11.30, per row:   3.2
psql: NOTICE:    intermediate: 18.34, per row:   4.5
psql: NOTICE:    intermediate: 2.5, per row:   1.9
psql: NOTICE:    intermediate: 6.68, per row:   4.5
psql:
trip_id | taxi_price
---------+------------
       1 |     28.24
       2 |     16.58
(2 rows)
```

The system starts with trip 1 and €2.50 (the init condition). Then, four kilometers are added. Overall, the price is now 2.50 + 4 x 2.2. Then, the next line is added, which will add 3.2 x 2.2, and so on. The first trip, therefore, costs €28.24.

Then, the next trip starts. Again, there is a fresh init condition, and PostgreSQL will call one function per line.

In PostgreSQL, an aggregate can automatically be used as a windowing function too. No additional steps are needed—you can use the aggregate directly:

```
test=# SELECT *,
       taxi_price(km) OVER (PARTITION BY trip_id ORDER BY km)
FROM   t_taxi;
psql: NOTICE:   intermediate: 2.5,  per row:   3.2
psql: NOTICE:   intermediate: 9.54,  per row:   4.0
psql: NOTICE:   intermediate: 18.34,  per row:   4.5
```

```
psql: NOTICE:   intermediate: 2.5,  per row:  1.9
psql: NOTICE:   intermediate: 6.68,  per row:  4.5
 trip_id | km  | taxi_price
---------+-----+------------
 1       | 3.2 |       9.54
 1       | 4.0 |      18.34
 1       | 4.5 |      28.24
 2       | 1.9 |       6.68
 2       | 4.5 |      16.58
(5 rows)
```

What the query does is give us the price up to a given point on the trip.

The aggregate we have defined will call one function per line. However, how would users be able to calculate an average? Without adding a FINALFUNC function, calculations like that are not possible. To demonstrate how FINALFUNC works, we must extend our example. Suppose the customer wants to give the taxi driver a 10% tip as soon as they leave the taxi. That 10% has to be added at the end, as soon as the total price is known. This is the point where FINALFUNC kicks in. This is how it works:

```
test=# DROP AGGREGATE taxi_price(numeric);
DROP AGGREGATE
```

First of all, the old aggregate is dropped. Then, FINALFUNC is defined. It will get the intermediate result as a parameter and do its magic:

```
test=# CREATE FUNCTION taxi_final (numeric)
    RETURNS numeric AS
$$
    SELECT $1 * 1.1;
$$
LANGUAGE sql IMMUTABLE;
CREATE FUNCTION
```

The calculation is pretty simple, in this case—as we stated previously, 10% is added to the final sum.

Once the function has been deployed, it is already possible to recreate the aggregate:

```
test=# CREATE AGGREGATE taxi_price (numeric)
(
    INITCOND = 2.5,
    SFUNC = taxi_per_line,
    STYPE = numeric,
    FINALFUNC = taxi_final
);
CREATE AGGREGATE
```

Finally, the price will simply be a bit higher than before:

```
test=# SELECT trip_id, taxi_price(km)
FROM    t_taxi
GROUP BY 1;
psql: NOTICE:   intermediate: 2.5, per row: 4.0
...
 trip_id | taxi_price
---------+------------
       1 |    31.064
       2 |    18.238
(2 rows)
```

PostgreSQL takes care of all of the grouping and so on automatically.

For simple calculations, simple data types can be used for the intermediate result. However, not all operations can be done by just passing simple numbers and text around. Fortunately, PostgreSQL allows the use of composite data types, which can be used as intermediate results.

Imagine that you want to calculate an average of some data, maybe a time series. An intermediate result might look as follows:

```
test=# CREATE TYPE my_intermediate AS (c int4, s numeric);
CREATE TYPE
```

Feel free to compose any arbitrary type that serves your purpose. Just pass it as the first parameter and add data as additional parameters as needed.

Adding support for parallel queries

What you have just seen is a simple aggregate, which has no support for parallel queries and so on. To solve those challenges, the following couple of examples are all about improvements and speedups.

When creating an aggregate, you can optionally define the following things:

```
PARALLEL { UNSAFE | RESTRICTED | SAFE }
```

By default, an aggregate does not support parallel queries. For performance reasons, it does make sense, however, to explicitly state what the aggregate is capable of:

- UNSAFE: In this mode, no parallel queries are allowed
- RESTRICTED: In this mode, the aggregate can be executed in parallel mode, but the execution is limited to the parallel group leader
- SAFE: In this mode, it provides full support for parallel queries

If you mark a function as SAFE, you have to keep in mind that the function must not have side effects. The execution order must not have an impact on the result of the query. Only then should PostgreSQL be allowed to execute operations in parallel. Examples of functions without side effects would be sin(x) and length(s). The IMMUTABLE functions are good candidates for this since they're guaranteed to return the same result given the same inputs. The STABLE function can work if certain restrictions apply.

Improving efficiency

The aggregates we've defined so far can already achieve quite a lot. However, if you are using sliding windows, the number of function calls will simply explode. This is what happens:

```
test=# SELECT
    taxi_price(x::numeric)OVER (ROWS BETWEEN 0 FOLLOWING AND 3
FOLLOWING)
FROM    generate_series(1, 5) AS x;
psql: NOTICE:  intermediate: 2.5,   per row:  1
psql: NOTICE:  intermediate: 4.7,   per row:  2
psql: NOTICE:  intermediate: 9.1,   per row:  3
psql: NOTICE:  intermediate: 15.7,   per row:  4
psql: NOTICE:  intermediate: 2.5,   per row:  2
psql: NOTICE:  intermediate: 6.9,   per row:  3
psql: NOTICE:  intermediate: 13.5,   per row:  4
psql: NOTICE:  intermediate: 22.3,   per row:  5
. . .
```

For every line, PostgreSQL will process the full window. If the sliding window is large, efficiency will fall. To fix that, our aggregates can be extended. Before that, the old aggregate can be dropped:

```
DROP AGGREGATE taxi_price(numeric);
```

Basically, two functions are needed. The msfunc function will add the next row in the window to the intermediate result:

```
CREATE FUNCTION taxi_msfunc(numeric, numeric)
    RETURNS numeric AS
$$
    BEGIN
    RAISE NOTICE 'taxi_msfunc called with % and %', $1, $2;
    RETURN $1 + $2;
    END;
$$ LANGUAGE 'plpgsql' STRICT;
```

The minvfunc function will remove the value falling out of the window from the intermediate result:

```
CREATE FUNCTION taxi_minvfunc(numeric, numeric) RETURNS numeric AS
$$
BEGIN
    RAISE NOTICE 'taxi_minvfunc called with % and %', $1, $2;
    RETURN $1 - $2;
END;
$$
LANGUAGE 'plpgsql' STRICT;
```

In this example, all we do is add and subtract. In a more sophisticated example, the calculation can be arbitrarily complex.

The following statement shows how the aggregate can be recreated:

```
CREATE AGGREGATE taxi_price (numeric)
(
    INITCOND = 0,
    STYPE   = numeric,
    SFUNC   = taxi_per_line,
    MSFUNC = taxi_msfunc,
    MINVFUNC = taxi_minvfunc,
    MSTYPE = numeric
);
```

Let's run the same query again now:

```
test# SELECT
    taxi_price(x::numeric) OVER   (
        ROWS   BETWEEN 0 FOLLOWING AND 3 FOLLOWING)
FROM      generate_series(1, 5) AS x;
psql: NOTICE:   taxi_msfunc called with 1 and 2
psql: NOTICE:   taxi_msfunc called with 3 and 3
psql: NOTICE:   taxi_msfunc called with 6 and 4
psql: NOTICE:   taxi_minfunc called with 10 and 1
psql: NOTICE:   taxi_msfunc called with 9 and 5
psql: NOTICE:   taxi_minfunc called with 14 and 2
psql: NOTICE:   taxi_minfunc called with 12 and 3
psql: NOTICE:   taxi_minfunc called with 9 and 4
```

The number of function calls has decreased dramatically. Only a fixed handful of calls per row have to be performed. There is no longer any need to calculate the same frame all over again.

Writing hypothetical aggregates

Writing aggregates is not hard and can be highly beneficial for performing more complex operations. In this section, the plan is to write a hypothetical aggregate, which has already been discussed in this chapter.

Implementing hypothetical aggregates is not too different from writing normal aggregates. The really hard part is figuring out when to actually use one. To make this section as easy to understand as possible, I have decided to include a trivial example: given a specific order, what would the result be if we added abc to the end of the string?

This is how it works:

```
CREATE AGGREGATE name  ( [ [ argmode ] [ argname ] arg_data_type [ ,
... ] ]
    ORDER  BY [ argmode ] [ argname ] arg_data_type
    [ , ...])
(
    SFUNC  = sfunc,
    STYPE  = state_data_type
    [ , SSPACE = state_data_size ]
    [ , FINALFUNC = ffunc   ]
    [ , FINALFUNC_EXTRA ]
    [ , INITCOND = initial_condition ]
    [ , PARALLEL = { SAFE  | RESTRICTED | UNSAFE } ]
    [ , HYPOTHETICAL ]
)
```

Two functions will be needed: sfunc and finalfunc. The sfunc function will be called for every line:

```
CREATE FUNCTION hypo_sfunc(text, text)
    RETURNS text  AS
$$
    BEGIN
    RAISE  NOTICE 'hypo_sfunc called with  % and %', $1, $2;
    RETURN $1 || $2;
    END;
$$ LANGUAGE 'plpgsql';
```

Two text parameters will be passed to the procedure. We use them for concatenation. The logic is the same as it was previously. Just like we did earlier, a final function call can be defined:

```
CREATE FUNCTION hypo_final(text, text,  text)
    RETURNS text  AS
$$
```

```
      BEGIN
      RAISE  NOTICE 'hypo_final called with  %, %, and %',
      $1, $2, $3;
      RETURN $1 || $2;
      END;
  $$ LANGUAGE 'plpgsql';
```

Once these functions are in place, the hypothetical aggregate can be created:

```
CREATE AGGREGATE whatif(text ORDER  BY text)
(
    INITCOND = 'START',
    STYPE  = text,
    SFUNC  = hypo_sfunc,
    FINALFUNC = hypo_final,
    FINALFUNC_EXTRA = true,
    HYPOTHETICAL
);
```

Note that the aggregate has been marked as hypothetical so that PostgreSQL will know what kind of aggregate it actually is.

Now that the aggregate has been created, it is possible to run it:

```
test=# SELECT whatif('abc'::text)
    WITHIN GROUP (ORDER BY id::text)
FROM      generate_series(1, 3) AS id;
psql: NOTICE:  hypo_sfunc called with  START  and 1
psql: NOTICE:  hypo_sfunc called with  START1 and 2
psql: NOTICE:  hypo_sfunc called with  START12 and 3
psql: NOTICE:  hypo_final called with  START123, abc,  and <NULL>
   whatif
-------------
  START123abc
(1 row)
```

The key to understanding all these aggregates is really to fully see what happens when each kind of function is called and how the overall machinery works.

The next topic we will deal with is related to recursions.

Handling recursions

Recursions are an important aspect and are supported by the most advanced SQL database engines, including PostgreSQL. Using recursions, many types of operations can be done fairly easily. So, let us dissect the most simplistic recursion and try to understand how recursion works. Here is an example:

```
test=# WITH RECURSIVE x(n) AS (
    SELECT  1 AS n, 'a'::text AS dummy
    UNION ALL
    SELECT  n + 1, dummy || 'a'
    FROM    x
    WHERE   n < 5
)
SELECT  *
FROM    x;
 n | dummy
---+-------
 1 | a
 2 | aa
 3 | aaa
 4 | aaaa
 5 | aaaaa
(5 rows)
```

The goal of this query is to recursively return numbers and compile a string at the end. Basically, the query consists of two parts: the WITH RECURSIVE part and the SELECT statement at the end starting the recursion. While the SELECT part at the end is trivial, the WITH RECURSIVE part requires a deeper inspection. If we look closely, the WITH statement contains UNION ALL. This is really important: the SELECT statement before UNION ALL represents the start condition of the recursion. In our case, we start with 1 and a. Two columns are produced by the first statement.

Then comes the second SQL statement. The important thing here is the FROM clause. It recursively calls x. Each iteration will increment the number by one and add a character to the end of the string. We abort when n reaches 5. Note that the last iteration will already display n + 1 so the last value returned is 5 and not 4.

All basic components of recursions are therefore to be found in the query: an init condition, a recursive call, and a condition to terminate.

UNION versus UNION ALL

In any recursion, loops can happen. The problem is that if the loop is infinite, your query will not terminate and will run forever. This is not desirable. UNION prevents such loops by preventing repeated calls using the same parameters.

This difference is really important because it can protect us from bugs in the data by just skipping over instead of entering an infinite loop. The following two examples show the difference in behavior depending on the type of recursion:

```
test=# WITH RECURSIVE x(n) AS (
    SELECT  1 AS n
    UNION ALL
    SELECT  n
    FROM    x
    WHERE   n < 5
)
SELECT  *
FROM    x;
^Cancel request sent
ERROR:  canceling statement due to user request
    ß runs forever, we have to quit
test=# WITH RECURSIVE x(n) AS (
    SELECT  1 AS n
    UNION
    SELECT  n
    FROM    x
    WHERE   n < 5
)
SELECT  *
FROM    x;
 --
  1
(1 row)
```

The first query never returns because we did not increment n, which leads to an identical recursive call. The second query exits quickly and returns just one row because PostgreSQL figures that it has seen those values before and can therefore terminate the recursion.

Inspecting a practical example

After this theoretical introduction, it is helpful to try out what we just learned by looking at a more practical example. Often, recursions are used to handle hierarchical data. The standard example is the organization of a company. All employees have a boss, and if we want to find out who is whose boss, recursion is a natural thing to use.

The first thing to do is to create a table:

```
CREATE TABLE t_manager
(
```

```
        id       serial,
        person   text,
        manager  text,
        UNIQUE (person, manager)
);
```

Often, hierarchical data is represented as a "slave/master" relationship. We simply store pairs of who is on top and who is below. The nodes on top of our tree have no "master" and are therefore set to NULL. Here is some sample data:

```
test=# INSERT INTO t_manager (person, manager)
VALUES ('eliza', NULL),
    ('ronald', 'eliza'),
    ('carlos', 'eliza'),
    ('manuel', 'ronald'),
    ('mike', 'ronald'),
    ('joe', 'carlos'),
    ('augustin', 'carlos'),
    ('jane', 'carlos')
;
```

The goal of the next query is to create a tree showing us exactly who is in which position:

```
test=# WITH RECURSIVE x AS (
    SELECT  person, manager, person AS hierarchy
    FROM    t_manager
    WHERE   manager IS NULL
    UNION ALL
    SELECT  t_manager.person, t_manager.manager,
            hierarchy || ' --> ' || t_manager.person
    FROM    t_manager, x
    WHERE   t_manager.manager = x.person
)
SELECT * FROM x;
  person   | manager |            hierarchy
----------+---------+--------------------------------
 eliza    |         | eliza
 ronald   | eliza   | eliza --> ronald
 carlos   | eliza   | eliza --> carlos
 manuel   | ronald  | eliza --> ronald --> manuel
 mike     | ronald  | eliza --> ronald --> mike
 joe      | carlos  | eliza --> carlos --> joe
 augustin | carlos  | eliza --> carlos --> augustin
 jane     | carlos  | eliza --> carlos --> jane
(8 rows)
```

What we are doing in this query is joining the recursive call with the raw data. This is a bit like a self-join. To make this work, we have to join the "current" boss with the "previous" normal employee. In other words, the join connects the current level with the previous level. In our end result, you can see the full hierarchy of the company in the third column.

Working with JSON and JSONB

As we conclude our in-depth exploration of recursion, it's time to pivot and delve into another pivotal topic: JSON. In recent years, JSON has emerged as a dominant force in data exchange, supplanting other formats, such as SOAP, plain XML, and custom APIs. Its versatility and ease of use have made it the de facto standard for exchanging data online, allowing developers to effortlessly transmit and receive data between applications. The simplicity and flexibility of JSON have also enabled its widespread adoption across industries, from finance and healthcare to social media and e-commerce.

The PostgreSQL community has recognized the importance of JSON in modern application development and has responded by implementing comprehensive JSON support into the database management system. This integration enables developers to easily store, retrieve, and manipulate JSON data within their applications, streamlining the development process and enhancing overall performance. With JSON support now built into PostgreSQL, developers can focus on building innovative applications that take advantage of this powerful data format.

As we move forward in the world of software development, it's clear that JSON will continue to play a central role in shaping the future of data exchange. Its flexibility, ease of use, and widespread adoption make it an ideal choice for developers looking to build robust, scalable applications that can seamlessly integrate with other systems. By incorporating JSON support into PostgreSQL, the community has provided developers with a powerful toolset for building innovative applications that can take advantage of this versatile data format.

In this section, you will be introduced to the basic concepts and we will show some basic operations that you can do using JSON documents. Keep in mind that JSON in PostgreSQL has become really powerful and JSON support is growing. Therefore, comprehensive coverage of the topic has become close to impossible. You have to keep that in mind when going through this chapter. There is more out there, and it is growing at a rapid pace.

Two data types have been added: `json` and `jsonb`. While the `json` data type validates the JSON document, it will store it as plain text (as it is). It does not store it in binary format. During insertions, there might be a small benefit, but if you want to access the document again later on, it will cost you dearly. Therefore, it makes sense to store data as `jsonb`, which is parsed and stored in binary format for easy access later on. What makes `jsonb` even more attractive is that many functions and operators only exist for the binary representation. An example of such a function is `jsonb_pretty`, which improves the readability of the data, but more on that a bit later.

Displaying and creating JSON documents

The first thing we have to understand is how to create JSON documents in the first place. To create some data, we can use VALUES, which is a SQL instruction to simply return a dataset of your choice (usually some constants). Here is how it works:

```
test=# VALUES (1, 2, 3), (4, 5, 6);
 column1 | column2 | column3
---------+---------+---------
       1 |       2 |       3
       4 |       5 |       6
(2 rows)
```

What we have here is two lines featuring three columns each. We can turn each row into a JSON document easily:

```
test=# SELECT row_to_json(x)
FROM (VALUES (1, 2, 3), (4, 5, 6)) AS x;
                row_to_json
-------------------------------------------
 {"column1":1,"column2":2,"column3":3}
 {"column1":4,"column2":5,"column3":6}
(2 rows)
```

The important part is that we can turn a generic data structure (in our case, x) into a JSON document. Basically, anything can be passed to the row_to_json function. The second important observation is that each row will be turned into one JSON document.

Often, we want the entire result set to be a single document. To achieve that, the json_agg function is what we need:

```
test=# SELECT json_agg(x)
FROM (VALUES (1, 2, 3), (4, 5, 6)) AS x;
                   json_agg
-------------------------------------------
 [{"column1":1,"column2":2,"column3":3}, +
  {"column1":4,"column2":5,"column3":6}]
(1 row)
```

The listing shows that a single document is returned.

> **Note**
>
> There is a + symbol at the end of the first line. This is *not* part of the JSON document, but it is added by psql to indicate the line break.

Often, it is easier for developers to preformat a JSON document. The `jsonb_pretty` function helps us to properly format the output, as shown in the next listing:

```
test=# SELECT jsonb_pretty(json_agg(x)::jsonb)
FROM    (VALUES (1, 2, 3), (4, 5, 6)) AS x;
      jsonb_pretty
----------------------
 [                      +
     {                  +
         "column1": 1,+
         "column2": 2,+
         "column3": 3 +
     },                 +
     {                  +
         "column1": 4,+
         "column2": 5,+
         "column3": 6 +
     }                  +
 ]
(1 row)
```

Keep in mind that the + symbols are again injected by `psql` and are not present in the result set sent by the database. If you are an application developer, this is not an issue.

Turning JSON documents into rows

JSON does not end up in a database by itself—we have to put it there. Inserting a document directly into a JSON column is easy. However, sometimes, we have to map a document to an existing table. Consider the following example:

```
test=# CREATE TABLE t_json (x int, y int);
CREATE TABLE
```

This is a very simple table. It only consists of two columns. The `json_populate_record` function helps us to map suitable JSON to the table:

```
test=# SELECT *
FROM json_populate_record(
    NULL::t_json,
    '{"x":54,"y":65}');
 x  | y
----+----
 54 | 65
(1 row)
```

The trick is to pass NULL as a parameter and cast it to the name of the table we want to map the document to, which is really powerful. If you have a table that matches your JSON document, at least partially, you are mostly done. It is really easy to insert data under those circumstances:

```
test=# INSERT INTO t_json
SELECT *
FROM  json_populate_record(NULL::t_json,
    '{"x":54,"y":65}');
INSERT 0 1
```

Here is proof that the data has been added:

```
test=# SELECT * FROM t_json;
 x  | y
----+----
 54 | 65
(1 row)
```

Accessing a JSON document

After learning how to actually create a JSON document, you will see how to access this data type, extract subtrees, and a lot more. Let us first create a table, insert a document, and dissect it:

```
test=# CREATE TABLE t_demo (id int, doc jsonb);
CREATE TABLE
test=# INSERT INTO t_demo
VALUES (1,
'{
    "product": "shoes",
    "colors": {
    "red": "red",
    "blue": "blue",
    "green": "green"
  }
}');
```

We inserted one row, and we will try to fetch this row in various ways:

```
test=# \x
Expanded display is on.
test=# SELECT jsonb_pretty(doc),
    jsonb_pretty(doc -> 'colors') FROM t_demo;
-[ RECORD 1 ]+-------------------------
jsonb_pretty | {                        +
             |     "colors": {          +
```

```
           |              "red": "red",    +
           |              "blue": "blue", +
           |              "green": "green"+
           |          },                  +
           |          "product": "shoes"  +
           |  }
jsonb_pretty | {                          +
           |          "red": "red",       +
           |          "blue": "blue",     +
           |          "green": "green"     +
           |  }
```

The - > operator will help us to find a subtree and return this part. The example here shows how the subtree containing colors can be extracted.

Of course, we can dig one level deeper and see what description there is for red:

```
test=# SELECT jsonb_pretty(doc -> 'colors' -> 'red')
FROM    t_demo;
-[ RECORD 1 ]+------
jsonb_pretty | "red"
```

As you can see, we can just call the operator again and apply it to the mini-JSON document. However, there is a little thing here that is worth noting: the data is quoted. There is a reason for that:

```
test=# SELECT pg_typeof(doc -> 'product')
FROM    t_demo;
 pg_typeof
-----------
 jsonb
(1 row)
```

It looks as if PostgreSQL has quoted the text column, but it is actually still a little JSON document. If we want to have the real value of the entry, we have to use the - >> operator:

```
test=# \x
Expanded display is off.
test=# SELECT doc -> 'product', doc ->> 'product'
FROM t_demo;
 ?column? | ?column?
----------+----------
 "shoes"  | shoes
(1 row)
```

Let us take a look at the data types from a relational PostgreSQL point of view:

```
test=# SELECT    pg_typeof(doc ->> 'colors'),
          pg_typeof(doc ->> 'product')
FROM    t_demo;
 pg_typeof | pg_typeof
-----------+-----------
 text      | text
(1 row)
```

This is really important: in both cases, we get a text document, even if we are dealing with an entire subtree. The data type has a couple of implications: if you are looking for other data types inside the JSON, you have to cast those fields to the data type you need (integer, numeric, date, and so on).

However, there is more. Consider the following example:

```
test=# SELECT    jsonb_typeof(doc -> 'colors'),
          jsonb_typeof(doc -> 'product')
FROM    t_demo;
 jsonb_typeof | jsonb_typeof
--------------+--------------
 object       | string
(1 row)
```

From a JSON point of view, we are dealing with objects (if we are talking about a subtree) and a JSON data type at the lowest level.

What is often needed is to loop over elements:

```
test=# SELECT jsonb_each(doc -> 'colors')
FROM    t_demo;
     jsonb_each
--------------------
 (red,"""red""")
 (blue,"""blue""")
 (green,"""green""")
(3 rows)
```

The jsonb_each function will loop over the subtree and return all elements as a composite type (the record data type). However, we can expand on this type and return those elements as separate fields:

```
test=# SELECT (jsonb_each(doc -> 'colors')).*
FROM    t_demo;
  key  |  value
-------+---------
 red   | "red"
```

```
blue   | "blue"
green  | "green"
(3 rows)
```

Note that the value is still a mini-JSON document, which is important because we might be dealing with a subtree in need of further processing. If you want to loop over all elements and extract text, consider the following code sample:

```
test=# SELECT (jsonb_each_text(doc -> 'colors')).*
FROM    t_demo;
  key  | value
-------+-------
 red   | red
 blue  | blue
 green | green
(3 rows)
```

The jsonb_each_text function will do the job and return the element as text.

Sometimes, it is sufficient to just extract the keys in the document or subtree. The way to fetch those keys is to use the jsonb_object_keys function:

```
test=# SELECT jsonb_object_keys(doc) FROM t_demo;
 jsonb_object_keys
-------------------
 colors
 product
(2 rows)
```

There are more functions to modify JSON documents. However, covering them all will take too long.

Making use of JSONPath

One of the more recent features of PostgreSQL is the ability to make use of JSONPath. But before we get started: what is JSONPath in the first place? **JSONPath** (also known as XPath for JSON) is a query language used to navigate and extract specific values from JSON data. Sounds like a database task? It is! JSONPath allows you to specify the path or location within a JSON document where you want to extract or manipulate data. It's similar to XPath, which is used with XML documents and which has been widely adopted.

A JSONPath expression typically starts with a dollar sign ($) followed by the path to the desired value. For example:

- $: The root of the JSON document

- $.name: The name property at the top level of the document

- $.address.street: The street property within an address object, which is located one level down from the root

JSONPath expressions can include various operators to navigate and filter data:

- ., /: Navigation operators that allow you to move down the JSON tree (for example, $.person.name)

- [ ]: Indexing operator for arrays

- @`: Property name or attribute operator

- ?: Filtering operator that allows you to filter data based on conditions (for example, $.people[?age<25])

JSONPath is widely supported by various programming languages and libraries but can also be accessed using PostgreSQL, as shown in the next example:

```
test=# SELECT jsonb_path_query('[1,2,3]', '$[last - 1]');
 jsonb_path_query
------------------
 2
(1 row)

test=# SELECT jsonb_path_query('[1,2,3]',
    '$[last ? (@.type() == "number")]');
 jsonb_path_query
------------------
 3
(1 row)
```

What we can see in the first two SQL statements is that we can easily extract sub-elements from the JSON document and retrieve those values. However, we can also validate data types, as shown in the next listing:

```
test=# SELECT jsonb_path_query('[1,2,3]',
    '$[last ? (@.type() == "string")]');
ERROR:  jsonpath array subscript is not a single numeric value
```

It is also possible to extract parts of the JSON document by addressing the subtree properly:

```
test=# SELECT jsonb_path_query('{"c": {"a": 2, "b":1}}',
    '$.** ? (@.a == (@.b + 1))');
 jsonb_path_query
------------------
 {"a": 2, "b": 1}
(1 row)
```

As you can see, this special syntax is fairly easy to use and gives us a great deal of flexibility and power.

Summary

In this chapter, you learned about the advanced features provided by SQL. On top of simple aggregates, PostgreSQL provides ordered sets, grouping sets, windowing functions, and recursions, as well as an interface that you can use to create custom aggregates. The advantage of running aggregations in the database is that code is easy to write and a database engine will usually have an edge when it comes to efficiency. We also covered the ever-more important topic of JSON and JSON processing in general (JSON, JSONPath, and so on).

In *Chapter 5, Log Files and System Statistics*, we will turn our attention to more administrative tasks, such as handling log files, understanding system statistics, and implementing monitoring.

5

Log Files and System Statistics

In *Chapter 4, Handling Advanced SQL*, you learned about advanced SQL and ways of viewing SQL in a different light. However, database work doesn't only consist of hacking up fancy SQL. Sometimes, it's about keeping things running professionally. To do that, it's highly important to keep an eye on system statistics, log files, and so on.

Monitoring is the key to running databases professionally. Fortunately, PostgreSQL has many features that can help you monitor your databases, and you'll learn how to use them in this chapter.

In this chapter, you'll learn about the following topics:

- Gathering runtime statistics
- Creating log files

By the end of this chapter, you'll be able to configure PostgreSQL's logging infrastructure properly and take care of log files in the most professional way possible.

Gathering runtime statistics

The first thing you have to understand is what features PostgreSQL's onboard statistics have to offer and how to use them. In my opinion, there's no way to improve performance and reliability without collecting the necessary data to make prudent decisions.

This section will guide you through PostgreSQL's runtime statistics and explain how you can extract more runtime information from your database setups.

PostgreSQL offers a large set of system views that allow administrators and developers alike to take a deep look into what's going on in their system. The trouble is that many people collect all this data but can't make real sense of it. The general rule is that there's no point in drawing a graph for something you don't understand anyway. Therefore, the goal of this section is to shed some light on what PostgreSQL has to offer to hopefully make it easier for users to take advantage of what there is for them to use.

pg_stat_activity – checking live traffic

Whenever I inspect a system to run it, fix it, or make some other improvements, there's a system view I prefer to inspect first, before digging deeper. I am, of course, talking about pg_stat_activity. The idea behind this view is to give you a chance to figure out what's going on right now.

Here's how it works:

```
test=# \d pg_stat_activity
            View "pg_catalog.pg_stat_activity"
        Column         |         Type    ...
-----------------------+--------------------- ...
 datid                 | oid ...
 datname               | name ...
 pid                   | integer ...
 leader_pid            | integer ...
 usesysid              | oid ...
 usename               | name ...
 application_name      | text ...
 client_addr           | inet ...
 client_hostname       | text  ...
 client_port           | integer ...
 backend_start         | timestamp with time zone ...
 xact_start            | timestamp with time zone ...
 query_start           | timestamp with time zone ...
 state_change          | timestamp with time zone ...
 wait_event_type       | text ...
 wait_event            | text ...
 state                 | text ...
 backend_xid           | xid ...
 backend_xmin          | xid ...
 query_id              | bigint ...
 query                 | text ...
 backend_type          | text  ..
```

Furthermore, pg_stat_activity will provide you with one line per active connection. You'll see the internal object ID of the database (datid), the name of the database somebody is connected to (datname), and the process ID serving this connection (pid). Some processes might also have leader_pid. What's this? In case you're running a parallel query, PostgreSQL will launch worker processes to help with the query. On top of that, PostgreSQL will tell you who's connected (usename; note the missing r) and that user's internal object ID (usesysid), which identifies the user inside the system catalog.

> **Important note**
> Remember, in PostgreSQL, everything has a number internally to which a real name is attached.

Then, there's a field called `application_name`, which is worth commenting on a bit more extensively. In general, `application_name` can be set freely by the end user, as follows:

```
test=# SET application_name
TO 'www.cybertec-postgresql.com';
SET
test=# SHOW application_name;
  application_name
----------------------
 www.cybertec-postgresql.com
 (1 row)
```

The point is this: let's assume that thousands of connections are coming from a single IP. Can you, as the administrator, tell what a specific connection is doing right now? You may not know all the SQL stuff by heart. If the client is kind enough to set an `application_name` parameter, it's a lot easier to see what the purpose of a connection is. In my example, I have set the name to the domain the connection belongs to. This makes it easy to find similar connections that may cause similar problems.

The next three columns (`client_*`) will tell you where a connection comes from. PostgreSQL will show IP addresses and (set the `log_hostname` variable in `postgresql.conf` to *on*) even hostnames.

Additionally, `backend_start` will tell you when a certain connection has started, and `xact_start` indicates when a transaction has started. Then, there are `query_start` and `state_change`. Back in the dark old days, PostgreSQL would only show active queries. At a time when queries took a lot longer than today, this made sense. On modern hardware, **online transaction processing** (**OLTP**) queries may only consume a fraction of a millisecond, so it's hard to catch such queries doing potential harm. The solution was to either show the active query or the previous query that was executed by the connection you're looking at.

Here's what you may see:

```
test=# SELECT pid, query_start, state_change, state, query
FROM    pg_stat_activity;
...
-[ RECORD 2 ]  +-------------------------------------------
pid            | 28001
query_start    | 2024-09-05 10:03:57.575593+01
state_change   | 2024-09-05 10:03:57.575595+01
state          | active
query          | SELECT pg_sleep(10000000);
```

In this case, you can see that `pg_sleep` is being executed in a second connection. As soon as this query is terminated, the output will change, as shown in the following code:

```
-[ RECORD 2 ]+----------------------------------------
pid          | 28001
query_start  | 2024-09-05 10:03:57.575593+01
state_change | 2024-09-05 10:05:10.388522+01
state        | idle
query        | SELECT pg_sleep(10000000);
```

The query is now marked as `idle`. The difference between `state_change` and `query_start` is the time the query needs to execute. Therefore, `pg_stat_activity` will give you a great overview of what's going on in your system right now. The new `state_change` field makes it a lot more likely for us to spot expensive queries.

The question now is this: Once you've found bad queries, how can you get rid of them? PostgreSQL provides two functions to take care of these things:

- `pg_cancel_backend`: The `pg_cancel_backend` function will terminate the query but will leave the connection in place
- `pg_terminate_backend`: The `pg_terminate_backend` function is a bit more radical and will kill the entire database connection, along with the query

If you want to disconnect all other users but yourself, here's how you can do this. Be careful when running this in production – it will terminate all connections and, therefore, might cause downtime:

```
test=# SELECT pg_terminate_backend(pid)
FROM    pg_stat_activity
WHERE   pid <> pg_backend_pid()
    AND backend_type = 'client backend';
 pg_terminate_backend
----------------------
 t
 t
(2 row)
```

We call the `terminate` function for every row matching the `WHERE` condition.

If you happen to be kicked out, the following message will be displayed:

```
test=# SELECT pg_sleep(10000000);
psql: FATAL: terminating connection due to administrator command
server closed the connection unexpectedly
This probably means that the server terminated abnormally before or
while processing the request. The
  connection to the server was lost. Attempting reset: succeeded.
```

Only `psql` will try to reconnect. This isn't true for most other clients – especially not for client libraries.

There's more important information here, such as `wait_event_type`, which will provide us some insights into what the backend is busy doing (for example, waiting on I/O, waiting on a lock, and so on).

If you want to look into some more in-depth debugging, consider checking out `backend_xmin`. It will show you some information about the transaction ID of your database process. Why is that important? Remember: `VACUUM` can recycle all rows that aren't visible by the oldest transaction anymore, and `backend_xmin` is important for exactly this purpose.

Inspecting databases

Once you've inspected the active database connections, you can dig deeper and inspect database-level statistics. The `pg_stat_database` view will return one line per database inside your PostgreSQL instance.

This is what you'll find there:

```
test=# \d pg_stat_database
          View "pg_catalog.pg_stat_database"
          Column              |           Type       ...
--------------------------+-------------------- ...
 datid                    | oid ...
 datname                  | name ...
 numbackends              | integer ...
 xact_commit              | bigint ...
 xact_rollback            | bigint  ...
 blks_read                | bigint ...
 blks_hit                 | bigint ...
 tup_returned             | bigint ...
 tup_fetched              | bigint ...
 tup_inserted             | bigint ...
 tup_updated              | bigint ...
 tup_deleted              | bigint ...
 conflicts                | bigint ...
 temp_files               | bigint ...
 temp_bytes               | bigint ...
 deadlocks                | bigint ...
 checksum_failures        | bigint ...
 checksum_last_failure    | timestamp with time zone ...
 blk_read_time            | double precision ...
 blk_write_time           | double precision ...
 session_time             | double precision ...
 active_time              | double precision ...
 idle_in_transaction_time | double precision ...
```

```
sessions                     | bigint ...
sessions_abandoned           | bigint ...
sessions_fatal               | bigint ...
sessions_killed              | bigint ...
stats_reset                  | timestamp with time zone ...
```

Next to the database ID and the database name is a column called `numbackends`, which shows the number of database connections that are currently open.

Then, there's `xact_commit` and `xact_rollback`. These two columns indicate whether your application tends to commit or roll back. The `blks_hit` and `blks_read` columns will tell you about cache hits and cache misses. When inspecting these two columns, keep in mind that we're mostly talking about shared buffer hits and shared buffer misses. At the database level, there's no reasonable way to distinguish between filesystem cache hits and real disk hits. At CYBERTEC (`https://www.cybertec-postgresql.com`), we like to see whether there are disk wait and cache misses at the same time in `pg_stat_database` to get an idea of what goes on in the system.

The `tup_` columns will tell you whether there's a lot of reading or a lot of writing going on in your system.

Then, we have `temp_files` and `temp_bytes`. These two columns are of incredible importance because they'll tell you whether your database has to write temporary files to disk, which will inevitably slow down operations. What can be the reasons for high temporary file usage? The main reasons are as follows:

- **Poor settings**: If your `work_mem` settings are too low, there's no way to do anything in RAM, and therefore PostgreSQL will go to disk.

- **Stupid operations**: It happens quite frequently that people torture their system with fairly expensive and pointless queries. If you see many temporary files on an OLTP system, consider checking for expensive queries.

- **Indexing and other administrative tasks**: Once in a while, indexes may be created or people may run DDLs. These operations can lead to temporary file I/O but aren't necessarily considered a problem (in many cases).

In short, temporary files can occur, even if your system is perfectly fine. However, it makes sense to keep an eye on them and ensure that temporary files aren't needed frequently. Too many temporary files can quickly fill up your disk space.

Finally, there are two more important fields: `blk_read_time` and `blk_write_time`. By default, these two fields are empty, and no data is collected. The idea behind these fields is to give you a way of seeing how much time was spent on I/O. The reason these fields are empty is that `track_io_timing` is off by default. This is for a good reason. Imagine that you want to check how long it takes to read 1 million blocks. To do that, you have to call the `time` function in your C library twice, which leads to 2 million additional function calls just to read 8 GB of data. It depends on the speed of your system as to whether this will lead to a lot of overhead or not.

Fortunately, there's a tool that can help you determine how expensive the timing is, as shown in the following code block. Make sure that pg_test_timing is in your $PATH variable or use a full path to run it:

```
[postgres@linux ~]$ pg_test_timing
Testing timing overhead for 3 seconds.
Per loop time including overhead: 23.16  nsec
Histogram of timing durations:
< usec   %       of total        count
  1              97.70300        126549189
  2              2.29506         2972668
  4              0.00024         317
  8              0.00008         101
  16             0.00160         2072
  32             0.00000         5
  64             0.00000         6
  128            0.00000         4
  256            0.00000         0
  512            0.00000         0
  1024           0.00000         4
  2048           0.00000         2
```

In my case, the overhead of turning track_io_timing on for a session in the postgresql. conf file is around 23 nanoseconds, which is fine. Professional high-end servers can provide you with numbers as low as 14 nanoseconds, while bad virtualization can return values of up to 1,400 nanoseconds or even 1,900 nanoseconds. If you're using a cloud service, you can expect around 100-120 nanoseconds (in most cases). If you're ever confronted with four-digit values, measuring the I/O timing may lead to real measurable overhead, which will slow down your system. The general rule is that on real hardware, timing isn't an issue; on virtual systems, check it out before you turn it on.

More and more fields are added over time. What's especially noteworthy is idle_in_transaction_ time. It contains vital information as it tells you how much time the system has spent on an idle transaction. Why is that relevant? The reason is that idle transactions are the single biggest source of table bloat. Remember, when a transaction is running, PostgreSQL can't easily remove rows using VACUUM – therefore, idle transactions matter and this column will give you deep insights if you want to figure out whether idle transactions are to blame for bloat or not.

Finally, we've got those session_* fields. Up to PostgreSQL 14, it wasn't possible to figure out how many connections had been established to PostgreSQL overall. Those new fields will tell us more about the number and life of database connections: how many sessions were created, how many got killed, and so on. All the information is there.

> **Tip**
>
> It's also possible to turn things on selectively by using ALTER DATABASE, ALTER USER, and so on.

Inspecting tables

Once you've gained an overview of what's going on in your databases, it may be a good idea to dig deeper and see what's going on in individual tables. Two system views are here to help you: pg_stat_user_tables and pg_statio_user_tables.

Here's the first one:

```
test=# \d pg_stat_user_tables
            View "pg_catalog.pg_stat_user_tables"
        Column          |              Type ...
------------------------+----------------------- ...
 relid                  | oid ...
 schemaname             | name ...
 relname                | name ...
 seq_scan               | bigint ...
 last_seq_scan          | timestamp with time zone ...
 seq_tup_read           | bigint ...
 idx_scan               | bigint ...
 last_idx_scan          | timestamp with time zone ...
 idx_tup_fetch          | bigint ...
 n_tup_ins              | bigint ...
 n_tup_upd              | bigint ...
 n_tup_del              | bigint ...
 n_tup_hot_upd          | bigint ...
 n_tup_newpage_upd      | bigint ...
 n_live_tup             | bigint ...
 n_dead_tup             | bigint ...
 n_mod_since_analyze    | bigint ...
 n_ins_since_vacuum     | bigint ...
 last_vacuum            | timestamp with time zone ...
 last_autovacuum        | timestamp with time zone ...
 last_analyze           | timestamp with time zone ...
 last_autoanalyze       | timestamp with time zone ...
 vacuum_count           | bigint ...
 autovacuum_count       | bigint ...
 analyze_count          | bigint ...
 autoanalyze_count      | bigint ...
```

By my judgment, `pg_stat_user_tables` is one of the most important but also one of the most misunderstood, or even ignored, system views. I have a feeling that many people read it but fail to extract the full potential of what can be seen here. When used properly, `pg_stat_user_tables` can, in some cases, be nothing short of a revelation.

Before we dig into the interpretation of data, it's important to understand which fields are there. First of all, there's one entry for each table, which will show us the number of sequential scans that happened on the table (`seq_scan`). Then, we have `seq_tup_read`, which tells us how many tuples the system has to read during those sequential scans.

> **Tip**
>
> Remember the `seq_tup_read` column; it contains vital information that can help you find performance problems.

The `idx_scan` field is next on the list. It will show us how often an index was used for this table. PostgreSQL will also show us how many rows those scans returned. Then, there are a couple of columns starting with `n_tup_`. These will tell us how much we inserted, updated, and deleted. The most important thing here is related to HOT UPDATE. When running UPDATE, PostgreSQL must copy a row to ensure that ROLLBACK will work correctly. So, HOT UPDATE is pretty good because it allows PostgreSQL to ensure that a row doesn't have to leave a block.

The copy of the row stays inside the same block, which is beneficial for performance in general. A fair amount of HOT UPDATE clauses indicates that you're on the right track in the case of an intense UPDATE workload. The perfect ratio between normal and HOT UPDATE can't be stated here for all use cases. You've got to think for yourself to figure out which workload benefits from many in-place operations. The general rule is that the more UPDATE-intense your workload is, the better it is to have many HOT UPDATE clauses.

Finally, there are some VACUUM statistics, which mostly speak for themselves.

Making sense of pg_stat_user_tables

Reading all of this data may be interesting; however, unless you can make sense of it, it's pretty pointless. One way to use `pg_stat_user_tables` is to detect which tables may need an index. One way to find this out is to use the following query:

```
SELECT schemaname, relname, seq_scan, seq_tup_read,
       seq_tup_read / seq_scan AS avg, idx_scan
FROM   pg_stat_user_tables
WHERE  seq_scan > 0
ORDER BY seq_tup_read DESC
LIMIT 25;
```

The idea is to find large tables that have been used frequently in a sequential scan. Those tables will naturally come out at the top of the list to bless us with enormously high `seq_tup_read` values, which can be mind-blowing.

> **Tip**
>
> Work your way from top to bottom and look for expensive scans. Keep in mind that sequential scans aren't necessarily bad. They appear naturally in backups, analytical statements, and so on without causing any harm. However, if you're running large sequential scans all the time, your performance will go down the drain.

Note that this query is golden – it will help you spot tables with missing indexes. My practical experience, which is nearly two decades' worth, has shown again and again that missing indexes are the single most important cause of bad performance. Therefore, the query you're looking at is like gold.

Once you're done looking for potentially missing indexes, consider taking a brief look at the caching behavior of your tables. To facilitate this, `pg_statio_user_tables` contains information about all kinds of things, such as the caching behavior of the table (`heap_blks_`), of your indexes (`idx_blks_`), and of **The Oversized-Attribute Storage Technique** (**TOAST**) tables. Finally, you can find out more about TID scans (which are simply scans that read data in physical order) with the following code, which is usually irrelevant to the overall performance of the system:

```
test=# \d pg_statio_user_tables
            View "pg_catalog.pg_statio_user_tables"
      Column       |  Type  | Collation | Nullable | Default
-------------------+--------+-----------+----------+---------
 relid             | oid    |           |          |
 schemaname        | name   |           |          |
 relname           | name   |           |          |
 heap_blks_read    | bigint |           |          |
 heap_blks_hit     | bigint |           |          |
 idx_blks_read     | bigint |           |          |
 idx_blks_hit      | bigint |           |          |
 toast_blks_read   | bigint |           |          |
 toast_blks_hit    | bigint |           |          |
 tidx_blks_read    | bigint |           |          |
 tidx_blks_hit     | bigint |           |          |
```

Although `pg_statio_user_tables` contains important information, it's usually the case that `pg_stat_user_tables` is more likely to provide you with relevant insights (such as a missing index and so on).

Digging into indexes

While pg_stat_user_tables is important for spotting missing indexes, it's sometimes necessary to find indexes that shouldn't exist. Recently, I was on a business trip to Germany and discovered a system that contained mostly pointless indexes (74% of the total storage consumption). While this may not be a problem if your database is really small, it does make a difference in the case of large systems – having hundreds of gigabytes of pointless indexes can seriously harm your overall performance.

Fortunately, pg_stat_user_indexes can be inspected to find those pointless indexes:

```
test=# \d pg_stat_user_indexes
                View "pg_catalog.pg_stat_user_indexes"
      Column     |                Type     ...
---------------+------------------------+ ...
  relid          | oid ...
  indexrelid     | oid ...
  schemaname     | name ...
  relname        | name ...
  indexrelname   | name ...
  idx_scan       | bigint ...
  last_idx_scan  | timestamp with time zone ...
  idx_tup_read   | bigint ...
  idx_tup_fetch  | bigint ...
```

This view tells us how often every index on every table in every schema has been used (idx_scan). To enrich this view a bit, I suggest using the following SQL query:

```
SELECT schemaname, relname, indexrelname, idx_scan,
       pg_size_pretty(pg_relation_size(indexrelid))
          AS idx_size,
       pg_size_pretty(sum(pg_relation_size(indexrelid))
             OVER (ORDER BY idx_scan, indexrelid))
          AS total
FROM   pg_stat_user_indexes
ORDER BY 6;
```

The output of this statement is very useful. It doesn't only contain information about how often an index was used – it also tells us how much space has been wasted for each index. Finally, it adds up all the space consumption in column 6. You can now go through the table and rethink all of those indexes that have rarely been used. It's hard to come up with a general rule regarding when to drop an index, so some manual checking makes a lot of sense.

> **Tip**
>
> Don't just blindly drop indexes. In some cases, indexes are simply not used because end users use the application differently from what's expected. If the end user changes (a new secretary is hired, for example), an index may very well turn into a useful object again.

There's also a view called `pg_statio_user_indexes`, which contains caching information about an index. Although it's interesting, it usually doesn't contain information that leads to big leaps forward.

Tracking the background writer

In this section, we'll take a look at the background writer statistics. As you may already know, database connections will, in many cases, not write blocks to disks directly. Instead, data is written by the background writer process or by the checkpointer.

To see how data is written, inspect the `pg_stat_bgwriter` view. Note that this view has been shortened drastically in PostgreSQL 17 as a lot of the information has been moved out:

```
test=# \d pg_stat_bgwriter
            View "pg_catalog.pg_stat_bgwriter"
      Column        |          Type           ...
------------------+---------------------+ ...
 buffers_clean     | bigint ...
 maxwritten_clean  | bigint  ...
 buffers_alloc     | bigint  ...
 stats_reset       | timestamp with time zone ...
```

How many were written by the background writer? This is what `buffers_clean` will tell us.

But there's more: `maxwritten_clean` tells us about the number of times the background writer stopped a cleaning scan because it had written too many buffers.

Finally, there's `buffers_alloc`, which contains the number of buffers that have been allocated.

Inspecting I/O statistics

As already stated, a lot of information has been moved out of `pg_stat_bgwriter`. The main question is, where did this information end up? The answer is in the `pg_stat_io` system view:

```
test=# \d pg_stat_io
            View "pg_catalog.pg_stat_io"
      Column       |          Type           ...
----------------+---------------------+ ...
 backend_type   | text ...
 object         | text ...
```

```
context          | text ...
reads            | bigint ...
read_time        | double precision ...
writes           | bigint ...
write_time       | double precision ...
writebacks       | bigint ...
writeback_time   | double precision ...
extends          | bigint ...
extend_time      | double precision ...
op_bytes         | bigint ...
hits             | bigint ...
evictions        | bigint ...
reuses           | bigint ...
fsyncs           | bigint ...
fsync_time       | double precision ...
stats_reset      | timestamp with time zone ...
```

The beauty of `pg_stat_io` is that it gives us a unified view of the entire I/O activity of the system. Everything there is can be found in one place. Let's take a look and see what we've got here. The first observation we can make is that the view shows us information about temporary as well as real objects:

```
test=# SELECT DISTINCT object FROM pg_stat_io;
    object
---------------
 temp relation
 relation
(2 rows)
```

We can also see in which context I/O has been happening. In general, PostgreSQL 17 knows four different types of context, as shown in the following listing:

```
test=# SELECT DISTINCT context FROM pg_stat_io;
  context
-----------
 vacuum
 normal
 bulkread
 bulkwrite
(4 rows)
```

The names of those contexts pretty much speak for themselves and let us diagnose under which circumstances I/O has happened. Was it VACUUM or maybe just a normal operation?

We'll see the number of operations as well as the time we need to perform those operations. Make sure that `track_io_timing` is on to make PostgreSQL track time in general.

In some cases, a table or an index doesn't contain enough space to add new data. That's when PostgreSQL writes an "extend," We can also track this activity easily. Finally, PostgreSQL tells us about cache behavior (cache hits as well as the number of blocks that have been removed from the I/O cache) and disk flush operations.

Tracking, archiving, and streaming

In this section, we'll take a look at some features related to **replication** and **transaction** log archiving. The first thing to inspect is `pg_stat_archiver`, which tells us about the archiver process of moving the transaction log (WAL) from the main server to a backup device:

```
test=# \d pg_stat_archiver
            View "pg_catalog.pg_stat_archiver"
       Column        |         Type ...
---------------------+----------------  ...
   archived_count    | bigint ...
 last_archived_wal   | text
 last_archived_time  | timestamp with time zone
   failed_count      | bigint
  last_failed_wal    | text
 last_failed_time    | timestamp with time zone
   stats_reset       | timestamp with time zone
```

Furthermore, `pg_stat_archiver` contains important information about your archiving process. First of all, it will inform you about the number of transaction log files that have been archived (`archived_count`). It will also know details of the last file that was archived and when that happened (`last_archived_wal` and `last_archived_time`).

While knowing the number of WAL files is certainly interesting, it isn't that important. Therefore, consider taking a look at `failed_count` and `last_failed_wal`. If your transaction log archiving failed, it will tell you about the latest file that failed and when that happened. It's recommended to keep an eye on those fields because otherwise, it may be possible that archiving will work without you even noticing.

If you're running a streaming replication, the following two views will be important for you: `pg_stat_replication` and `pg_stat_wal_receiver`. The `pg_stat_replication` view will provide information about the streaming process. One entry per WAL sender process will be visible. If there's no single entry, then this means there's no transaction log streaming going on, which may not be what you want.

Let's take a look at `pg_stat_replication`:

```
test=# \d pg_stat_replication
            View "pg_catalog.pg_stat_replication"
       Column        |          Type ...
```

```
------------------+---------------  ...
 pid              | integer ...
 usesysid         | oid
 usename          | name
 application_name | text
 client_addr      | inet
 client_hostname  | text
 client_port      | integer
 backend_start    | timestamp with time zone
 backend_xmin     | xid
 state            | text
 sent_lsn         | pg_lsn
 write_lsn        | pg_lsn
 flush_lsn        | pg_lsn
 replay_lsn       | pg_lsn
 write_lag        | interval
 flush_lag        | interval
 replay_lag       | interval
 sync_priority    | integer
 sync_state       | text
 reply_time       | timestamp with time zone
```

Here, you'll find columns that indicate the username that's connected via the streaming replication. Then, there's the application name, along with the connection data (client_*). Here, PostgreSQL will tell us when the streaming connection started. In production, a young connection can point to a network problem or something even worse (reliability issues and so on). The state column shows in which state the other side of the stream is. We'll cover this in more detail in *Chapter 10*, *Making Sense of Backups and Replication*.

There are fields here telling us how much of the transaction log has been sent over the network connection (sent_lsn), how much has been sent to the kernel (write_lsn), how much has been flushed to disk (flush_lsn), and how much has already been replayed (replay_lsn). Finally, the sync status is listed. Since PostgreSQL 10.0, there are additional fields that already contain the time difference between the nodes. The *_lag fields contain intervals, which give some indication of the actual time difference between your servers.

PostgreSQL 13 has added some more information to the pg_stat_replication_slots view: the spill_* fields tell us how logical decoding behaves. Sometimes, logical decoding has to spill to disk, which, in turn, can cause performance issues. By inspecting the spill_* fields, we can see how many transactions (spill_txns) have to spill to disk, how often (spill_count), and how much (spill_bytes).

While `pg_stat_replication` can be queried on the sending server of a replication setup, `pg_stat_wal_receiver` can be consulted on the receiving end. It provides similar information and allows this information to be extracted on the replica.

Here's the definition of the view:

```
test=# \d pg_stat_wal_receiver
            View "pg_catalog.pg_stat_wal_receiver"
        Column            |            Type ...
--------------------------+-----------------  ...
 pid                      | integer ...
 status                   | text
 receive_start_lsn        | pg_lsn
 receive_start_tli        | integer
 written_lsn              | pg_lsn
 flushed_lsn              | pg_lsn
 received_tli             | integer
 last_msg_send_time       | timestamp with time zone
 last_msg_receipt_time    | timestamp with time zone
 latest_end_lsn           | pg_lsn
 latest_end_time          | timestamp with time zone
 slot_name                | text
 sender_host              | text
 sender_port              | integer
 conninfo                 | text
```

First of all, PostgreSQL tells us the process ID of the WAL receiver process. Then, the view shows us the status of the connection in use. Next, `receive_start_lsn` tells us the transaction log position that was used when the WAL receiver was started. In addition to this, `receive_start_tli` contains the timeline that was in use when the WAL receiver was started. At some point, you may want to know the latest WAL position and timeline. To get those two numbers, use `received_lsn` and `received_tli`.

In the next two columns, there are two timestamps: `last_msg_send_time` and `last_msg_receipt_time`. The first one states when a message was last sent and the second one when it was received.

Here, `latest_end_lsn` contains the last transaction log position that was reported to the WAL sender process at `latest_end_time`. Then, there's the `slot_name` field and an obfuscated version of the connection information. In PostgreSQL 11, additional fields have been added – the `sender_host`, `sender_port`, and `conninfo` fields tell us about the host that the WAL receiver is connected to.

Checking SSL connections

Many users running PostgreSQL use SSL to encrypt connections from the server to the client. More recent versions of PostgreSQL provide a view so that we can gain an overview of those encrypted connections – that is, pg_stat_ssl:

```
test=# \d pg_stat_ssl
               View "pg_catalog.pg_stat_ssl"
    Column    |  Type   | Collation | Nullable | Default
--------------+---------+-----------+----------+---------
 pid          | integer |           |          |
 ssl          | boolean |           |          |
 version      | text    |           |          |
 cipher       | text    |           |          |
 bits         | integer |           |          |
 client_dn    | text    |           |          |
 client_serial| numeric |           |          |
 issuer_dn    | text    |           |          |
```

Every process is represented by the process ID. If a connection uses SSL, the second column is set to true. The third and fourth columns will define the version, as well as the cipher. Finally, there's the number of bits that are used by the encryption algorithm, including an indicator of whether compression is used or not, as well as the **distinguished name** (**DN**) field from the client certificate.

Inspecting transactions in real time

Thus far, some statistics tables have been discussed. The idea behind all of them is to see what's going on in the system. But what if you're a developer who wants to inspect an individual transaction? We have pg_stat_xact_user_tables to help us with this. It doesn't contain system-wide transactions; it only contains data about your current transaction. This is shown in the following code:

```
test=# \d pg_stat_xact_user_tables
        View "pg_catalog.pg_stat_xact_user_tables"
    Column    |  Type  ...
--------------+--------...
 relid        | oid ...
 schemaname   | name   ...
 relname      | name   ...
 seq_scan     | bigint ...
 seq_tup_read | bigint ...
 idx_scan     | bigint ...
 idx_tup_fetch| bigint ...
 n_tup_ins    | bigint ...
 n_tup_upd    | bigint ...
 n_tup_del    | bigint ...
```

```
n_tup_hot_upd | bigint   ...
n_tup_newpage_upd | bigint   ...
```

The content of `pg_stat_xact_user_tables` is identical to what you can see in `pg_stat_user_tables`. However, the context is a bit different.

Developers can look into a transaction just before it commits to see whether it has caused any performance issues. It helps us distinguish the overall data from what has just been caused by our application.

The ideal way for application developers to use this view is to add a function call in the application before a commit to track what the transaction has done.

This data can then be inspected so that the output of the current transaction can be distinguished from the overall workload.

Tracking VACUUM and CREATE INDEX progress

In PostgreSQL 9.6, the community introduced a system view that many people have been waiting for. For many years, people have wanted to track the progress of a vacuum process to see how long things may take.

Due to this, `pg_stat_progress_vacuum` was invented to address this issue. The following listing shows what kind of information you can obtain:

```
test=# \d pg_stat_progress_vacuum
          View "pg_catalog.pg_stat_progress_vacuum"
          Column          |  Type ...
--------------------------+-------- ...
 pid                      | integer ...
 datid                    | oid     ...
 datname                  | name    ...
 relid                    | oid     ...
 phase                    | text    ...
 heap_blks_total          | bigint  ...
 heap_blks_scanned        | bigint  ...
 heap_blks_vacuumed       | bigint  ...
 index_vacuum_count       | bigint  ...
 max_dead_tuple_bytes     | bigint  ...
 dead_tuple_bytes         | bigint  ...
 num_dead_item_ids        | bigint  ...
 indexes_total            | bigint  ...
 indexes_processed        | bigint  ...
```

Most of the columns speak for themselves, so I won't go into too much detail here. There are just a couple of things that should be kept in mind. First of all, the process isn't linear – it can jump quite a bit. In addition to that, a vacuum is usually pretty fast, so progress can be rapid and hard to track.

Starting with PostgreSQL 12, there's also a way to see what CREATE INDEX is doing. The pg_ stat_progress_create_index view is the counterpart to pg_progress_vacuum. Here's the definition of the system view:

```
test=# \d pg_stat_progress_create_index
        View "pg_catalog.pg_stat_progress_create_index"
          Column          |  Type    ...
------------------------+------   ...
 pid                    | integer ...
 datname                | name
 relid                  | oid
 index_relid            | oid
 command                | text
 phase                  | text
 lockers_total          | bigint
 lockers_done           | bigint
 current_locker_pid     | bigint
 blocks_total           | bigint
 blocks_done            | bigint
 tuples_total           | bigint
 tuples_done            | bigint
 partitions_total       | bigint
 partitions_done        | bigint
```

The content of this table helps us get an idea of how far CREATE INDEX has proceeded. To show you what the content of this table looks like, I've created a fairly large table that can be indexed:

```
test=# CREATE TABLE t_index (x numeric);
CREATE TABLE

test=# INSERT INTO t_index
SELECT * FROM generate_series(1, 50000000);
INSERT 0 50000000

test=# CREATE INDEX idx_numeric ON t_index (x);
CREATE INDEX
```

There are various phases during the index's creation. First, PostgreSQL must scan the table you want to index, which is represented in the system view as follows:

```
test=# SELECT * FROM pg_stat_progress_create_index;
-[ RECORD 1 ]-------+------------------------------
 pid                | 805
 datid              | 16546
 datname            | test
```

```
relid                 | 24576
index_relid           | 0
command               | CREATE INDEX
phase                 | building index: scanning table
lockers_total         | 0
lockers_done          | 0
current_locker_pid    | 0
blocks_total          | 221239
blocks_done           | 59872
tuples_total          | 0
tuples_done           | 0
partitions_total      | 0
partitions_done       | 0
```

Once this is done, PostgreSQL will build the real index, which can also be seen inside the system table, as shown in the following code listing:

```
test=# SELECT * FROM pg_stat_progress_create_index;
-[ RECORD 1 ]
--------------------+----------------------------------------
pid                 | 29191
datid               | 16410
datname             | test
relid               | 24600
index_relid         | 0
command             | CREATE INDEX
phase               | building index: loading tuples in  tree
lockers_total       | 0
lockers_done        | 0
current_locker_pid  | 0
blocks_total        | 0
blocks_done         | 0
tuples_total        | 50000000
tuples_done         | 4289774
partitions_total    | 0
partitions_done     | 0
```

In my listing, close to 10% of the loading process has been done, as shown in the tuples_* columns toward the end of the listing.

Using pg_stat_statements

Now that we've discussed the first couple of views, it's time to turn our attention to one of the most important views, which can be used to spot performance problems. I am, of course, speaking about pg_stat_statements. The idea is to have information about queries on your system. This helps us figure out which types of queries are slow and how often queries are called.

To use this module, we need to follow three steps:

1. Add pg_stat_statements to shared_preload_libraries in the postgresql. conf file.

2. Restart the database server.

3. Run CREATE EXTENSION pg_stat_statements in the databases of our choice.

Let's inspect the definition of the view that's continued to grow over time:

```
test=# \d pg_stat_statements
                View "public.pg_stat_statements"
        Column              |          Type    ...
------------------------+--------------  ...
  userid                    | oid ...
  dbid                      | oid ...
  toplevel                  | boolean ...
  queryid                   | bigint ...
  query                     | text ...
  plans                     | bigint ...
  total_plan_time           | double precision ...
  min_plan_time             | double precision ...
  max_plan_time             | double precision ...
  mean_plan_time            | double precision ...
  stddev_plan_time          | double precision ...
  calls                     | bigint ...
  total_exec_time           | double precision ...
  min_exec_time             | double precision ...
  max_exec_time             | double precision ...
  mean_exec_time            | double precision ...
  stddev_exec_time          | double precision ...
  rows                      | bigint ...
  shared_blks_hit           | bigint ...
  shared_blks_read          | bigint ...
  shared_blks_dirtied       | bigint ...
  shared_blks_written       | bigint ...
  local_blks_hit            | bigint ...
  local_blks_read           | bigint ...
  local_blks_dirtied        | bigint ...
  local_blks_written        | bigint ...
  temp_blks_read            | bigint ...
  temp_blks_written         | bigint ...
```

```
shared_blk_read_time   | double precision ...
shared_blk_write_time  | double precision ...
local_blk_read_time    | double precision ...
local_blk_write_time   | double precision ...
temp_blk_read_time     | double precision ...
temp_blk_write_time    | double precision ...
wal_records            | bigint ...
wal_fpi                | bigint ...
wal_bytes              | numeric ...
jit_functions          | bigint ...
jit_generation_time    | double precision ...
jit_inlining_count     | bigint ...
jit_inlining_time      | double precision ...
jit_optimization_count | bigint ...
jit_optimization_time  | double precision ...
jit_emission_count     | bigint ...
jit_emission_time      | double precision ...
jit_deform_count       | bigint ...
jit_deform_time        | double precision ...
stats_since            | timestamp with time zone ...
minmax_stats_since     | timestamp with time zone ...
```

Here, `pg_stat_statements` provides simply fabulous information that gives you excellent insights into what the database is doing. For every user in every database, it provides one line per query. By default, it tracks 5,000 statements (this can be changed by setting `pg_stat_statements.max`).

Queries and parameters are separated. PostgreSQL will put placeholders into the query. This allows identical queries, which just use different parameters, to be aggregated. For example, `SELECT ... FROM x WHERE y = 10` will be turned into `SELECT ... FROM x WHERE y = ?`.

For each query, PostgreSQL will tell us the total time it has consumed (`total_exec_time`), along with the number of calls it has made (`calls`). The standard deviation is especially noteworthy because it will tell us whether a query has stable or fluctuating runtimes (`stddev_exec_time`). Unstable runtimes can occur for various reasons:

- If the data isn't fully cached in RAM, queries that have to go to disk will take a lot longer than their cached counterparts

- Different parameters can lead to different plans and result sets

- Concurrency and locking can have an impact

In addition, PostgreSQL gives us insights into planning behavior. In case planning time is an issue, this is highly important. For small queries, planning can be quite expensive (compared to the overall runtime). PostgreSQL will also tell us about the caching behavior of a query. The `shared_*` columns show us how many blocks came from the cache (_hit) or from the operating system (_read). If many blocks come from the operating system, the runtime of a query may fluctuate.

The next block of columns is all about local buffers, which are memory blocks that are allocated by the database connection directly.

On top of all this information, PostgreSQL provides information about temporary file I/O. Note that temporary file I/O will naturally happen when a large index is built or when some other large DDL is executed. However, temporary files are usually a very bad thing to have in OLTP as they will slow down the entire system by potentially blocking the disk. A high amount of temporary file I/O can point to some undesirable things. The following are three common scenarios:

- Undesirable work_mem settings (OLTP)
- Suboptimal maintenance_work_mem settings (DDLs)
- Queries that shouldn't have been run in the first place

Finally, there are two fields containing information about I/O timing. By default, these two fields are empty. The reason for this is that measuring timing can involve quite a lot of overhead on some systems. Therefore, the default value for track_io_timing is false – remember to turn it on if you need this data.

What's also new from PostgreSQL 13 and beyond is information about WAL generation – for example, you can find out how much WAL has been produced (the number of records and bytes). This can give you valuable insights into database performance.

Finally, there's a lot of information about JIT compilation. We can see how many functions were compiled, how much time was spent on JIT compilation, and a lot more.

Once the module has been enabled, PostgreSQL will be collecting data, and you can use the view.

> **Tip**
> Never run SELECT * FROM pg_stat_statements in front of a customer. It has been known for people to start pointing at queries they happened to know and for them to explain why, who, what, when, and so on. When you use this view, always create a sorted output so that the most relevant information can be seen instantly.

The following query can prove to be very helpful to gain an overview of what's happening on the database server. Without knowing what's going on, debugging is close to impossible. So, pg_stat_statements is a very good way to figure out what's slow and what isn't:

```
SELECT  round((100 * total_exec_time /
          sum(total_exec_time)
                OVER ())::numeric, 2) percent,
        round(total_exec_time::numeric, 2) AS total,
```

```
        calls,
        round(mean_exec_time::numeric, 2) AS mean,
        substring(query, 1, 40)
FROM    pg_stat_statements
ORDER BY total_exec_time DESC
LIMIT 10;
```

We'll get the following result:

```
percent |    total   | calls |    mean  |        substring
--------+------------+-------+----------+----------------------------------------
  66.27 | 319648.78  | 55859 |     5.72 | UPDATE pgbench_accounts SET abalance = a
  18.54 |  89423.28  |     1 | 89423.28 | copy pgbench_accounts from stdin
   6.37 |  30729.70  |     1 | 30729.70 | vacuum analyze pgbench_accounts
   6.20 |  29886.45  |     1 | 29886.45 | alter table pgbench_accounts add primary
   1.92 |   9270.97  | 55859 |     0.17 | UPDATE pgbench_branches SET bbalance = b
   0.37 |   1770.88  | 55859 |     0.03 | UPDATE pgbench_tellers SET tbalance = tb
   0.13 |    608.56  | 55859 |     0.01 | SELECT abalance FROM pgbench_accounts WH
   0.10 |    493.33  | 55859 |     0.01 | INSERT INTO pgbench_history (tid, bid, a
   0.05 |    239.06  |     1 |   239.06 | vacuum analyze pgbench_branches
   0.02 |    112.91  |     1 |   112.91 | vacuum analyze pgbench_tellers
(10 rows)
```

Figure 5.1 – Inspecting runtime information

The preceding code shows the top 10 queries and their runtime, including a percentage. It also makes sense to display the average execution time of the queries so that you can decide whether the runtime of those queries is too high or not.

Work your way down the list and inspect all the queries that seem to run too long on average.

Keep in mind that working through the top 1,000 queries is usually not worth it. In most cases, the first few queries are already responsible for most of the load on the system.

> **Tip**
>
> In my example, I used a substring to shorten the query so that it fits on one page. I don't recommend this if you want to see what's going on.

At this point, I want to use this situation to point out how important pg_stat_statements is. It's by far the easiest way to track down performance problems. A slow query log can never be as useful as pg_stat_statements because a slow query log will only point to individual slow queries – it won't show us problems that are caused by tons of medium queries. Therefore, it's recommended to always turn this module on. The overhead is really small and in no way harms the overall performance of the system.

By default, 5,000 types of queries are tracked. In most reasonably sane applications, this will be enough.

To reset the data, consider using the following instruction:

```
test=# SELECT pg_stat_statements_reset();
 pg_stat_statements_reset
--------------------------

(1 row)
```

Resetting statistics once in a while can make a lot of sense to ensure that you can see up-to-date information and not some historical old distortions.

Creating log files

Now that we've taken a deep look at the system views provided by PostgreSQL, it's time to configure logging. Fortunately, PostgreSQL provides us with an easy way to work with log files and helps people set up a good configuration easily.

Collecting logs is important because it can point to errors and potential database problems. In this section, you'll learn how to configure logging properly.

The postgresql.conf file contains all the parameters you need so that you're provided with all the necessary information.

In this section, we'll go through some of the most important entries in the postgresql.conf file that we can use to configure logging and see how logging can be used most beneficially.

Before we get started, I want to say a few words about logging in PostgreSQL in general. On Unix systems, PostgreSQL will send log information to stderr by default. However, stderr isn't a good place for logs to go because you'll want to inspect the log stream at some point. Therefore, you should work through this chapter and adjust things to your needs. Let's take a look and see how this can be done.

Defining log destination and rotation

Configuring logging is easy but it requires a little bit of knowledge. Let's go through the postgresql.conf file and see what can be done:

```
#------------------------------------------------------------
# REPORTING AND LOGGING
#------------------------------------------------------------
# - Where to Log -
#log_destination = 'stderr'
     # Valid values are combinations of
     # stderr, csvlog, syslog, and eventlog,
     # depending on platform. csvlog
     # requires logging_collector to be on.
```

```
    # This is used when logging to stderr:
#logging_collector = off
    # Enable capturing of stderr, jsonlog,
    # and csvlog into log files. Required
    # to be on for csvlogs and jsonlogs.
    # (change requires restart)
```

The first configuration option defines how the log is processed. By default, it will go to `stderr` (on Unix). On Windows, the default is `eventlog`, which is the Windows onboard tool that's used to handle logging. Alternatively, you can choose to go with `csvlog` or `syslog`.

If you want to make PostgreSQL log files, you should go for `stderr` and turn `logging collector` on. PostgreSQL will then create log files.

The logical question now is, what will the names of those log files be, and where will those files be stored? Fortunately, `postgresql.conf` has the answer:

```
# These are only used if logging_collector is on:
#log_directory = 'pg_log'
                # directory where log files are written,
                # can be absolute or relative to PGDATA
#log_filename = 'postgresql-%Y-%m-%d_%H%M%S.log'
                # log file name pattern,
                # can include strftime() escapes
```

Here, `log_directory` will tell the system where to store the log. If you're using an absolute path, you can explicitly configure where logs will go. If you prefer the logs to be in the PostgreSQL data directly, simply go for a relative path. The advantage of this is that the data directory will be self-contained, and you can move it without having to worry.

In the next step, you can define the filename that PostgreSQL is supposed to use. PostgreSQL is very flexible and allows you to use all the shortcuts provided by `strftime`. To give you an idea of how powerful this feature is, a quick count on my platform reveals that `strftime` provides 43 (!) placeholders to create the filename. Everything users usually need is certainly possible.

Once the filename has been defined, it makes sense to briefly think about cleanup. The following settings will be available:

```
#log_truncate_on_rotation = off
#log_rotation_age = 1d
#log_rotation_size = 10MB
```

By default, PostgreSQL will keep producing log files if files are older than 1 day or larger than 10 MB. Additionally, `log_truncate_on_rotation` specifies whether you want to append data to a log file or not. Sometimes, `log_filenames` is defined in a way that it becomes cyclic. The `log_truncate_on_rotation` parameter defines whether to overwrite or append to the file that already exists. Given the default log file, this will, of course, not happen.

One way to handle auto-rotation is to use something such as `postgresql_%a.log`, along with `log_truncate_on_rotation = on`. The `%a` part means that the day of the week will be used inside the log file. The advantage here is that the day of the week repeats every 7 days. Therefore, the log will be kept for a week and recycled. If you're aiming for weekly rotation, a 10 MB file size may not be enough. So, consider turning the maximum file size off.

Configuring syslog

Some people prefer to use `syslog` to collect log files. PostgreSQL offers the following configuration parameters:

```
# These are relevant when logging to syslog:
#syslog_facility = 'LOCAL0'
#syslog_ident = 'postgres'
#syslog_sequence_numbers = on
#syslog_split_messages = on
```

The `syslog` tool is pretty popular among sysadmins. Fortunately, it's easy to configure: you set a facility and an identifier. If `log_destination` is set to `syslog`, then you don't need to do anything else.

Logging slow queries

The log can also be used to track down individual slow queries. Back in the old days, this was pretty much the only way to spot performance problems.

How does it work? Basically, `postgresql.conf` has a variable called `log_min_duration_statement`. If this is set to a value greater than 0, every query exceeding our chosen setting will make it to the log:

```
# log_min_duration_statement = -1
```

Most people see the slow query log as the ultimate source of wisdom. However, I would like to add a word of caution. There are many slow queries, and they just happen to eat up a lot of CPU: **index creation**, **data exports**, **analytics**, and so on.

These long-running queries are expected and, in many cases, aren't the root of all evil. It's frequently the case that many shorter queries are to blame. Here's an example: 1,000 queries x 500 milliseconds is worse than 2 queries x 5 seconds. The slow query log can be misleading in some cases.

Still, it doesn't mean that it's pointless – it just means that it's *a* source of information and not *the* source of information.

Defining what and how to log

After taking a look at some basic settings, it's time to decide what to log. By default, only errors will be logged. However, this may not be enough. In this section, you'll learn about what can be logged and what a logline will look like.

By default, PostgreSQL doesn't log information about checkpoints. The following setting is here to change exactly that:

```
#log_checkpoints = off
```

The same applies to connections; whenever a connection is established or destroyed properly, PostgreSQL can create log entries, as follows:

```
#log_connections = off
#log_disconnections = off
```

In most cases, it doesn't make sense to log connections since extensive logging significantly slows down the system. Analytical systems won't suffer much. However, OLTP may be seriously impacted.

If you want to see how long statements take, consider switching the following setting to *on*:

```
#log_duration = off
```

Here, `log_duration` will add time to all statements while `log_min_duration_statement` will only be a threshold of when to log a statement at all (to reduce the volume of logs produced).

Let's move on to one of the most important settings. We haven't defined the layout of the messages yet, and so far, the `log` files contain errors in the following form:

```
test=# SELECT 1/0;
psql: ERROR: division by zero
```

The log will state ERROR, along with the error message. Before PostgreSQL 10.0, there wasn't a timestamp, username, and so on. You had to change the value immediately to make sense of the logs. In PostgreSQL 10.0, the default value has changed to something much more reasonable. To change that, take a look at `log_line_prefix`:

```
#log_line_prefix = '%m [%p] '
# special values:
#    %a = application name
#    %u = user name
#    %d = database name
#    %r = remote host and port
#    %h = remote host
```

```
#     %p = process ID
#     %t = timestamp without milliseconds
#     %m = timestamp with milliseconds
#     %n = timestamp with milliseconds (as a Unix epoch)
#     %i = command tag
#     %e = SQL state
#     %c = session ID
#     %l = session line number
#     %s = session start timestamp
#     %v = virtual transaction ID
#     %x = transaction ID (0 if none)
#     %q = stop here in non-session processes
#     %% = <%>
```

As we can see, `log_line_prefix` is pretty flexible and allows you to configure the logline to exactly match your needs. In general, it's a good idea to log a timestamp. Otherwise, it's close to impossible to see when something bad has happened. I also like to know the username, the transaction ID, and the database. However, it's up to you to decide what you need.

Sometimes, slowness is caused by bad locking behavior. Users blocking each other can cause bad performance, and it's important to sort out those issues to ensure high throughput. In general, locking-related issues can be hard to track down.

The `log_lock_waits` parameter can help detect such issues. If a lock is held longer than `deadlock_timeout`, then a line will be sent to the log, provided that the following configuration variable is turned on:

```
#log_lock_waits = off
```

Finally, it's time to tell PostgreSQL what to log. So far, only errors, slow queries, and the like have been sent to the log. However, `log_statement` has four possible settings, as shown in the following block:

```
#log_statement = 'none'
 # none, ddl, mod, all
```

Note that none means that only errors will be logged, ddl means that errors, as well as DDLs (CREATE TABLE, ALTER TABLE, and so on), will be logged, mod will already include data changes, and all will send every statement to the log.

Be aware that all can lead to a lot of logging information, which can slow down your system. This will send replication-related commands to the log:

```
#log_replication_commands = off
```

> **Important note**
>
> For more information on replication, visit the following website: `https://www.postgresql.org/docs/current/protocol-replication.html`.

It can frequently be the case that performance problems are caused by temporary file I/O. To see which queries cause problems, the following setting can be used:

```
#log_temp_files = -1
#   log temporary files  equal  or larger
#   than  the specified size  in kilobytes;
#   -1 disables, 0 logs  all temp  files
```

While `pg_stat_statements` contains aggregated information, `log_temp_files` will point to specific queries causing issues. It usually makes sense to set this one to a reasonably low value. The correct value depends on your workload, but maybe 4 MB is a good start.

By default, PostgreSQL will write log files in the time zone where the server is located. However, if you're running a system that's spread all over the world, it makes sense to adjust the time zone so that you can go and compare log entries, as shown in the following code:

```
log_timezone = 'Europe/Vienna'
```

Keep in mind that, on the SQL side, you'll still see the time in your local time zone. However, if this variable is set, log entries will be in a different time zone.

If logging is turned on, it can lead to enormous amounts of logs, which, in turn, reduces database performance. Three parameters have been added to control the number of logs produced:

```
log_min_duration_sample = -1
log_statement_sample_rate = 1.0
log_transaction_sample_rate = 0.0
```

The sample rates define how many of those desired log entries will make it to the log stream. The idea is to reduce the number of logs while still maintaining the usefulness of those settings as such.

Logging is key to seeing what's going on in the database. However, we recommend configuring logging wisely to avoid excessive log production and thus slowdowns. Extract as much information as needed but avoid excess.

Monitoring replication conflicts

If you're using PostgreSQL, you might want to get information about replication conflicts:

```
#log_recovery_conflict_waits = off
# log standby recovery conflict waits
# >= deadlock_timeout
```

Often, a replica must terminate a query because of a replication conflict. One way to figure out that those errors happen is to use `log_recovery_conflict_waits`. It will send a message to the log if the conflict persists longer than `deadlock_timeout`.

If you're suffering from extensive replication conflicts, consider checking out `hot_standby_feedback` to prevent those errors.

Summary

This chapter was all about system statistics. First, you learned how to extract information from PostgreSQL and how to use system statistics beneficially. Without proper monitoring, achieving good and reliable operations is close to impossible. It's important to keep an eye on runtime parameters and database vitals to avoid trouble. Then, you learned about PostgreSQL monitoring, which can be used to optimize your database.

We also discussed the most important views in detail. *Chapter 6, Optimizing Queries for Good Performance*, is all about query optimization. You'll learn how to inspect queries and how they're optimized.

Optimizing Queries for Good Performance

In *Chapter 5, Log Files and System Statistics*, you learned how to read system statistics and how to make use of what PostgreSQL provides. Now that we're armed with this knowledge, this chapter is all about good query performance. Everybody is looking for good query performance. Therefore, it's important to address this topic in depth.

In this chapter, you'll learn about the following topics:

- Learning what the PostgreSQL optimizer does
- Understanding execution plans
- Understanding and fixing joins
- Enabling and disabling optimizer settings
- Partitioning data
- Adjusting parameters for good query performance
- Making use of parallel queries
- Introducing **just-in-time** (**JIT**) compilation

By the end of this chapter, we'll be able to write better and faster queries. If the queries still aren't very good, we should be able to understand why this is the case. We'll also be able to use the new techniques we'll learn about to partition data.

Learning what the PostgreSQL optimizer does

Before even attempting to think about query performance, it makes sense to familiarize yourself with what the PostgreSQL query optimizer does. Having a deeper understanding of what's going on under the hood makes a lot of sense because it helps you see what the database is really up to. Keep in mind that the optimizer is a part of PostgreSQL. It's constantly evolving and more optimizations are being added as we speak. It's impossible to cover every corner of the software but it's vital to have at least some basic understanding of what's happening under the hood deep inside the "engine room" of PostgreSQL.

A practical example – how the query optimizer handles a sample query

To demonstrate how the optimizer works, I've compiled an example. It's something that I've used over the years for PostgreSQL training. Let's assume that there are three tables, as follows:

```
CREATE TABLE a (aid int, ...);     -- 100 million rows
CREATE TABLE b (bid int, ...);     -- 200 million rows
CREATE TABLE c (cid int, ...);     -- 300 million rows
```

Let's also assume that those tables contain millions, or maybe hundreds of millions, of rows. In addition to that, there are indexes:

```
CREATE INDEX idx_a ON a (aid);
CREATE INDEX idx_b ON b (bid);
CREATE INDEX idx_c ON c (cid);
CREATE VIEW v AS SELECT *
    FROM a, b
    WHERE aid = bid;
```

Finally, there's a view that joins the first two tables together.

Let's suppose that the end user wants to run the following query. What will the optimizer do with this query? What choices does the planner have?

```
SELECT *
FROM   v, c
WHERE v.aid = c.cid
    AND cid = 4;
```

Before looking at the actual optimization process, we'll focus on some of the options that the planner has.

> **Note**
>
> While reading this chapter, keep in mind that we'll be discussing basic optimizer strategies. So, in case you see execution plans that don't exactly match what you see, consider that all examples have been made with a "no parallel query environment" and that we're explaining basic concepts, not exact plans.

Evaluating join options

The planner has a couple of options here, so let's take this opportunity to understand what can go wrong if straightforward approaches are used.

Suppose the planner just steams ahead and calculates the output of the view. What's the best way to join 100 million rows with 200 million rows?

In this section, a few (not all) join options will be discussed to show you what PostgreSQL can do.

> **Note**
>
> This is a generic introduction. The goal is to show many of the basic concepts here. Many of those algorithms are also available for parallel queries. The key here is to understand the basic ideas and implications from an optimization point of view.

Nested loops

One way to join two tables is to use a **nested loop**. The principle here is simple. Here's some pseudocode:

```
for x in table1:
    for y in table2:
        if x.field == y.field
            issue row
        else
            keep doing
```

Nested loops are often used if one of the sides is very small and contains only a limited set of data. In our example, a nested loop would lead to 100 million x 200 million iterations through the code. This isn't an option because the runtime would simply explode.

A nested loop is generally O(n*n), so it's only efficient if one side of the join is very small. In this example, this isn't the case, so a nested loop can be ruled out for calculating the view.

Hash joins

The second option is a **hash join**. The following strategy could be applied to solve our little problem. The following listing shows how a hash join works:

```
Hash join
    Sequential scan table 1
    Sequential scan table 2
```

Both sides can be hashed, and the hash keys can be compared, leaving us with the result of the join. The problem here is that all of the values have to be hashed and stored somewhere.

Merge joins

Finally, there's the **merge join**. The idea here is to use sorted lists to join the results. If both sides of the join are sorted, the system can just take the rows from the top, see whether they match, and return them. The main requirement here is that the lists are sorted. Here's a sample plan:

```
Merge join
  Sort table 1
     Sequential scan table 1
  Sort table 2
     Sequential scan table 2
```

To join these two tables (`table 1` and `table 2`), data must be provided in sorted order. In many cases, PostgreSQL will just sort the data. However, there are other options we can use to provide the join with sorted data. One way is to consult an index, as shown in the following example:

```
Merge join
    Index scan table 1
    Index scan table 2
```

One side of the join, or both sides, can use sorted data coming from lower levels of the plan. If the table is accessed directly, an index is an obvious choice for this, but only if the returned result set is significantly smaller than the entire table. Otherwise, we'll encounter almost double the overhead because we have to read the entire index and then the entire table. If the result set is a large portion of the table, a sequential scan is more efficient, especially if it's accessed in the primary key order.

The beauty of a merge join is that it can handle a lot of data. The downside is that data has to be sorted or taken from an index at some point.

Sorting is $O(n * \log(n))$. Therefore, sorting 300 million rows to perform the join isn't attractive either.

Applying transformations

Doing the obvious thing (joining the view first) makes no sense at all. A nested loop would send the execution time through the roof. A hash join has to hash millions of rows, and a nested loop has to sort 300 million rows. All three options are unsuitable here. The way out is to apply logical transformations to make the query fast. In this section, you'll learn what the planner does to speed up the query. A couple of steps will need to be performed by the optimizer to reach higher efficiency:

1. **Inline the view**: The first transformation that the optimizer does is inline the views. Here's what happens:

    ```
    SELECT *
    FROM
    (
        SELECT *
    ```

```
      FROM a, b
      WHERE aid = bid
  ) AS v, c
  WHERE v.aid = c.cid
      AND cid = 4;
```

The view is inlined and transformed into a subselect. What does this one buy us? Nothing. All it does is open the door for further optimization, which will be a game-changer for this query.

2. **Flatten subselects**: The next thing we need to do is flatten the subselects, which means integrating them into the main query. By getting rid of subselects, a couple more options that we can utilize to optimize the query will appear.

Here's what the query will look like after flattening the subselects:

```
SELECT    *
FROM    a, b, c
WHERE a.aid = c.cid
  AND aid = bid
  AND cid = 4;
```

Now, a normal join offers the option to apply many more optimizations. Without this inlining step, this would be impossible. Let's see which optimizations are now available.

> **Important note**
> We could have rewritten this SQL on our own, but the planner will take care of those transformations for us anyway. The optimizer can now perform further optimizations.

Applying equality constraints

The following process creates equality constraints. The idea is to detect additional constraints, join options, and filters. Let's take a deep breath and take a look at the following logic:

- If `aid = cid` and `aid = bid`, we know that `bid = cid`

- If `cid = 4` and all the others are equal, we know that `aid` and `bid` have to be 4 as well

This leads to the following query:

```
SELECT *
FROM a, b, c
WHERE a.aid = c.cid
    AND aid = bid
    AND cid = 4
```

```
      AND bid = cid
      AND aid = 4
      AND bid = 4
```

The importance of this optimization can't be stressed enough. What the planner did here was open the door for two additional indexes that weren't visible in the original query.

By being able to use indexes on all three columns, the query is now a lot cheaper. The optimizer has the option to just retrieve a couple of rows from the index and use whatever join option makes sense.

However, we have to be a bit careful in this area: equality constraints work for *equals* but not for other operators. Consider the following example:

```
test=# explain SELECT *
FROM       pg_class
WHERE      oid = 1
AND oid = reltype;
              QUERY PLAN
-------------------------------------------------
 Index Scan using pg_class_oid_index on pg_class
  (cost=0.28..8.29 rows=1 width=767)
    Index Cond: (oid = '1'::oid)
    Filter: (reltype = '1'::oid)
(3 rows)


test=# explain SELECT *
FROM       pg_class
WHERE      oid < 1
AND oid = reltype;
                    QUERY PLAN
-------------------------------------------------
 Index Scan using pg_class_oid_index on pg_class
  (cost=0.28..7.79 rows=1 width=767)
    Index Cond: (oid < '1'::oid)
    Filter: (oid = reltype)
(3 rows)
```

As we can see, the plan is different. The < operator doesn't make it to the second column.

Exhaustive searching

Now that those formal transformations have been done, PostgreSQL will perform an exhaustive search. It will try out all the possible plans and come up with the cheapest solution to your query. PostgreSQL knows which indexes are possible and just uses the cost model to determine how to do things in the best way possible.

During an exhaustive search, PostgreSQL will also try to determine the best join order. In the original query, the join order was fixed to A → B and A → C. However, using those equality constraints, we could join B → C and join A later. All of these options are open to the planner.

Checking out execution plans

Now that all of the optimization options have been discussed, it's time to see what kind of execution plan is produced by PostgreSQL.

First, let's try using the query with fully analyzed but empty tables:

```
test=# SET max_parallel_workers_per_gather TO 0;
SET
test=# explain SELECT *
FROM      v, c
WHERE     v.aid = c.cid
AND cid = 4;
                           QUERY PLAN
-----------------------------------------------------------
 Nested Loop  (cost=12.77..74.50 rows=2197 width=12)
   ->  Nested Loop  (cost=8.51..32.05 rows=169 width=8)
         ->  Bitmap Heap Scan on a
             (cost=4.26..14.95 rows=13 width=4)
               Recheck Cond: (aid = 4)
               ->  Bitmap Index Scan on idx_a
         (cost=0.00..4.25 rows=13 width=0)
                     Index Cond: (aid = 4)
         ->  Materialize  (cost=4.26..15.02
                     rows=13 width=4)
               ->  Bitmap Heap Scan on b
         (cost=4.26..14.95 rows=13 width=4)
                     Recheck Cond: (bid = 4)
                     ->  Bitmap Index Scan on idx_b
                         (cost=0.00..4.25 rows=13 width=0)
                         Index Cond: (bid = 4)
   ->  Materialize  (cost=4.26..15.02 rows=13 width=4)
         ->  Bitmap Heap Scan on c
             (cost=4.26..14.95 rows=13 width=4)
               Recheck Cond: (cid = 4)
               ->  Bitmap Index Scan on idx_c
                   (cost=0.00..4.25 rows=13 width=0)
                     Index Cond: (cid = 4)
 (16 rows)
```

Here, we can see the plan that was produced using empty tables. However, let's check out what happens if we add data:

```
test=# INSERT INTO a SELECT * FROM generate_series(1, 1000000);
INSERT 0 1000000
test=# INSERT INTO b SELECT * FROM generate_series(1, 1000000);
INSERT 0 1000000
test=# INSERT INTO c SELECT * FROM generate_series(1, 1000000);
INSERT 0 1000000
test=# ANALYZE ;
ANALYZE
```

As shown in the following code, the plan has changed. However, what's important is that, in both plans, you'll see filters being automatically applied to all the columns in the query. PostgreSQL's equality constraints have done their job:

```
test=# explain SELECT * FROM v, c WHERE v.aid = c.cid AND cid = 4;
                            QUERY PLAN
-----------------------------------------------------------------
 Nested Loop (cost=1.27..13.35 rows=1 width=12)
   -> Nested Loop (cost=0.85..8.89 rows=1 width=8)
         -> Index Only Scan using idx_a on a
      (cost=0.42..4.44 rows=1 width=4)
               Index Cond: (aid = 4)
         -> Index Only Scan using idx_b on b
      (cost=0.42..4.44 rows=1 width=4)
               Index Cond: (bid = 4)
   -> Index Only Scan using idx_c on c
      (cost=0.42..4.44 rows=1 width=4)
         Index Cond: (cid = 4)
 (8 rows)
```

> **Important note**
>
> The plans shown in this chapter aren't necessarily 100% identical to what you'll observe. Depending on how much data you've loaded, there may be slight variations. Costs may also depend on physically aligning data on the disk (order on disk). Please keep this in mind when running these examples.

As you can see, PostgreSQL will use three indexes. It's also interesting to see that PostgreSQL decides to go for a nested loop to join the data. This makes perfect sense because there's virtually no data coming back from the index scans. Therefore, using a loop to join things is perfectly feasible and highly efficient.

Making the process fail

So far, you've seen what PostgreSQL can do for you and how the optimizer helps speed up queries. PostgreSQL is pretty smart, but it needs smart users. There are some cases where the end user cripples the entire optimization process by doing stupid things. Let's drop the view by using the following command:

```
test=# DROP VIEW v;
DROP VIEW
```

With that, the view has been recreated. Note that OFFSET 0 has been added to the end of the view (the purpose of OFFSET is to skip a couple of rows from the result). Let's take a look at the following example:

```
test=# CREATE OR REPLACE VIEW v AS
SELECT *
FROM a, b
WHERE aid = bid
OFFSET 0;
 CREATE VIEW
```

While this view is logically equivalent to the example that was shown previously, the optimizer has to treat things differently. Every OFFSET other than 0 will change the result, and therefore the view has to be calculated. The entire optimization process is crippled by adding things such as OFFSET.

> **Important note**
>
> The PostgreSQL community has decided to not optimize this pattern. If you used OFFSET 0 in a view, the planner wouldn't strip it out. People are simply not supposed to do that. We'll use this just as an example to observe how certain operations can cripple performance and that we, as developers, should be aware of the underlying optimization process. However, if you happen to know how PostgreSQL works, this trick can be used for optimization.

Here's the new plan if the view contained OFFSET 0:

```
test=# EXPLAIN SELECT *
FROM    v, c
WHERE   v.aid = c.cid
AND cid = 4;
                            QUERY PLAN
---------------------------------------------------------------
 Nested Loop (cost=1.62..79463.79 rows=1 width=12)
   -> Subquery Scan on v (cost=1.19..79459.34
         rows=1  width=8)
         Filter: (v.aid = 4)
```

```
        -> Merge Join (cost=1.19..66959.34
              rows=1000000 width=8)
              Merge Cond: (a.aid = b.bid)
              -> Index Only Scan using idx_a on a
                   (cost=0.42..25980.42
                    rows=1000000 width=4)
              -> Index Only Scan using idx_b on b
                 (cost=0.42..25980.42 rows=1000000 width=4)
  -> Index Only Scan using idx_c on c
        (cost=0.42..4.44 rows=1 width=4)
          Index Cond: (cid = 4)
(9 rows)
```

Just take a look at the costs that have been predicted by the planner – they've skyrocketed from two-digit numbers to a staggering one. This query is going to provide bad performance.

There are various ways to cripple performance, but it makes sense to keep the optimization process in mind.

Constant folding

Many more optimizations in PostgreSQL take place behind the scenes that contribute to overall good performance. One of these features is called **constant folding**. The idea is to turn expressions into constants, as shown in the following example:

```
test=# explain SELECT * FROM a WHERE aid = 3 + 1;
                        QUERY PLAN
-----------------------------------------------------------
 Index Only Scan using idx_a on a
   (cost=0.42..4.44 rows=1 width=4)
     Index Cond: (aid = 4)
(2 rows)
```

As you can see, PostgreSQL will try to look for 4. Since aid is indexed, PostgreSQL will go for an index scan. Note that our table has just one column, so PostgreSQL even figured out that all the data it needs can be found in the index.

What happens if the expression is on the left-hand side?

```
test=# SET max_parallel_workers_per_gather TO DEFAULT;
SET
test=# explain SELECT * FROM a WHERE aid - 1 = 3;
                        QUERY PLAN
-----------------------------------------------------------
 Gather (cost=1000.00..12175.00 rows=5000 width=4)
```

```
    Workers Planned: 2
    -> Parallel Seq Scan on a
          (cost=0.00..10675.00 rows=2083 width=4)
          Filter: ((aid - 1) = 3)
(4 rows)
test=# SET max_parallel_workers_per_gather TO 0;
SET
test=# explain SELECT * FROM a WHERE aid - 1 = 3;
                      QUERY PLAN
-------------------------------------------------------
 Seq Scan on a (cost=0.00..19425.00 rows=5000 width=4)
   Filter: ((aid - 1) = 3)
(2 rows)
```

In this case, the index lookup code will fail, and PostgreSQL has to go for a sequential scan. I've included two examples here – a parallel plan as well as a single core plan.

For the sake of simplicity, all the plans shown from now on are single-core ones.

Understanding function inlining

As we already outlined in this section, many optimizations help speed up queries. One of them is called **function inlining**. PostgreSQL can inline immutable SQL functions. The main idea is to reduce the number of function calls that have to be made to speed things up.

Here's an example of a function that can be inlined by the optimizer:

```
test=# CREATE OR REPLACE FUNCTION ld(int)
RETURNS numeric AS
$$
    SELECT log(2, $1);
$$
LANGUAGE 'sql' IMMUTABLE;
CREATE FUNCTION
```

This is a normal SQL function marked as IMMUTABLE. This is perfect optimization fodder for the optimizer. To make it simple, all my function does is calculate a logarithm:

```
test=# SELECT ld(1024);
        ld
--------------------
 10.0000000000000000
(1 row)
```

As you can see, the function works as expected.

To demonstrate how things work, we'll recreate the table with less content to speed up the index creation process:

```
test=# TRUNCATE a;
TRUNCATE TABLE
```

After that, the TRUNCATE data can be added again, and the index can be applied:

```
test=# INSERT INTO a SELECT * FROM generate_series(1, 10000);
INSERT 0 10000
test=# CREATE INDEX idx_ld ON a (ld(aid));
CREATE INDEX
```

As expected, the index that's created on the function will be used just like any other index. However, let's take a closer look at the indexing condition:

```
test=# EXPLAIN SELECT * FROM a WHERE ld(aid) = 10;
                          QUERY PLAN
-----------------------------------------------------------
 Bitmap Heap Scan on a (cost=4.67..52.77 rows=50 width=4)
   Recheck Cond: (log('2'::numeric,
           (aid)::numeric) = '10'::numeric)
   -> Bitmap Index Scan on idx_ld
       (cost=0.00..4.66 rows=50 width=0)
       Index Cond: (log('2'::numeric,
           (aid)::numeric) = '10'::numeric)
(4 rows)
test=# ANALYZE;
ANALYZE
test=# EXPLAIN SELECT * FROM a WHERE ld(aid) = 10;
                          QUERY PLAN
-----------------------------------------------------------
 Index Scan using idx_ld on a
       (cost=0.29..8.30 rows=1 width=4)
   Index Cond: (log('2'::numeric, (aid)::numeric) = '10'::numeric)
(2 rows)
```

The important observation here is that the indexing condition looks for the log function instead of the ld function. The optimizer has completely gotten rid of the function call. It's also worth mentioning that fresh optimizer statistics can be of real importance to generate an efficient plan.

Logically, this opens the door for the following query:

```
test=# EXPLAIN SELECT * FROM a WHERE log(2, aid) = 10;
                          QUERY PLAN
-----------------------------------------------------------
```

```
Index Scan using idx_ld on a
    (cost=0.29..8.30 rows=1 width=4)
  Index Cond: (log('2'::numeric,
    (aid)::numeric) = '10'::numeric)
(2 rows)
```

The optimizer managed to inline the function and provided us with an index scan that's far superior to an expensive sequential operation.

Introducing join pruning

PostgreSQL also provides an optimization called **join pruning**. The idea is to remove joins if they aren't required by the query. This can come in handy if queries are generated by some middleware or **object-relational mapping (ORM)**. If a join can be removed, it naturally speeds things up dramatically and leads to less overhead.

The question now is, how does join pruning work? Here's an example:

```
CREATE TABLE x (id int, PRIMARY KEY (id));
CREATE TABLE y (id int, PRIMARY KEY (id));
```

First of all, two tables are created. Make sure that both sides of the join condition are unique. Those constraints will be important in a minute.

Now, we can write a simple query:

```
test=# EXPLAIN SELECT *
FROM  x LEFT JOIN y ON (x.id = y.id)
WHERE x.id = 3;
                        QUERY PLAN
-------------------------------------------------------
 Nested Loop Left Join  (cost=0.31..16.36 rows=1 width=8)
   Join Filter: (x.id = y.id)
   ->  Index Only Scan using x_pkey on x
       (cost=0.15..8.17 rows=1 width=4)
         Index Cond: (id = 3)
   ->  Index Only Scan using y_pkey on y
       (cost=0.15..8.17 rows=1 width=4)
         Index Cond: (id = 3)
(6 rows)
```

As you can see, PostgreSQL will join those tables directly. So far, there are no surprises. However, the following query has been modified slightly. Instead of selecting all the columns, it only selects those columns on the left-hand side of the join:

```
test=# EXPLAIN SELECT x.*
FROM  x LEFT JOIN y ON (x.id = y.id)
```

```
WHERE  x.id = 3;
                          QUERY PLAN
---------------------------------------------------------------
 Index Only Scan using x_pkey on x
     (cost=0.15..8.17 rows=1 width=4)
   Index Cond: (id = 3)
(2 rows)
```

PostgreSQL will go for a direct inside scan and skip the join completely. There are two reasons why this is possible and logically correct:

- No columns are selected from the right-hand side of the join; thus, looking those columns up doesn't buy us anything

- The right-hand side is unique, which means that joining can't increase the number of rows due to duplicates on the right-hand side

If joins can be pruned automatically, then the queries may be a magnitude faster. The beauty here is that an increase in speed can be achieved by just removing columns that may not be required by the application in any case.

Speedup set operations

Set operations combine the results of more than one query into a single result set. They include UNION, INTERSECT, and EXCEPT. PostgreSQL implements all of them and offers many important optimizations to speed them up.

The planner can push restrictions down into the set operation, opening the door for fancy indexing and speedups in general. Let's take a look at the following query, which shows us how this works:

```
test=# EXPLAIN SELECT *
FROM
(
    SELECT aid AS xid
    FROM a
    UNION ALL
    SELECT bid FROM b
) AS y
WHERE xid = 3;
                             QUERY PLAN
---------------------------------------------------------------
 Append (cost=0.29..8.76 rows=2 width=4)
   -> Index Only Scan using idx_a on a
         (cost=0.29..4.30 rows=1 width=4)
           Index Cond: (aid = 3)
```

```
        -> Index Only Scan using idx_b on b
              (cost=0.42..4.44 rows=1 width=4)
              Index Cond: (bid = 3)
 (5 rows)
```

What you can see here is that two relations have been added to each other. The trouble is that the only restriction is outside the subselect. However, PostgreSQL figures out that the filter can be pushed further down the plan. Therefore, `xid = 3` is attached to `aid` and `bid`, giving us the option to use indexes on both tables. By avoiding the sequential scan on both tables, the query will run a lot faster.

> **Important note**
>
> There's a distinction between the UNION clause and the UNION ALL clause. The UNION ALL clause will just blindly append the data and deliver the results of both tables.

The UNION clause is different as it will filter out duplicates. The following plan shows how that works:

```
test=# EXPLAIN SELECT *
FROM
(
      SELECT aid AS xid
      FROM a
      UNION SELECT bid
      FROM b
) AS y
WHERE xid = 3;
                              QUERY PLAN
---------------------------------------------------------------- Unique
(cost=8.79..8.80 rows=2 width=4)
   -> Sort  (cost=8.79..8.79 rows=2 width=4)
           Sort Key: a.aid
           -> Append  (cost=0.29..8.78 rows=2 width=4)
               -> Index Only Scan using idx_a on a
                   (cost=0.29..4.30 rows=1 width=4)
                      Index Cond: (aid = 3)
               -> Index Only Scan using idx_b on b
                   (cost=0.42..4.44 rows=1 width=4)
                      Index Cond: (bid = 3)
 (8 rows)
```

The execution plan already looks very attractive. Two index scans can be seen. PostgreSQL has to add a `Sort` node on top of the `Append` node to ensure that duplicates can be filtered later on.

> **Important note**
>
> Many developers who aren't fully aware of the difference between the UNION clause and the UNION ALL clause complain about bad performance because they're unaware that PostgreSQL has to filter out duplicates, which is especially painful in the case of large datasets.

In this section, some of the most important optimizations have been discussed. Keep in mind that a lot more is going on inside the planner. However, once the most important steps are understood, it's easier to write proper queries.

Understanding execution plans

Now that we've dug into some important optimizations that are implemented in PostgreSQL, let's take a closer look at execution plans. You've already seen some execution plans in this book. However, to make full use of plans, it's important to develop a systematic approach when it comes to reading this information.

Approaching plans systematically

The first thing you have to know is that an EXPLAIN clause can do quite a lot for you, and I highly recommend making full use of these features.

As you may already know, an EXPLAIN ANALYZE clause will execute the query and return the plan, including real runtime information. Here's an example:

```
test=# EXPLAIN ANALYZE SELECT *
FROM
(
    SELECT *
    FROM b
    LIMIT 1000000
) AS b
ORDER BY cos(bid);
                            QUERY PLAN
-------------------------------------------------------------- Sort
(cost=146173.34..148673.34 rows=1000000 width=12)
      (actual time=494.028..602.733 rows=1000000 loops=1)
   Sort Key: (cos((b.bid)::double precision))
   Sort Method: external merge Disk: 25496kB
   -> Subquery Scan on b
      (cost=0.00..29425.00 rows=1000000 width=12)
      (actual time=6.274..208.224 rows=1000000 loops=1)
         -> Limit (cost=0.00..14425.00
                rows=1000000 width=4)
            (actual time=5.930..105.253
```

```
                  rows=1000000 loops=1)
            -> Seq Scan on b b_1
        (cost=0.00..14425.00 rows=1000000 width=4)
                  (actual time=0.014..55.448
                      rows=1000000 loops=1)
 Planning Time: 0.170 ms
 JIT:
   Functions: 3
   Options: Inlining false, Optimization false,
    Expressions true, Deforming true
   Timing: Generation 0.319 ms, Inlining 0.000 ms,
    Optimization 0.242 ms,
           Emission 5.196 ms, Total 5.757 ms
 Execution Time: 699.903 ms
 (12 rows)
```

The plan looks a bit scary, but don't panic – we'll go through it step by step. When reading a plan, make sure that you read it from the inside out. In our example, execution starts with a sequential scan on b. There are two blocks of information here: the **cost block** and the **actual time block**. While the cost block contains estimations, the actual time block is hard evidence: it shows the real execution time. What you can also see here is that since PostgreSQL 12, JIT compilation has been on by default. The query is already time-consuming enough to justify JIT compilation.

> **Important note**
> The costs shown on your system may not be identical. A small difference in the optimizer's statistics can cause differences. The important thing here is the way the plan has to be read.

The data coming from Seq Scan is then passed on to the Limit node, which ensures that there isn't much data. Note that each stage of execution will also show us the number of rows involved. As you can see, PostgreSQL will only fetch 1 million rows from the table in the first place; the Limit node ensures that this will happen. Finally, the data is sorted, which takes a lot of time. The most important thing when looking at the plan is to figure out where time is lost. The best way to do that is to take a look at the actual time block and try to figure out where time jumps. In this example, the sequential scan takes some time, but it can't be sped up significantly. Instead, we can see that time skyrockets as sorting starts.

Making EXPLAIN more verbose

In PostgreSQL, the output of an EXPLAIN clause can be beefed up a little to provide you with more information. To extract as much as possible out of a plan, consider turning the following options on:

```
test=# EXPLAIN (analyze, verbose, costs, timing, buffers)
SELECT * FROM a ORDER BY random();
```

```
                        QUERY PLAN
--------------------------------------------------------------
  Sort  (cost=834.39..859.39 rows=10000 width=12)
          (actual time=4.124..4.965 rows=10000 loops=1)
    Output: aid, (random())
    Sort Key: (random())
    Sort Method: quicksort Memory: 853kB
    Buffers: shared hit=45
    -> Seq Scan on public.a
            (cost=0.00..170.00 rows=10000 width=12)
            (actual time=0.057..1.457 rows=10000 loops=1)
            Output: aid, random()
            Buffers: shared hit=45
  Planning Time: 0.109 ms
  Execution Time: 5.895 ms
(10 rows)
```

Here, `analyze true` will execute the query, as shown previously. Then, `verbose true` will add some more information to the plan (such as column information) and `costs true` will show information about costs. Note that `timing true` is equally important as it will provide us with good runtime data so that we can see where in the plan time gets lost. Finally, there's `buffers true`, which can be very enlightening. In my example, it reveals that we needed to access thousands of buffers to execute the query.

After this introduction, it's time to take a look at some additional topics, including how to spot problems in a plan.

Spotting problems

Given all the information that was shown in *Chapter 5, Log Files and System Statistics*, it's already possible to spot a couple of potential performance problems that are very important in real life.

Spotting changes in runtime

When looking at a plan, there are always two questions that you have to ask yourself:

- Is the runtime shown by the EXPLAIN ANALYZE clause justified for the given query?
- If the query is slow, where does the runtime jump?

In my case, the sequential scan is rated at 1.457 milliseconds. The sort is done after 4.965 milliseconds, so the sort takes roughly 5 milliseconds to complete and is therefore responsible for most of the runtime that's needed by the query.

Looking for jumps in the execution time of the query will reveal what's going on. Depending on which type of operation will burn too much time, you have to act accordingly. Providing some general advice isn't possible here because there are simply too many things that can cause issues.

Inspecting estimates

However, there's something that should always be done: *we should make sure that estimates and real numbers are reasonably close together*. In some cases, the optimizer will make poor decisions because the estimates are way off for some reason. Sometimes, estimates can be off because the system statistics aren't up to date. Therefore, running an ANALYZE clause is a good thing to start with. However, optimizer statistics are mostly taken care of by the autovacuum daemon, so it's worth considering other options that are causing bad estimates.

Take a look at the following example, which helps us add some data to a table:

```
test=# CREATE TABLE t_estimate AS
SELECT * FROM generate_series(1, 10000) AS id;
SELECT 10000
```

After loading the 10000 rows, the optimizer statistics are created:

```
test=# ANALYZE t_estimate;
ANALYZE
```

Let's take a look at the estimates now:

```
test=# EXPLAIN ANALYZE SELECT *
FROM    t_estimate
WHERE   cos(id) < 4;
                            QUERY PLAN
-------------------------------------------------------------
 Seq Scan on t_estimate
        (cost=0.00..220.00 rows=3333 width=4)
        (actual time=0.010..4.006 rows=10000 loops=1)
   Filter: (cos((id)::double precision) < '4'::double precision)
 Planning time: 0.064 ms
 Execution time: 4.701 ms
(4 rows)
```

In many cases, PostgreSQL may not be able to process the WHERE clause properly because it only has statistics on columns, not on expressions. What we can see here is a nasty underestimation of the data that's returned from the WHERE clause.

Of course, the amount of data can also be overestimated, as shown in the following code:

```
test=# EXPLAIN ANALYZE
SELECT *
FROM    t_estimate
WHERE   cos(id) > 4;
                              QUERY PLAN
----------------------------------------------------------------
 Seq Scan on t_estimate
     (cost=0.00..220.00 rows=3333 width=4)
     (actual time=3.802..3.802 rows=0 loops=1)
     Filter: (cos((id)::double precision) >
        '4'::double precision)
     Rows Removed by Filter: 10000
 Planning time: 0.037 ms
 Execution time: 3.813 ms
(5 rows)
```

If something like this happens deep inside the plan, the process may very well create a bad plan. Therefore, making sure that estimates are within a certain range makes perfect sense.

Fortunately, there's a way to get around this problem. Consider the following code block:

```
test=# CREATE INDEX idx_cosine ON t_estimate (cos(id));
CREATE INDEX
```

This listing shows how a functional index can be created.

Creating an index will make PostgreSQL track the statistics of the expression:

```
test=# ANALYZE t_estimate;
ANALYZE
```

Apart from the fact that this plan will ensure significantly better performance, it will also fix statistics, even if the index isn't used, as shown in the following code:

```
test=# EXPLAIN ANALYZE SELECT * FROM t_estimate WHERE cos(id) > 4;
                              QUERY PLAN
----------------------------------------------------------------
 Index Scan using idx_cosine on t_estimate
     (cost=0.29..8.30 rows=1 width=4)
     (actual time=0.002..0.002 rows=0 loops=1)
     Index Cond: (cos((id)::double precision) >
        '4'::double precision)
```

```
 Planning time: 0.095 ms
 Execution time: 0.011 ms
(4 rows)
```

However, there's more to incorrect estimates than meets the eye. One problem that's often underestimated is called **cross-column correlation**. Consider a simple example involving two columns:

- 20% of people like to ski

- 20% of people are from Africa

If we want to count the number of skiers in Africa, mathematics says that the result will be 0.2 x 0.2 = 4% of the overall population. However, there's no snow in Africa. Therefore, the real result will surely be lower. The observations, Africa and skiing, aren't statistically independent. In many cases, the fact that PostgreSQL keeps column statistics that don't span more than one column can lead to bad results.

Of course, the planner does a lot to prevent these things from happening as often as possible. Nevertheless, it can be an issue.

Starting with PostgreSQL 10.0, we have multivariate statistics, which has put an end to cross-column correlation once and for all.

Inspecting buffer usage

However, the plan itself isn't the only thing that can cause issues. In many cases, dangerous things are hidden on some other level. Memory and caching can lead to undesired behavior, which is often hard to understand for end users who aren't trained to see the problem that will be described in this section.

Here's an example that depicts the process of randomly inserting data into the table. The query will generate some randomly ordered data and add it to a new table:

```
test=# CREATE TABLE t_random AS
SELECT *
FROM    generate_series(1, 10000000) AS id
ORDER BY random();
SELECT 10000000
test=# ANALYZE t_random;
ANALYZE
```

With that, we've generated a simple table containing 10 million rows and created the optimizer statistics.

In the next step, a simple query that's retrieving only a handful of rows is executed:

```
test=# EXPLAIN (
    analyze true, buffers true, costs true, timing true)
SELECT * FROM t_random WHERE id < 1000;
            QUERY PLAN
```

```
-------------------------------------------------------------
Seq Scan on t_random
  (cost=0.00..169247.71 rows=1000 width=4)
  (actual time=0.976..856.663 rows=999 loops=1)
  Filter: (id < 1000)
  Rows Removed by Filter: 9999001
  Buffers: shared hit=2080
      read=42168 dirtied=14248 written=13565
Planning Time: 0.099 ms
Buffers: shared hit=5 dirtied=1
Execution Time: 856.808 ms
(7 rows)
```

Before inspecting the data, make sure that you've executed the query twice. Of course, it makes sense to use an index here. However, in this query, PostgreSQL has 2080 blocks inside the cache and 42168 aren't to be found in shared buffers (they had to be taken from the operating system).

Now, two things can happen:

- If you're lucky, the operating system will land a couple of cache hits and the query will be fast

- If the filesystem cache isn't lucky, those blocks have to be taken from disk

This may seem obvious; it can, however, lead to wild swings in the execution time. A query that runs entirely in the cache can be 100 times faster than a query that has to slowly collect random blocks from disk.

Let's try to outline this problem by using a simple example. Suppose we have a phone system that stores 10 billion rows (which isn't uncommon for large phone carriers). Data flows in at a rapid rate, and users want to query this data. If you have 10 billion rows, the data will only partially fit into memory, and, therefore, a lot of stuff will naturally end up coming from the disk.

Let's run a simple query to learn how PostgreSQL looks up a phone number:

```
SELECT * FROM data WHERE phone_number = '+12345678';
```

Even if you're on the phone, your data will be spread all over the place. If you end a phone call just to start the next call, thousands of people will do the same, so the odds that two of your calls will end up in the very same 8,000 block is close to zero. Just imagine, for the time being, that 100,000 calls are going on at the same time. On disk, data will be randomly distributed. If your phone number shows up often, it means that for each row, at least one block has to be fetched from disk (assuming there's a very low cache hit rate). Let's say 5,000 rows are returned. Assuming that you have to go to disk 5,000 times, it leads to something such as the following:

5,000 x 5 milliseconds = 25 seconds of execution time

> **Important note**
>
> The execution time of this query may vary between milliseconds and, say, 30 seconds, depending on how much has been cached by the operating system or by PostgreSQL.
>
> Keep in mind that every server restart will naturally clean out the PostgreSQL and filesystem caches, which can lead to real trouble following a node failure.

Fixing high buffer usage

The question that begs an answer is, *how can I improve this situation?* One way to do this is to run a CLUSTER clause:

```
https://www.postgresql.org/docs/15/sql-cluster.html CLUSTER [ ( option
[, ...] ) ] [ table_name [ USING index_name ] ]

where option can be one of:

    VERBOSE [ boolean ]
```

The CLUSTER clause will rewrite the table in the same order as a btree index. If you're running an analytical workload, this can make sense. However, in an OLTP system, the CLUSTER clause may not be feasible because a table lock is required while the table is being rewritten.

Consider checking out pg_squeeze as well, which is an extension to reorganize a table without extensive table locking.

Fixing high buffer usage is important as it can lead to considerable performance gains. Therefore, it makes sense to keep an eye on those issues at all times. So, let's move on to the next topic and understand how the optimizer handles joins.

Understanding and fixing joins

Joins are important; everybody needs them regularly. Consequently, joins are also relevant for maintaining or achieving good performance. To ensure that you can write good joins, we'll also learn about joining in this book.

Getting joins right

Before we dive into optimizing joins, it's important to take a look at some of the most common problems that arise with joins and which of them should sound alarm bells for you.

Here's an example of a simple table structure to demonstrate how joins work (make sure the table we used before has been deleted):

```
test=# CREATE TABLE a (aid int);
CREATE TABLE
```

```
test=# CREATE TABLE b (bid int);
CREATE TABLE
test=# INSERT INTO a VALUES (1), (2), (3);
INSERT 0 3
test=# INSERT INTO b VALUES (2), (3), (4);
INSERT 0 3
```

Two tables containing a couple of rows have been created.

The following example shows a simple outer join:

```
test=# SELECT * FROM a LEFT JOIN b ON (aid = bid);
 aid | bid
-----+-----
   1 |
   2 |   2
   3 |   3
(3 rows)
```

As you can see, PostgreSQL will take all the rows from the left-hand side and only list the ones that fit the join.

The following example may come as a surprise to many people:

```
test=# SELECT *
FROM   a LEFT JOIN b
    ON (aid = bid AND bid = 2);
 aid | bid
-----+-----
   1 |
   2 |   2
   3 |
(3 rows)
```

No, the number of rows doesn't decrease – it will stay constant. Most people assume that there will only be one row in the join, but this isn't true and will lead to some hidden issues.

Consider the following query, which performs a simple join:

```
test=# SELECT avg(aid), avg(bid)
FROM a LEFT JOIN b
    ON (aid = bid AND bid = 2);
        avg         |        avg
--------------------+--------------------
 2.0000000000000000 | 2.0000000000000000
(1 row)
```

Most people assume that the average is calculated based on a single row. However, as we stated earlier, this isn't the case. Queries such as this are often considered a performance problem because, for some reason, PostgreSQL doesn't index the table on the left-hand side of the join. Of course, we aren't looking at a performance problem here – we're looking at a semantic issue. Often, people writing outer joins don't know what they're asking PostgreSQL to do. So, my advice is to always question the semantic correctness of an outer join before attacking the performance problem that's reported by the client.

I can't stress enough how important this kind of work is to ensure that your queries are correct and do exactly what's needed.

Processing outer joins

After verifying that your queries are correct from a business point of view, it makes sense to check what the optimizer can do to speed up your outer joins. The most important thing is that PostgreSQL can, in many cases, reorder inner joins to speed things up dramatically. However, in the case of outer joins, this isn't always possible. Only a handful of reordering operations are allowed:

```
(A leftjoin B on (Pab)) innerjoin C on (Pac) = (A innerjoin C on
(Pac)) leftjoin B on (Pab)
```

Here, Pac is a predicate referencing A and C, and so on (in this case, Pac can't reference B; otherwise, the transformation is nonsensical):

- `(A leftjoin B on (Pab)) leftjoin C on (Pac) = (A leftjoin C on (Pac)) leftjoin B on (Pab)`

- `(A leftjoin B on (Pab)) leftjoin C on (Pbc) = (A leftjoin (B leftjoin C on (Pbc)) on (Pab)`

The last rule only holds if the Pbc predicate must fail for all null B rows (that is, Pbc is strict for at least one column of B). If Pbc isn't strict, the first form may produce some rows with non-null C columns, while the second form would make those entries null.

While some joins can be reordered, a typical type of query can't benefit from join reordering. Consider the following code snippet, which has some special properties:

```
SELECT ...
  FROM a LEFT JOIN b ON (aid = bid)
    LEFT JOIN c ON (bid = cid)
    LEFT JOIN d ON (cid = did)
...
```

Join reordering isn't going to do us any good here (because it's impossible).

The way to approach this is to check whether all the outer joins are necessary. In many cases, it happens that people write outer joins without actually needing them. Often, the business case doesn't even call for outer joins. Following this section, it's necessary to dig into some more planner options.

Understanding the join_collapse_limit variable

During the planning process, PostgreSQL tries to check all the possible join orders. In many cases, this can be pretty expensive because there can be many permutations, which naturally slows down the planning process.

The `join_collapse_limit` variable is here to give developers a tool to work around these problems and define how a query should be processed more straightforwardly.

To show you what this setting is all about, we'll compile a little example:

```
SELECT * FROM tab1, tab2, tab3
WHERE tab1.id = tab2.id
      AND tab2.ref = tab3.id;
SELECT * FROM tab1 CROSS JOIN tab2
CROSS JOIN tab3
WHERE tab1.id = tab2.id
      AND tab2.ref = tab3.id;
SELECT * FROM tab1 JOIN (tab2 JOIN tab3
   ON (tab2.ref = tab3.id))
   ON (tab1.id = tab2.id);
```

These three queries are identical and treated by the planner in the same way. The first query consists of implicit joins. The last one only consists of explicit joins. Internally, the planner will inspect those requests and order joins accordingly to ensure the best runtime possible. The question here is, how many explicit joins will PostgreSQL plan implicitly? This is exactly what you can tell the planner by setting the `join_collapse_limit` variable. The default value is reasonably good for normal queries. However, if your query contains a very high number of joins, playing around with this setting can reduce planning time considerably. Reducing planning time can be essential to maintaining good throughput.

To see how the `join_collapse_limit` variable changes the plan, we'll write this simple query:

```
test=# EXPLAIN WITH x AS
(
  SELECT *
  FROM  generate_series(1, 1000) AS id
)
SELECT *
FROM x AS a
  JOIN x AS b ON (a.id = b.id)
  JOIN x AS c ON (b.id = c.id)
```

```
JOIN x AS d ON (c.id = d.id)
JOIN x AS e ON (d.id = e.id)
JOIN x AS f ON (e.id = f.id);
```

Try running the query with different settings and see how the plan changes. Unfortunately, the plan is too long to copy here, so it's impossible to include the actual changes in this section.

Having dealt with collapse limits, let's take a look at some additional planner options.

Enabling and disabling optimizer settings

So far, the most important optimizations that are performed by the planner have been discussed in detail. PostgreSQL has improved a lot over the years. Still, something can go south, and users have to convince the planner to do the right thing.

To modify plans, PostgreSQL offers a couple of runtime variables that will have a significant impact on planning. The idea is to give the end user a chance to make certain types of nodes in the plan more expensive than others. What does that mean in practice? Here's a simple plan:

```
test=# explain SELECT *
FROM generate_series(1, 100) AS a,
    generate_series(1, 100) AS b
WHERE a = b;
                          QUERY PLAN
-------------------------------------------------------------
 Hash Join  (cost=2.25..4.63 rows=100 width=8)
   Hash Cond:  (a.a = b.b)
   -> Function Scan on generate_series a
      (cost=0.00..1.00 rows=100 width=4)
   -> Hash  (cost=1.00..1.00 rows=100 width=4)
         -> Function Scan on generate_series b
            (cost=0.00..1.00 rows=100 width=4)
(5 rows)
```

Here, PostgreSQL will scan the functions and perform a hash join. Let's run the same query in PostgreSQL 11 or older and look at the execution plan:

```
                          QUERY PLAN
-------------------------------------------------------------
 Merge Join  (cost=119.66..199.66 rows=5000 width=8)
   Merge Cond:  (a.a = b.b)
   -> Sort  (cost=59.83..62.33 rows=1000 width=4)
         Sort Key: a.a
         -> Function Scan on generate_series a
```

```
                    (cost=0.00..10.00 rows=1000 width=4)
  -> Sort (cost=59.83..62.33 rows=1000 width=4)
        Sort Key: b.b
        -> Function Scan on generate_series b
           (cost=0.00..10.00 rows=1000 width=4)
(8 rows)
```

Can you see the difference between these two plans? In PostgreSQL 12, the estimate of the set-returning function is already correct. In the older version, the optimizer still estimates that a set-returning function will always return 100 rows. In PostgreSQL, there are optimizer support functions that can help estimate the result set. Therefore, the plan in PostgreSQL 12 and beyond is vastly superior to the old plan.

What we can see in the new plan is that hashjoin is performed, which is, of course, the most efficient way to do things. However, what if we're smarter than the optimizer? Fortunately, PostgreSQL has the means to overrule the optimizer. You can set variables in a connection that change the default cost estimates. Here's how it works:

```
test=# SET enable_hashjoin TO off;
SET
test=# explain SELECT *
FROM generate_series(1, 100) AS a,
    generate_series(1, 100) AS b
WHERE a = b;
                           QUERY PLAN
-------------------------------------------------------------
 Merge Join  (cost=8.65..10.65 rows=100 width=8)
   Merge Cond: (a.a = b.b)
   -> Sort  (cost=4.32..4.57 rows=100 width=4)
         Sort Key: a.a
         -> Function Scan on generate_series a
            (cost=0.00..1.00 rows=100 width=4)
   -> Sort  (cost=4.32..4.57 rows=100 width=4)
         Sort Key: b.b
         -> Function Scan on generate_series b
            (cost=0.00..1.00 rows=100 width=4)
(8 rows)
```

PostgreSQL assumes that the hashjoin functions are bad and makes them infinitely expensive. Hence, it falls back to a merge join. However, we can turn merge joins off as well:

```
test=# SET enable_mergejoin TO off;
SET
test=# explain SELECT *
```

```
FROM generate_series(1, 100) AS a,
    generate_series(1, 100) AS b
WHERE a = b;
                            QUERY PLAN
-------------------------------------------------------- Nested Loop
(cost=0.01..226.00 rows=100 width=8)
  Join Filter: (a.a = b.b)
    -> Function Scan on generate_series a
        (cost=0.00..1.00 rows=100 width=4)
  -> Function Scan on generate_series b
        (cost=0.00..1.00 rows=100 width=4)
(4 rows)
```

PostgreSQL is slowly running out of options. The following example shows what happens if we turn off nested loops as well:

```
test=# SET enable_nestloop TO off;
SET
test=# explain SELECT *
FROM generate_series(1, 100) AS a,
    generate_series(1, 100) AS b
WHERE a = b;
                            QUERY PLAN
------------------------------------------------------- Nested Loop
    (cost=10000000000.00..10000000226.00 rows=100 width=8)
  Join Filter: (a.a = b.b)
  ->  Function Scan on generate_series a
        (cost=0.00..1.00 rows=100 width=4)
  ->  Function Scan on generate_series b
        (cost=0.00..1.00 rows=100 width=4)
 JIT:
  Functions: 10
  Options: Inlining true, Optimization true,
    Expressions true, Deforming true
(7 rows)
```

The important thing is that turning them off doesn't mean off – it just means that the cost is set by the optimizer so that it's insanely expensive. If PostgreSQL has no cheaper options, it will fall back to the ones we turned off. Otherwise, there would no longer be any way to execute SQL.

So, what settings influence the planner? The following switches are available:

```
# - Planner Method Configuration -
#enable_async_append = on
#enable_bitmapscan = on
```

```
#enable_gathermerge = on
#enable_hashagg = on
#enable_hashjoin = on
#enable_incremental_sort = on
#enable_indexscan = on
#enable_indexonlyscan = on
#enable_material = on
#enable_memoize = on
#enable_mergejoin = on
#enable_nestloop = on
#enable_parallel_append = on
#enable_parallel_hash = on
#enable_partition_pruning = on
#enable_partitionwise_join = off
#enable_partitionwise_aggregate = off
#enable_presorted_aggregate = on
#enable_seqscan = on
#enable_sort = on
#enable_tidscan = on
#enable_group_by_reordering = on
```

While these settings can be beneficial, please understand that these tweaks should be handled with care. They should only be used to speed up individual queries and not turn off things globally. Switching off options can turn against you fairly quickly and destroy performance. Therefore, it makes sense to think twice before changing these parameters.

What we can see here is that partition-wise operations are turned off by default. This is done to reduce planning time. However, if you happen to run excessive analytic queries, it can make a lot of sense to turn those settings on.

However, an exhaustive search isn't the only way to optimize queries. There's also a genetic query optimizer, something that will be covered in the next section.

Understanding genetic query optimization

The result of the planning process is key to achieving superior performance. As we've seen in this chapter, planning is far from straightforward and involves various complex calculations. The more tables that are touched by a query, the more complicated planning will become. The more tables there are, the more choices the planner will have. Logically, the planning time will increase. At some point, planning will take so long that performing the classical exhaustive search is no longer feasible. On top of that, the errors that occur during planning are so big that finding the theoretically best plan doesn't necessarily lead to the best plan in terms of runtime.

Genetic query optimization (GEQO) can come to the rescue in such cases. So, what is GEQO? The idea derives inspiration from nature and resembles the natural process of evolution.

PostgreSQL will approach this problem just like a traveling salesman problem and encode the possible joins as integer strings. For example, 4 - 1 - 3 - 2 means joining 4 and 1 first, then 3, and then 2. The numbers represent the relations' IDs.

First, the genetic optimizer will generate a random set of plans. Those plans are then inspected. The bad ones are discarded, and new ones are generated based on the genes of the good ones. This way, even better plans are potentially generated. This process can be repeated as often as desired. At the end of the day, we're left with a plan that's expected to be a lot better than just using a random plan. GEQO can be turned on and off by adjusting the geqo variable, as shown in the following lines of code:

```
test=# SHOW geqo;
 geqo
------
 on
(1 row)
test=# SET geqo TO off;
SET
```

The listing shows how GEQO can be turned on and off. By default, the geqo variable kicks in if a statement exceeds a certain level of complexity, which is controlled by the following variable:

```
test=# SHOW geqo_threshold;
 geqo_threshold
----------------
 12
(1 row)
```

If your queries are so large that you start to reach this threshold, it certainly makes sense to play with this setting to see how plans are changed by the planner if you change those variables.

As a general rule, however, I would suggest avoiding GEQO for as long as possible and trying to fix things first by attempting to somehow fix the join order by using the join_collapse_limit variable. Note that every query is different, so it certainly helps to experiment and gain more experience by learning how the planner behaves under different circumstances.

> **Important note**
>
> If you want to learn more about joins, please refer to the following link: https://www.slideshare.net/slideshow/postgresql-joining-1-million-tables/45740963.

In the next section, we'll take a look at partitioning, which is a method for breaking large datasets into smaller chunks.

Partitioning data

Given a default of 8,000 blocks, PostgreSQL can store up to 32 TB of data inside a single table. If you compile PostgreSQL with 32,000 blocks, you can even put up to 128 TB into a single table. However, large tables such as this aren't necessarily convenient anymore, and it can make sense to partition tables to make processing easier and, in some cases, a bit faster. Starting from version 10.0, PostgreSQL offers improved partitioning, which offers end users significantly easier handling of data partitioning.

In this chapter, the old means of partitioning, as well as the new features that are available as of PostgreSQL 13.0, will be covered. As we speak, features in partitioning are being added in all areas so that people can expect more and better partitioning in all future versions of PostgreSQL. The first thing you'll learn is how to work with classical PostgreSQL inheritance.

Creating inherited tables

First, we'll take a closer look at the outdated method of partitioning data. Keep in mind that understanding this technique is important in gaining a deeper overview of what PostgreSQL does behind the scenes.

Before digging deeper into the advantages of partitioning, I want to show you how partitions can be created. The entire thing starts with a parent table that we can create by using the following command:

```
test=# CREATE TABLE t_data (
    id       serial,
    t        date,
    payload  text
);
CREATE TABLE
```

In this example, the parent table has three columns. The date column will be used for partitioning, but we'll learn more about that a bit later.

Now that the parent table is in place, the child tables can be created. This is how it works:

```
test=# CREATE TABLE t_data_2016 () INHERITS (t_data);
CREATE TABLE
test=# \d t_data_2016
                        Table "public.t_data_2016"
  Column |   Type   | Collation | Nullable | Default
 --------+----------+-----------+----------+----
  id      | integer |           | not null
 |                        nextval('t_data_id_seq'::regclass)
```

```
 t       | date    |           |         |
 payload | text    |           |         |
Inherits: t_data
```

The table is called `t_data_2016` and inherits from `t_data`. This means that no extra columns are added to the child table. As you can see, inheritance means that all the columns from the parents are available in the child table. Also, note that the `id` column will inherit the sequence from the parent so that all the children can share the very same numbering.

Let's create some more tables:

```
test=# CREATE TABLE t_data_2015 () INHERITS (t_data);
CREATE TABLE
test=# CREATE TABLE t_data_2014 () INHERITS (t_data);
CREATE TABLE
```

So far, all of the tables are identical and just inherit from the parent. However, there's more: child tables can have more columns than parents. Adding more fields is simple:

```
test=# CREATE TABLE t_data_2013 (special text) INHERITS (t_data);
CREATE TABLE
```

In this case, a special column has been added. It has no impact on the parent; it just enriches the children and allows them to hold more data.

After creating a handful of tables, a row can be added:

```
test=# INSERT INTO t_data_2015 (t, payload)
VALUES ('2015-05-04', 'some data');
INSERT 0 1
```

The most important thing now is that the parent table can be used to find all the data in the child tables:

```
test=# SELECT * FROM t_data;
 id |     t      | payload
----+------------+-----------
  1 | 2015-05-04 | some data
(1 row)
```

Querying the parent allows you to gain access to everything below the parent simply and efficiently.

To understand how PostgreSQL does partitioning, it makes sense to take a look at the plan:

```
test=# EXPLAIN SELECT * FROM t_data;
                            QUERY PLAN
------------------------------------------------------------- Append
(cost=0.00..106.16 rows=4411 width=40)
```

```
    -> Seq Scan on t_data t_data_1
       (cost=0.00..0.00 rows=1 width=40)
    -> Seq Scan on t_data_2016 t_data_2
     (cost=0.00..22.00 rows=1200 width=40)
    -> Seq Scan on t_data_2015 t_data_3
        (cost=0.00..22.00 rows=1200 width=40)
    -> Seq Scan on t_data_2014 t_data_4
        (cost=0.00..22.00 rows=1200 width=40)
    -> Seq Scan on t_data_2013 t_data_5
        (cost=0.00..18.10 rows=810 width=40)
 (6 rows)
```

What happens is relatively straightforward: PostgreSQL will take all tables and simply append them to each other. Therefore, inheritance and partitioning are merely set operations. Note that all relations are independent and are just connected logically through the system catalog (which means by appending them all), but what if there was a way to make optimizer decisions smarter?

Applying table constraints

What happens if filters are applied to the table? What will the optimizer decide to do to execute this query in the most efficient way possible? The following example shows us how the PostgreSQL planner will behave:

```
test=# EXPLAIN SELECT *
FROM    t_data
WHERE   t = '2016-01-04';
                              QUERY PLAN
------------------------------------------------------------
 Append (cost=0.00..95.24 rows=23 width=40)
   -> Seq Scan on t_data t_data_1
         (cost=0.00..0.00 rows=1 width=40)
         Filter: (t = <2016-01-04'::date)
   -> Seq Scan on t_data_2016 t_data_2
         (cost=0.00..25.00 rows=6 width=40)
         Filter: (t = <2016-01-04'::date)
   -> Seq Scan on t_data_2015 t_data_3
         (cost=0.00..25.00 rows=6 width=40)
         Filter: (t = <2016-01-04'::date)
   -> Seq Scan on t_data_2014 t_data_4
         (cost=0.00..25.00 rows=6 width=40)
         Filter: (t = <2016-01-04'::date)
   -> Seq Scan on t_data_2013 t_data_5
         (cost=0.00..20.12 rows=4 width=40)
         Filter: (t = <2016-01-04'::date)
 (11 rows)
```

PostgreSQL will apply the filter to all the partitions in the structure. It doesn't know that the table name is somehow related to the content of the tables. To the database, names are just names and have nothing to do with what we're looking for. This makes sense, of course, since there's no mathematical justification for doing anything else.

The point now is, how can we teach the database that the 2016 table only contains 2016 data, that the 2015 table only contains 2015 data, and so on? Table constraints are here to do exactly that. They teach PostgreSQL about the content of those tables and, therefore, allow the planner to make smarter decisions than before. This feature is called **constraint exclusion** and helps to dramatically speed up queries in many cases.

The following listing shows how table constraints can be created:

```
test=# ALTER TABLE t_data_2013
ADD CHECK (t < '2014-01-01');
ALTER TABLE
test=# ALTER TABLE t_data_2014
ADD CHECK (t >= '2014-01-01' AND t < '2015-01-01');
ALTER TABLE
test=# ALTER TABLE t_data_2015
ADD CHECK (t >= '2015-01-01' AND t < '2016-01-01');
ALTER TABLE
test=# ALTER TABLE t_data_2016
ADD CHECK (t >= '2016-01-01' AND t < '2017-01-01');
ALTER TABLE
```

For each table, a CHECK constraint can be added.

> **Important note**
> PostgreSQL will only create the constraint if all the data in those tables is perfectly correct and if every single row satisfies the constraint. There's no such thing as an invalid constraint.

In PostgreSQL, these constraints can overlap – this isn't forbidden and can make sense in some cases. However, it's usually better to have non-overlapping constraints because PostgreSQL has the option to prune more tables.

Here's what happens after adding those table constraints:

```
test=# EXPLAIN SELECT *
FROM    t_data
WHERE   t = '2016-01-04';
                            QUERY PLAN
-------------------------------------------------------------
 Append (cost=0.00..25.04 rows=7 width=40)
```

```
    -> Seq Scan on t_data t_data_1
        (cost=0.00..0.00 rows=1 width=40)
        Filter: (t = <2016-01-04'::date)
    -> Seq Scan on t_data_2016 t_data_2
        (cost=0.00..25.00 rows=6 width=40)
        Filter: (t = <2016-01-04'::date)
(5 rows)
```

The planner will be able to remove many of the tables from the query and only keep those that potentially contain the data. This query can greatly benefit from a shorter and more efficient plan. In particular, if those tables are really large, removing them can boost speed considerably.

In the next section, you'll learn how to modify those structures.

Modifying inherited structures

Once in a while, data structures have to be modified. The ALTER TABLE clause is here to do precisely that. The question here is, how can partitioned tables be modified?

All you have to do is tackle the parent table and add or remove columns. PostgreSQL will automatically propagate those changes through to the child tables and ensure that changes are made to all the relations, as follows:

```
test=# ALTER TABLE t_data ADD COLUMN x int;
ALTER TABLE
test=# \d t_data_2016
                    Table "public.t_data_2016"
  Column  |   Type   | Collation | Nullable | Default
----------+----------+-----------+----------+---------
 id       | integer  |           | not null |
              nextval('t_data_id_seq'::regclass)
 t        | date     |           |          |
 payload  | text     |           |          |
 x        | integer  |           |          |
Check constraints:
    "t_data_2016_t_check" CHECK (t >= '2016-01-01'::date AND t <
'2017-01-01'::date)
Inherits: t_data
```

As you can see, the column is added to the parent and automatically added to the child table here.

Note that this works for columns as well. Indexes are a different story. In an inherited structure, every table has to be indexed separately. If you add an index to the parent table, it will only be present on the parent – it won't be deployed on those child tables. Indexing all of those columns in all of those tables is your task; PostgreSQL isn't going to make those decisions for you. Of course, this can be seen as a feature or as a limitation. On the upside, you could say that PostgreSQL gives you the flexibility to index things separately and, therefore, potentially more efficiently. However, people may also argue that deploying all those indexes one by one is a lot more work.

Moving tables in and out of partitioned structures

Suppose you have an inherited structure. Data is partitioned by date, and you want to provide the most recent years to the end user. At some point, you may want to remove some data from the scope of the user without actually touching it. You may want to put data into some sort of archive.

PostgreSQL provides a simple means to achieve exactly that. First, a new parent can be created:

```
test=# CREATE TABLE t_history (LIKE t_data);
CREATE TABLE
```

The LIKE keyword allows you to create a table that has the same layout as the t_data table. If you've forgotten which columns the t_data table contains, this may come in handy as it saves you a lot of work. It's also possible to include indexes, constraints, and defaults.

Then, the table can be moved away from the old parent table and put below the new one. Here's how it works:

```
test=# ALTER TABLE t_data_2013 NO INHERIT t_data;
ALTER TABLE
test=# ALTER TABLE t_data_2013 INHERIT t_history;
ALTER TABLE
```

The entire process can, of course, be done in a single transaction to ensure that the operation stays atomic.

Cleaning up data

One advantage of partitioned tables is the ability to clean data up quickly. Let's assume that we want to delete an entire year. If the data is partitioned accordingly, a simple DROP TABLE clause can do the job:

```
test=# DROP TABLE t_data_2014;
DROP TABLE
```

As you can see, dropping a child table is easy. But what about the parent table? There are dependent objects, so PostgreSQL naturally errors out to make sure that nothing unexpected happens:

```
test=# DROP TABLE t_data;
ERROR: cannot drop table t_data because other objects depend on it
DETAIL: default for table t_data_2013 column id depends on
    sequence t_data_id_seq
table t_data_2016 depends on table t_data
```

```
table t_data_2015 depends on table t_data
HINT: Use DROP ... CASCADE to drop the dependent objects too.
```

The DROP TABLE clause will warn us that there are dependent objects and will refuse to drop those tables. The following example shows us how to use a cascaded DROP TABLE clause:

```
test=# DROP TABLE t_data CASCADE;
NOTICE: drop cascades to 3 other objects
DETAIL: drop cascades to default value for column id of table t_
data_2013
drop cascades to table t_data_2016
drop cascades to table t_data_2015
DROP TABLE
```

The CASCADE clause is needed to force PostgreSQL to remove those objects, along with the parent table.

Following this introduction to classical means, let's look at advanced PostgreSQL 17.x partitioning.

Understanding PostgreSQL 17.x partitioning

A lot of functionality has been added to PostgreSQL since partitioning was introduced, and many things you've seen in the old world have been automated or made easier since then. However, let's go through those things in a more organized way. Partitioning is an ever-growing field and every new version has its new unique and distinct features that are increasingly hard to cover.

Keep in mind that what you're about to see works in PostgreSQL 17 and isn't necessarily possible in older versions of PostgreSQL. Every version adds new features (see https://www.postgresql.org/about/featurematrix/). As stated before, partitioning is constantly being worked on and, therefore, new features are being added.

For many years, the PostgreSQL community has been working on built-in partitioning. Finally, PostgreSQL 10.0 offered the first implementation of in-core partitioning. In PostgreSQL 10, the partitioning functionality was still pretty basic; therefore, a lot of stuff has been improved since then.

Handling partitioning strategies

Three types of partitioning exist in PostgreSQL. Depending on your use case, the right strategy can be chosen.

Here's a list of what's currently available in PostgreSQL:

- Range partitioning
- List partitioning
- Hash partitioning

What's the purpose of those various types? Range partitioning is ideal if you want to partition time series data. You might want to store every year in a different partition. List partitioning is preferred if your dataset only contains a certain list of values. You might want to store pending offers in one partition and signed offers in some other partition, or you might want to create one partition per country (or a list of countries). Hash partitioning is more desired if you want to spread data evenly. This happens if you want to balance your I/O and spread it out to various devices. Let's inspect those various features in more detail.

Using range partitioning

To show you how range partitioning works, I've compiled a simple example featuring range partitioning, as follows:

```
CREATE TABLE data (
    payload   integer
)    PARTITION BY RANGE (payload);
CREATE TABLE negatives PARTITION
    OF data FOR VALUES FROM (MINVALUE) TO (0);
CREATE TABLE positives PARTITION
    OF data FOR VALUES FROM (0) TO (MAXVALUE);
```

In this example, one partition will hold all the negative values, while the other one will take care of the positive values. While creating the parent table, you can simply specify how you want to partition data.

Once the parent table has been created, it's time to create the partitions. To do that, the PARTITION OF clause has to be added. In PostgreSQL 10, there are still some limitations. The most important one is that a tuple (a row) can't move from one partition to the other, as follows:

```
UPDATE data SET payload = -10 WHERE payload = 5
```

Fortunately, this restriction has been lifted, and PostgreSQL 11+ can move a row from one partition to the other. However, keep in mind that moving data between partitions may not be the best idea in general.

Let's take a look and see what happens under the hood:

```
test=# INSERT INTO data VALUES (5);
INSERT 0 1
test=# SELECT * FROM data;
 payload
---------
       5
(1 row)
test=# SELECT * FROM positives;
 payload
```

```
---------
        5
(1 row)
```

As we can see, the data is moved to the correct partition. If we change the value, you'll see that the partition also changes. The following listing shows an example of this:

```
test=# UPDATE data
SET     payload = -10
WHERE   payload = 5
RETURNING *;
 payload
---------
  -10
(1 row)
UPDATE 1
test=# SELECT * FROM negatives;
 payload
---------
  -10
(1 row)
```

Every row has been put into the correct table, as shown in the previous listing.

The next important aspect is related to indexing. In PostgreSQL 10, every table (every partition) had to be indexed separately. This is no longer true in PostgreSQL 11 and higher. Let's try this out and see what happens:

```
test=# CREATE INDEX idx_payload ON data (payload);
CREATE INDEX
test=# \d positives
              Table "public.positives"
 Column  |  Type   | Collation | Nullable | Default
---------+---------+-----------+----------+---------
 payload | integer |           |          |
Partition of: data FOR VALUES FROM (0) TO (MAXVALUE)
Indexes:
    "positives_payload_idx" btree (payload)
```

As you can see, the index has also been added to the child table automatically, which is a really important feature of PostgreSQL 11 and has widely been appreciated by users moving their applications to PostgreSQL 11 and beyond.

Another important feature is the ability to create a default partition. To show you how that works, we can drop one of our two partitions:

```
test=# DROP TABLE negatives;
DROP TABLE
```

Now, a default partition for the data table can be created easily:

```
test=# CREATE TABLE p_def PARTITION OF data DEFAULT;
CREATE TABLE
```

All the data that doesn't fit anywhere will end up in this default partition, which ensures that creating the right partition can never be forgotten. Experience has shown that the existence of a default partition makes applications a lot more reliable as time goes by.

Utilizing list partitioning

List partitioning is useful if you're dealing with a finite list of values. Typical examples are countries, categories, genders, and so on. Those values are known in advance and are, therefore, ideal partitioning criteria.

To show how this works, I've compiled a simple example that partitions revenue by country:

```
BEGIN;
CREATE TABLE t_turnover (
    id          serial,
    country     text,
    t           timestamptz,
    task        text,
    turnover    numeric
) PARTITION BY LIST (country);

CREATE TABLE t_austria
    PARTITION OF t_turnover FOR VALUES IN ('Austria');

CREATE TABLE t_usa
    PARTITION OF t_turnover FOR VALUES IN ('USA');

CREATE TABLE t_ger_swiss
    PARTITION OF t_turnover FOR VALUES IN ('Germany', 'Switzerland');
COMMIT;
```

As you can see, we have one partition by country. However, it's also possible to use an IN list in case more than one value should be packed into the same partition. In this example, this has been done for Germany and Switzerland.

The main question that arises now is, how can we handle data that doesn't fit into the partitioning schema? The answer is that we can introduce a *default* partition. Here's how it works:

```
test=# CREATE TABLE t_rest PARTITION OF t_turnover DEFAULT;
CREATE TABLE
```

All data that doesn't fit into any other partition will end up in the default partition. Note that, without creating this partition, we can't insert data that doesn't fit into a partition.

In this example, I'll use a little trick to insert:

```
test=# \x
Expanded display is on.
test=# INSERT INTO t_turnover (country, t, task, turnover)
VALUES ('Uganda', now(), 'Some task', 200)
RETURNING tableoid::regclass, *;
-[ RECORD 1 ]+---------------------------
tableoid | t_rest
id       | 2
country  | Uganda
t        | 2022-11-01 09:35:38.991547+01
task     | Some task
turnover | 200
INSERT 0 1
```

The `tableoid` column is a hidden column that contains the OID of the table we're inserting into. We can, of course, cast this value to `regclass`, which will turn the data into a human-readable string. This reveals that we're inserting into the default partition of this table.

Handling hash partitions

Finally, there's hash partitioning. When is it needed? So far, we've seen partitioning methods that make use of lists and ranges. In other words, we've used methods that broke data into known groups. However, often, we want to split data into even groups. Countries are usually not evenly large groups, so to achieve even groups, we can use hashes. Let's take a look:

```
CREATE TABLE t_data (a int, b int) PARTITION BY HASH (a);

CREATE TABLE t_hash_0 PARTITION OF t_data
    FOR VALUES WITH (MODULUS 4, REMAINDER 0);

CREATE TABLE t_hash_1 PARTITION OF t_data
    FOR VALUES WITH (MODULUS 4, REMAINDER 1);
```

```
CREATE TABLE t_hash_2 PARTITION OF t_data
    FOR VALUES WITH (MODULUS 4, REMAINDER 2);

CREATE TABLE t_hash_3 PARTITION OF t_data
    FOR VALUES WITH (MODULUS 4, REMAINDER 3);
```

In this case, our data table has no obvious and useful partition criteria. Therefore, we used a hash. The goal is to have four partitions, so we used the hash value and did a *modulo 4*. The remainder will identify the partition. Here's the partitioned table in action:

```
test=# INSERT INTO t_data VALUES (8, 29)
RETURNING tableoid::regclass, *;
 tableoid | a | b
----------+---+----
 t_hash_1 | 8 | 29
(1 row)
INSERT 0 1
```

Often, it's necessary to detach or attach a partition. Note that this isn't only relevant for hash partitions but is also important if you're dealing with any other partitioning mechanism.

PostgreSQL allows us to remove and add partitions easily. The following example shows that we can remove a single partition and attach it again:

```
test=# ALTER TABLE t_data
DETACH PARTITION t_hash_3;

ALTER TABLE
test=# ALTER TABLE t_data
ATTACH PARTITION t_hash_3
FOR VALUES WITH (MODULUS 4, REMAINDER 3);
ALTER TABLE
```

In recent versions of PostgreSQL, there's also a way to detach and re-attach using the CONCURRENTLY keyword. The idea is to reduce the impact of locking on your operations.

In this section, you learned about partitioning. In the next section, you'll be guided through some more advanced performance parameters.

Adjusting parameters for good query performance

Writing good queries is the first step to achieving good performance. Without a good query, you'll most likely suffer from bad performance. Therefore, writing good and intelligent code will give you the greatest edge possible. Once your queries have been optimized from a logical and semantic point of view, good memory settings can provide you with a nice final increase in speed.

In this section, we'll learn about what more memory can do for you and how PostgreSQL can use it for your benefit. Again, this section assumes that we're using single-core queries to make the plans more readable. To ensure that there's always just one core at work, use the following command:

```
test=# SET max_parallel_workers_per_gather TO 0;
SET
```

Here's a simple example demonstrating what memory parameters can do for you:

```
test=# CREATE TABLE t_test (id serial, name text);
CREATE TABLE
test=# INSERT INTO t_test (name)
SELECT 'hans' FROM generate_series(1, 100000);
INSERT 0 100000
test=# INSERT INTO t_test (name)
SELECT 'paul' FROM generate_series(1, 100000);
INSERT 0 100000
```

Here, we're adding 100000 rows containing hans to the table. After, 100000 rows containing paul will be loaded. Altogether, there will be 2 million unique IDs, but just two different names.

Let's run a simple query by using PostgreSQL's default memory settings:

```
test=# SELECT name, count(*) FROM t_test GROUP BY 1;
 name  | count
-------+--------
 hans  | 100000
 paul  | 100000
(2 rows)
```

Two rows will be returned, which shouldn't come as a surprise. The important thing here isn't the result but what PostgreSQL is doing behind the scenes:

```
test=# explain analyze SELECT name, count(*)
FROM      t_test
GROUP BY 1;
                            QUERY PLAN
-------------------------------------------------------------
HashAggregate  (cost=4082.00..4082.02 rows=2 width=13)
   (actual time=49.150..49.152 rows=2 loops=1)
    Group Key: name
    Batches: 1  Memory Usage: 24kB
    -> Seq Scan on t_test
        (cost=0.00..3082.00 rows=200000 width=5)
   (actual time=0.023..12.739 rows=200000 loops=1)
 Planning Time: 0.127 ms
```

```
Execution Time: 49.203 ms
(6 rows)
```

PostgreSQL figured out that the number of groups is very small. Therefore, it creates a hash, adds one hash entry per group, and starts to count. Due to the low number of groups, the hash is really small, and PostgreSQL can quickly do the count by incrementing the numbers for each group.

What happens if we group by ID and not by name? The number of groups will skyrocket. In PostgreSQL 13, an improvement has been implemented – hashes can now spill to disk:

```
test=# EXPLAIN ANALYZE SELECT id, count(*)
FROM    t_test
GROUP BY 1;
                        QUERY PLAN
-----------------------------------------------------------
 HashAggregate
   (cost=14332.00..17894.50 rows=200000 width=12)
   (actual time=66.883..96.415 rows=200000 loops=1)
    Group Key: id
    Planned Partitions: 4  Batches: 5
    Memory Usage: 8257kB  Disk Usage: 3688kB
    ->  Seq Scan on t_test
        (cost=0.00..3082.00 rows=200000 width=4)
        (actual time=0.011..11.805 rows=200000 loops=1)
 Planning Time: 0.342 ms
 Execution Time: 103.035 ms
```

The execution plan in the previous listing gives us some nice insights and shows which operations are needed.

In PostgreSQL, the fallback strategy was to use `GroupAggregate`. You can simulate the old behavior easily:

```
test=# SET enable_hashagg TO off;
SET
```

The alternative plan is shown in the following code snippet:

```
test=# EXPLAIN ANALYZE SELECT id, count(*)
FROM    t_test
GROUP BY 1;
                        QUERY PLAN
-----------------------------------------------------------
 GroupAggregate
   (cost=28428.64..31928.64 rows=200000 width=12)
```

```
    (actual time=43.887..82.789 rows=200000 loops=1)
     Group Key: id
     ->  Sort  (cost=28428.64..28928.64 rows=200000 width=4)
          (actual time=43.874..52.021 rows=200000 loops=1)
            Sort Key: id
            Sort Method: external merge  Disk: 2360kB
            ->  Seq Scan on t_test
                (cost=0.00..3082.00 rows=200000 width=4)
                (actual time=0.035..19.334 rows=200000 loops=1)
  Planning Time: 0.164 ms
  Execution Time: 89.536 ms
 (8 rows)
```

PostgreSQL figures out that the number of groups is now a lot larger and quickly changes its strategy. The problem is that a hash containing so many entries doesn't fit into memory. Therefore, the alternative strategy is to sort on disk:

```
test=# SHOW work_mem;
 work_mem
----------
 4MB
(1 row)
```

As we can see, the work_mem variable governs the size of the hash that's used by the GROUP BY clause. Since there are too many entries, PostgreSQL has to find a strategy that doesn't require that we hold the entire dataset in memory. The solution is to sort the data by ID and group it. Once the data has been sorted, PostgreSQL can move down the list and form one group after the other. If the first type of value is counted, the partial result is read and can be emitted. Then, the next group can be processed. Once the value in the sorted list changes when moving down, it will never show up again; hence, the system knows that a partial result is ready.

To speed up the query, a higher value for the work_mem variable can be set on the fly (and, of course, globally):

```
test=# SET work_mem TO '1 GB';
SET
```

Now, the plan will, once again, feature a fast and efficient hash aggregate:

```
test=# SET enable_hashagg TO on;
SET
test=# EXPLAIN ANALYZE SELECT id, count(*) FROM t_test GROUP BY 1;
                     QUERY PLAN
-----------------------------------------------------------
 HashAggregate
```

```
        (cost=4082.00..6082.00 rows=200000 width=12)
   (actual time=64.807..80.279 rows=200000 loops=1)
     Group Key: id
     Batches: 1  Memory Usage: 28689kB
     -> Seq Scan on t_test
        (cost=0.00..3082.00 rows=200000 width=4)
     (actual time=0.037..12.104 rows=200000 loops=1)
  Planning Time: 0.836 ms
  Execution Time: 86.612 ms
```

PostgreSQL knows (or at least assumes) that data will fit into memory and switch to the faster plan. As you can see, the execution time is lower. The query won't be as fast as in the GROUP BY name case because many more hash values have to be calculated, but you'll be able to see a nice and reliable benefit in the vast majority of cases. As stated previously, this behavior is a bit version-dependent.

Speeding up sorting

The work_mem variable doesn't only speed up grouping. It can also have a very nice impact on simple things such as sorting, which is an essential mechanism that's been mastered by every database system in the world.

The following query shows a simple operation using the default setting of 4 MB:

```
test=# SET work_mem TO '4 MB';
SET
test=# EXPLAIN ANALYZE SELECT * FROM t_test ORDER BY name, id;
                        QUERY PLAN
-----------------------------------------------------------
Sort  (cost=24111.14..24611.14 rows=200000 width=9)
   (actual time=51.298..64.231 rows=200000 loops=1)
     Sort Key: name, id
     Sort Method: external merge  Disk: 3736kB
     -> Seq Scan on t_test
     (cost=0.00..3082.00 rows=200000 width=9)
     (actual time=0.016..17.042 rows=200000 loops=1)
  Planning Time: 0.212 ms
  Execution Time: 72.544 ms
 (6 rows)
```

PostgreSQL needs 17.0 milliseconds to read the data and over 40 milliseconds to sort it. Due to the low amount of memory available, sorting has to be performed using temporary files. The external merge Disk method only requires small amounts of RAM but has to send intermediate data to a comparatively slow storage device, which, of course, leads to poor throughput.

Increasing the `work_mem` variable setting will make PostgreSQL use more memory for sorting:

```
test=# SET work_mem TO '1 GB';
SET
test=# EXPLAIN ANALYZE SELECT *
FROM    t_test
ORDER BY name, id;
                        QUERY PLAN
-----------------------------------------------------------
Sort  (cost=20691.64..21191.64 rows=200000 width=9)
    (actual time=40.354..47.480 rows=200000 loops=1)
       Sort Key: name, id
   Sort Method: quicksort  Memory: 12395kB
   -> Seq Scan on t_test
       (cost=0.00..3082.00 rows=200000 width=9)
   (actual time=0.041..18.213 rows=200000 loops=1)
 Planning Time: 0.181 ms
 Execution Time: 54.279 ms
```

Since there's enough memory now, the database will do all the sorting in memory – therefore, speeding up the process dramatically. The sort takes just around 30 milliseconds now, which is a relevant improvement compared to the query we had previously. More memory will lead to faster sorting and will speed up the system.

So far, you've seen two mechanisms that can be used to sort data: `external merge Disk` and `quicksort Memory`. In addition to these two mechanisms, there's a third algorithm, `top-N heapsort Memory`. It can be used to provide you with only the `top-N` rows:

```
test=# EXPLAIN ANALYZE SELECT *
FROM    t_test
ORDER BY name, id
LIMIT 10;
                        QUERY PLAN
-----------------------------------------------------------
 Limit (cost=7403.93..7403.95 rows=10 width=9)
        (actual time=31.837..31.838 rows=10 loops=1)
       -> Sort (cost=7403.93..7903.93 rows=200000 width=9)
           (actual time=31.836..31.837 rows=10 loops=1)
           Sort Key: name, id
           Sort Method: top-N heapsort Memory: 25kB
           -> Seq Scan on t_test
               (cost=0.00..3082.00 rows=200000 width=9)
               (actual time=0.011..13.645 rows=200000...)
```

```
 Planning time: 0.053 ms
 Execution time: 31.856 ms
(7 rows)
```

The algorithm is lightning-fast, and the entire query will be done in just over 30 milliseconds. The sorting part is now only 18 milliseconds and is, therefore, almost as fast as reading the data in the first place.

In PostgreSQL 13, a new algorithm has been added:

```
test=# CREATE INDEX idx_id ON t_test (id);
CREATE INDEX
test=# explain analyze SELECT * FROM t_test ORDER BY id, name;
                            QUERY PLAN
-------------------------------------------------------------
 Incremental Sort
   (cost=0.46..15289.42 rows=200000 width=9)
   (actual time=0.047..71.622 rows=200000 loops=1)
    Sort Key: id, name
    Presorted Key: id
    Full-sort Groups: 6250 Sort Method: quicksort
    Average Memory: 26kB Peak Memory: 26kB
   -> Index Scan using idx_id on t_test
       (cost=0.42..6289.42 rows=200000 width=9)
       (actual time=0.032..37.965 rows=200000 loops=1)
 Planning Time: 0.165 ms
 Execution Time: 83.681 ms
(7 rows)
```

Incremental sort is used if data is already sorted by some variables. In this case, idx_id will return data sorted by id. All we have to do is sort the already sorted data by name.

Note that the work_mem variable is allocated per operation. Theoretically, a query may need the work_mem variable more than once. It isn't a global setting – it's really per operation. Therefore, you have to set it carefully.

The one thing that we need to keep in mind is that many books claim that setting the work_mem variable too high on an OLTP system may cause your server to run out of memory. Yes, if 1,000 people sort 100 MB at the same time, this can result in memory failures. However, do you expect the disk to be able to handle that? I doubt it. The solution is only to rethink what you're doing. Concurrently sorting 100 MB 1,000 times shouldn't happen in an OLTP system anyway. Consider deploying proper indexes, writing better queries, or simply rethinking your requirements. Under any circumstances, concurrently sorting so much data so often is a bad idea – stop before those things stop your application.

Speeding up administrative tasks

Most operations have to do some sorting or memory allocation of some kind. The administrative ones, such as the CREATE INDEX clause, don't rely on the `work_mem` variable and use the `maintenance_work_mem` variable instead. Here's how it works:

```
test=# DROP INDEX idx_id;
DROP INDEX
test=# SET maintenance_work_mem TO '1 MB';
SET
test=# \timing
Timing is on.
test=# CREATE INDEX idx_id ON t_test (id);
CREATE INDEX
Time:  104.268 ms
```

As you can see, creating an index on 2 million rows takes around 100 milliseconds, which is really slow. Therefore, the `maintenance_work_mem` variable can be used to speed up sorting, which is essentially what the CREATE INDEX clause does:

```
test=# SET maintenance_work_mem TO '1 GB';
SET
test=# CREATE INDEX idx_id2 ON t_test (id);
CREATE INDEX
Time:  46.774 ms
```

The speed has now doubled just because sorting has been improved so much.

More administrative jobs can benefit from more memory. The most prominent ones are the VACUUM clause (to clean out indexes) and the ALTER TABLE clause. The rules for the `maintenance_work_mem` variable are the same as they are for the `work_mem` variable. The setting is per operation, and only the required memory is allocated on the fly.

In PostgreSQL 11, an additional feature was added to the database engine: PostgreSQL is now able to build `btree` indexes in parallel, which can dramatically speed up the indexing of large tables. The parameter that's in charge of configuring parallelism is as follows:

```
test=# SHOW max_parallel_maintenance_workers;
 max_parallel_maintenance_workers
-----------------------------------
 2
(1 row)
```

As you can see, `max_parallel_maintenance_workers` controls the maximum number of worker processes that can be used by CREATE INDEX. As for every parallel operation, PostgreSQL will determine the number of workers based on table sizes. When indexing large tables, index creation can see drastic improvements. I did some extensive testing and summarized my findings in one of my blog posts: `https://www.cybertec-postgresql.com/en/postgresql-parallel-create-index-for-better-performance/`. Here, you'll learn about some important performance insights related to index creation.

However, index creation isn't the only thing that supports concurrency.

Making use of parallel queries

From version 9.6, PostgreSQL has supported parallel queries. This support for parallelism has been improved gradually over time, and version 11 has added even more functionality to this important feature. In this section, we'll take a look at how parallelism works and what can be done to speed things up.

Before digging into the details, it's necessary to create some sample data, as follows:

```
test=# CREATE TABLE t_parallel AS
SELECT *
FROM   generate_series(1, 25000000) AS id;
SELECT 25000000
```

After loading the initial data, we can run our first parallel query. A simple count will show what a parallel query looks like in general:

```
test=# explain SELECT count(*) FROM t_parallel;
                          QUERY PLAN
-----------------------------------------------------------
 Finalize Aggregate
     (cost=241829.17..241829.18 rows=1 width=8)
   -> Gather (cost=241828.96..241829.17 rows=2 width=8)
         Workers Planned: 2
         -> Partial Aggregate
     (cost=240828.96..240828.97 rows=1 width=8)
               -> Parallel Seq Scan on t_parallel
         (cost=0.00..214787.17 rows=10416717 width=0)
 (5 rows)
```

Let's take a detailed look at the execution plan of the query. First, PostgreSQL performs a parallel sequential scan. This implies that PostgreSQL will use more than one CPU to process the table (block by block) and it will create partial aggregates. The job of the `Gather` node is to collect the data and pass it on to do the final aggregation. The `Gather` node is the end of parallelism. It's important to mention that parallelism is (currently) never nested. There can never be a `Gather` node inside another `Gather` node. In this example, PostgreSQL has decided on two worker processes. Why's that?

Let's consider the following variable:

```
test=# SHOW max_parallel_workers_per_gather;
 max_parallel_workers_per_gather
---------------------------------
 2
(1 row)
```

Here, `max_parallel_workers_per_gather` limits the number of worker processes allowed below the `Gather` node to 2. The important thing is that if a table is small, it will never use parallelism. The size of a table has to be at least 8MB, as defined by the following configuration setting:

```
test=# SHOW min_parallel_table_scan_size;
 min_parallel_table_scan_size
------------------------------
 8MB
(1 row)
```

Now, the rule for parallelism is that the size of the table has to triple for PostgreSQL to add one more worker process. In other words, to get four additional workers, you need at least 81 times as much data. This makes sense because the size of your database goes up 100 times, and the storage system is usually not 100 times faster. Therefore, the number of useful cores is somewhat limited.

However, our table is fairly large:

```
test=# \d+
                       List of relations
 Schema |    Name     | Type  | Owner | Persistence |  Size
--------+-------------+-------+-------+-------------+--------
 public | t_parallel  | table | hs    | permanent   | 864 MB
(1 row)
```

In this example, `max_parallel_workers_per_gather` limits the number of cores. If we change this setting, PostgreSQL will decide on more cores:

```
test=# SET max_parallel_workers_per_gather TO 10;
SET
test=# explain SELECT count(*) FROM t_parallel;
                              QUERY PLAN
-----------------------------------------------------------------
 Finalize Aggregate (cost=174120.82..174120.83 rows=1 width=8)
   -> Gather (cost=174120.30..174120.81 rows=5 width=8)
         Workers Planned: 5
```

```
      -> Partial Aggregate
          (cost=173120.30..173120.31 rows=1 width=8)
          -> Parallel Seq Scan on t_parallel
                (cost=0.00..160620.24
                  rows=5000024 width=0)
JIT:
  Functions: 4
  Options: Inlining false, Optimization false, Expressions true,
Deforming true
(8 rows)
```

In this case, we get 5 workers (just as expected).

However, there are cases in which you'll want the number of cores being used for a certain table to be a lot higher. Just imagine a 200 GB database that has 1 TB of RAM and only a single user. This user could use up all the CPU without harming anybody else. In this case, ALTER TABLE can be used to overrule what we've just discussed:

```
test=# ALTER TABLE t_parallel SET (parallel_workers = 9);
ALTER TABLE
```

If you want to overrule the x3 rule to determine the number of desired CPUs, you can use ALTER TABLE to hardcode the number of CPUs explicitly.

Note that max_parallel_workers_per_gather will still be effective and serve as the upper limit.

If you look at the plan, you'll see that the number of cores will be considered (take a look at Workers Planned to see this information):

```
test=# explain SELECT count(*) FROM t_parallel;
                          QUERY PLAN
-----------------------------------------------------------
 Finalize Aggregate (cost=146343.32..146343.33
      rows=1 width=8)
   -> Gather (cost=146342.39..146343.30 rows=9 width=8)
        Workers Planned: 9
        -> Partial Aggregate
        (cost=145342.39..145342.40 rows=1 width=8)
              -> Parallel Seq Scan on t_parallel
        (cost=0.00..138397.91 rows=2777791 width=0)
JIT:
  Functions: 4
  Options: Inlining false, Optimization false, Expressions true,
Deforming true
(8 rows)
Time: 2.454 ms
```

However, that doesn't mean that those cores are used:

```
test=# explain analyze SELECT count(*) FROM t_parallel;
                             QUERY PLAN
-----------------------------------------------------------
 Finalize Aggregate
        (cost=146343.32..146343.33 rows=1 width=8)
        (actual time=1375.606..1375.606 rows=1 loops=1)
    -> Gather (cost=146342.39..146343.30 rows=9 width=8)
             (actual time=1374.411..1376.442 rows=8 loops=1)
        Workers Planned: 9
        Workers Launched: 7
        -> Partial Aggregate
            (cost=145342.39..145342.40 rows=1 width=8)
            (actual time=1347.573..1347.573 rows=1 loops=8)
            -> Parallel Seq Scan on t_parallel
               (cost=0.00..138397.91 rows=2777791 width=0)
               (actual time=0.049..844.601 rows=3125000 loops=8)
 Planning Time: 0.028 ms
 JIT:
   Functions: 18
   Options: Inlining false, Optimization false, Expressions
true,    Deforming true
   Timing: Generation 1.703 ms, Inlining 0.000 ms,
     Optimization 1.119 ms,
     Emission 14.707 ms, Total 17.529 ms
 Execution Time: 1164.922 ms
(12 rows)
```

As you can see, only seven cores were launched, even though nine processes were planned. What's the reason for this? In this example, two more variables come into play:

```
test=# SHOW max_worker_processes;
 max_worker_processes
----------------------
 8
(1 row)
test=# SHOW max_parallel_workers;
 max_parallel_workers
----------------------
 8
(1 row)
```

The first process tells PostgreSQL how many worker processes are generally available. The max_parallel_workers parameter states how many workers are available for parallel queries. Why are there two parameters? Background processes aren't only used by the parallel query infrastructure – they can also be used for other purposes, and therefore, most developers decide to use two parameters.

In general, we at Cybertec (https://www.cybertec-postgresql.com) tend to set max_worker_processes to the number of CPUs in the server. This is because it seems that using more is usually not beneficial.

What's PostgreSQL able to do in parallel?

As we've already mentioned in this section, the support for parallelism has gradually improved since the early times of PostgreSQL. In every version, new functionality has been added.

The following are the most important operations that can be done in parallel:

- Parallel sequential scans
- Parallel index scans (B-trees only)
- Parallel bitmap heap scans
- Parallel joins (all types of joins)
- Parallel SELECT DISTINCT
- Parallel B-trees creation (CREATE INDEX)
- Parallel aggregation
- Parallel append
- VACUUM
- CREATE INDEX

In the case of CREATE INDEX, parallel B-tree creation is available. However, other index types don't enjoy the same level of sophistication yet. Normal sort operations aren't fully parallel yet. To control the amount of parallelism, we need to apply the following parameter:

```
test=# SHOW max_parallel_maintenance_workers;
 max_parallel_maintenance_workers
----------------------------------
 2
(1 row)
```

The rules for parallelism are the same as they are for normal operations.

If you want to speed up your index creation, consider checking out one of my blog posts relating to index creation and performance: `https://www.cybertec-postgresql.com/en/postgresql-parallel-create-index-for-better-performance/`.

Parallelism in practice

Now that we've introduced the basics of parallelism, let's learn what it means in the real world. Let's take a look at the following query:

```
test=# explain SELECT * FROM t_parallel;
                         QUERY PLAN
-----------------------------------------------------------
 Seq Scan on t_parallel
   (cost=0.00..360621.20 rows=25000120 width=4)
(1 row)
```

Why does PostgreSQL not use a parallel query? The table is sufficiently large and the PostgreSQL worker is available, so why doesn't it use a parallel query? The answer is that interprocess communication is really expensive. If PostgreSQL has to ship rows between processes, a query can be slower than in single-process mode. The optimizer uses cost parameters to punish interprocess communication:

```
#parallel_tuple_cost = 0.1
```

Every time a tuple is moved between processes, 0.1 points will be added to the calculation.

In a real example, it's also important to see that more cores doesn't automatically lead to more speed. A delicate balancing act is required to find the perfect number of cores.

Introducing just-in-time (JIT) compilation

JIT compilation has been one of the hot topics in PostgreSQL recently. It's been a major undertaking, and the first results look promising. However, let's start with the fundamentals: what's JIT compilation all about? When you run a query, PostgreSQL has to figure out a lot of stuff at runtime. When PostgreSQL itself is compiled, it doesn't know which kind of query you will run next, so it has to be prepared for all kinds of scenarios.

The core is generic, meaning that it can do all kinds of stuff. However, when you're in a query, you just want to execute the current query as fast as possible – not some other random stuff. The point is, at runtime, you know a lot more about what you have to do than at compile time (that is, when PostgreSQL is compiled). That's exactly the point: when JIT compilation is enabled, PostgreSQL will check your query, and if it happens to be time-consuming enough, highly optimized code for your query will be created on the fly (just in time).

Configuring JIT

To use JIT, it must be added at compile time (when running `./configure`). The following configuration options are available:

```
--with-llvm build with LLVM based JIT support
...
LLVM_CONFIG path to llvm-config command
```

Some Linux distributions ship an extra package containing support for JIT. If you want to make use of JIT, make sure those packages are installed.

Once you've made sure that JIT is available, the following configuration parameters will be available so that you can fine-tune JIT compilation for your queries:

```
#jit = on                              # allow JIT compilation
#jit_provider = 'llvmjit'              # JIT implementation to use
#jit_above_cost = 100000               # perform JIT compilation if
                                       # available
                                       # and query more expensive,
                                       # -1 disables
#jit_optimize_above_cost = 500000 # optimize JITed functions
                                       # if query is
                                       # more expensive, -1 disables
#jit_inline_above_cost = 500000    # attempt to inline operators and
                                       # functions if query is
                                       # more expensive,
                                       # -1 disables
```

Here, `jit_above_cost` means that JIT is only considered if the expected cost is at least 100,000 units. Why is that relevant? If a query isn't sufficiently long, the overhead of compilation can be a lot higher than the potential gain. Therefore, only optimization is attempted. However, there are two more parameters: deep optimizations are attempted if the query is considered to be more expensive than 500,000 units. In this case, function calls will be inlined.

At this point, PostgreSQL only supports **Low-Level Virtual Machine (LLVM)** as a JIT backend. Maybe additional backends will be available in the future as well. For now, LLVM does a really good job and covers most of the environments that are used in professional contexts.

Running queries

To show you how JIT works, we'll compile a simple example. Let's begin by creating a big table – one that contains a lot of data. Remember, JIT compilation is only useful if the operation is sufficiently large. To begin with, 50 million rows should suffice. The following example shows how to populate the table:

```
jit=# CREATE TABLE t_jit AS
SELECT (random()*10000)::int AS x,
    (random()*100000)::int AS y,
    (random()*1000000)::int AS z
FROM generate_series(1, 50000000) AS id;
SELECT 50000000
jit=# VACUUM ANALYZE t_jit;
VACUUM
```

In this case, we'll use the `random` function to generate some data. To show you how JIT works and to make execution plans easier to read, you can turn off parallel queries. JIT works fine with parallel queries, but execution plans tend to be a lot longer:

```
jit=# SET max_parallel_workers_per_gather TO 0;
SET
jit=# SET jit TO off;
SET
jit=# explain (analyze, verbose)
SELECT avg(z+y-pi()),
    avg(y-pi()), max(x/pi())
FROM    t_jit
WHERE   ((y+z))>((y-x)*0.000001);
                              QUERY PLAN
------------------------------------------------------------
 Aggregate  (cost=1936901.68..1936901.69 rows=1 width=24)
            (actual time=20617.425..20617.425 rows=1 loops=1)
   Output: avg(((z + y))::double precision -
       <3.14159265358979'::double precision)),
          avg(((y)::double precision -
      '3.14159265358979'::double precision)),
         max(((x)::double precision /
      '3.14159265358979'::double precision))
     -> Seq Scan on public.t_jit
   (cost=0.00..1520244.00 rows=16666307 width=12)
           (actual time=0.061..15322.555 rows=50000000 loops=1)
          Output: x, y, z
          Filter: (((t_jit.y + t_jit.z))::numeric >
```

```
      ((((t_jit.y - t_jit.x))::numeric * 0.000001))
 Planning Time: 0.078 ms
 Execution Time: 20617.473 ms
(7 rows)
```

In this case, the query took 20 seconds.

> **Important note**
>
> I used a VACUUM function to ensure that all the hint bits and so on have been set properly to ensure a fair comparison between a JIT query and a normal query.

Let's repeat this test with JIT enabled:

```
jit=# SET jit TO on;
SET
jit=# explain (analyze, verbose)
SELECT avg(z+y-pi()), avg(y-pi()), max(x/pi())
FROM   t_jit
WHERE  ((y+z))>((y-x)*0.000001);
                              QUERY PLAN
---------------------------------------------------------------
 Aggregate (cost=1936901.68..1936901.69 rows=1 width=24)
         (actual time=15585.788..15585.789 rows=1 loops=1)
   Output: avg((((z + y))::double precision -
     '3.14159265358979'::double precision)),
         avg(((y)::double precision -
     '3.14159265358979'::double precision)),
         max(((x)::double precision /
     '3.14159265358979'::double precision))
     -> Seq Scan on public.t_jit
     (cost=0.00..1520244.00 rows=16666307 width=12)
     (actual time=81.991..13396.227 rows=50000000 loops=1)
         Output: x, y, z
         Filter: ((((t_jit.y + t_jit.z))::numeric >
     (((t_jit.y - t_jit.x))::numeric * 0.000001))
 Planning Time: 0.135 ms
 JIT:
   Functions: 5
 Options: Inlining true, Optimization true, Expressions true,
   Deforming true
   Timing: Generation 2.942 ms, Inlining 15.717 ms,
   Optimization 40.806 ms,
   Emission 25.233 ms,
```

```
    Total 84.698 ms
 Execution Time: 15588.851 ms
(11 rows)
```

In this case, you can see that the query is a lot faster than before, which is already significant. In some cases, the benefits can be even bigger. However, keep in mind that recompiling code is also associated with some additional effort, so it doesn't make sense for every kind of query.

Understanding the PostgreSQL optimizer can be very beneficial in providing good performance. It makes sense to delve into these topics to ensure good performance.

Summary

In this chapter, several query optimizations were discussed. You learned about the optimizer and various internal optimizations, such as constant folding, view inlining, joins, and much more. We also covered some more optimization techniques, such as JIT compilation and parallel queries. All of these optimizations contribute to good performance and help speed things up considerably.

Now that we've covered this introduction to optimizations, in *Chapter 7*, *Writing Stored Procedures*, we'll talk about stored procedures. You'll learn about all the options PostgreSQL has with which we can handle user-defined code.

7

Writing Stored Procedures

In *Chapter 6*, *Optimizing Queries for Good Performance*, we learned a lot about the optimizer, as well as the optimizations going on in the system. In this chapter, we will learn about stored procedures and how to use them efficiently and easily. We will also inspect how optimization and stored procedures go together. You will learn about what a stored procedure is made up of, which languages are available, and how you can speed things up nicely. On top of that, you will be introduced to some of the more advanced features of PL/pgSQL, and you will learn how to write good server-side code.

The following topics will be covered in this chapter:

- Understanding stored procedure languages
- Exploring various stored procedure languages
- Improving functions
- Using functions for various purposes

By the end of this chapter, you will be able to write good, efficient stored procedures.

Understanding stored procedure languages

When it comes to stored procedures and functions, PostgreSQL differs quite significantly from other database systems. Most database engines force you to use a certain programming language to write server-side code. Microsoft SQL Server offers Transact-SQL, while Oracle encourages you to use PL/SQL. PostgreSQL doesn't force you to use a certain language; instead, it allows you to decide on what you know and like the best.

The reason PostgreSQL is so flexible is actually quite interesting in a historical sense, too. Many years ago, one of the most well-known PostgreSQL developers, Jan Wieck, who had written countless patches back in its early days, came up with the idea of using **Tool Command Language (Tcl)** as the server-side programming language. The trouble was that nobody wanted to use Tcl, and nobody wanted to have this stuff in the database engine. The solution to the problem was to make the language interface so flexible that basically any language could be easily integrated with PostgreSQL. At this point, the CREATE LANGUAGE clause was born. Here is the syntax of CREATE LANGUAGE:

```
test=# \h CREATE LANGUAGE
Command:     CREATE LANGUAGE
Description: define a new procedural language
Syntax:
CREATE [ OR REPLACE ] [ TRUSTED ] [ PROCEDURAL ]
    LANGUAGE name
    HANDLER call_handler [ INLINE inline_handler ]
            [ VALIDATOR valfunction ]
CREATE [ OR REPLACE ] [ TRUSTED ] [ PROCEDURAL ]
            LANGUAGE name

URL: https://www.postgresql.org/docs/17/sql-createlanguage.html
```

Nowadays, many different languages can be used to write functions and stored procedures. The flexibility that's been added to PostgreSQL has really paid off; we can now choose from a rich set of programming languages.

How exactly does PostgreSQL handle languages? If we take a look at the syntax of the CREATE LANGUAGE clause, we will see a few keywords:

- HANDLER: This function is actually the glue between PostgreSQL and any external language that you want to use. It is in charge of mapping PostgreSQL data structures to whatever is needed by the language and helps pass the code around.

- VALIDATOR: This is the police officer of the infrastructure. If it is available, it will be in charge of delivering tasty syntax errors to the end user. Many languages are able to parse code before actually executing it. PostgreSQL can use that and tell you whether a function is correct or not when you create it. Unfortunately, not all languages can do this, so in some cases, you will still be left with problems showing up at runtime.

- INLINE: If this is present, PostgreSQL will be able to run anonymous code blocks utilizing this handler function.

After checking those options, we can move on to understand some fundamental differences between functions and procedures.

Understanding the fundamentals of stored procedures versus functions

Before we dig into the anatomy of a stored procedure, it is important to talk about functions and procedures in general. The term stored procedure has traditionally been used to actually talk about a function. Thus, it is essential that we understand the difference between a function and a procedure.

A function is part of a normal SQL statement and is not allowed to start or commit transactions. Here is an example:

```
SELECT func(id) FROM large_table;
```

Suppose func(id) is called 50 million times. If you use the function called COMMIT, what exactly should happen? It is impossible to simply end a transaction in the middle of a query and launch a new one. The entire concept of transactional integrity, consistency, and so on would be violated.

In contrast, a procedure can control transactions and even run multiple transactions one after the other. However, you cannot run it inside a SELECT statement. Instead, you have to invoke CALL. The following listing shows the syntax of the CALL command:

```
test=# \h CALL
Command:     CALL
Description: invoke a procedure
Syntax:
CALL name ( [ argument ] [, ...] )

URL: https://www.postgresql.org/docs/17/sql-call.html
```

Therefore, there is a fundamental distinction between functions and procedures. The terminology that you will find on the internet is not always clear. However, you have to be aware of those important differences. In PostgreSQL, functions have been around since the very beginning. However, the concept of a procedure, as outlined in this section, is important because we are talking about important distinctions. In this chapter, we will take a look at functions and procedures in detail. Let's begin by understanding the anatomy of a function.

The anatomy of a function

Before we dig into a specific language, we will look at the anatomy of a typical function. For demonstration purposes, let's look at the following function, which just adds two numbers:

```
test=# CREATE OR REPLACE FUNCTION mysum(int, int)
RETURNS int AS
'
    SELECT $1 + $2;
' LANGUAGE 'sql';
CREATE FUNCTION
```

The first thing to observe is that this function is written in SQL. PostgreSQL needs to know which language we are using, so we have to specify that in the definition.

Note that the code of the function is passed to PostgreSQL as a string ('). This is somewhat noteworthy because it allows a function to become a black box to the execution machinery.

In other database engines, the code of the function is not a string but is directly attached to the statement. This simple abstraction layer is what gives the PostgreSQL function manager all its power. Inside the string, you can basically use all that the programming language of your choice has to offer.

In this example, we will simply add up two numbers that have been passed to the function. Two integer variables are in use. The important part here is that PostgreSQL provides you with function overloading. In other words, the mysum(int, int) function is not the same as the mysum(int8, int8) function.

PostgreSQL sees these things as two distinct functions. Function overloading is a good feature; however, you have to be very careful not to accidentally deploy too many functions if your parameter list happens to change from time to time. Always make sure that functions that are not needed anymore are really deleted.

The CREATE OR REPLACE FUNCTION clause will not change the parameter list. Therefore, you can use it only if the signature does not change. It will either error out or simply deploy a new function.

Let's run the mysum function:

```
test=# SELECT mysum(10, 20);
 mysum
-------
 30
(1 row)
```

The result here is 30, which is not really surprising. After this introduction to functions, it is important to focus on the next major topic, quoting.

Introducing dollar quoting

Passing code to PostgreSQL as a string is very flexible. However, using single quotes can be an issue. In many programming languages, single quotes show up frequently. To be able to use these quotes, you have to escape them when passing the string to PostgreSQL. For many years, this has been the standard procedure. Fortunately, those old times have passed by, and new means of passing the code to PostgreSQL are available. One of these is dollar quoting, as shown in the following code:

```
test=# CREATE OR REPLACE FUNCTION mysum(int, int)
RETURNS int AS
$$
    SELECT $1 + $2;
$$ LANGUAGE 'sql';
CREATE FUNCTION
```

Instead of using quotes to start and end strings, you can simply use $$. Currently, two languages have assigned a meaning to $$. In Perl, as well as in Bash scripts, $$ represents the process ID. To overcome this little obstacle, we can use $ before almost anything to start and end the string. The following example shows how that works:

```
test=# CREATE OR REPLACE FUNCTION mysum(int, int)
RETURNS int AS
$body$
    SELECT $1 + $2;
$body$ LANGUAGE sql;
CREATE FUNCTION
```

All this flexibility allows you to overcome the problem of quoting once and for all. As long as the start string and the end string match, there won't be any problems.

Making use of anonymous code blocks

So far, we have written the simplest stored procedures possible and also learned how to execute code. However, there is more to code execution than just full-blown functions. In addition to functions, PostgreSQL allows the use of anonymous code blocks. The idea is to run code that is needed only once. This kind of code execution is especially useful for dealing with administrative tasks. Anonymous code blocks don't take parameters and are not permanently stored in the database since they don't have names.

Here is a simple example showing an anonymous code block in action:

```
test=# DO
$$
BEGIN
    RAISE NOTICE 'current time: %', now();
END;
$$ LANGUAGE plpgsql;
NOTICE:   current time: 2024-10-15 16:29:08.640934+01
DO
```

In this example, the code only issues a message and quits. Again, the code block has to know which language it uses. This string is passed to PostgreSQL using simple dollar quoting.

New-style SQL functions

However, there is more. There is a feature that has become way more popular recently. I am of course talking about the idea of "new style function". Before we dive into the details, the best way to start is to take a look at an example:

```
test=# CREATE FUNCTION f_new_style(a text, b date)
RETURNS boolean
LANGUAGE SQL
BEGIN ATOMIC
```

```
      RETURN a = 'abcd' AND b > '2025-01-01';
END;
```

What we see here is that we don't pass the code as a string and we are not using dollar-quoting. Instead, we can see `BEGIN ATOMIC` and a simple SQL statement. The idea here is to give users the chance to write simple SQL functions (no other languages) and skip all the markup because PostgreSQL is able to parse the code directly – it is just SQL after all.

Running the function works as follows:

```
test=# SELECT f_new_style('abcd', '2029-05-04');
 f_new_style
-------------
 t
(1 row)
```

New-style SQL functions offer an easy way to write simple code.

Using functions and transactions

As you know, everything that PostgreSQL exposes in userland is a transaction. The same, of course, applies if you are writing functions. A function is always part of the transaction you are in. It is not autonomous, just like an operator or any other operation.

Here is an example:

```
test=# SELECT now(), mysum(id, id)
FROM generate_series(1, 3) AS gs(id);
              now               | mysum
--------------------------------+-------
 2024-10-16 08:49:19.356442+02 |     2
 2024-10-16 08:49:19.356442+02 |     4
 2024-10-16 08:49:19.356442+02 |     6
(3 rows)
```

All three function calls happen in the same transaction. This is important to understand because it implies that you cannot do too much transactional flow control inside a function. What happens when the second function call commits? It just cannot work.

However, Oracle has a mechanism that allows autonomous transactions. The idea is that even if a transaction rolls back, some parts might still be needed, and they should be kept. A classic example is as follows:

1. Start a function to look up secret data.

2. Add a log line to the document to state that somebody has modified this important secret data.

3. Commit the log line but roll back the change.

4. Preserve the information, stating that an attempt has been made to change data.

Autonomous transactions can be used to solve problems such as this one. The idea is to be able to commit a transaction inside the main transaction independently. In this case, the entry in the log table will prevail, while the change will be rolled back.

Autonomous transactions are not implemented. However, there are already patches floating around that implement this feature. It is still to be seen when these features will make it to the core.

To give you an impression of how things will most likely work, here is a code snippet based on the first patches:

```
...
AS
$$
DECLARE
   PRAGMA AUTONOMOUS_TRANSACTION;
BEGIN
     FOR i IN 0..9 LOOP
         START TRANSACTION;
         INSERT INTO test1 VALUES (i);
         IF i % 2 = 0 THEN
             COMMIT;
         ELSE
             ROLLBACK;
         END IF;
     END LOOP;
     RETURN 42;
END;
$$;
...
```

The point of this example is to show you that we can decide whether to commit or roll back the autonomous transaction on the fly.

Exploring various stored procedure languages

As we've already stated in this chapter, PostgreSQL gives you the power to write functions and store procedures in various languages. The following options are available and are shipped along with the PostgreSQL core:

- SQL

- PL/pgSQL

- PL/Perl and PL/PerlU

- PL/Python3U

- PL/Tcl and PL/TclU

SQL is the obvious choice for writing functions, and it should be used whenever possible, as it gives the most freedom to the optimizer. However, if you want to write slightly more complex code, PL/pgSQL might be the language of your choice.

PL/pgSQL offers flow control and much more. In this chapter, some of the more advanced and lesser-known features of PL/pgSQL will be shown, but do keep in mind that this chapter is not meant to be a complete tutorial on PL/pgSQL.

The core contains code to run server-side functions in Perl. Basically, the logic is the same here. Code will be passed as a string and executed by Perl. Remember that PostgreSQL does not speak Perl; it merely has the code to pass things on to the external programming language.

Maybe you have noticed that Perl and Tcl are available in two flavors: **trusted language** (PL/Perl and PL/Tcl) and **untrusted language** (PL/PerlU and PL/TclU). The difference between a trusted and an untrusted language is actually an important one. In PostgreSQL, a language is loaded directly into the database connection. Therefore, the language is able to do quite a lot of critical stuff. To get rid of security problems, the concept of trusted languages was invented. The idea is that a trusted language is restricted to the very core of the language, therefore, it is not possible to do the following:

- Include libraries

- Open network sockets

- Perform system calls of any kind, which would include opening files

Perl offers something called **taint mode**, which is used to implement security in PostgreSQL. Perl will automatically restrict itself to trusted mode and error out if a security violation is about to happen. In untrusted mode, everything is possible; therefore, only the superuser is allowed to run untrusted code.

If you want to run trusted as well as untrusted code, you have to activate both languages, that is, **plperl** and **plperlu** (**pltcl** and **pltclu**, respectively).

Python is currently only available as an untrusted language; therefore, administrators have to be very careful when it comes to security in general. A function running in untrusted mode can bypass all the security mechanisms that are enforced by PostgreSQL. Just keep in mind that Python is running as part of your database connection and is in no way responsible for security.

Let's get started with the most awaited topic of this chapter.

Introducing PL/pgSQL

In this section, you will be introduced to some of the more advanced features of PL/pgSQL, which are important for writing proper and highly efficient code.

Before we dive into some more advanced topics, we can take a look at some more simple things.

Structuring PL/pgSQL code

Before we dig deeper, we want to return to the anatomy of a simple function. In the case of PL/pgSQL, we are talking about a **block-oriented language**. What does it mean in real life? The first thing you can see is a DECLARE block. In this block, variables are declared. Then there is a BEGIN block, which contains the real code:

```
CREATE OR REPLACE FUNCTION investment_calculator(
    IN v_amount numeric, IN v_interest numeric,
    IN v_years int)
RETURNS numeric AS
$$
DECLARE
    v_sum    ALIAS FOR $1;
    v_result numeric := 0;
BEGIN
    v_result := v_amount
                  * pow(1 + v_interest, v_years);
    RETURN v_result;
END;
$$ LANGUAGE 'plpgsql';
```

In our example, there is a bit more to see. What you see in real life is often the concept of IN/OUT parameters. We can name those parameters passed to a function and use them directly instead of using $1 and $2. What is also possible is to use aliases. v_sum can be used just like v_amount, so the effect of an alias and a named parameter is pretty much the same from a coding standpoint.

Of course, assigning code to a variable before returning it is not necessary. We can directly return the result of the expression. However, it serves as an example so that we can see how things work.

Let us call the function:

```
test=# SELECT investment_calculator(1000, 0.1, 2);
 investment_calculator
-----------------------
 1210.0000000000000000
(1 row)
```

The result is not that much of a surprise.

Performance considerations

Before diving deeper into PL/pgSQL and its language concepts, it makes sense to understand some basic performance considerations: in PostgreSQL, you can choose between many different languages. However, not all of them are created equal. If you are looking for good performance, it makes sense to stick to SQL whenever necessary. PL/pgSQL is a good language but it does come with a bit of overhead. For simple operations that don't need flow control, use SQL – it will be a lot faster.

To prove this point, I have implemented a second incarnation of this function doing the same thing in SQL:

```
CREATE OR REPLACE FUNCTION
    simple_invest(numeric, numeric, numeric)
RETURNS numeric AS
$$
    SELECT $1 * pow(1 + $2, $3);
$$ LANGUAGE 'sql';
```

Comparing the performance of those functions is easy. In my example, I have simply used generate_series to run the function 1 million times:

```
test=# explain analyze
SELECT investment_calculator(x, 0.1, 2)
FROM generate_series(1, 1000000) AS x;
                    QUERY PLAN
-----------------------------------------------------------
 Function Scan on generate_series x
    (cost=0.00..262500.00 rows=1000000 width=32)
    (actual time=83.927..1237.593 rows=1000000 loops=1)
 Planning Time: 0.073 ms
 JIT:
    Functions: 4
    Options: Inlining false, Optimization false,
  Expressions true, Deforming true
    Timing: Generation 1.354 ms, Inlining 0.000 ms,
    Optimization 4.150 ms, Emission 10.002 ms,
        Total 15.507 ms
 Execution Time: 1345.603 ms
(7 rows)
```

We need 1.3 seconds to generate 1 million rows and to call the function. Let us do the same thing using the plain SQL function:

```
test=# explain analyze SELECT simple_invest(x, 0.1, 2)
FROM generate_series(1, 1000000) AS x;
```

```
                    QUERY PLAN
------------------------------------------------------------
 Function Scan on generate_series x
   (cost=0.00..15000.00 rows=1000000 width=32)
   (actual time=69.795..281.639 rows=1000000 loops=1)
 Planning Time: 0.114 ms
 Execution Time: 310.512 ms
(3 rows)
```

It took 0.31 seconds – that is a major difference that should be kept in mind. Of course, not all functions can be written in plain SQL and it would not make sense to do so either. However, for simple functions, it can make a major difference because the optimizer can inline things and optimize them.

Loops and flow control

Flow control is not something you can easily do in SQL. PL/pgSQL will definitely be needed to achieve more complex operations.

In the next example, we want to add some sanity checks to our incoming data:

```
CREATE OR REPLACE FUNCTION investment_calculator(
    IN v_amount numeric, IN v_interest numeric,
    IN v_years int)
RETURNS numeric AS
$$
  BEGIN
    IF  v_years < 1
    THEN
    RAISE EXCEPTION 'use values > 1 year instead of %',
     v_years;
    ELSEIF  v_years > 100
    THEN
    RAISE WARNING 'predicting more than 100 years is not recommended';
    ELSE
    RETURN v_amount * pow(1 + v_interest, v_years);
    END IF;
    RETURN NULL;
  END;
$$ LANGUAGE 'plpgsql';
```

In PL/pgSQL, you can use simple IF/ELSE syntax. What is important here is that we did not add a DECLARE block this time, as we can get away without declaring variables.

Let us call the function:

```
test=# SELECT investment_calculator(1000, 0.1, -2);
ERROR:  use values > 1 year instead of -2
CONTEXT:  PL/pgSQL function investment_calculator(numeric, numeric,
integer) line 5 at RAISE
```

RAISE EXCEPTION will trigger an error, exit the function, and cause the entire SQL statement to fail, while RAISE WARNING will simply trigger a log message to be sent out:

```
test=# SELECT investment_calculator(1000, 0.1, 2344523);
WARNING:  predicting more than 100 years is not recommended
 investment_calculator
-----------------------

(1 row)
```

In this case, the code returns NULL and warns us that the period is simply too long.

Let's now move on to handling quoting and the string format.

Handling quoting and the string format

One of the most important things in database programming is quoting. If you don't use proper quoting, you will surely get into trouble with SQL injection and open unacceptable security holes.

What is SQL injection?

Let's consider the following example:

```
CREATE FUNCTION broken(text) RETURNS void AS
$$
DECLARE
  v_sql text;
BEGIN
  v_sql := 'SELECT schemaname
        FROM pg_tables
        WHERE tablename = ''' || $1 || '''';
  RAISE NOTICE 'v_sql: %', v_sql;
  RETURN;
END;
$$ LANGUAGE 'plpgsql';
```

In this example, the SQL code is simply pasted together without ever worrying about security. All we are doing here is using the | | operator to concatenate strings. This works fine if you run normal queries.

Consider the following example, showing some broken code:

```
SELECT broken('t_test');
```

However, you have to be prepared for people trying to exploit your systems.

Consider the following example:

```
SELECT broken('''; DROP  TABLE  t_test; ');
```

Running the function with this parameter will show a problem.

The following code shows classic SQL injection:

```
NOTICE: v_sql: SELECT schemaname FROM  pg_tables
WHERE tablename = ''; DROP TABLE t_test; '
CONTEXT: PL/pgSQL function broken(text) line  6 at RAISE
 broken
 --------
(1 row)
```

Dropping a table when you just want to do a lookup is not a desirable thing to do. It is definitely not acceptable to make the security of your application depend on the parameters that are passed to your statements.

To avoid SQL injection, PostgreSQL offers various functions; these should be used at all times to ensure that your security stays intact:

```
test=# SELECT  quote_literal(E'o''reilly'),
quote_ident(E'o''reilly');
 quote_literal  | quote_ident
----------------+-------------
  'o''reilly'   | "o'reilly"
(1 row)
```

The `quote_literal` function will escape a string in such a way that nothing bad can happen anymore. It will add all the quotes around the string and will escape problematic characters inside the string. Therefore, there is no need to start and end the string manually.

The second function that's shown here is `quote_ident`. It can be used to quote object names properly. Note that double quotes are used, which is exactly what is needed to handle table names. The following example shows how to use complex names:

```
test=# CREATE TABLE "Some stupid name" ("ID" int);
CREATE TABLE
test=# \d "Some stupid name"
Table "public.Some stupid name"
```

```
 Column |  Type   | Collation | Nullable | Default
--------+---------+-----------+----------+---------
 ID     | integer |           |          |
```

Normally, all of the table names in PostgreSQL are lowercase. However, if double quotes are used, object names can contain capital letters. In general, it is not a good idea to use this kind of trickery, as you would have to use double quotes all the time, which can be a bit inconvenient.

Now that you've had a basic introduction to quoting, it is important to take a look at how NULL values are handled. The following code shows how NULL is treated by the quote_literal function:

```
test=# SELECT quote_literal(NULL);
 quote_literal
---------------

(1 row)
```

If you call the quote_literal function on a NULL value, it will simply return NULL. There is no need to take care of quoting in this case. PostgreSQL provides even more functions to explicitly take care of a NULL value:

```
test=# SELECT
    quote_nullable(123),
    quote_nullable(NULL);
 quote_nullable | quote_nullable
----------------+----------------
 '123'          | NULL
(1 row)
```

It is not only possible to quote strings and object names; it is also possible to use PL/pgSQL onboard to format and prepare entire queries. The beauty here is that you can use the format function to add parameters to a statement.

Here is how it works:

```
CREATE FUNCTION simple_format() RETURNS text AS
$$
DECLARE
  v_string text;
  v_result text;
BEGIN
  v_string := format('SELECT schemaname|| ''.''
    || tablename
          FROM pg_tables
          WHERE %I = $1
```

```
             AND %I = $2', 'schemaname', 'tablename');
   EXECUTE v_string USING 'public', 't_test'
   INTO v_result;
   RAISE NOTICE 'result: %', v_result;
   RETURN v_string;
END;
$$ LANGUAGE 'plpgsql';
```

The names of the fields are passed to the `format` function. Finally, the `USING` clause of the `EXECUTE` statement is there to add the parameters to the query, which is then executed. Again, the beauty here is that no SQL injection can happen.

Here is what happens when the `simple_format` function is called:

```
test=# SELECT simple_format ();
NOTICE: result: public.t_test
            simple_format
-------------------------------------------
 SELECT schemaname|| '.' || tablename        +
        FROM pg_tables          +
        WHERE schemaname = $1 +
                 AND tablename = $2
(1 row)
```

As you can see, the debug message correctly displays the table, including the schema, and correctly returns the query. However, the `format` function can do a lot more. Here are some examples:

```
test=# SELECT format('Hello, %s %s','PostgreSQL', 17);
      format
---------------------
 Hello, PostgreSQL 17
(1 row)


test=# SELECT
    format('Hello, %s %10s',
    'PostgreSQL', 17);
      format
---------------------
 Hello, PostgreSQL 17
(1 row)
```

The `format` function is able to use format options as shown in the example. `%10s` means that the string we want to add will be padded by adding blanks.

In some cases, it can be necessary to use a variable more than once. The following example shows two parameters, which are added more than once to the string that we want to create. What you can do is use $1, $2, and so on to identify the entries in the argument list:

```
test=# SELECT format('%1$s, %1$s, %2$s', 'one', 'two');
   format
---------------
 one, one, two
(1 row)
```

The `format` function is very powerful and super important when you want to avoid SQL injection, and you should make good use of this powerful feature.

Let us cover managing scopes next.

Managing scopes

After dealing with quoting and basic security (SQL injection) in general, we will focus on another important topic: **scopes**.

Just like most popular programming languages, PL/pgSQL uses variables depending on their context. Variables are defined in the DECLARE statement of a function. In addition, however, PL/pgSQL allows you to nest a DECLARE statement:

```
CREATE FUNCTION scope_test () RETURNS int AS
$$
DECLARE
    i int := 0;
BEGIN
    RAISE NOTICE 'i1: %', i;
    DECLARE
        i int;
    BEGIN
        RAISE NOTICE 'i2: %', i;
    END;
    RETURN i;
END;
$$ LANGUAGE 'plpgsql';
```

In the DECLARE statement, the i variable is defined, and a value is assigned to it. Then, i is displayed. The output will, of course, be 0. Then, a second DECLARE statement starts. It contains an additional incarnation of i, which is not assigned a value. Therefore, the value will be NULL. Note that PostgreSQL will now display the inner i.

Here is what happens:

```
test=# SELECT scope_test();
NOTICE:  i1: 0
NOTICE:  i2: <NULL>
 scope_test
------------
    0
(1 row)
```

As expected, the debug messages will show 0 and NULL.

PostgreSQL allows you to use all kinds of tricks. However, it is strongly recommended that you keep your code simple and easy to read.

Understanding advanced error handling

For programming languages, in every program and in every module, error handling is an important thing. Everything is expected to go wrong once in a while, and therefore it is vital to handle errors properly and professionally. In PL/pgSQL, you can use EXCEPTION blocks to handle errors. The idea is that if the BEGIN block does something wrong, the EXCEPTION block will take care of it and handle the problem correctly. Just like many other languages, such as Java, you can react to different types of errors and catch them separately.

In the following example, the code might run into a division-by-zero problem. The goal is to catch this error and react accordingly:

```
CREATE FUNCTION error_test1(int, int)
   RETURNS int AS
$$
BEGIN
    RAISE NOTICE 'debug message: % / %', $1, $2;
    BEGIN
        RETURN $1 / $2;
    EXCEPTION
        WHEN division_by_zero THEN
            RAISE NOTICE 'division by zero detected: %', sqlerrm;
        WHEN others THEN
            RAISE NOTICE 'some other error: %', sqlerrm;
    END;
    RAISE NOTICE 'all errors handled';
    RETURN 0;
END;
$$ LANGUAGE 'plpgsql';
```

The `BEGIN` block can clearly throw an error because there can be a division by zero. However, the `EXCEPTION` block catches the error that we are looking at and also takes care of all other potential problems that can unexpectedly pop up.

Technically, this is more or less the same as a savepoint; therefore, the error does not cause the entire transaction to fail completely. Only the block that is causing the error will be subject to a mini rollback.

By inspecting the `sqlerrm` variable, you can also have direct access to the error message itself. Let's run the code:

```
test=# SELECT error_test1(9, 0);
NOTICE:  debug message: 9 / 0
NOTICE:  division by zero  detected: division by zero
NOTICE:  all errors handled
 error_test1
-------------
     0
(1 row)
```

PostgreSQL catches the exception and shows the message in the `EXCEPTION` block. It is kind enough to show us the line containing the error. This makes it a whole lot easier to debug and fix the code if it is broken.

In some cases, it also makes sense to raise your own exception. As you might expect, this is quite easy to do:

```
RAISE unique_violation USING MESSAGE = 'Duplicate user ID: ' || user_
id;
```

Apart from this, PostgreSQL offers many predefined error codes and exceptions.

The following page contains a complete list of these error messages: `https://www.postgresql.org/docs/current/errcodes-appendix.html`.

Making use of GET DIAGNOSTICS

Many people who have used Oracle in the past might be familiar with the `GET DIAGNOSTICS` clause. The idea behind the `GET DIAGNOSTICS` clause is to allow users to see what is going on in the system. While the syntax might appear a bit strange to people who are used to modern code, it is still a valuable tool that can improve your applications.

From my point of view, there are two main tasks that the `GET DIAGNOSTICS` clause can be used for:

- Inspecting the row count
- Fetching context information and getting a backtrace

Inspecting the row count is definitely something that you will need during everyday programming. Extracting context information is useful if you want to debug applications.

The following example shows how the GET DIAGNOSTICS clause can be used inside your code:

```
CREATE FUNCTION get_diag()
    RETURNS int AS
$$
DECLARE
    rc int;
    _sqlstate text;
    _message text;
    _context text;
BEGIN
    EXECUTE 'SELECT * FROM generate_series(1, 10)';
    GET DIAGNOSTICS rc = ROW_COUNT;
    RAISE NOTICE 'row count: %', rc;
    SELECT rc / 0;
EXCEPTION
    WHEN OTHERS THEN
        GET STACKED DIAGNOSTICS
            _sqlstate = returned_sqlstate,
            _message = message_text,
            _context = pg_exception_context;
        RAISE NOTICE 'sqlstate: %, message: %, context: [%]',
            _sqlstate,
            _message,
            replace(_context, E'n', ' <- ');
    RETURN rc;
END;
$$ LANGUAGE 'plpgsql';
```

The first thing after declaring those variables is to execute a SQL statement and ask the GET DIAGNOSTICS clause for a row count, which is then displayed in a debug message. Then, the function forces PL/pgSQL to error out. Once this happens, we will use the GET DIAGNOSTICS clause to extract information from the server to display it.

Here is what happens when we call the get_diag function:

```
test=# SELECT get_diag();
NOTICE:   row count: 10
CONTEXT:   PL/pgSQL function get_diag() line  12 at RAISE
NOTICE:   sqlstate: 22012,
message: division by zero,
context: [SQL  statement "SELECT rc / 0"
```

```
<- PL/pgSQL function get_diag() line  14 at
SQL statement]
CONTEXT:  PL/pgSQL function get_diag() line  22 at RAISE
 get_diag
----------
 10
(1 row)
```

As you can see, the GET DIAGNOSTICS clause gives us detailed information about the activities in the system.

Using cursors to fetch data in chunks

If you execute SQL, the database will calculate the result and send it to your application. Once the entire result set has been sent to the client, the application can continue doing its job. The problem is this: what happens if the result set is so large that it doesn't fit into the memory anymore? What if the database returns 10 billion rows? The client application usually cannot handle so much data at once, and actually, it shouldn't. The solution to this problem is a cursor. The idea behind a cursor is that data is generated only when it is needed (when FETCH is called). Therefore, the application can already start to consume data while it is being generated by the database. On top of that, much less memory is required to perform this operation.

When it comes to PL/pgSQL, cursors also play a major role. Whenever you loop over a result set, PostgreSQL will automatically use a cursor internally. The advantage is that the memory consumption of your applications will be reduced dramatically, and there is hardly a chance of ever running out of memory due to the large amounts of data that are processed. There are various ways to use cursors.

Here is the most simplistic example of using a cursor inside a function:

```
CREATE OR REPLACE FUNCTION c(int)
  RETURNS setof text AS
$$
DECLARE
    v_rec record;
BEGIN
    FOR v_rec IN
        SELECT tablename
        FROM pg_tables
        LIMIT $1
    LOOP
        RETURN NEXT v_rec.tablename;
    END LOOP;
    RETURN;
END;
$$ LANGUAGE 'plpgsql';
```

This code is interesting for two reasons:

- First of all, it is a **set returning function** (**SRF**). It produces an entire column and not just a single row. The way to achieve this is to use the set of variables instead of just the data type. The RETURN NEXT clause will build up the result set until we have reached the end. The RETURN clause will tell PostgreSQL that we want to leave the function and that we have the results.

- The second important issue is that looping over the cursor will automatically create an internal cursor. In other words, there is no need to be afraid that you could potentially run out of memory. PostgreSQL will optimize the query so that it tries to produce the first 10% of the data (defined by the cursor_tuple_fraction variable) as fast as possible.

The query will return something like this (almost random rows basically):

```
test=# SELECT * FROM c(3);
    c
--------------
 t_test
 pg_statistic
 pg_type
(3 rows)
```

In this example, there will simply be a list of random tables. If the result differs on your side, this is somewhat expected.

What you have just seen is, in my opinion, the most frequent and most common way to use implicit cursors in PL/pgSQL.

The following example shows an older mechanism that many people from an Oracle background might know of:

```
CREATE OR REPLACE FUNCTION d(int)
  RETURNS setof text AS
$$
DECLARE
    v_cur refcursor;
    v_data text;
BEGIN
    OPEN v_cur FOR
        SELECT tablename
        FROM pg_tables
        LIMIT $1;
    WHILE true LOOP
        FETCH v_cur INTO v_data;
        IF FOUND THEN
            RETURN NEXT v_data;
```

```
            ELSE
                  RETURN;
            END IF;
        END LOOP;
    END;
    $$ LANGUAGE 'plpgsql';
```

In this example, the cursor is explicitly declared and opened. Inside, the loop data is then explicitly fetched and returned to the caller. Basically, the query does exactly the same thing. It is merely a matter of taste in regard to what syntax developers prefer.

Do you still have the feeling that you don't know enough about cursors yet? There's more; here is a third option to do exactly the same thing:

```
CREATE OR REPLACE FUNCTION e(int)
    RETURNS setof text AS
$$
DECLARE
        v_cur CURSOR (param1 int) FOR
            SELECT tablename
            FROM pg_tables
            LIMIT param1;
        v_data text;
BEGIN
        OPEN v_cur ($1);
        WHILE true LOOP
            FETCH v_cur INTO v_data;
            IF FOUND THEN
                RETURN NEXT v_data;
            ELSE
                  RETURN;
            END IF;
        END LOOP;
    END;
    $$ LANGUAGE 'plpgsql';
```

In this case, the cursor is fed with an integer parameter that comes directly from the function call ($1).

Sometimes, a cursor is not used up by the stored procedure itself but returned for later use. In this case, you can return a simple refcursor as the return value:

```
CREATE OR REPLACE FUNCTION cursor_test(c refcursor)
    RETURNS refcursor AS
$$
BEGIN
```

```
    OPEN c FOR
        SELECT *
        FROM generate_series(1, 10) AS id;
    RETURN c;
END;
$$ LANGUAGE plpgsql;
```

The logic here is quite simple. The name of the cursor is passed to the function. Then, the cursor is opened and returned. The beauty here is that the query behind the cursor can be created on the fly and compiled dynamically.

The application can fetch from the cursor just like from any other application. Here is how it works:

```
test=# BEGIN;
BEGIN
test=# SELECT cursor_test('mytest');
 cursor_test
-------------
 mytest
(1 row)


test=# FETCH NEXT FROM mytest;
 id
----
 1
(1 row)


test=# FETCH NEXT FROM mytest;
 id
----
 2
(1 row)
```

Note that it works only when a transaction block is used. Without an explicit transaction, the cursor will error out.

In this section, we have learned that cursors will only produce data as it is consumed. This holds true for most queries. However, there is a catch to this example; whenever an SRF is used, the entire result has to be materialized. It is not created on the fly but, instead, at once. The reason for this is that SQL must be able to rescan a relation, which is easily possible in the case of a normal table. However, for functions, the situation is different. Therefore, an SRF is always calculated and materialized, making the cursor in this example totally useless. In other words, we need to be careful while writing functions. In some cases, the danger is hidden in the nifty details.

Utilizing composite types

In most other database systems, stored procedures are only used with primitive data types, such as integers, numeric, varchar, and so on. However, PostgreSQL is very different. We can use all the data types that are available to us. This includes primitive, composite, and custom types of data. There are simply no restrictions as far as data types are concerned. To unleash the full power of PostgreSQL, composite types are highly important and are often used by extensions found on the internet. The following example shows how a composite type can be passed to a function and how it can be used internally. Finally, the composite type will be returned again, as shown in the following code block:

```
CREATE TYPE my_cool_type AS (s text, t text);

CREATE FUNCTION f(my_cool_type)
  RETURNS my_cool_type AS
$$
DECLARE
    v_row my_cool_type;
BEGIN
    RAISE NOTICE 'schema: (%) / table: (%)', $1.s, $1.t;

    SELECT schemaname, tablename
    INTO v_row
    FROM pg_tables
    WHERE tablename = trim($1.t)
      AND schemaname = trim($1.s)
    LIMIT 1;

    RETURN v_row;
END;
$$ LANGUAGE 'plpgsql';
```

The main issue here is that you can simply use `$1.field_name` in order to access the composite type. Returning the composite type is not difficult, either.

You just have to assemble the composite type variable on the fly and return it, just like any other data type. You can even easily use arrays or even more complex structures.

The following code shows what PostgreSQL will return:

```
test=# SELECT (f).s, (f).t
FROM   f ('("public", "t_test")'::my_cool_type);
NOTICE:  schema: (public) / table: ( t_test)
   s    |    t
--------+---------
 public | t_test
(1 row)
```

Let's next move on to cover writing triggers in PL/pgSQL.

Writing triggers in PL/pgSQL

Server-side code is especially popular if you want to react to certain events that are happening in the database. A trigger allows you to call a function if an INSERT, UPDATE, DELETE, or TRUNCATE clause happens on a table. The function that is called by the trigger can then modify the data that's changed in your table or simply perform a necessary operation.

In PostgreSQL, triggers have become more powerful over the years, and they now provide a rich set of features:

```
test=# \h CREATE TRIGGER
Command:     CREATE TRIGGER
Description: define a new trigger
Syntax:
CREATE [ OR REPLACE ] [ CONSTRAINT ] TRIGGER name
       { BEFORE | AFTER | INSTEAD OF } { event [ OR ... ] }
    ON table_name
    [ FROM referenced_table_name ]
    [ NOT DEFERRABLE | [ DEFERRABLE ]
    [ INITIALLY IMMEDIATE | INITIALLY DEFERRED ] ]
    [ REFERENCING { { OLD | NEW } TABLE [ AS ] transition_relation_
name } [ ... ] ]
    [ FOR [ EACH ] { ROW | STATEMENT } ]
    [ WHEN ( condition ) ]
    EXECUTE { FUNCTION | PROCEDURE } function_name ( arguments )

where event can be one of:

    INSERT
    UPDATE [ OF column_name [, ... ] ]
    DELETE
    TRUNCATE

URL: https://www.postgresql.org/docs/17/sql-createtrigger.html
```

The first thing to observe is that a trigger is always fired for a table or a view and calls a function. It has a name, and it can happen before or after an event. The beauty of PostgreSQL is that you can have umpteen triggers on a single table. While this will not come as a surprise to hardcore PostgreSQL users, I want to point out that this is not possible in many expensive commercial database engines that are still in use around the world.

If there is more than one trigger on the same table, then the following rule, which was introduced many years ago in PostgreSQL 7.3, will be useful: triggers are fired in alphabetical order. First, all of those BEFORE triggers happen in alphabetical order. Then, PostgreSQL performs the row operation for which the trigger has been fired and continues executing after the triggers in alphabetical order. In other words, the execution order of triggers is absolutely deterministic, and the number of triggers is basically unlimited.

Triggers can modify data before or after the actual modification has happened. In general, this is a good way to verify data and to error out if some custom restrictions are violated.

The following example shows a trigger that is fired in the INSERT clause and that changes the data that's added to the table:

```
CREATE TABLE    t_sensor (
       id              serial,
       ts              timestamp,
       temperature  numeric
);
```

Our table just stores a couple of values. The goal now is to call a function as soon as a row is inserted:

```
CREATE OR REPLACE FUNCTION trig_func()
RETURNS trigger AS
$$
BEGIN
    IF NEW.temperature < -273 THEN
        NEW.temperature := 0;
    END IF;
    RETURN NEW;
END;
$$ LANGUAGE 'plpgsql';
```

As we stated previously, the trigger will always call a function, which allows you to use nicely abstract code. The important thing here is that the trigger function has to return a trigger. To access the row that you are about to insert, you can access the NEW variable.

The INSERT and UPDATE triggers always provide a NEW variable. UPDATE and DELETE will offer a variable called OLD. These variables contain the row that you are about to modify.

In my example, the code checks whether the temperature is too low. If it is and the value is not okay, it is dynamically adjusted. To ensure that the modified row can be used, NEW is simply returned. If there is a second trigger called after this one, the next function call will already see the modified row.

In the next step, the trigger can be created by using the CREATE TRIGGER command:

```
CREATE TRIGGER sensor_trig
BEFORE INSERT ON t_sensor
FOR EACH  ROW
EXECUTE PROCEDURE trig_func();
```

Here is what the trigger will do:

```
test=# INSERT INTO t_sensor (ts,  temperature)
VALUES ('2024-08-04 19:12', -300)
RETURNING *;
 id |          ts          | temperature
----+----------------------+-------------
 1  | 2024-08-04 19:12:00  |  0
(1 row)
INSERT 0 1
```

As you can see, the value has been adjusted correctly. The content of the table shows 0 for the temperature.

If you are using triggers, you should be aware of the fact that a trigger knows a lot about itself. It can access a couple of variables that allow you to write more sophisticated code and, therefore, achieve better abstraction.

Let's drop the trigger first:

```
test=# DROP TRIGGER sensor_trig ON t_sensor;
DROP TRIGGER
```

The trigger is successfully dropped.

Then, a new function can be added:

```
CREATE OR REPLACE FUNCTION trig_demo()
  RETURNS trigger AS
$$
BEGIN
    RAISE NOTICE 'TG_NAME: %', TG_NAME;
    RAISE NOTICE 'TG_RELNAME: %', TG_RELNAME;
    RAISE NOTICE 'TG_TABLE_SCHEMA: %', TG_TABLE_SCHEMA;
    RAISE NOTICE 'TG_TABLE_NAME: %', TG_TABLE_NAME;
    RAISE NOTICE 'TG_WHEN: %', TG_WHEN;
    RAISE NOTICE 'TG_LEVEL: %', TG_LEVEL;
    RAISE NOTICE 'TG_OP: %', TG_OP;
    RAISE NOTICE 'TG_NARGS: %', TG_NARGS;
    -- RAISE NOTICE 'TG_ARGV: %', TG_NAME;
```

```
    RETURN NEW;
END;
$$ LANGUAGE plpgsql;

CREATE TRIGGER sensor_trig
    BEFORE INSERT ON t_sensor
    FOR EACH ROW
    EXECUTE PROCEDURE trig_demo();
```

All of the variables that are used here are predefined and are available by default. All our code does is display them so that we can see their content:

```
test=# INSERT INTO t_sensor (ts, temperature)
VALUES ('2024-08-04 19:12', -300)
RETURNING *;
NOTICE: TG_NAME: demo_trigger
NOTICE: TG_RELNAME: t_sensor
NOTICE: TG_TABLE_SCHEMA: public
NOTICE: TG_TABLE_NAME: t_sensor
NOTICE: TG_WHEN: BEFORE
NOTICE: TG_LEVEL: ROW
NOTICE: TG_OP: INSERT
NOTICE: TG_NARGS: 0
 id |n.      ts              | temperature
----+--------------------+-------------
  2  n| 2024-08-04 19:12:00 | -300
(1 row)
INSERT 0 1
```

What we see here is that the trigger knows its name, the table it has been fired for, and a lot more. To apply similar actions on various tables, these variables help to avoid duplicate code by just writing a single function. This can then be used for all the tables that we are interested in.

So far, we have seen simple row-level triggers, which are fired once per statement. Statement-level triggers have been around for a while already. In a statement trigger, it is possible to make use of transition tables, which contain all the changes that were made:

The following code contains a complete example showing how a transition table can be used:

```
CREATE OR REPLACE FUNCTION transition_trigger()
  RETURNS TRIGGER AS $$
DECLARE
    v_record record;
BEGIN
    IF (TG_OP = 'INSERT') THEN
```

```
        RAISE NOTICE 'new data: ';
        FOR v_record IN SELECT * FROM new_table LOOP
            RAISE NOTICE '%', v_record;
        END LOOP;
    ELSE
        RAISE NOTICE 'old data: ';
        FOR v_record IN SELECT * FROM old_table LOOP
            RAISE NOTICE '%', v_record;
        END LOOP;
    END IF;

    RETURN NULL; -- result is ignored since
                 -- this is an AFTER trigger
END;
$$ LANGUAGE plpgsql;

CREATE TRIGGER transition_test_trigger_ins
    AFTER INSERT ON t_sensor
    REFERENCING NEW TABLE AS new_table
    FOR EACH STATEMENT
    EXECUTE PROCEDURE transition_trigger();

CREATE TRIGGER transition_test_trigger_del
    AFTER DELETE ON t_sensor
    REFERENCING OLD TABLE AS old_table
    FOR EACH STATEMENT
    EXECUTE PROCEDURE transition_trigger();
```

In this case, we need two trigger definitions because we cannot just squeeze everything into just one definition. Inside the trigger function, the transition table is easy to use: it can be accessed just like a normal table.

Let's test the code of the trigger by inserting some data:

```
INSERT INTO t_sensor
SELECT  *, now(), random() * 20
FROM    generate_series(1, 5);
DELETE FROM t_sensor;
```

In my example, the code will simply issue NOTICE for each entry in the transition table:

```
NOTICE: new data:
NOTICE: (1,"2024-08-04 19:47:14.129151",10.4552665632218)
NOTICE: (2,"2024-08-04 19:47:14.129151",12.8670312650502)
NOTICE: (3,"2024-08-04 19:47:14.129151",14.3934494629502)
```

```
NOTICE: (4,"2024-08-04 19:47:14.129151",4.35718866065145)
NOTICE: (5,"2024-08-04 19:47:14.129151",10.9121138229966)
INSERT 0 5
NOTICE: old data:
NOTICE: (1,"2024-08-04 19:47:14.129151",10.4552665632218)
NOTICE: (2,"2024-08-04 19:47:14.129151",12.8670312650502)
NOTICE: (3,"2024-08-04 19:47:14.129151",14.3934494629502)
NOTICE: (4,"2024-08-04 19:47:14.129151",4.35718866065145)
NOTICE: (5,"2024-08-04 19:47:14.129151",10.9121138229966)
DELETE 5
```

Keep in mind that it is not necessarily a good idea to use transition tables for billions of rows. PostgreSQL really is scalable, but at some point, you will see that there are performance implications as well.

Writing stored procedures in PL/pgSQL

Now, let's move on, and learn how to write procedures. In this section, you will learn how to write real stored procedures, which were introduced in PostgreSQL 11. To create a procedure, you have to use CREATE PROCEDURE. The syntax of this command is remarkably similar to CREATE FUNCTION. There are just a few minor differences, which can be seen in the following syntax definition:

```
test=# \h CREATE PROCEDURE
Command:     CREATE PROCEDURE
Description: define a new procedure
Syntax:
CREATE [ OR REPLACE ] PROCEDURE
    name ( [ [ argmode ] [ argname ] argtype
      [ { DEFAULT | = } default_expr ] [, ...] ] )
  { LANGUAGE lang_name
    | TRANSFORM { FOR TYPE type_name } [, ... ]
    | [ EXTERNAL ] SECURITY INVOKER | [ EXTERNAL ] SECURITY DEFINER
    | SET configuration_parameter { TO value | = value | FROM CURRENT
  }
    | AS 'definition'
    | AS 'obj_file', 'link_symbol'
    | sql_body
  } ...

URL: https://www.postgresql.org/docs/17/sql-createprocedure.html
```

The following example shows a stored procedure that runs two transactions. The first transaction is COMMIT and, therefore, creates two tables. The second procedure is ROLLBACK:

```
test=# CREATE PROCEDURE test_proc()
LANGUAGE plpgsql
```

```
AS $$
BEGIN
    CREATE TABLE a (aid int);
    CREATE TABLE b (bid int);
    COMMIT;

    CREATE TABLE c (cid int);
    ROLLBACK;
END;
$$;C
CREATE PROCEDURE
```

As we can see, a procedure can do explicit transaction handling. The idea behind a procedure is to be able to run batch jobs and other operations, which are hard to do in a function.

To run the procedure, you have to use CALL, as shown in the following example (make sure those tables are dropped before in case they still exist):

```
test=# CALL test_proc();
CALL
```

The first two tables were committed. The third table hasn't been created because of the rollback inside the procedure:

```
test=# \d
 List of relations
 Schema | Name | Type  | Owner
--------+------+-------+-------
 public | a    | table | hs
 public | b    | table | hs
(2 rows)
```

Procedures are one of the most important features that were introduced in PostgreSQL 11, and they make a significant contribution to the efficiency of software development.

Introducing PL/Perl

There is a lot more to say about PL/pgSQL. However, not everything can be covered in one book, and some issues are definitely beyond the scope of this book, so it is time to move on to the next procedural language. PL/Perl has been adopted by many people as the ideal language for string crunching. As you might know, Perl is famous for its string manipulation capabilities and is, therefore, still fairly popular after all these years. If you want to use PL/Perl, make sure that you have installed those PostgreSQL packages from your favorite repository (Debian, RPM, and so on).

To enable PL/Perl, you have two choices:

```
test=# CREATE EXTENSION plperl;
CREATE EXTENSION
test=# CREATE EXTENSION plperlu;
CREATE EXTENSION
```

You can deploy trusted or untrusted Perl. If you want both, you have to enable both languages.

To show you how PL/Perl works, I have implemented a function that simply parses an email address and returns true or false. Here is how it works:

```
test=# CREATE OR REPLACE FUNCTION verify_email(text)
RETURNS boolean AS
$$
if ($_[0] =~ /^[a-z0-9.]+@[a-z0-9.-]+$/) {
    return true;
}
return false;
$$ LANGUAGE 'plperl';
CREATE FUNCTION
```

A test parameter is passed to the function. Inside the function, all those input parameters can be accessed using $_. In this example, the regular expression is executed, and the function is returned.

The function can be called, just like any other procedure written in any other language. The following listing shows how the function can be called:

```
test=# SELECT verify_email('hs@cybertec.at');
 verify_email
--------------
 t
(1 row)


test=# SELECT verify_email('totally wrong');
 verify_email
--------------
 f
(1 row)
```

The previous listing shows that the function validates the code correctly. Keep in mind that you cannot load packages and so on if you are inside a trusted function. For example, if you want to use the w command to find words, Perl will internally load utf8.pm, which, of course, is not allowed.

Using PL/Perl for data type abstraction

As stated already in this chapter, functions in PostgreSQL are pretty universal and can be used in many different contexts:

If you want to use functions to improve your data quality, you can use a CREATE DOMAIN clause:

```
test=# \h CREATE DOMAIN
Command:     CREATE DOMAIN
Description: define a new domain
Syntax:
CREATE DOMAIN name [ AS ] data_type
    [ COLLATE collation ]
    [ DEFAULT expression ]
    [ domain_constraint [ ... ] ]

where domain_constraint is:

[ CONSTRAINT constraint_name ]
{ NOT NULL | NULL | CHECK (expression) }

URL: https://www.postgresql.org/docs/17/sql-createdomain.html
```

In this example, the PL/Perl function will be used to create a domain called email, which, in turn, can be used as a data type.

The following code shows how the domain can be created:

```
test=# CREATE DOMAIN email AS text
CHECK (verify_email(VALUE) = true);
CREATE DOMAIN
```

The CREATE DOMAIN command creates the additional type and automatically applies check constraints to make sure that the restriction is consistently used all over the database.

As we mentioned previously, the domain functions just like a normal data type:

```
test=# CREATE TABLE t_email
(
    Id serial,
    Data email
);
CREATE TABLE
```

The Perl function ensures that nothing that violates our checks can be inserted into the database, as the following example demonstrates successfully:

```
test=# INSERT INTO t_email (data)
VALUES ('somewhere@example.com');
INSERT 0 1
test=# INSERT INTO  t_email (data)
VALUES ('somewhere_wrong_example.com');
ERROR:  value  for domain email  violates check constraint "email_
check"
```

Perl might be a good option to do string crunching, but, as always, you have to decide whether you want this code directly in the database or not.

Deciding between PL/Perl and PL/PerlU

So far, the Perl code has not caused any security-related problems because all we did was use regular expressions. The question here is, what if somebody tries to do something nasty inside the Perl function?

As we've stated already, PL/Perl will simply error out, as you can see in the next listing:

```
test=# CREATE OR REPLACE FUNCTION test_security()
RETURNS boolean AS
$$
use strict;
my $fp = open("/etc/password", "r");
return false;
$$ LANGUAGE 'plperl';
ERROR:  'open' trapped by operation mask  at line
CONTEXT:  compilation of PL/Perl function "test_security"
```

The listing shows that PL/Perl will complain as soon as you try to create the function, and an error will be displayed instantly.

If you really want to run untrusted code in Perl, you have to use PL/PerlU, as shown in the following code block:

```
test=# CREATE OR REPLACE FUNCTION first_line()
RETURNS text AS
$$
open(my $fh, '<:encoding(UTF-8)', "/etc/passwd")
    or elog(NOTICE, "Could not open file '/etc/passwd': $!");
my $row = <$fh>;
close($fh);
return $row;
$$ LANGUAGE plperlu;
```

```
CREATE FUNCTION
```

The procedure stays the same. It returns a string. However, it is allowed to do everything. The only difference is that the function is marked as `plperlu`.

The result is somewhat unsurprising:

```
test=# SELECT first_line();
 first_line
---------------------------------
 root:x:0:0:root:/root:/bin/bash+
(1 row)
```

The first line will be displayed as expected.

What is important to discuss in the next section is to actually apply our knowledge about the SPI.

Making use of the SPI interface

Once in a while, your Perl procedure has to carry out some database work. Remember, the function is part of the database connection. Therefore, it is pointless to actually create a database connection. To talk to the database, the PostgreSQL server infrastructure provides the **Server Programming Interface** (**SPI**), which is a C interface that you can use to talk to database internals. All procedural languages that help you to run server-side code use this interface to expose the functionality. PL/Perl does the same, and in this section, you will learn how to use the Perl wrapper around the SPI interface.

The most important thing that you might want to do is simply run SQL and retrieve the number of rows that have been fetched. The `spi_exec_query` function is here to do exactly that. The first parameter that's passed to the function is the `query` parameter. The second parameter has the number of rows that you actually want to retrieve. For simplicity, I decided to fetch all of them. The following code shows an example of this:

```
test=# CREATE OR REPLACE FUNCTION spi_sample(int)
RETURNS void AS
$$
my $rv = spi_exec_query(
    "SELECT * FROM generate_series(1, $_[0])",
    $_[0]
);
elog(NOTICE, "rows fetched: " . $rv->{processed});
elog(NOTICE, "status: " . $rv->{status});
return;
$$ LANGUAGE plperl;
```

The SPI will execute the query and display the number of rows. The important thing here is that all of the stored procedure languages provide a means to send log messages. In the case of PL/Perl, this function is called `elog`, which takes two parameters. The first one defines the importance of the message (`INFO`, `NOTICE`, `WARNING`, `ERROR`, and so on), and the second parameter contains the actual message.

The following message shows what the query returns:

```
test=# SELECT spi_sample(9);
NOTICE:   rows   fetched: 9
NOTICE:   status: SPI_OK_SELECT
 spi_sample
------------
(1 row)
```

The call to the SPI works out nicely, and the status is displayed.

Using the SPI for set-returning functions

In many cases, you don't just want to execute some SQL and forget about it. In most cases, a procedure will loop over the result and do something with it. The following example shows how you can loop over the output of a query. On top of that, I decided to beef up the example a bit and make the function return a composite data type. Working with composite types in Perl is very easy because you can simply stuff the data into a hash and return it.

The `return_next` function will gradually build up the result set until the function is terminated with a simple `return` statement.

The example in the following code generates a table consisting of random values:

```
CREATE TYPE random_type AS (a float8, b float8);

CREATE OR REPLACE FUNCTION spi_srf_perl(int)
  RETURNS setof random_type AS
$$
my $rv = spi_query(
    "SELECT random() AS a, random() AS b
     FROM generate_series(1, $_[0])"
);
while (defined (my $row = spi_fetchrow($rv))) {
    elog(NOTICE, "data: " . $row->{a} . " / " . $row->{b});
    return_next({a => $row->{a}, b => $row->{b}});
}
return;
$$ LANGUAGE plperl;
CREATE FUNCTION
```

First, the `spi_query` function is executed, and a loop using the `spi_fetchrow` function is started. Inside the loop, the composite type will be assembled and stuffed into the result set.

As expected, the function will return a set of random values:

```
test=# SELECT * FROM  spi_srf_perl(3);
NOTICE:  data:  0.154673356097192 / 0.278830723837018
CONTEXT:  PL/Perl function "spi_srf_perl"
NOTICE:  data:  0.615888888947666 / 0.632620786316693
CONTEXT:  PL/Perl function "spi_srf_perl"
NOTICE:  data:  0.910436692181975 / 0.753427186980844
CONTEXT:  PL/Perl function "spi_srf_perl"
   a_col              |  b_col
--------------------+--------------------
 0.154673356097192  | 0.278830723837018
 0.615888888947666  | 0.632620786316693
 0.910436692181975  | 0.753427186980844
(3 rows)
```

Keep in mind that set-returning functions have to be materialized so that the entire result set can be stored in memory.

Escaping in PL/Perl and support functions

So far, we have only used integers, so SQL injection or special table names were not an issue. Additionally, the following list contains a set of functions that are available to write server-side code:

- `quote_literal`: This returns a string quote as a string literal
- `quote_nullable`: This quotes a string
- `quote_ident`: This quotes SQL identifiers (object names, and so on)
- `decode_bytea`: This decodes a PostgreSQL byte array field
- `encode_bytea`: This encodes data and turns it into a byte array
- `encode_literal_array`: This encodes an array of literals
- `encode_typed_literal`: This converts a Perl variable into the value of the data type that's passed as a second argument and returns a string representation of this value
- `encode_array_constructor`: This returns the content of the referenced array as a string in array constructor format
- `looks_like_number`: This returns `true` if a string looks like a number
- `is_array_ref`: This returns `true` if something is an array reference

These functions are always available, and they can be called directly without having to include a library.

Sharing data across function calls

Sometimes, it is necessary to share data across calls. The infrastructure has the means to do that. In Perl, a hash can be used to store whatever data is needed. Take a look at the following example:

```
CREATE FUNCTION perl_shared(text) RETURNS int AS
$$
if (!defined $_SHARED{$_[0]}) {
    $_SHARED{$_[0]} = 0;
} else {
    $_SHARED{$_[0]}++;
}
return $_SHARED{$_[0]};
$$ LANGUAGE plperl;
```

The $_SHARED variable will be initialized with 0 as soon as we figure out that the key that's been passed to the function is not there yet. For every other call, 1 is added to the counter, leaving us with the following output:

```
test=# SELECT perl_shared('some_key'
FROM  generate_series(1, 3);
 perl_shared
-------------
           0
           1
           2
(3 rows)
```

In the case of a more complex statement, the developer usually doesn't know what order the functions will be called in. It is important to keep that in mind. In most cases, you cannot rely on an execution order.

Writing triggers in Perl

Every stored procedure language that is shipped with the core of PostgreSQL allows you to write triggers in that language. The same, of course, applies to Perl. Since the length of this chapter is limited, I have decided not to include an example of a trigger written in Perl but instead to point you to the official PostgreSQL documentation: https://www.postgresql.org/docs/current/plperl-triggers.html.

Basically, writing a trigger in Perl doesn't differ from writing one in PL/pgSQL. All predefined variables are in place, and as far as return values are concerned, the rules apply in every stored procedure language.

Introducing PL/Python

If you don't happen to be a Perl expert, PL/Python might be the right thing for you. Python has been part of the PostgreSQL infrastructure for a long time and is, therefore, a solid, well-tested implementation.

When it comes to PL/Python, there is one thing to be mindful of: PL/Python is only available as an untrusted language. From a security point of view, it is important to keep that in mind at all times. Note that back in the old days, we used to support Python 2. However, those days are long gone. From now on, it will only be Python 3.

To enable PL/Python, you can run the following line from your command line and test the name of the database that you want to use with PL/Python:

```
test=# CREATE LANGUAGE plpython3u;
CREATE EXTENSION
```

Once the language is enabled, it is possible to write code.

Alternatively, you can use a `CREATE LANGUAGE` clause. Also, keep in mind that in order to use server-side languages, PostgreSQL packages that contain those languages are needed (`postgresql-plpython-$(VERSIONNUMBER)` and so on).

Writing simple PL/Python code

In this section, you will learn how to write simple Python procedures. The example that we'll discuss here is quite simple: if you are visiting a client by car in Austria, you can deduct 0.42 euros per kilometer in expenses in order to reduce your income tax. So, what the function does is take the number of kilometers and return the amount of money that we can deduct from our tax bill. Here is how it works:

```
CREATE OR REPLACE FUNCTION calculate_deduction(km float)
RETURNS numeric AS
$$
if km <= 0:
    plpy.error('invalid number of kilometers')
else:
    return km * 0.42
$$ LANGUAGE plpython3u;
```

The function ensures that only positive values are accepted. Finally, the result is calculated and returned. As you can see, the way that a Python function is passed to PostgreSQL doesn't really differ from Perl or PL/pgSQL.

Using the SPI interface

Like all procedural languages, PL/Python gives you access to the SPI interface.

The following example shows how numbers can be added up:

```
CREATE FUNCTION add_numbers(rows_desired integer)
RETURNS integer AS
$$
mysum = 0
cursor = plpy.cursor("SELECT * FROM generate_series(1, %d) AS id" %
(rows_desired))
while True:
    rows = cursor.fetch(rows_desired)
    if not rows:
        break
    for row in rows:
        mysum += row['id']
return mysum
$$ LANGUAGE plpython3u;
```

When you try this example out, make sure that the call to the cursor is actually a single line. Python is all about indentation, so it does make a difference if your code consists of one or two lines.

Once the cursor has been created, we can loop over it and add up those numbers. The columns inside those rows can easily be referenced using column names.

Calling the function will return the desired result:

```
test=# SELECT add_numbers(10);
 add_numbers
-------------
          55
(1 row)
```

If you want to inspect the result set of a SQL statement, PL/Python offers various functions, allowing you to retrieve more information from the result. Again, those functions are wrappers around what SPI offers at the C level.

The following function inspects a result more closely:

```
CREATE OR REPLACE FUNCTION result_diag(rows_desired integer)
RETURNS integer AS
$$
rv = plpy.execute("SELECT * FROM generate_series(1, %d) AS id" %
(rows_desired))
plpy.notice(rv.nrows())
```

```
plpy.notice(rv.status())
plpy.notice(rv.colnames())
plpy.notice(rv.coltypes())
plpy.notice(rv.coltypmods())
return 0
$$ LANGUAGE plpython3u;
```

Let's review these functions:

- The `nrows()` function will display the number of rows

- The `status()` function tells us whether everything worked out fine

- The `colnames()` function returns a list of columns

- The `coltypes()` function returns the object IDs of the data types in the result set

23 is the internal number of integers, as shown in the following code:

```
test=# SELECT typname FROM pg_type WHERE oid = 23;
 typname
---------
  int4
(1 row)
```

Then comes `typmod`. Consider something like `varchar(20)`: the configuration part of the type is what `typmod` is all about.

Finally, there is a function to return the entire thing as a string for debugging purposes. Calling the function will return the following result:

```
test=# SELECT result_diag(3);
NOTICE:   3
NOTICE:   5
NOTICE:   ['id']
NOTICE:   [23]
NOTICE:   [-1]
 result_diag
-------------
       0
(1 row)
```

The listing shows what our diagnosis function returns. There are many more functions in the SPI interface that can help you execute SQL.

Handling errors

Once in a while, you might have to catch an error. Of course, this is also possible in Python. The following example shows how this works:

```
CREATE OR REPLACE FUNCTION trial_error()
RETURNS text AS
$$
try:
    rv = plpy.execute("SELECT surely_a_syntax_error")
except plpy.SPIError:
    return "we caught the error"
else:
    return "all fine"
$$ LANGUAGE plpython3u;
```

You can use a normal `try` or `except` block, and access `plpy` to treat the error that you want to catch. The function can then return normally without destroying your transaction, as follows:

```
test=# SELECT trial_error();
 trial_error
--------------------
 we caught the error
(1 row)
```

Remember, PL/Python has full access to the internals of PostgreSQL. Therefore, it can also expose all kinds of errors in your procedure. Here is an example:

```
except spiexceptions.DivisionByZero:
  return "found a division by zero"
except spiexceptions.UniqueViolation:
  return "found a unique violation"
except plpy.SPIError, e:
  return "other error, SQLSTATE %s" % e.sqlstate
```

The code shows how various Python errors can be caught. Catching errors in Python is really easy and can help prevent your functions from failing.

In this section, you have learned about Python error handling. In the next section, we will dive a bit deeper and see how we can help the optimizer.

Improving functions

So far, you have seen how to write basic functions and triggers in various languages. Of course, many more languages are supported. Some of the most prominent ones are PL/R (R is a powerful statistics package) and PL/v8 (which is based on the Google JavaScript engine). However, those languages are beyond the scope of this chapter (regardless of their usefulness).

In this section, we will focus on improving the performance of a function. There are a few ways by which we can speed up processing:

- Reducing the number of function calls
- Using cached plans
- Giving hints to the optimizer

In this section, all three of these topics will be discussed. Let's get started with reducing the number of function calls and see how this can be done.

Reducing the number of function calls

In many cases, performance is bad because functions are called way too often. In my opinion—and I cannot stress this point enough—calling things too often is the main reason for bad performance. When creating a function, you can choose from three types: **volatile**, **stable**, and **immutable**. Here is an example of those three types of functions in action:

```
test=# SELECT random(), random();
       random       |      random
--------------------+-------------------
 0.276252629235387  | 0.710661871358752
(1 row)


test=# SELECT now(), now();
             now            |             now
----------------------------  --+----------------------------
  2024-10-20 16:23:40.960+02 | 2024-10-20 16:23:40.960+02
(1 row)


test=# SELECT pi();
      pi
-----------------
 3.14159265358979
(1 row)
```

A volatile function means that the function cannot be optimized away. It has to be executed over and over again. A volatile function can also be the reason why a certain index is not used. By default, every function is considered to be volatile.

A stable function will always return the same data within the same transaction. It can be optimized and calls can be removed. The now() function is a good example of a stable function; within the same transaction, it returns the same data.

Immutable functions are the gold standard because they allow for most optimizations as they always return the same result if they are given the same input. As a first step to optimizing functions, always make sure that they are marked correctly by adding volatile, stable, or immutable to the end of the definition.

In the next subsection, you will learn about cached plans.

Using cached plans

In PostgreSQL, a query is executed using four stages:

1. **Parser**: This checks the syntax.
2. **Rewrite system**: This takes care of rules.
3. **Optimizer/planner**: This optimizes the query.
4. **Executor**: This executes the plan that is provided by the planner.

If the query is short, the first three steps are relatively time-consuming compared to the real execution time. Therefore, it makes sense to cache execution plans. PL/pgSQL basically does all the plan caching for you automatically behind the scenes. You don't have to worry about it. PL/Perl and PL/Python will give you the choice.

The SPI interface provides functions so that you can handle and run prepared queries, so the programmer has a choice regarding whether a query should be prepared or not. In the case of long queries, it actually makes sense to use unprepared queries. Short queries should always be prepared in order to reduce internal overheads.

Assigning costs to functions

From the optimizer's point of view, a function is basically just like an operator. PostgreSQL will also treat the costs in the same way as if it were a standard operator. The problem is this: adding two numbers is usually cheaper than intersecting costlines using a PostGIS-provided function. The thing is that the optimizer doesn't know whether a function is cheap or expensive.

Fortunately, we can tell the optimizer to make functions cheaper or more expensive. Here is the syntax of CREATE FUNCTION:

```
test=# \h CREATE FUNCTION
Command: CREATE FUNCTION
Description: Define a new function
Syntax:
```

```
CREATE [ OR REPLACE ] FUNCTION
...
    | COST   execution_cost
    | ROWS   result_rows
...
```

The COST parameter indicates how much more expensive than a standard operator your operator really is. It is a multiplier for cpu_operator_cost and is not a static value. In general, the default value is 100 unless the function has been written in C. Now that we have learned all about functions, let's explore more about them in the following section.

Using functions for various purposes

In PostgreSQL, stored procedures can be used for pretty much everything. In this chapter, you have already learned about the CREATE DOMAIN clause and so on, but it is also possible to create your own operators, type casts, and even collations.

In this section, you will see how a simple type cast can be created and how it can be used to your advantage. To define a type cast, consider taking a look at the CREATE CAST clause. The syntax of this command is shown in the following code:

```
test=# \h CREATE CAST
Command:     CREATE CAST
Description: define a new cast
Syntax:
CREATE CAST (source_type AS target_type)
    WITH FUNCTION function_name [ (argument_type [, ...]) ]
    [ AS ASSIGNMENT | AS IMPLICIT ]

CREATE CAST (source_type AS target_type)
    WITHOUT FUNCTION
    [ AS ASSIGNMENT | AS IMPLICIT ]

CREATE CAST (source_type AS target_type)
    WITH INOUT
    [ AS ASSIGNMENT | AS IMPLICIT ]

URL: https://www.postgresql.org/docs/17/sql-createcast.html
```

Using this stuff is very simple. You simply tell PostgreSQL which procedure it is supposed to call in order to cast whatever type to your desired data type.

In standard PostgreSQL, you cannot cast an IP address to a Boolean. Therefore, it makes for a good example.

First, the stored procedure has to be defined:

```
CREATE FUNCTION inet_to_boolean(inet)
RETURNS boolean AS
$$
BEGIN
    RETURN true;
END;
$$ LANGUAGE plpgsql;
```

For simplicity, it returns true. However, you can use any code in any language to do the actual transformation.

In the next step, it is already possible to define the CAST type:

```
CREATE CAST (inet  AS boolean)
WITH FUNCTION inet_to_boolean(inet) AS IMPLICIT;
```

The first thing we need to do is tell PostgreSQL that we want to cast inet to boolean. Then, the function is listed, and we tell PostgreSQL that we prefer an implicit cast.

It is a simple and straightforward process, and we can test the cast as follows:

```
test=# SELECT '192.168.0.34'::inet::boolean;
 bool
------
 t
(1 row)
```

The type cast was successful.

The same logic can also be applied to define collations. Again, a stored procedure can be used to perform whatever the collation needs to do:

```
test=# \h CREATE COLLATION
Command:     CREATE COLLATION
Description: define a new collation
Syntax:
CREATE COLLATION [ IF NOT EXISTS ] name (
    [ LOCALE = locale, ]
    [ LC_COLLATE = lc_collate, ]
    [ LC_CTYPE = lc_ctype, ]
    [ PROVIDER = provider, ]
    [ DETERMINISTIC = boolean, ]
    [ RULES = rules, ]
    [ VERSION = version ]
```

```
)
CREATE COLLATION [ IF NOT EXISTS ] name FROM existing_collation

URL: https://www.postgresql.org/docs/17/sql-createcollation.html
```

The syntax of CREATE COLLATION is really simple. While creating collations is possible, it is still one of those features that is rarely used.

Stored procedures and functions offer a lot more. Many things are possible and can be done nicely and efficiently.

Summary

In this chapter, you learned how to write stored procedures. After a theoretical introduction, our attention was focused on some selected features of PL/pgSQL. In addition to that, you learned how to use PL/Perl and PL/Python, which are two important languages that PostgreSQL provides. Of course, there are many more languages available. However, due to the limitations of the scope of this book, they could not be covered in detail. If you want to know more, check out the following website: https://wiki.postgresql.org/wiki/PL_Matrix. We also learned how to improve function calls and how we can use them for various other purposes to speed up applications and do a lot more.

In *Chapter 8*, *Managing PostgreSQL Security*, you will learn about PostgreSQL security. You will learn how to manage users and permissions in general, and on top of that, you will also learn about network security.

Managing PostgreSQL Security

8

In *Chapter 7, Writing Stored Procedures*, we learned about stored procedures and writing server-side code. After being introduced to many other important topics, it is now time to shift to PostgreSQL security as well as certification-related issues. Here, we will learn how to secure a server and configure permissions to avoid security breaches. Security is an important aspect and is getting increasingly important as applications are exposed to more and more internal, as well as external, threats.

The following topics will be covered in this chapter:

- Managing network security
- Digging into row-level security
- Inspecting and handling permissions
- Reassigning objects and dropping users

By the end of the chapter, we will be able to professionally configure PostgreSQL security. Let's now start with managing network security.

Managing network security

Security is a complex thing, and we have to approach this topic systematically to ensure success. One of the key aspects is **network security**, which is the first topic we want to focus on. However, before we dive head first into network security, it makes sense to consider a mental model for managing PostgreSQL security in general.

Here is my personal mental model, which has served me well over the years:

- **Bind addresses**: The `listen_addresses` in the `postgresql.conf` file
- **Host-based access control**: The `pg_hba.conf` file
- **Instance-level permissions**: Users, roles, database creation, login, and replication
- **Database-level permissions**: Connecting and creating schemas, and more

- **Schema-level permissions**: Using a schema and creating objects inside a schema
- **Table-level permissions**: Selecting, inserting, updating, and more
- **Column-level permissions**: Allowing or restricting access to columns
- **Row-Level Security** (**RLS**): Restricting access to rows

In order to read a value (a cell in a table), PostgreSQL has to ensure that we have sufficient permissions on every level. The entire chain of permissions has to be correct. My little model has served me well over the years in debugging security-related problems over and over again in real-world applications. It will hopefully help you to use a more systematic approach, thereby leading to more security.

Understanding bind addresses and connections

When configuring a PostgreSQL server, one of the first things that you need to do is to define remote access. By default, PostgreSQL does not accept remote connections. The important thing here is that PostgreSQL does not even reject the connection, because it simply does not listen on the port. If we try to connect, the error message will actually come from the operating system, because PostgreSQL does not care at all.

Assuming that there is a database server using the default configuration on 192.168.0.123, the following will happen:

```
[hs@test ~]$ telnet 192.168.0.123 5432
Trying 192.168.0.123...
telnet: connect to address 192.168.0.123: Connection refused
telnet: Unable to connect to remote host
```

Telnet (a really old tool to initiate low-level communication over **Transmission Control Protocol** (**TCP**)) tries to create a connection on port 5432 and is instantly rejected by the remote box. From the outside, it looks as if PostgreSQL is not running at all.

The key to success can be found in the postgresql.conf file:

```
# - Connection Settings -
# listen_addresses = 'localhost'
  # what IP address(es) to listen on;
  # comma-separated list of addresses;
  # defaults to 'localhost'; use '*' for all
  # (change requires restart)
```

The listen_addresses setting will tell PostgreSQL which addresses to listen on. Technically speaking, those addresses are bind addresses. What does that actually mean? Suppose that we have four network cards in our machine. We can listen on, say, three of those **Internet Protocol** (**IP**) addresses. PostgreSQL takes requests to those three cards into account and does not listen on the fourth one. The port is simply closed.

> **Setting listen_addresses correctly**
>
> We have to put our server's IP address into `listen_addresses`, not the IPs of the clients.

If you put * in PostgreSQL, you will listen to every IP address assigned to your machine.

> **Make sure your server is restarted**
>
> Keep in mind that changing `listen_addresses` requires a PostgreSQL service restart. It cannot be changed on the fly without a restart.

However, there are more settings related to connection management that are very important to understand. They are as follows:

```
#port = 5432
                    # (change requires restart)
max_connections = 100
                    # (change requires restart)
#superuser_reserved_connections = 3
                    # (change requires restart)
#unix_socket_directories = '/tmp'
                    # comma-separated list
                    # of directories
                    # (change requires restart)
#unix_socket_group = ''
                    # (change requires restart)
#unix_socket_permissions = 0777
                    # begin with 0 to use octal notation
                    # (change requires restart)
```

First of all, PostgreSQL listens to a single TCP port, the default value of which is 5432. Keep in mind that PostgreSQL will listen on a single port only. Whenever a request comes in, the postmaster will fork and create a new process to handle the connection. By default, up to 100 normal connections are allowed. On top of that, three additional connections are reserved for superusers. This means that we can either have 97 connections plus 3 superusers, or 100 superuser connections. To get started, we will first take a look at connections and performance.

> **Note**
>
> Note that these connection-related settings will also need a restart. The reason for this is that a static amount of memory is allocated to shared memory, which cannot be changed on the fly.

Inspecting connections and performance

While doing PostgreSQL consulting, many people ask me whether raising the connection limit will have an impact on database performance in general. The answer is not much, as there is always some overhead due to context switches. It makes little difference as to how many connections there are. However, what does make a difference is the number of open snapshots. The more open snapshots there are, the greater the overhead on the database side. In other words, we can increase `max_connections` cheaply. In the next section, we will learn how to avoid TCP for security reasons.

> **Inspecting the impact of max_connections on performance**
>
> If you are interested in some real-world data, consider taking a look at `https://www.cybertec-postgresql.com/max_connections-performance-impacts/`.

Living in a world without TCP

In some cases, we might not want to use a network. It often happens that a database will only talk to a local application anyway. Maybe our PostgreSQL database has been shipped along with our application, or maybe we just don't want the risk of using a network. In this case, Unix sockets are what you need. Unix sockets are a network-free means of communication. Your application can connect through a Unix socket locally without exposing anything to the outside world.

What we need, however, is a directory. By default, PostgreSQL will use the `/tmp` directory. However, if more than one database server is running per machine, each one will need a separate data directory to live in.

Apart from security, there are various reasons why not using a network might be a good idea. One of these reasons is performance. Using Unix sockets is a lot faster than going through the loopback device (`127.0.0.1`). If that sounds surprising, don't worry; it is for many people. However, the overhead of a real network connection should not be underestimated if you are only running very small queries.

To depict what this really means, I have included a simple benchmark.

We will create a `script.sql` file. This is a simple script that creates a random number and selects it. It is the most simplistic statement possible. There is nothing simpler than fetching a number.

So, let's run this simple benchmark on a normal laptop. To do so, we shall write a small thing called `script.sql`. It will be used by the following benchmark:

```
[hs@linux ~]$ cat /tmp/script.sql
SELECT 1
```

Then, we can simply run `pgbench` to execute the SQL statement over and over again. The `-f` option allows us to pass the name of the SQL to the script. `-c 10` means that we want 10 concurrent connections to be active for five seconds (`-T 5`). The benchmark is running as the `postgres` user and is supposed to use the postgres database, which should be there by default. Note that the following examples will work on **Red Hat Enterprise Linux** (**RHEL**) derivatives. Debian-based systems will use different paths:

```
[hs@linux ~]$ pgbench -f /tmp/script.sql
                -c 10 -T 5
                -U postgres postgres 2> /dev/null
transaction type: /tmp/script.sql
scaling factor: 1
query mode: simple
number of clients: 10
number of threads: 1
duration: 5 s
number of transactions actually processed: 871407
latency average = 0.057 ms
tps = 174278.158426 (including connections establishing)
tps = 174377.935625 (excluding connections establishing)
```

As we can see, no hostname is passed to pgbench, so the tool connects locally to the Unix socket and runs the script as fast as possible. On this 4-core Intel box, the system was able to achieve around 174,000 transactions per second.

What happens if the -h localhost is added? The performance will change, as you can see in the following code snippet:

```
[hs@linux ~]$ pgbench -f /tmp/script.sql
                -h localhost -c 10 -T 5
                -U postgres postgres 2> /dev/null
transaction type: /tmp/script.sql
scaling factor: 1
query mode: simple
number of clients: 10
number of threads: 1
duration: 5 s
number of transactions actually processed: 535251
latency average = 0.093 ms
tps = 107000.872598 (including connections establishing)
tps = 107046.943632 (excluding connections establishing)
```

The throughput will drop like a stone to around 107000 transactions per second. The difference is clearly related to the networking overhead.

> **Handling parallel dumps**
>
> By using the -j option (the number of threads assigned to pgbench), we can squeeze some more transactions out of our systems. However, it does not change the overall picture of the benchmark in our situation. In other tests, it does because pgbench can be a real bottleneck if you don't provide enough CPU power.

As we can see, networking can not only be a security issue but also a performance issue. However, performance is not the only important aspect. As we are talking primarily about security here, the next piece of the puzzle is all about pg_hba.conf.

Managing the pg_hba.conf file

After configuring bind addresses, we can move on to the next level. The pg_hba.conf file will tell PostgreSQL how to authenticate people coming over the network. In general, the pg_hba.conf file entries have the following layout:

```
# local DATABASE USER METHOD [OPTIONS]
# host DATABASE USER ADDRESS METHOD [OPTIONS]
# hostssl DATABASE USER ADDRESS METHOD [OPTIONS]
# hostnossl DATABASE USER ADDRESS METHOD [OPTIONS]
# hostgssenc DATABASE USER ADDRESS METHOD [OPTIONS]
# hostnogssenc DATABASE USER ADDRESS METHOD [OPTIONS]
```

There are several types of rules that can be put into the pg_hba.conf file:

- local: This can be used to configure local Unix socket connections.

- host: This can be used for **Secure Socket Layer (SSL)** and non-SSL connections.

- hostssl: This is only valid for SSL connections. To make use of this option, SSL must be compiled into the server, which is the case if we are using prepackaged versions of PostgreSQL. In addition to that, ssl = on has to be set in the postgresql.conf file. This file is called when the server is started.

- hostnossl: This works for non-SSL connections.

- hostgssenc: This rule defines that a connection is only created when **Generic Security Service Application Program Interface (GSSAPI)** encryption can be done. Otherwise, it will fail.

- hostnogssenc: This rule is the exact opposite of hostgssenc.

A list of rules can be incorporated into the pg_hba.conf file. Here is an example:

```
# TYPE DATABASE USER ADDRESS METHOD
# "local" is for Unix domain socket connections only
local all all trust
```

```
# IPv4 local connections:
host    all    all    127.0.0.1/32    trust
# IPv6 local connections:
host    all    all    ::1/128        trust
```

You can see three simple rules:

- The local record says that all users from local Unix sockets for all databases are to be trusted. The `trust` method means that no password has to be sent to the server and people can log in directly.

- The other two rules say that the same applies to connections from the `127.0.0.1` localhost and `::1/128`, which is an IPv6 address.

As connecting without a password is certainly not the best choice for remote access, PostgreSQL provides various authentication methods that can be used to configure the `pg_hba.conf` file flexibly. Here is a list of possible authentication methods:

- `trust`: This allows authentication without providing a password. The desired user has to be available on the PostgreSQL side.

- `reject`: The connection will be rejected.

- `md5` and `password`: The connections can be created using a password. `md5` means that the password is encrypted when it is sent over the wire. In the case of passwords, the credentials are sent in plaintext, which should no longer be done on a modern system.

> **Note**
> `md5` is no longer considered safe. You should use `scram-sha-256` instead of PostgreSQL 10 and beyond.

- `scram-sha-256`: This setting is the successor of `md5` and uses a far more secure hash than the previous version.

- `gss` and `sspi`: They use GSSAPI or **Security Support Provider Interface** (**SSPI**) authentication. This is only possible for TCP/IP connections. The idea here is to allow for single sign-on.

- `ident`: This obtains the operating system username of the client by contacting the `ident` server of the client and checking whether it matches the requested database username.

- `peer`: Suppose we are logged in as `abc` on Unix. If `peer` is enabled, we can only log in to PostgreSQL as `abc`. If we try to change the username, we will be rejected. The beauty of this is that `abc` won't need a password in order to authenticate. The idea here is that only the database administrator can log in to the database on a Unix system and not somebody else who just has the password or a Unix account on the same machine. This only works for local connections.

- `pam`: This uses the **Pluggable Authentication Modules** (**PAM**) library. This is especially important if you want to use a means of authentication that is not provided by PostgreSQL out of the box. To use PAM, create a file called `/etc/pam.d/postgresql` on your Linux system and put the desired PAM that you are planning to use into the `config` file. Using the PAM library, we can even authenticate against less common components. However, it can also be used to connect to Active Directory.

- `ldap`: This configuration allows you to authenticate using the **Lightweight Directory Access Protocol** (**LDAP**). Note that PostgreSQL will only ask LDAP for authentication; if a user is present only on the LDAP side and not on the PostgreSQL side, you cannot log in. You should also note that PostgreSQL has to know where your LDAP server is. All of this information has to be stored in the `pg_hba.conf` file, as outlined in the official documentation at `https://www.postgresql.org/docs/devel/auth-ldap.html`.

- `radius`: The **Remote Authentication Dial-In User Service** (**RADIUS**) is a means of performing single sign-on. Again, parameters are passed using configuration options.

- `cert`: This authentication method uses SSL client certificates to perform authentication, and therefore, it is possible only if SSL is used. The advantage here is that no password has to be sent. The `CN` attribute of the certificate will be compared to the requested database username and, if they match, the login will be allowed. A map can be used to allow user mapping.

Rules can simply be listed one after the other. The important thing here is that the order does make a difference, as shown in the following example:

```
host    all    all    192.168.1.0/24     scram-sha-256
host    all    all    192.168.1.54/32    reject
```

When PostgreSQL walks through the `pg_hba.conf` file, it will use the first rule that matches. So, if our request is coming from `192.168.1.54`, the first rule will always match before we make it to the second one. This means that `192.168.1.54` will be able to log in if the password and username are correct; therefore, the second rule is pointless.

If we want to exclude the IP, we need to ensure that those two rules are swapped. In the next section, we will take a look at SSL and how you can use it easily.

Inspecting the content of pg_hba.conf via SQL

Now that we have seen how to configure the `pg_hba.conf` file, it is important to understand how we can actually check its content via SQL. Why is this feature relevant? In a modern environment that is often containerized or fully virtualized, it is not really possible to have access to the filesystem as was common many years ago. Therefore, this information has to be exposed in a way that makes data accessible without the need to run shell commands. In the latest version, a new view has been added that closes this gap and shows us exactly what those pg_hba.conf settings look like:

```
test=# \d pg_hba_file_rules
          View "pg_catalog.pg_hba_file_rules"
    Column     |  Type   | Collation | Nullable | Default
---------------+---------+-----------+----------+---------
 rule_number   | integer |           |          |
 file_name     | text    |           |          |
 line_number   | integer |           |          |
 type          | text    |           |          |
 database      | text[]  |           |          |
 user_name     | text[]  |           |          |
 address       | text    |           |          |
 netmask       | text    |           |          |
 auth_method   | text    |           |          |
 options       | text[]  |           |          |
 error         | text    |           |          |
```

Basically, the content is quite straightforward and mimics what we have just seen in the previous section. The following listing shows what the content might look like:

```
test=# \x
Expanded display is on.
test=# SELECT * FROM pg_hba_file_rules;
-[ RECORD 1 ]---------------------------------------
rule_number | 1
file_name   | /Users/hs/db17/pg_hba.conf
line_number | 117
type        | local
database    | {all}
user_name   | {all}
address     |
netmask     |
auth_method | trust
options     |
error       |
-[ RECORD 2 ]---------------------------------------
rule_number | 2
file_name   | /Users/hs/db17/pg_hba.conf
line_number | 119
type        | host
database    | {all}
user_name   | {all}
```

```
address     | 127.0.0.1
netmask     | 255.255.255.255
auth_method | trust
options     |
error       |
```

What is really nice here is that we can not only see the position of the file but also things such as line numbers and errors. What we have here is a comprehensive and easy-to-digest overview that can give us excellent insights.

Handling SSL

PostgreSQL allows the transfer between the server and the client to be encrypted. Encryption is highly beneficial, especially if we are communicating over long distances. SSL offers a simple and secure way to ensure that nobody is able to listen to your communication.

In this section, we will learn how to set up SSL:

1. The first thing to do is to set the `ssl` parameter to `on` in the `postgresql.conf` file when the server starts. In the next step, we can put SSL certificates into the `$PGDATA` directory. If we don't want the certificates to be in some other directory, we need to change the following parameters:

    ```
    #ssl_cert_file = 'server.crt'
            # (change requires restart)
    #ssl_key_file = 'server.key'
            # (change requires restart)
    #ssl_ca_file = ''
            # (change requires restart)
    #ssl_crl_file = ''
            # (change requires restart)
    ```

    If we want to use self-signed certificates, we need to run the following command:

    ```
    openssl req -new -text -out server.req
    ```

2. Answer the questions that are asked by OpenSSL. Make sure that you enter the local hostname as the common name. We can leave the password empty. This call will generate a key that is passphrase-protected; it will not accept a passphrase that is fewer than four characters long.

3. To remove the passphrase (as you must if you want an automatic startup of the server), run the following code:

    ```
    openssl rsa -in privkey.pem -out server.key
    rm privkey.pem
    ```

4. Enter the old passphrase to unlock the existing key. Now, use the following code to turn the certificate into a self-signed certificate and copy the key and certificate to where the server will look for them:

```
openssl req -x509 -in server.req -text
    -key server.key -out server.crt
```

5. After doing this, make sure that the files have the correct set of permissions:

```
chmod og-rwx server.key
```

6. Once the proper rules have been put into the pg_hba.conf file, you can use SSL to connect to your server. To verify that you are using SSL, consider checking out the pg_stat_ssl function. It will tell you about every connection and whether it uses SSL, and will provide some important information about encryption:

```
test=# \d pg_stat_ssl
               View "pg_catalog.pg_stat_ssl"
     Column     |   Type   | Collation | Nullable |
----------------+----------+-----------+----------+
 pid            | integer  |           |          |
 ssl            | boolean  |           |          |
 version        | text     |           |          |
 cipher         | text     |           |          |
 bits           | integer  |           |          |
 client_dn      | text     |           |          |
 client_serial  | numeric  |           |          |
 issuer_dn      | text     |           |          |
```

If the ssl field for a process contains true, PostgreSQL does what we would expect it to do:

```
postgres=# select * from pg_stat_ssl;
-[ RECORD 1 ]
----------------+------------
 pid            | 20075
 ssl            | t
 version        | TLSv1.2
 cipher         | ECDHE-RSA-AES256-GCM-SHA384
 bits           | 256
 clientdn       |
 client_serial  |
 issuer_dn      |
```

Once you have configured SSL, it is time to take a look at instance-level security.

Handling instance-level security

So far, we have configured bind addresses and we have told PostgreSQL which means of authentication to use for which IP ranges. Up until now, the configuration has been purely network-related.

In this section, we can shift our attention to *permissions* at the instance level. The most important thing to know is whether users in PostgreSQL exist at the instance level. If we create a user, it is not just visible inside one database; it can be seen by all the databases. A user might have permission to access just a single database, but users are essentially created at the instance level.

For those of you who are new to PostgreSQL, there is one more thing you should keep in mind: users and roles are the same thing. The CREATE ROLE and CREATE USER clauses have different default values (the only difference is that roles do not get the LOGIN attribute by default), but at the end of the day, users and roles are the same. Therefore, the CREATE ROLE and CREATE USER clauses support the very same syntax. The following listing contains the syntax overview of CREATE USER:

```
test=# \h CREATE USER
Command:     CREATE USER
Description: define a new database role
Syntax:
CREATE USER name [ [ WITH ] option [ ... ] ]
Where option can be:
      SUPERUSER | NOSUPERUSER
    | CREATEDB | NOCREATEDB
    | CREATEROLE | NOCREATEROLE
    | INHERIT | NOINHERIT
    | LOGIN | NOLOGIN
    | REPLICATION | NOREPLICATION
    | BYPASSRLS | NOBYPASSRLS
    | CONNECTION LIMIT connlimit
    | [ ENCRYPTED ] PASSWORD 'password' | PASSWORD NULL
    | VALID UNTIL 'timestamp'
    | IN ROLE role_name [, ...]
    | IN GROUP role_name [, ...]
    | ROLE role_name [, ...]
    | ADMIN role_name [, ...]
    | USER role_name [, ...]
    | SYSID uid
URL: https://www.postgresql.org/docs/17/sql-createuser.html
```

Let's discuss those syntax elements one by one. The first thing that we can see is that a user can be a superuser or a normal user. If somebody is marked as SUPERUSER, there are no longer any restrictions that a normal user has to face. A SUPERUSER user can drop objects (for example, databases) as they wish.

The next important thing is that it takes permissions on the instance level to create a new database.

> **Important note**
>
> Note that when somebody creates a database, this user will automatically be the owner of the database.

The rule is this: the creator is always automatically the owner of an object (unless specified otherwise, as can be done with the CREATE DATABASE clause). The beauty of this is that the object owners can also drop an object again.

> **Important note**
>
> The CREATEROLE or NOCREATEROLE clause defines whether somebody is allowed to create new users/roles.

The next important thing is the INHERIT or NOINHERIT clause. If the INHERIT clause is set (which is the default value), a user can inherit permissions from some other user. Using inherited permissions allows us to use roles, which is a good way to abstract permissions. For example, we can create the role of bookkeeper and make many other roles inherit from bookkeeper. The idea is that we only have to tell PostgreSQL once what a bookkeeper role is allowed to do, even if we have many people working in accounting.

The LOGIN or NOLOGIN clause defines whether a role is allowed to log in to the instance.

> **Important note**
>
> Note that the LOGIN clause is not enough to actually connect to a database. To do that, more permissions are required.

At this point, we are trying to make it to the instance, which is the gate to all the databases inside the instance. Let's get back to our example. bookkeeper might be marked as NOLOGIN because we want people to log in with their real names. All your accountants (say, Joe and Jane) might be marked with the LOGIN clause but can inherit all the permissions from the bookkeeper role. A structure such as this makes it easy to ensure that all bookkeepers will have the same permissions while ensuring their individual activity is operated and logged under their separate identities.

If we are planning to run PostgreSQL with streaming replication, we can do all the transaction log streaming as a superuser. However, this is not recommended from a security point of view. As an assurance that we don't have to be a superuser to stream WAL, PostgreSQL allows us to give replication rights to a normal user, which can then be used to do the streaming. It is common practice to create a special user just for the purpose of managing streaming.

As we will see later in this chapter, PostgreSQL provides a feature called **row-level security**, or **RLS**. The idea is that we can exclude rows from the scope of a user. If a user is explicitly supposed to bypass RLS, set this value to BYPASSRLS. The default value is NOBYPASSRLS.

Sometimes, it makes sense to restrict the number of connections allowed for a user. CONNECTION LIMIT allows us to do exactly that. Note that overall, there can never be more connections than defined in the postgresql.conf file (max_connections). However, we can always restrict certain users to a lower value.

By default, PostgreSQL will store encrypted passwords in the system table, which is a good default behavior. However, suppose you are doing a training course; 10 students are attending and everybody is connected to your box. You can be 100% certain that one of those people will forget their password once in a while. As your setup is not security critical, you might decide to store the password in plaintext so that you can easily look it up and give it to a student. This feature might also come in handy if you are testing software.

Often, we already know that somebody will leave the organization fairly soon. The VALID UNTIL clause allows us to automatically lock out a specific user if their account has expired.

The IN ROLE clause lists one or more existing roles to which the new role will be immediately added as a new member. This helps to avoid additional manual steps. An alternative to IN ROLE is IN GROUP.

The ROLE clause will define the roles that are automatically added as members of the new role.

The ADMIN clause is the same as the ROLE clause.

Finally, we can use the SYSID clause to set a specific ID for the user (this is similar to what some Unix administrators do for usernames at the operating system level). Once in a while, a user has to be modified. The following section explains how this can be done.

Creating and modifying users

After this theoretical introduction, it is time to actually create users and see how things can be used in a practical example. Let's begin with creating a role named bookkeeper:

```
test=# CREATE ROLE  bookkeeper NOLOGIN;
CREATE ROLE
test=# CREATE ROLE  joe LOGIN;
CREATE ROLE
test=# GRANT  bookkeeper TO joe;
GRANT ROLE
```

The first thing that has been done here is that a role called bookkeeper has been created.

Note that we don't want people to log in as bookkeeper, so the role is marked as NOLOGIN.

> **CREATE ROLE versus CREATE USER**
>
> You should also note that NOLOGIN is the default attribute if you use the CREATE ROLE clause. If you prefer the CREATE USER clause, the default setting is LOGIN.

Then, the joe role is created and marked as LOGIN. Finally, the bookkeeper role is assigned to the joe role, so that they can do everything that bookkeeper is actually allowed to do.

Once the users are in place, we can test what we have so far:

```
[hs@linux ~]$ psql test -U bookkeeper
psql: FATAL:  role "bookkeeper" is not permitted to log in
```

As expected, the bookkeeper role is not allowed to log in to the system. What happens if the joe role tries to log in? Have a look at the following code snippet:

```
[hs@linux ~]$ psql test -U joe
...
test=>
```

This will actually work as expected. However, note that the command prompt has changed. This is just a way for PostgreSQL to show you that you are not logged in as a superuser.

Once a user has been created, it might be necessary to modify it. One thing we might want to change is the password. In PostgreSQL, users are allowed to change their own passwords. Here is how it works:

```
test=> ALTER  ROLE  joe PASSWORD 'abc';
ALTER  ROLE
test=> SELECT current_user;
 current_user
--------------
 joe
(1 row)
```

> **Handling passwords carefully**
>
> Be aware of the fact that ALTER ROLE changes the attributes of a role. PASSWORD will actually make the password show up in the log file if **Data Definition Language** (DDL) logging has been configured. This is not too desirable. It is better to change the password using a visual tool. In this case, there is some C-level support (in the client library) that ensures that the password is never sent over the wire in plaintext. Using ALTER ROLE directly to change the password is not a good idea at all because it will yield too much information:
>
> ```
> 2024-07-15 16:43:17.336 CEST [27680] STATEMENT: ALTER ROLE joe
> PASSWORD 'abc';
> ```
>
> ```
> 2024-07-15 16:43:25.049 CEST [27695] FATAL: role "bookkeeper"
> is not permitted to log in
> ```

The ALTER ROLE clause (or ALTER USER) will allow us to change most of the settings that can be set during user creation. However, there is even more to managing users. In many cases, we want to assign special parameters to a user. The ALTER USER clause gives us the means to do that:

```
ALTER USER { role_specification | ALL }
  [ IN DATABASE database_name ]
  SET configuration_parameter { TO | = } { value | DEFAULT }
ALTER USER { role_specification | ALL }
  [ IN DATABASE database_name ]
  SET configuration_parameter FROM CURRENT
ALTER USER { role_specification | ALL }
  [ IN DATABASE database_name ]
  RESET configuration_parameter
ALTER USER { role_specification | ALL }
  [ IN DATABASE database_name ] RESET ALL
```

The syntax is fairly straightforward. To depict why this is really useful, I have added a real-world example. Let's suppose that Joe happens to live on the island of Mauritius. When he logs in, he wants to be in his own time zone, even though his database server is located in Europe. Let's set the time zone on a per-user basis:

```
test=> ALTER  ROLE  joe SET TimeZone = 'UTC-4';
ALTER  ROLE
test=> SELECT now();
            now
-------------------------------
2024-05-06 17:08:30.268385+02
(1 row)
test=> \q
[hs@linux ~]$ psql  test  -U joe
...
test=> SELECT now();
            now
-------------------------------
2024-05-06 19:09:02.492889+04
(1 row)
```

The ALTER ROLE clause will modify the user. As soon as joe reconnects, the time zone will already be set for him.

> **Important note**
>
> The time zone is not changed immediately. You should either reconnect or use a SET ...
> TO DEFAULT clause.

The important thing here is that this is also possible for some memory parameters, which have already been covered earlier in this book, such as `work_mem`.

Defining database-level security

After configuring users at the instance level, it is possible to dig deeper and see what can be done at the database level. The first major question that arises is this: we explicitly allowed `joe` to log in to the database instance, but who or what allowed `joe` to actually connect to one of the databases? Maybe you don't want `joe` to access all the databases in your system. Restricting access to certain databases is exactly what we can achieve at this level.

For databases, the following permissions can be set using a GRANT clause:

```
GRANT { { CREATE | CONNECT | TEMPORARY | TEMP } [, ...] | ALL [
PRIVILEGES ] }
    ON DATABASE database_name [, ...]
    TO role_specification [, ...] [ WITH GRANT OPTION ]
    [ GRANTED BY role_specification ]
```

There are two major permissions at the database level that deserve close attention:

- CREATE: This allows somebody to create a schema inside the database. Note that a CREATE clause does not allow for the creation of tables; it is about schemas. In PostgreSQL, a table resides inside a schema, so you have to get to the schema level first in order to be able to create a table.

- CONNECT: This allows somebody to connect to a database.

The question now is this: nobody has explicitly assigned any CONNECT permissions to the `joe` role, so where do those permissions actually come from? The answer is `public`, which is similar to in the Unix world. If the world is allowed to do something, so is `joe`, who is part of the general public.

The main thing is that `public` is not a role in the sense that it can be dropped and renamed. We can simply see it as the equivalent of everybody on the system.

So, to ensure that not everybody can connect to any database at any time, the CONNECT permission may have to be revoked from the general public. To do so, we can connect as a superuser and fix the problem:

```
[hs@linux ~]$ psql  test  -U postgres
...
test=# REVOKE ALL ON DATABASE test FROM public;
REVOKE
test=# \q
[hs@linux ~]$ psql test -U joe
psql: FATAL:  permission denied for database "test"
DETAIL:  User does not have CONNECT privilege.
```

As we can see, the joe role is no longer allowed to connect. At this point, only superusers have access to test.

In general, it is a good idea to revoke permissions from the postgres database even before other databases are created. The idea behind this is that those permissions won't be in all those newly created databases anymore. If somebody needs access to a certain database, the rights have to be explicitly granted. The rights are no longer automatically there.

Say we want to allow the joe role to connect to the test database; try the following as a superuser:

```
[hs@linux ~]$ psql test -U postgres
...
test=# GRANT CONNECT ON DATABASE test TO bookkeeper;
GRANT
test=# \q
[hs@linux ~]$ psql test -U joe
...
test=>
```

There are two choices here:

- We can allow the joe role directly so that only the joe role will be able to connect.
- Alternatively, we can grant permissions to the bookkeeper role. Remember, the joe role will inherit all the permissions from the bookkeeper role, so if we want all accountants to be able to connect to the database, assigning permissions to the bookkeeper role seems to be an attractive idea.

It is not risky if we grant permissions to the bookkeeper role, because the role is not allowed to log in to the instance in the first place, so it purely serves as a source of permissions.

Adjusting schema-level permissions

Once we are done configuring the database level, it makes sense to take a look at the schema level.

What is important here is that we are facing two types of behaviors:

- PostgreSQL 14 and older
- PostgreSQL 15 and newer

It is important to keep in mind that the default behavior has changed in PostgreSQL. Let us see the behavior in PostgreSQL 14 and older.

PostgreSQL 14 and older

Let's run a small test:

```
test=> CREATE DATABASE test;
ERROR:  permission denied to create database
test=> CREATE USER  xy;
ERROR:  permission denied to create role
test=> CREATE SCHEMA sales;
ERROR:  permission denied for database test
```

As we can see, `joe` is having a bad day and nothing but connecting to the database is allowed.

However, there is a small exception, and it comes as a surprise to many people:

```
test=> CREATE TABLE t_broken (id int);
CREATE TABLE
test=> \d
          List  of relations
 Schema  |   Name    |  Type   | Owner
---------+-----------+---------+-------
 public  | t_broken  | table   | joe
(1 rows)
```

By default, `public` is allowed to work with the public schema, which is always around. If you are seriously interested in securing your database, make sure that this problem is taken care of. Otherwise, normal users will potentially spam your public schema with all kinds of tables, and the entire setup might suffer. You should also keep in mind that if somebody is allowed to create an object, that person is also its owner. Ownership means that all permissions are automatically available to the creator, including the permissions for the destruction of the object.

To take those permissions away from `public`, run the following line as a superuser:

```
test=# REVOKE ALL ON SCHEMA public FROM public;
REVOKE
```

This is really important in pre-15 deployments and should be done under all circumstances. From now on, nobody can put things into your public schema without the correct permissions. The next listing is proof of that:

```
[hs@linux ~]$ psql test -U joe
...
test=> CREATE TABLE  t_data (id int);
ERROR: no schema has been selected to create in
LINE 1: CREATE TABLE t_data (id int);
```

As we can see, the command will fail. The important thing here is the error message that will be displayed. PostgreSQL does not know where to put these tables. By default, it will try to put the table into one of the following schemas:

```
test=> SHOW search_path ;
 search_path
-----------------
 "$user", public
(1 row)
```

As there is no schema called joe, this is not an option, so PostgreSQL will try the public schema. As there are no permissions, it will complain that it does not know where to put the table.

PostgreSQL 15 and beyond

In PostgreSQL 15 and beyond, the behavior has changed. It is now necessary to explicitly set the permissions for the public schema to avoid the following error:

```
test=> CREATE TABLE  public.t_data (id int);
ERROR:  permission denied for schema public
LINE  1: CREATE TABLE  public.t_data (id int);
```

In this case, we will get the error message that we expect. PostgreSQL denies access to the public schema.

The next logical question now is this: which permissions can be set at the schema level to give some more power to the joe role? Let's see:

```
GRANT { { CREATE | USAGE } [, ...] | ALL [ PRIVILEGES ] }
    ON SCHEMA schema_name [, ...]
    TO role_specification [, ...] [ WITH GRANT OPTION ]
    [ GRANTED BY role_specification ]
```

CREATE means that somebody can put objects into a schema. USAGE means that somebody is allowed to enter the schema. Note that entering the schema does not mean that something inside the schema can actually be used; those permissions have not been defined yet. This just means that the user can see the system catalog for this schema.

To allow the joe role to access the table it created previously, the following line will be necessary (executed as a superuser):

```
test=# CREATE TABLE t_broken (id int);
CREATE TABLE
test=# GRANT USAGE ON SCHEMA public TO bookkeeper;
GRANT
```

The joe role is now able to read its table as expected:

```
[hs@linux ~]$ psql test -U joe
test=> SELECT count(*) FROM t_broken;
 count
-------
     0
(1 row)
```

The joe role is also able to add and modify rows because it happens to be the owner of the table. However, although it can do quite a lot of things already, the joe role is not yet almighty. Consider the following statement:

```
test=> ALTER TABLE t_broken RENAME TO t_useful;
ERROR:  permission denied for schema public
```

Let's take a closer look at the actual error message. As we can see, the message complains about the permissions on the schema, not about the permissions on the table itself (remember, the joe role owns the table). To fix the problem, it has to be tackled at the schema level and not the table level. Run the following line as a superuser:

```
test=# GRANT CREATE ON SCHEMA public TO bookkeeper;
GRANT
```

CREATE permissions on the public schema are assigned to bookkeeper.

The joe role can now change the name of its table to something more meaningful:

```
[hs@linux ~]$ psql test -U joe
test=> ALTER TABLE t_broken RENAME TO t_useful;
ALTER TABLE
```

Keep in mind that this is necessary if DDLs are used. In my daily work as a PostgreSQL support service provider, I have seen a couple of issues where this turned out to be a problem.

Working with tables

After taking care of bind addresses, network authentication, users, databases, and schemas, we have finally made it to the table level. The following code snippet shows which permissions can be set for a table:

```
GRANT { { SELECT | INSERT | UPDATE | DELETE | TRUNCATE |
  REFERENCES | TRIGGER | MAINTAIN }
    [, ...] | ALL [ PRIVILEGES ] }
    ON { [ TABLE ] table_name [, ...]
```

```
        | ALL TABLES IN SCHEMA schema_name [, ...] }
    TO role_specification [, ...] [ WITH GRANT OPTION ]
    [ GRANTED BY role_specification ]
```

Let me explain these permissions one by one:

- SELECT: This allows you to read a table.

- INSERT: This allows you to add rows to the table (this also includes copy and other commands; it is not only relevant to the INSERT clause). Note that if you are allowed to insert, you are not automatically allowed to read. The SELECT and INSERT clauses are required in order to be able to read the data that you have inserted.

- UPDATE: This modifies the content of a table.

- DELETE: This is used to remove rows from a table.

- TRUNCATE: This allows you to use the TRUNCATE clause. Note that the DELETE and TRUNCATE clauses are two separate permissions because the TRUNCATE clause will lock the table, which is not done by the DELETE clause (not even if there is no WHERE condition).

- REFERENCES: This allows the creation of foreign keys. It is necessary to have this privilege on both the referencing and referenced columns; otherwise, the creation of the key won't work.

- TRIGGER: This allows for the creation of triggers.

- MAINTAIN: This allows you to run VACUUM, ANALYZE, CLUSTER, REFRESH MATERIALIZED VIEW, REINDEX, and LOCK TABLE on a relation. It assists in reducing the need for superuser and owner permissions.

Making use of GRANT

The nice thing about the GRANT clause is that we can set permissions on all tables in a schema at the same time.

This greatly simplifies the process of adjusting permissions. It is also possible to use the WITH GRANT OPTION clause. The idea is to ensure that normal users can pass on permissions to others, which has the advantage of being able to reduce the workload of the administrators quite significantly. Just imagine a system that provides access to hundreds of users. It can start to be a lot of work to manage all those people, and therefore, administrators can appoint people to manage a subset of the data themselves.

Handling column-level security

In some cases, not everybody is allowed to see all the data. For example, just imagine a bank. Some people might see all the information about a bank account, while others might be limited to only a subset of the data. In a real-world situation, somebody might not be allowed to read the balance column, while somebody else might not be able to see the interest rates of people's loans.

Another example would be that people are allowed to see other people's social media profiles, but not their pictures or some other private information. The question now is this: how can column-level security be used?

To demonstrate this, we will add a column to the existing table belonging to the joe role:

```
test=> ALTER TABLE t_useful ADD COLUMN name text;
ALTER TABLE
```

The table now consists of two columns. The goal of the example is to ensure that a user can see only one of those columns:

```
test=> \d t_useful
    Table  "public.t_useful"
 Column |   Type   | Modifiers
--------+----------+-----------
 id     | integer  |
 name   | text     |
```

As a superuser, let's create a user and give them access to the schema containing our table:

```
test=# CREATE ROLE paul LOGIN;
CREATE ROLE
test=# GRANT CONNECT ON DATABASE test TO paul;
GRANT
test=# GRANT USAGE ON SCHEMA public TO paul;
GRANT
```

Do not forget to give CONNECT rights to the new guy, paul, because earlier in the chapter, CONNECT was revoked from public. Explicit granting is therefore absolutely necessary to ensure that we can get to the table.

The SELECT permissions can be given to the paul role. Here is how it works:

```
test=# GRANT  SELECT (id)  ON t_useful TO paul;
GRANT
```

This is already enough. It is already possible to connect to the database as the paul user and read the column:

```
[hs@linux ~]$ psql test -U paul
...
test=> SELECT id FROM t_useful;
 id
----
(0 rows)
```

If we are using column-level permissions, there is an important thing to keep in mind. We should stop using SELECT * as it will no longer work:

```
test=> SELECT * FROM t_useful;
ERROR:  permission denied for relation t_useful
```

* still means all columns, but as there is no way to access all columns, things will error out instantly.

Configuring default privileges

So far, a lot of stuff has already been configured. The trouble is, what happens if new tables are added to the system? It can be quite painful and risky to process these tables one by one and to set the proper permissions. Wouldn't it be nice if those things were to just happen automatically? This is exactly what the ALTER DEFAULT PRIVILEGES clause does. The idea is to give users an option to make PostgreSQL automatically set the desired permissions as soon as an object comes into existence. It is now impossible to simply forget to set those rights.

The following listing shows the first part of the syntax specification:

```
test=# \h ALTER DEFAULT
Command:     ALTER DEFAULT PRIVILEGES
Description: define default access privileges
Syntax:
ALTER DEFAULT PRIVILEGES
    [ FOR { ROLE | USER } target_role [, ...] ]
    [ IN SCHEMA schema_name [, ...] ]
    abbreviated_grant_or_revoke
where abbreviated_grant_or_revoke is one of:
GRANT { { SELECT | INSERT | UPDATE | DELETE | TRUNCATE |
        REFERENCES | TRIGGER | MAINTAIN}
    [, ...] | ALL [ PRIVILEGES ] }
    ON TABLES
    TO { [ GROUP ] role_name | PUBLIC } [, ...]
        [ WITH GRANT OPTION ]
 ...
```

The syntax works in a similar manner to the GRANT clause and is therefore easy and intuitive to use. To show us how it works, I compiled a simple example. The idea is that if the joe role creates a table, the paul role will automatically be able to use it. The following listing shows how default privileges can be assigned (as a superuser):

```
test=# ALTER DEFAULT PRIVILEGES FOR ROLE joe
        IN SCHEMA public GRANT ALL ON TABLES TO paul;
ALTER DEFAULT PRIVILEGES
```

In my example, all tables in the `public` schema are granted all permissions.

Let's now connect as the `joe` role and create a table:

```
[hs@linux ~]$ psql  test  -U joe
...
test=> CREATE TABLE  t_user (
        id       serial,
        name     text,
        passwd   text
);
CREATE TABLE
```

As you can see, the table can now be created successfully.

Connecting as the `paul` role will prove that the table has been assigned to the proper set of permissions:

```
[hs@linux ~]$ psql test -U paul
...
test=> SELECT * FROM  t_user;
 id | name | passwd
----+------+--------
(0 rows)
```

The table can also be read nicely and PostgreSQL does not error out.

Digging into row-level security

Up to this point, a table has always been shown as a whole. When the table contained a million rows, it was possible to retrieve a million rows from it. If somebody had the right to read a table, it meant the entire table. In many cases, this is not enough. It is often required for a user to not be allowed to see all the rows.

Consider the following real-world example, where an accountant is doing accounting work for many people. The table containing tax rates should really be visible to everybody, as everybody has to pay the same rates. However, when it comes to the actual transactions, the accountant might want to ensure that everybody is only allowed to see their own transactions. Person *A* should not be allowed to see person *B*'s data. In addition to that, it might also make sense that the boss of a division is allowed to see all the data in their part of the company.

RLS has been designed to do exactly this and enables you to build multi-tenant systems in a fast and simple way. The way to configure those permissions is to come up with policies. The `CREATE POLICY` command is here to provide us with a means to write these rules. Let's have a look at an example of the `CREATE POLICY` command:

```
test=# \h CREATE POLICY
Command:     CREATE POLICY
```

```
Description: define a new row-level security policy
     for a table
Syntax:
CREATE POLICY name ON table_name
    [ AS { PERMISSIVE | RESTRICTIVE } ]
    [ FOR { ALL | SELECT | INSERT | UPDATE | DELETE } ]
    [ TO { role_name | PUBLIC | CURRENT_ROLE |
           CURRENT_USER | SESSION_USER } [, ...] ]
    [ USING ( using_expression ) ]
    [ WITH CHECK ( check_expression ) ]
URL: https://www.postgresql.org/docs/17/sql-createpolicy.html
```

The syntax is not hard to understand. However, an example is, of course, provided. To depict how a policy can be written, let's first log in as a superuser and create a table containing a couple of entries:

```
test=# CREATE TABLE t_person (gender text, name text);
CREATE TABLE
test=# INSERT INTO t_person
VALUES
    ('male', 'joe'),
    ('male', 'paul'),
    ('female', 'sarah'),
    (NULL, 'R2-D2');
INSERT 0 4
```

A table is created and data is successfully added. Access is then granted to the joe role, as can be seen in the following code:

```
test=# GRANT ALL ON t_person TO joe;
GRANT
```

So far, everything is pretty normal, and the joe role will be able to actually read the entire table, as there is no RLS in place. But let's see what happens if RLS is enabled for the table:

```
test=# ALTER TABLE t_person ENABLE ROW LEVEL SECURITY;
ALTER TABLE
```

There is a denial, and all default policies are in place, so the joe role will actually get an empty table:

```
test=> SELECT * FROM t_person;
 gender | name
--------+------
(0 rows)
```

The default policy makes a lot of sense, as users are forced to explicitly set permissions.

Now that the table is under RLS control, policies can be written as a superuser:

```
test=# CREATE POLICY joe_pol_1
ON t_person
FOR SELECT
TO joe
USING (gender = 'male');
CREATE POLICY
```

Logging in as the joe role and selecting all the data will return just two rows:

```
test=> SELECT * FROM  t_person;
 gender  | name
---------+------
 male    | joe
 male    | paul
(2 rows)
```

Let's inspect the policy we have just created in a more detailed way. The first thing that we can see is that the policy actually has a name. It is also connected to a table and allows for certain operations (in this case, the SELECT clause). Then comes the USING clause. This defines what the joe role will be allowed to see. The USING clause is, therefore, a mandatory filter attached to every query to only select the rows that our user is supposed to see.

There is also one important side note: if there is more than just a single policy, PostgreSQL will use an OR condition. In short, more policies will make you see more data by default. In PostgreSQL 9.6, this was always the case. However, with the introduction of PostgreSQL 10.0, the user can choose whether conditions should be connected by means of OR or AND. The following two options are available:

```
PERMISSIVE | RESTRICTIVE
```

By default, PostgreSQL is PERMISSIVE, so OR connections are at work. If we decide to use RESTRICTIVE, then those clauses will be connected with AND.

Now, suppose that, for some reason, it has been decided that the joe role is also allowed to see robots. There are two choices to achieve our goal. The first option is to simply use the ALTER POLICY clause to change the existing policy:

```
test=# \h ALTER POLICY
Command:     ALTER POLICY
Description: change the definition of a row-level
     security policy
Syntax:
ALTER POLICY name ON table_name RENAME TO new_name

ALTER POLICY name ON table_name
```

```
        [ TO { role_name | PUBLIC | CURRENT_ROLE |
              CURRENT_USER | SESSION_USER } [, ...] ]
        [ USING ( using_expression ) ]
        [ WITH CHECK ( check_expression ) ]
    URL: https://www.postgresql.org/docs/17/sql-alterpolicy.html
```

This listing shows the syntax of ALTER POLICY. It is pretty similar to CREATE POLICY.

The second option is to create a second policy, as shown in the following example:

```
test=# CREATE POLICY joe_pol_2
ON t_person
FOR SELECT TO joe
USING  (gender IS NULL);
CREATE POLICY
```

Creating the policy worked out successfully. The beauty is that those policies are simply connected using an OR condition, as stated before, unless RESTRICTIVE is used. Therefore, PostgreSQL will now return three rows instead of two:

```
test=> SELECT * FROM  t_person;
 gender  | name
---------+-------
  male   | joe
  male   | paul
         | R2-D2
(3 rows)
```

The R2-D2 role is now also included in the result, as it matches the second policy.

To depict how PostgreSQL runs the query, I have decided to include an execution plan of the query:

```
test=> explain SELECT * FROM t_person;
                        QUERY PLAN
----------------------------------------------------------------
 Seq Scan on t_person (cost=0.00..21.00 rows=9 width=64)
    Filter: ((gender IS NULL) OR (gender = <male'::text))
(2 rows)
```

As we can see, both the USING clauses have been added as mandatory filters to the query. You may have noticed in the syntax definition that there are two types of clauses:

- USING: This clause filters rows that already exist. This is relevant to the SELECT and UPDATE clauses.

- CHECK: This clause filters new rows that are about to be created, so they are relevant to the INSERT and UPDATE clauses, and other clauses.

Here is what happens if we try to insert a row:

```
test=> INSERT INTO t_person VALUES ('male', 'kaarel');
ERROR:  new row violates row-level security policy for table "t_
person"
```

As there is no policy for the INSERT clause, the statement will naturally error out. Here is the policy to allow insertions:

```
test=# CREATE POLICY joe_pol_3
ON t_person
FOR INSERT TO joe
WITH CHECK (gender IN ('male', 'female'));
CREATE POLICY
```

The joe role is allowed to add males and females to the table, which is shown in the following listing:

```
test=> INSERT INTO t_person VALUES ('female', 'maria');
INSERT 0 1
```

However, there is also a catch. Consider the following example:

```
test=> INSERT INTO  t_person VALUES ('female', 'maria') RETURNING *;
ERROR:  new row violates row-level security policy for table "t_
person"
```

Remember, there is only a policy to select males. The trouble here is that the statement will return a female, which is not allowed, as the joe role is under a male-only policy.

The RETURNING * clause will only work for males:

```
test=> INSERT INTO  t_person VALUES ('male', 'max') RETURNING *;
 gender | name
--------+------
 male   | max
(1 row)
INSERT 0 1
```

If we don't want this behavior, we have to write a policy that actually contains a proper USING clause. RLS is an important component in every database-side security system. Once we have defined our RLS policy, it makes sense to step back and see how you can inspect permissions.

Inspecting and handling permissions

When all of the permissions have been set, it is sometimes necessary to know who has which permissions. It is vital for administrators to find out who is allowed to do what. Unfortunately, this process is not so easy and requires a bit of knowledge. Usually, I am a big fan of command-line usage. However, in the case of the permission system, it can really make sense to use a graphical user interface to do things.

Before I show you how to read PostgreSQL permissions, let's assign rights to the role named joe so that we can inspect them in the next step:

```
test=# GRANT ALL ON t_person TO joe;
GRANT
```

Information about permissions can be retrieved using the z command in psql:

```
test=# \x
Expanded display is on.
test=# \z t_person
Access privileges
-[ RECORD 1 ]-----+----------------------------------------
Schema            | public
Name              | t_person
Type              | table
Access privileges | postgres=arwdDxtm/postgres
+
                  | joe=arwdDxtm/postgres
Column privileges |
Policies          | joe_pol_1 (r):
+                 | (u):  (gender = 'male'::text)
+                 | to: joe
+                 | joe_pol_2 (r):
+                 | (u): (gender IS NULL)
+                 | to: joe
+                 | joe_pol_3 (a):
+                 | (c): (gender = ANY (ARRAY['male'::text,
                        'female'::text]))
 +                | to: joe
```

This will return all those policies, along with information about joe's access privileges. Unfortunately, those shortcuts are hard to read, and I have a feeling that they are not widely understood by administrators. In this example, the joe role has obtained arwdDxtm from PostgreSQL. What do those shortcuts actually mean? Let's see:

- a: This appends for the INSERT clause

- r: This reads for the SELECT clause

- w: This writes for the UPDATE clause

- d: This deletes for the DELETE clause

- D: This is used for the TRUNCATE clause (when this was introduced, t was already taken)

- x: This is used for references

- t: This is used for triggers

- m: This is to allow the MAINTAIN clause

If you don't know this code, there is also a second way to make things more readable. Consider the following function call:

```
test=# SELECT * FROM  aclexplode('{joe=arwdDxtm/postgres}');
 grantor | grantee | privilege_type | is_grantable
---------+---------+----------------+--------------
      10 |   18481 | INSERT         | f
      10 |   18481 | SELECT         | f
      10 |   18481 | UPDATE         | f
      10 |   18481 | DELETE         | f
      10 |   18481 | TRUNCATE       | f
      10 |   18481 | REFERENCES     | f
      10 |   18481 | TRIGGER        | f
      10 |   18481 | MAINTAIN       | f
(8 rows)
```

As we can see, the set of permissions is returned as a simple table, which makes life really easy. For those of you who still consider inspecting permissions in PostgreSQL somewhat cumbersome, there is an additional solution that we at Cybertec (https://www.cybertec-postgresql.com) have implemented recently – pg_permission. The idea is to provide you with simple views to inspect the security system in greater depth.

To download pg_permission, visit our GitHub repository page at https://github.com/cybertec-postgresql/pg_permission.

You can easily clone the repository, as shown in the following listing:

```
git clone https://github.com/cybertec-postgresql/pg_permission.git
Cloning into 'pg_permission'...
remote: Enumerating objects: 164, done.
remote: Counting objects: 100% (53/53), done.
remote: Compressing objects: 100% (30/30), done.
remote: Total 164 (delta 18), reused 46 (delta 12), pack-reused 111
Receiving objects: 100% (164/164), 44.86 KiB | 1.36 MiB/s, done.
Resolving deltas: 100% (70/70), done.
```

Once that is done, enter the directory and just run `make install`. Those two things are already enough to deploy the extension. Here is how the extension can be enabled:

```
test=# CREATE EXTENSION pg_permissions;
 CREATE EXTENSION
```

`pg_permission` will deploy a handful of views, which are all structured identically. The following view shows what the structure looks like:

```
test=# \d all_permissions
 View "public.all_permissions"
    Column     |   Type    | Collation | Nullable | Default
---------------+-----------+-----------+----------+---------
 object_type   | obj_type  |           |          |
 role_name     | name      |           |          |
 schema_name   | name      |           |          |
 object_name   | text      | C         |          |
 column_name   | name      |           |          |
 permission    | perm_type |           |          |
 granted       | boolean   |           |          |
Triggers:
 permissions_trigger INSTEAD OF UPDATE ON all_permissions
                     FOR EACH ROW EXECUTE FUNCTION permissions_
trigger_func()
```

`all_permissions` is simply a view that provides you with an overall view of all permissions. You can simply filter by object type and so on to dig into the details. What is also interesting is that there is a trigger on this view, so if you want to change permissions, you can simply run `UPDATE` on all those views, while `pg_permissions` will change the permissions on the system for you. In the next section, you will learn how to reassign ownership.

Reassigning objects and dropping users

After assigning permissions and restricting access on various levels, users may be dropped from the system. Unsurprisingly, the commands to do this are `DROP ROLE` and `DROP USER`. Here is the syntax of `DROP ROLE`:

```
test=# \h DROP ROLE
Command: DROP ROLE
Description: remove a database role
Syntax:
 DROP ROLE [ IF EXISTS ] name [, ...]


URL: https://www.postgresql.org/docs/17/sql-droprole.html
```

We can now give DROP ROLE a try. The following listing shows how this works:

```
test=# DROP ROLE joe;
ERROR:  role  "joe"  cannot be dropped because some  objects depend on
it
DETAIL:  target of policy joe_pol_3 on table t_person
target of policy joe_pol_2 on table t_person
target of policy joe_pol_1 on table t_person
privileges for table t_person
owner of table t_user
owner of sequence t_user_id_seq
owner of default privileges on new relations belonging to role joe in
schema public
owner of table t_useful
```

PostgreSQL will issue error messages because a user can only be removed if everything has been taken away from them. This makes sense for the following reason: just suppose that somebody owns a table. What should PostgreSQL do with that table? Somebody has to own it.

To reassign tables from one user to the next, consider taking a look at the REASSIGN clause:

```
test=# \h REASSIGN
Command: REASSIGN OWNED
Description: change the ownership of database objects
      owned by a database role
Syntax:
 REASSIGN OWNED BY { old_role | CURRENT_ROLE |
                     CURRENT_USER |
                     SESSION_USER } [, ...]
             TO { new_role | CURRENT_ROLE |
                  CURRENT_USER |
                  SESSION_USER }

 URL: https://www.postgresql.org/docs/17/sql-reassign-owned.html
```

The syntax is, again, quite simple, and helps to simplify the handover process. Here is an example:

```
test=# REASSIGN OWNED  BY joe TO postgres;
REASSIGN OWNED
```

So, let's try to drop the joe role again:

```
test=# DROP ROLE joe;
ERROR:  role "joe" cannot be dropped because some objects depend on it
DETAIL:  target of policy joe_pol_3 on table t_person target of policy
joe_pol_2 on table t_person
```

```
target of policy joe_pol_1 on table t_person privileges for table t_
person
owner of default privileges on new relations belonging to role joe in
schema public
```

As we can see, the list of problems has been reduced significantly. What we can do now is resolve all of those problems one after the other, and then drop the role. There is no shortcut; the only way to make this more efficient is to make sure that as few permissions as possible are assigned to real people (users with `LOGIN` permissions). Try to abstract as much as you can into roles, which, in turn, can be used by many people. If individual permissions are not assigned to real people, things tend to be easier in general.

Summary

Database security is a wide field, and a single chapter can hardly cover all of the aspects of PostgreSQL security. Many things, such as SELinux and `SECURITY DEFINER/INVOKER`, were left untouched. However, in this chapter, we learned about the most common things that we will face as PostgreSQL developers and database administrators. We also learned how to avoid the basic pitfalls, and how to make our systems more secure. What is important to understand is that security matters and that PostgreSQL provides you with all the means necessary to secure your database.

In *Chapter 9*, *Handling Backup and Recovery*, we will learn about PostgreSQL streaming replication and incremental backups. The chapter will also cover failover scenarios.

Handling Backup and Recovery

In *Chapter 8*, *Managing PostgreSQL Security*, we took a look at all that we need to know about securing PostgreSQL in the most simplistic and beneficial way possible. The topics that we will cover in this chapter are backup and recovery. Creating backups should be a regular task, and every administrator should keep an eye on this vital exercise. The same is true for recovery, which should be tested and taken care of on a regular basis. Fortunately, PostgreSQL provides easy means to create backups and in PostgreSQL 17, we can make use of many great features that have been added over time.

Therefore, in this chapter, we will cover the following topics:

- Performing simple dumps
- Handling various formats
- Replaying backups
- Handling global data

By the end of this chapter, you will be able to set up proper backup mechanisms.

Performing simple dumps

Backups and data exports are important because, without backups, you are effectively putting your database at risk in the case of crashes and storage-related issues. If you are running through a PostgreSQL setup, there are basically two main methods of performing backups:

- Logical dumps (extracting a SQL script that represents your data)
- Transaction log shipping

The idea behind transaction log shipping is to archive binary changes made to the database. Most people claim that transaction log shipping is the only real way to create backups. However, in my opinion, this is not necessarily true.

Many people rely on pg_dump to simply extract a textual representation of the data. Interestingly, pg_dump is also the oldest method of creating a backup and has been around since the very early days of the PostgreSQL project (transaction log shipping was added much later). Every PostgreSQL administrator becomes familiar with pg_dump sooner or later, so it is important to know how it really works and what it does.

Running pg_dump

In the first part of this section, you will learn some basic things about pg_dump. The first thing we want to do is create a simple textual dump, as shown in the following code block:

```
[hs@linuxpc ~]$ pg_dump test > /tmp/dump.sql
```

This is the most simplistic backup you can imagine. Basically, pg_dump logs in to the local database instance, connects to a database called test, and starts to extract all of the data, which will then be sent to stdout and redirected to the file. The beauty here is that the standard output gives you all of the flexibility of a Unix system. You can easily compress the data using a pipe or do whatever you want to do with it.

In some cases, you might want to run pg_dump as a different user. All PostgreSQL client programs support a consistent set of command-line parameters to pass the user information. If you just want to set the user, use the -U flag, as follows:

```
[hs@linuxpc ~]$ pg_dump -U whatever_powerful_user test > /tmp/dump.sql
```

The following set of parameters can be found in all PostgreSQL client programs:

```
... Connection options:
  -d, --dbname=DBNAME database to dump
  -h, --host=HOSTNAME database
      server host or socket directory
  -p, --port=PORT database server port number
  -U, --username=NAME connect as specified database user
  -w, --no-password never prompt for password
  -W, --password force password prompt (should
                          happen automatically)
  --role=ROLENAME do SET ROLE before dump
...
```

You can just pass the information you want to pg_dump, and if you have the right level of permission, PostgreSQL will fetch the data. The important thing here is to see how the program really works. Basically, pg_dump connects to the database and opens a large, repeatable read transaction that simply reads all of the data committed before the start of the transaction. Remember, a repeatable read ensures that PostgreSQL creates a consistent snapshot of the data, which does not change throughout the transactions. In other words, a dump is always consistent—no foreign keys will be violated. The output is a snapshot of data as it was when the dump started. Consistency is a key factor here. It also implies that changes made to the data when the dump is running won't make it to the backup anymore.

> **Important note**
>
> A dump simply reads everything—therefore, there are no separate permissions to be able to dump something. As long as you can read it, you can back it up.

Also, note that the backup is in a textual format by default. This means that you can safely extract data from, say, Solaris, and move it to another CPU architecture. In the case of binary copies, this is clearly not possible, as the on-disk format depends on your CPU architecture.

Passing passwords and using the service file

If you take a close look at the connection parameters shown in the previous section, you will notice that there is no way to pass a password to `pg_dump`. You can enforce a password prompt, but you cannot pass the parameter to `pg_dump` using a command-line option.

The reason for this is simply because the password might show up in the process table and be visible to other people. The question now is this: If `pg_hba.conf`, which is on the server, enforces a password, how can the client program provide it?

There are various means of doing this. Here are three:

- Using environment variables
- Using `.pgpass` to pass connection information
- Using service files

In this section, we will learn about all three methods.

Using environment variables

One way to pass all kinds of parameters is to use environment variables. If information is not explicitly passed to `pg_dump`, it will look for the missing information in predefined environment variables. A list of all potential settings can be found at `https://www.postgresql.org/docs/17/static/libpq-envars.html`.

The following overview shows some of the environment variables that are commonly needed for backups:

- `PGHOST`: This tells the system which host to connect to
- `PGPORT`: This defines the TCP port to be used
- `PGUSER`: This tells a client program about the desired user

- PGPASSWORD: This contains the password to be used

- PGDATABASE: This is the name of the database to connect to

The advantage of these environments is that the password won't show up in the process table. However, there's more.

Consider the following example:

```
psql  -U ... -h ... -p ... -d ...
```

Given that you are a system administrator, would you really want to type a long piece of code such as this a couple of times every day? If you are working with the very same host again and again, just set those environment variables and connect with plain SQL. The following listing shows how to connect to the database by using environment variables to control the desired behavior:

```
[hs@linuxpc ~]$ export PGHOST=localhost
[hs@linuxpc ~]$ export PGUSER=hs
[hs@linuxpc ~]$ export PGPASSWORD=abc
[hs@linuxpc ~]$ export PGPORT=5432
[hs@linuxpc ~]$ export PGDATABASE=test
[hs@linuxpc ~]$ psql
psql (17.0)
Type "help" for help.
```

As you can see, there are no command-line parameters anymore. Just type `psql` and you are in.

> **Important note**
>
> All applications based on the standard PostgreSQL C language client library (`libpq`) will understand these environment variables, so you can use them not only for `psql` and `pg_dump` but also many other applications.

Using .pgpass to pass connection information

A very common way to store login information is via the use of the `.pgpass` files. The idea is simple: Put a file called `.pgpass` into your home directory and put your login information there. The format is simple. The following listing contains the basic format:

```
hostname:port:database:username:password
```

An example would be the following:

```
192.168.0.45:5432:mydb:xy:abc
```

PostgreSQL offers some nice additional functionality, in which most fields can contain `*`.

Here is an example:

```
*:*:*:xy:abc
```

The * character implies that on every host, on every port, for every database, the user called xy will use abc as the password. To make PostgreSQL use the .pgpass file, make sure that the right file permissions are in place. Without the following lines, things won't work properly:

```
chmod 0600 ~/.pgpass
```

chmod sets the file-level permissions. These are necessary to protect the files. Furthermore, .pgpass can also be used on a Windows system. In that case, the file can be found in the %APPDATA%\postgresql\pgpass.conf path.

Using service files

However, .pgpass is not the only file you can use. You can also make use of service files. Here's how they work: if you want to connect to the very same servers over and over again, you can create a .pg_service.conf file. It will hold all of the connection information you need.

Here is an example of a .pg_service.conf file:

```
Mac:~  hs$ cat .pg_service.conf
# a sample service
[hansservice]
host=localhost
port=5432
dbname=test
user=hs
password=abc
[paulservice]
host=192.168.0.45
port=5432
dbname=xyz
user=paul
password=cde
```

To connect to one of the services, just set the environment and connect the following:

```
iMac:~ hs$ export PGSERVICE=hansservice
```

A connection can now be established without passing parameters to psql:

```
iMac:~ hs$ psql
psql (17.0)
Type "help" for help.
test=#
```

As you can see, the login works without additional command-line parameters. Alternatively, you can use the following command:

```
psql service=hansservice
```

Now that we have learned how to pass passwords and connection information, let's move on to learning how to extract subsets of data.

Extracting subsets of data

So far, we have seen how to dump an entire database. However, this may not be what we want to do. In many cases, we just want to extract a subset of tables or schemas. Fortunately, pg_dump can help us to do that while also providing several switches:

- -a: This only dumps the data and does not dump the data structure
- -s: This dumps the data structure but skips the data
- -n: This only dumps a certain schema
- -N: This dumps everything but excludes certain schemas
- -t: This only dumps certain tables
- -T: This dumps everything but certain tables (this makes sense if you want to exclude logging tables and so on)

Partial dumps can be very useful to speed things up considerably. Now that we have learned how to perform simple dumps, let's learn how to handle various file formats.

Handling various formats

So far, we have seen that pg_dump can be used to create text files. The problem here is that a text file can only be replayed completely, so if we have saved an entire database, we can only replay the entire thing. In most cases, this is not what we want to do. Therefore, PostgreSQL has additional formats that offer more functionality.

At this point, four formats are supported:

```
-F, --format=c|d|t|p  output file  format
      (custom, directory, tar, plain  text  (default))
```

Those options have the following meaning:

- c: Custom format
- d: Directory format

- t: Tar format

- p: Plain text format

We have already seen plaintext, which is just normal text. On top of that, we can use a custom format. The idea behind a custom format is to get a compressed dump, including a table of contents. Here are two ways to create a custom format dump:

```
[hs@linuxpc ~]$ pg_dump -Fc test > /tmp/dump.fc
[hs@linuxpc ~]$ pg_dump -Fc test -f /tmp/dump.fc
```

In addition to the table of contents, the compressed dump has one more advantage: it is a lot smaller. The rule of thumb is that a custom format dump is around 90% smaller than the database instance you are about to back up. Of course, this is highly dependent on the number of indexes, but for many database applications, this rough estimation will hold.

Once the backup is created, we can inspect the backup file:

```
[hs@linuxpc ~]$ pg_restore --list /tmp/dump.fc
;
; Archive created at 2024-09-04 10:52:13 CEST
;      dbname: test
;      TOC Entries: 58
;      Compression: gzip
;      Dump Version: 1.16-0
;      Format: CUSTOM
;      Integer: 4 bytes
;      Offset: 8 bytes
;      Dumped from database version: 17.0
;      Dumped by pg_dump version: 17.0
;
;
; Selected TOC Entries:
;
4; 3079 386162 EXTENSION - pg_stat_statements
2971; 0 0 COMMENT - EXTENSION pg_stat_statements
2; 3079 386070 EXTENSION - pg_trgm
2972; 0 0 COMMENT - EXTENSION pg_trgm
226; 1259 385938 TABLE public a hs
227; 1259 385941 TABLE public b hs
228; 1259 385944 TABLE public c hs
...
```

Note that pg_restore --list will return the table of contents of the backup.

Using a custom format is a good idea as the backup will shrink in size. However, there's more: the -Fd command will create a backup in the directory format. Instead of a single file, you will now get a directory containing a couple of files:

```
[hs@linuxpc ~]$ mkdir /tmp/backup
[hs@linuxpc ~]$ pg_dump -Fd test -f /tmp/backup/
[hs@linuxpc ~]$ cd /tmp/backup/
[hs@linuxpc backup]$ ls -lh
total  86M
-rw-rw-r--. 1 hs hs   85M Jan   4 15:54  3095.dat.gz
-rw-rw-r--. 1 hs hs   107 Jan   4 15:54  3096.dat.gz
-rw-rw-r--. 1 hs hs  740K Jan   4 15:54  3097.dat.gz
-rw-rw-r--. 1 hs hs    39 Jan   4 15:54  3098.dat.gz
-rw-rw-r--. 1 hs hs  4.3K Jan   4 15:54  toc.dat
```

One advantage of the directory format is that we can use more than one core to perform the backup. In the case of a plain or custom format, only one process will be used by pg_dump. The directory format changes that rule. The following example shows how we can tell pg_dump to use four cores (or jobs):

```
[hs@linuxpc backup]$ rm -rf *
[hs@linuxpc backup]$ pg_dump -Fd test -f /tmp/backup/ -j 4
```

In this section, you learned about basic textual dumps. In the next section, you will learn about backup replay.

> **Important note**
>
> The more objects there are in our database, the greater the chance there is for a potential speed-up.

Replaying backups

Having a backup is pointless unless you have tried to actually replay it. Fortunately, this is easy to do. If you have created a plaintext backup, simply take the SQL file and execute it. The following example shows how that can be done:

```
psql your_db < your_file.sql
```

A plaintext backup is simply a text file containing everything. We can always simply replay a text file.

If you have decided on a custom format or directory format, you can use pg_restore to replay the backup. Additionally, pg_restore allows you to do all kinds of fancy things, such as replaying just part of a database. In most cases, however, you will simply replay the entire database. In this example, we will create an empty database and just replay a custom format dump:

```
[hs@linuxpc backup]$ createdb new_db
[hs@linuxpc backup]$ pg_restore -d new_db -j 4 /tmp/dump.fc
```

Note that `pg_restore` will add data to an existing database. If your database is not empty, `pg_restore` might error out but continue.

Again, `-j` is used to throw more than one process. In this example, four cores are used to replay the data; however, this only works when more than one table is being replayed.

> **Important note**
> If you are using a directory format, you can simply pass the name of the directory instead of the file.

As far as performance is concerned, dumps are a good solution if you are working with small or medium amounts of data. There are two major downsides:

- We will get a snapshot, so everything since the last snapshot will be lost
- Rebuilding a dump from scratch is comparatively slow compared to binary copies because all of the indexes have to be rebuilt

We will take a look at binary backups in *Chapter 10, Making Sense of Backups and Replication*. Replaying backups is easy, but there is more to it than meets the eye. The following section handles global data. What does that mean?

Handling global data

In the previous sections, we learned about `pg_dump` and `pg_restore`, which are two vital programs when it comes to creating backups. The thing is, `pg_dump` creates database dumps—it works at the database level. If we want to back up an entire instance, we have to use `pg_dumpall` or dump all of the databases separately. Before we dig into that, it makes sense to see how `pg_dumpall` works:

```
pg_dumpall > /tmp/all.sql
```

`pg_dumpall` will connect to one database after the other and send stuff to `stdout`, where you can process it with Unix. Note that `pg_dumpall` can be used just like `pg_dump`. However, it has some downsides. It does not support a custom or directory format and therefore does not offer multi-core support. This means that we will be stuck with one thread.

However, there is more to `pg_dumpall`. Keep in mind that users live at the instance level. If you create a normal database dump, you will get all of the permissions, but you won't get all of the CREATE USER statements. `globals` are not included in a normal dump—they will only be extracted by `pg_dumpall`.

If we only want `globals`, we can run `pg_dumpall` using the `-g` option:

```
pg_dumpall -g > /tmp/globals.sql
```

In most cases, you might want to run `pg_dumpall -g` along with a custom or directory format dump to extract your instances. A simple backup script might look like this:

```sh
#!/bin/sh
BACKUP_DIR=/tmp/
pg_dumpall -g > $BACKUP_DIR/globals.sql
for x in $(psql -c "SELECT datname FROM  pg_database
    WHERE  datname NOT IN ('postgres', 'template0', 'template1')"
postgres -A -t)
do
pg_dump -Fc $x > $BACKUP_DIR/$x.fc done
```

It will first dump `globals` and then loop through the list of databases to extract them one by one in a custom format.

Let's summarize the chapter.

Summary

In this chapter, we learned about creating backups and dumps in general. So far, binary backups have not been covered, but you are already able to extract textual backups from the server so that you can save and replay your data in the most simplistic way possible. Data protection is important, and backups are vital to ensure data security. Remember, without backups, you are running the risk of total data loss.

In *Chapter 10*, *Making Sense of Backups and Replication*, you will learn about transaction log shipping, streaming replication, and binary backups. You will also learn how to use PostgreSQL's onboard tools to replicate instances.

10
Making Sense of Backups and Replication

In *Chapter 9*, *Handling Backup and Recovery*, we learned a lot about backup and recovery, which is essential for administration. However, in large-scale systems, logical backups might not be what you're looking for since they take a lot of time to implement, something that increases with the amount of data being handled. Therefore, we want to focus our attention on important topics such as binary backups and more advanced topics. This chapter is all about PostgreSQL's transaction log and what we can do with it to improve our setup and make things more secure.

In this chapter, we'll cover the following topics:

- Understanding the transaction log
- Transaction log archiving and recovery
- Setting up asynchronous replication
- Upgrading to synchronous replication
- Making use of replication slots
- Making use of the CREATE PUBLICATION and CREATE SUBSCRIPTION commands

By the end of this chapter, you'll be able to set up transaction log archiving and implement **point-in-time recovery** (**PITR**), including incremental backups, and replication. In addition to that, you'll be able to understand basic concepts to handle high availability and apply them in a real-world environment. Keep in mind that this chapter could never be a comprehensive guide to replication; it's only a short introduction. There's a lot more information out there, especially in the high-availability area and in the entirely new field of PostgreSQL on Kubernetes/OpenShift, which seems to be one of the most relevant database topics nowadays.

Understanding the transaction log

Every modern database system provides functionality to make sure that a system can survive a crash if something goes wrong or somebody pulls the plug. This is true for filesystems and database systems alike.

PostgreSQL also provides a means to ensure that a crash can't harm the integrity of data or the data itself. It guarantees that if the power cuts out, the system will always be able to come back on again and do its job.

The means of providing this kind of security is achieved by **write-ahead logging** (**WAL**). The idea is to not write into a data file directly but instead to write to the log first. Why is this important? Imagine that we're writing some data, as follows:

```
INSERT INTO data ... VALUES ('12345678');
```

Let's assume that this data was written directly to the data file. If the operation fails midway, the data file will be corrupted. It might contain half-written rows, columns without index pointers, missing commit information, and so on. Since hardware doesn't guarantee atomic writes of large chunks of data, we must find a way to make this more robust. By writing to the log instead of writing to the file directly, this problem can be solved.

> **Important note**
> In PostgreSQL, the transaction log consists of records that are chained together. Each record represents a "change" in a table, an index, a file, or any other relevant component.

A single write can consist of various records that all have a checksum and are connected by the WAL header. A single transaction might contain a B-tree, an index, a storage manager, commit records, and a lot more. Each type of object has its own WAL entries to ensure that the object can survive a crash. If a crash occurs, PostgreSQL will start up and repair the data files based on the transaction log to ensure that no permanent corruption is allowed to happen.

With this introduction out of the way, let's understand the transaction log in general.

Looking at the transaction log

In PostgreSQL, WAL can usually be found in the pg_wal directory in the data directory, unless specified otherwise on initdb.

The following listing shows what the pg_wal directory looks like:

```
[pg_wal]$ ls -l
total 1343496
-rw-------  1 hs   staff   16777216 Oct  3 19:31 00000001000000000000002A
-rw-------  1 hs   staff   16777216 Oct  3 19:28 00000001000000000000002B
-rw-------  1 hs   staff   16777216 Oct  3 19:28 00000001000000000000002C
-rw-------  1 hs   staff   16777216 Oct  3 19:28 00000001000000000000002D
-rw-------  1 hs   staff   16777216 Oct  3 19:28 00000001000000000000002E
-rw-------  1 hs   staff   16777216 Oct  3 19:28 00000001000000000000002F
-rw-------  1 hs   staff   16777216 Oct  3 19:28 000000010000000000000030
-rw-------  1 hs   staff   16777216 Oct  3 19:28 000000010000000000000031
```

Figure 10.1 – The content of the pg_wal directory

What we can see is that the transaction log is a 16 MB file that consists of 24 digits. The numbering is hexadecimal. As we can see, 2F is followed by 30. The files are always a fixed size.

> **Important note**
> One thing to note is that, in PostgreSQL, the number of transaction log files isn't related to the size of a transaction. You can have a very small set of transaction log files and still run a multi-**terabyte** (**TB**) transaction easily.

Traditionally, the WAL directory typically consists of 16 MB files. However, since the introduction of PostgreSQL, the size of a WAL segment can now be set with initdb. In some cases, this can speed things up. Let's see how this works. The following example shows us how the WAL file's size can be changed to 32 MB:

```
initdb -D /pgdata --wal-segsize=32
```

Understanding checkpoints

As I mentioned earlier, every change is written to WAL in binary format (it doesn't contain SQL). The problem is that the database server can't keep writing to WAL forever as it will consume more and more space over time. So, at some point, the transaction log has to be recycled. This is done by a **checkpoint**, which happens automatically in the background.

The idea is that, when the data is written, it goes to the transaction log, and then a dirty buffer is put into shared buffers. Those dirty buffers have to go to disk and are written out to the data files by the background writer or during a checkpoint. As soon as all of the dirty buffers up to that point have been written, the transaction log can be deleted.

> **Important note**
>
> Please, never *ever* delete transaction log files manually. In the event of a crash, the database server won't be able to start up again, and the amount of disk space needed will be reclaimed anyway as new transactions come in. Never touch the transaction log manually. PostgreSQL takes care of things on its own, and doing things in there manually is harmful.

Optimizing the transaction log

Checkpoints happen automatically and are triggered by the server. However, there are configuration settings that decide when a checkpoint is initiated. The following parameters, which can be found in the `postgresql.conf` file, are in charge of handling checkpoints:

```
#checkpoint_timeout = 5min            # range 30s-1d
#max_wal_size = 1GB
#min_wal_size = 80MB
```

There are two reasons to initiate a checkpoint:

- We might run out of time or space
- The maximum time between two checkpoints is defined by the `checkpoint_timeout` variable

The amount of space provided to store the transaction logs will vary between the `min_wal_size` and `max_wal_size` variables. PostgreSQL will automatically trigger checkpoints in such a way that the amount of space needed will be between those two numbers.

> **Important note**
>
> The `max_wal_size` variable is a soft limit and PostgreSQL may (under heavy load) temporarily need a bit more space. In other words, if our transaction log is on a separate disk, it makes sense to make sure that there's a bit more space available to store `WAL`. Often, people ask how much `WAL` might overshoot the limit. This is hard to determine. However, we've seen substantially larger `WAL` directories.

Large checkpoint distances will decrease the amount of `WAL` created. Yes, that's right – larger checkpoint distances will lead to less `WAL`.

The reason for this is simple: whenever a block is touched after a checkpoint for the first time, it has to be sent to `WAL` completely. If the block is changed more often, only the changes make it to the log. Larger distances cause fewer full-page writes, which, in turn, reduces the amount of `WAL` created in the first place. The difference can be quite substantial, as can be seen in one of my blog posts at `https://www.cybertec-postgresql.com/en/checkpoint-distance-and-amount-of-wal/`.

PostgreSQL also allows us to configure whether checkpoints should be short and intense, or whether they should be spread out over a longer period. The default value is `0.9`, which means that the checkpoint should be done in such a way that the process has finished 90% between the current checkpoint and the next one. The following listing shows how to set `checkpoint_completion_target`:

```
#checkpoint_completion_target = 0.9
```

This value means that the checkpoint is stretched out and less intensive. In many cases, a higher value has proven beneficial for flattening out I/O spikes caused by intense checkpointing. A higher value is always better and therefore the default value of 0.9 is fine.

As we've already stated in this chapter, `WAL` is handled by the database server automatically. In the default setting, old `WAL` files are renamed and recycled. While this is good for traditional filesystems, it might not be the best possible option if you happen to use a **copy-on-write** (**COW**) filesystem such as `btrfs` or similar.

Therefore, the following parameter is relevant:

```
wal_recycle = on
```

If you're on a traditional filesystem, `on` is just fine; if you're using a COW filesystem, consider giving `off` a try for better performance.

However, performance isn't the only important topic. Let's also take a look at log archiving and recovery.

Transaction log archiving and recovery

After our brief introduction to the transaction log in general, it's time to focus on the process of transaction log archiving. As we've already seen, the transaction log contains a sequence of binary changes that are made to the storage system. So, why not use it to replicate database instances and do a lot of other cool stuff, such as archiving?

Configuring for archiving

The first thing we want to do in this chapter is create a configuration to perform standard PITR. There are a couple of advantages of using PITR over ordinary dumps:

- We'll lose less data because we can restore it to a certain point in time and not just to the fixed backup point.

- Restoring will be faster because indexes don't have to be created from scratch. They're just copied over and are ready to use.

Configuration for PITR is easy. Just a handful of changes have to be made in the postgresql. conf file, as shown here:

```
wal_level = replica      # used to be "hot_standby"
                         # in older versions
max_wal_senders = 10     # at least 2, better at least 2
```

The wal_level variable says that the server is supposed to produce enough transaction logs to allow for PITR. If the wal_level variable is set to minimal, the transaction log will only contain enough information to recover a single node setup – it isn't rich enough to handle replication.

The max_wal_senders variable allows us to stream WAL from the server and limits the number of active streams in the process. It will allow us to use pg_basebackup to create an initial backup instead of traditional file-based copying. The advantage here is that pg_basebackup is a lot easier to use.

The idea behind WAL streaming is that the transaction log that's created is copied to a safe place for storage. There are two means of transporting WAL:

- Using pg_receivewal
- Using the filesystem as a means to archive it

In this section, we'll look at how to set up the second option. During normal operations, PostgreSQL keeps writing to those WAL files. When we have archive_mode = on in the postgresql. conf file, PostgreSQL will call the archive_command variable for every single file.

A configuration might look as follows. First, a directory storing those transaction log files can be created:

```
mkdir /archive
chown postgres.postgres archive
```

The following entries can be changed in the postgresql.conf file:

```
archive_mode = on
archive_command = 'cp %p /archive/%f'
```

A restart will enable archiving, but let's configure the pg_hba.conf file first to reduce downtime to an absolute minimum.

> **Important note**
> We can put any command into the archive_command variable.

Many people use `rsync`, `scp`, and other options to transport their `WAL` files to a safe location. If our script returns 0, PostgreSQL will assume that the file has been archived. If anything else is returned, PostgreSQL will try to archive the file again. This is necessary because the database engine has to ensure that no files are lost. To perform the recovery process, we have to have every file available; not a single file is allowed to go missing. In the next section, we'll adjust the configuration in the `pg_hba.conf` file.

Using archiving libraries

In recent versions of PostgreSQL, an important new feature has been added: archiving libraries. To integrate backup tools more tightly into a system, it's easier to run them as a library than to run an executable for every 16 MB segment that has to be archived. This allows us to integrate tools and backup solutions way more tightly with PostgreSQL:

```
#archive_library = ''   # library to use to archive
                        # a logfile segment
                        # (empty string indicates
                        # archive_command should
                        # be used)
```

The idea is to allow people writing backup software to become a part of the server. In the future, we expect many backup software vendors to make use of this functionality.

Configuring the pg_hba.conf file

Now that the `postgresql.conf` file has been configured successfully, it's necessary to configure the `pg_hba.conf` file for streaming. Note that this is only necessary if we're planning to use `pg_basebackup`, which is a state-of-the-art tool for creating base backups.

The options we have in the `pg_hba.conf` file are the same ones that we already saw in *Chapter 8, Managing PostgreSQL Security*. There's just one major issue to keep in mind, which can be understood with the help of the following code:

```
# Allow replication connections from localhost,
# by a user with the replication privilege.
local   replication   postgres                    trust
host    replication   postgres   127.0.0.1/32     trust
host    replication   postgres   ::1/128          trust
```

We can define standard `pg_hba.conf` file rules. The important thing is that the second column says `replication`. Normal rules aren't enough – it's really important to add explicit replication permissions. Also, keep in mind that we don't have to do this as a superuser. We can create a specific user who's only allowed to perform login and replication.

Current versions are already configured in the way we've outlined in this section. Local replication works when out-of-the-box remote IPs have to be added to pg_hba.conf.

Now that the pg_hba.conf file has been configured correctly, PostgreSQL can be restarted.

Creating base backups

After teaching PostgreSQL how to archive those WAL files, it's time to create the first backup. The idea is to have a backup and replay the WAL files based on it to reach any point in time.

To create an initial backup, we can turn to pg_basebackup, which is a command-line tool used to perform backups. Let's call pg_basebackup and see how it works:

```
pg_basebackup -D /some_target_dir
        -h localhost
        --checkpoint=fast
        --wal-method=stream
```

As we can see, we'll use four parameters here:

- -D: Where do we want the base backup to live? PostgreSQL requires an empty directory. At the end of the backup, we'll see a copy of the server's data directory (the destination).

- -h: This indicates the IP address or the name of the primary (the source). This is the server you want to back up.

- --checkpoint=fast: Usually, pg_basebackup waits for the primary to create a checkpoint. The reason for this is that the replay process has to start somewhere. A checkpoint ensures that data has been written up to a certain point, so PostgreSQL can safely jump in there and start the replay process. It can also be done without the --checkpoint=fast parameter. However, it might take a while before pg_basebackup starts to copy data in this case. Checkpoints can be up to 1 hour apart, which can delay our backups unnecessarily.

- --wal-method=stream: By default, pg_basebackup connects to the primary server and starts copying files over. Now, keep in mind that those files are modified while they're being copied. Therefore, the data reaching the backup is inconsistent. This inconsistency can be repaired during the recovery process using WAL. However, the backup itself isn't consistent. By adding the --wal- method=stream parameter, it's possible to create a self-contained backup; it can be started directly without the need to replay the transaction log. This is a nice method if we just want to clone an instance and not use PITR. Fortunately, --wal-method=stream is already the default in PostgreSQL, but in the case of older versions, this is recommended (there's no need to worry in the case of PostgreSQL 17 and beyond).

Now, let's take a look at bandwidth management.

Reducing the bandwidth of backups

When pg_basebackup starts, it tries to finish its work as quickly as possible. If we have a good network connection, pg_basebackup can fetch hundreds of megabytes a second from the remote server. If our server has a weak I/O system, this could mean that pg_basebackup could suck up all the resources easily, and end users might experience bad performance because their I/O requests are simply too slow.

To control the maximum transfer rate, pg_basebackup offers the -r option, which is described by the following item:

```
-r, --max-rate=RATE
    maximum transfer rate to transfer data directory
    (in kB/s, or use suffix "k" or "M")
```

When we create a base backup, we need to make sure that the disk system on the primary can stand the load. Therefore, adjusting our transfer rate can make a lot of sense.

Mapping tablespaces

Usually, pg_basebackup can be called directly if we're using an identical filesystem layout on the target system. If this isn't the case, pg_basebackup allows you to map the primary's filesystem layout to the desired layout. The -T option allows us to do the mappings:

```
-T, --tablespace-mapping=OLDDIR=NEWDIR
    relocate tablespace in OLDDIR to NEWDIR
```

> **Important note**
>
> If your system is small, it could be a good idea to keep everything in one tablespace. Tablespaces only really make sense if they can help you add more physical disks to a server. It makes no sense when you're constrained by the network bandwidth or if data on your SAN ends on the same disk anyway.

This is also true if I/O isn't the problem (maybe because you're only managing a few gigabytes of data).

Using different formats

The pg_basebackup command-line tool can create various formats. By default, it will put data in an empty directory. Essentially, it will connect to the source server, create a .tar file over a network connection, and put data into the desired directory.

The trouble with this approach is that pg_basebackup will create many files, which isn't suitable if we want to move the backup to an external backup solution such as Tivoli Storage Manager. The following listing shows the valid output formats supported by pg_basebackup:

```
-F, --format=p|t                output format (plain (default), tar)
```

To create a single file, we can use the -F=t option. By default, it will create a file called base.tar, which can then be managed more easily. The downside, of course, is that we have to inflate the file again before performing PITR.

Defining backup targets

It's now possible to define a backup destination. By default, PostgreSQL will send the backup to the client. It will be stored on the machine that executes pg_basebackup. However, this might not be the desired behavior:

```
-t, --target=TARGET[:DETAIL]
  backup target (if other than client)
```

At the moment, there are three backup targets:

- client: Standard behaviors
- server: Store the backup on the server (for example, server:/some/path)
- backhole: Send the backup to /dev/null

This adds a lot of flexibility to the command because the new feature decouples the backup destination from the backup tool itself.

Tracking pg_basebackup

If you're saving a huge database, pg_basebackup might take a while. Be aware of the fact that if you're saving a 1 TB database using a 1 GB per second network connection, we're still talking about something that will take around 20 minutes to complete. This is a lot of time. Therefore, it can be useful to track the progress of pg_basebackup and see what it's doing. Fortunately, PostgreSQL provides a system view that gives you all the information you'll need to monitor things:

```
test=# \d pg_stat_progress_basebackup
        View "pg_catalog.pg_stat_progress_basebackup"
        Column          |   Type   | ...
------------------------+----------+-...
 pid                    | integer ...
 phase                  | text ...|
 backup_total           | bigint   ...
```

```
backup_streamed        | bigint  ...
tablespaces_total      | bigint ...
tablespaces_streamed   | bigint  ...
```

You can see how much data has already been sent, which gives a good indication of when the base backup might finish.

Testing transaction log archiving

Before we dive into the actual replay process, it makes sense to check out archiving to make sure that it's working perfectly and as expected. We can do this by using a simple `ls` command, as shown in the following code:

```
[hs@MacBook-Air-2 archive]$ ls -l
total 4030472

. . .
-rw-------   1 hs   wheel   16777216 Oct   7 18:50
000000010000000000000014
-rw-------   1 hs   wheel   16777216 Oct   7 18:50
000000010000000000000015
-rw-------   1 hs   wheel        343 Oct   7 18:50 000000010000000000000001
5.00000028.backup
-rw-------   1 hs   wheel   16777216 Oct   7 18:51
000000010000000000000016
-rw-------   1 hs   wheel   16777216 Oct   7 18:51
000000010000000000000017
-rw-------   1 hs   wheel   16777216 Oct   7 18:51
000000010000000000000018

. . .
```

As soon as there's any serious activity in a database, `WAL` files should be sent to the archive.

In addition to just checking for files, the following view can be useful:

```
test=# \d pg_stat_archiver
            View "pg_catalog.pg_stat_archiver"
      Column        |            Type             | Modifiers
--------------------+-----------------------------+-----------
 archived_count     | bigint                      |
 last_archived_wal  | text                        |
 last_archived_time | timestamp with time zone    |
 failed_count       | bigint                      |
 last_failed_wal    | text                        |
 last_failed_time   | timestamp with time zone    |
 stats_reset        | timestamp with time zone    |
```

The pg_stat_archiver system view is very useful for figuring out whether and when archiving has stalled for whatever reason. It will tell us about the number of files already archived (archived_ count). We can also see what the final file was and when the event happened. Finally, the pg_stat_ archiver system view can tell us when archiving has gone wrong, which is vital information. Unfortunately, the error code or message isn't shown in the table, but since archive_command can be an arbitrary command, it's easy to log.

There's one more thing to see in the archive. As we described previously, it's important to check that the files have been archived. But there's more – when the pg_basebackup command-line tool is called, we'll see a .backup file in the stream of WAL files. It's small and contains only some information about the base backup itself – it's purely informative and isn't needed by the replay process. However, it gives us some vital clues. When we start to replay the transaction log later on, we can delete all WAL files that are older than the .backup file. In this case, our backup file is called 00000001000000 0000000015.00000028.backup. This means that the replay process starts somewhere within the . . .0015 file (at position . . .28). It also means that we can delete all files older than . . .0015. Older WAL files won't be needed for recovery anymore. Keep in mind that we can keep more than just one backup around, so I'm only referring to the current backup.

Now that we know how archiving works, we can turn our attention to the replay process.

Replaying the transaction log

So far, we've adjusted the postgresql.conf file (wal_level, max_wal_senders, archive_ mode, and archive_command) and allowed the pg_basebackup command to be used in the pg_hba.conf file. Then, the database was restarted, and a base backup was successfully produced.

Keep in mind that base backups can only happen while the database is fully operational – only a brief restart is required to change the max_wal_senders and wal_level variables.

Now that the system is working properly, we might face a crash that we'll want to recover from. Therefore, we can perform PITR to restore as much data as possible. The first thing we've got to do is take the base backup and put it in the desired location.

> **Important note**
>
> It can be a good idea to save the old database cluster. Even if it's broken, our PostgreSQL support company might need it to track down the reason for the crash. You can still delete it later on, once you've got everything up and running again.

Given the preceding filesystem layout, we might want to do something like this:

```
cd /some_target_dir
cp -Rv * /data
```

We're assuming that the new database server will be located in the /data directory. Make sure that the directory is empty before you copy the base backup over.

So, let's see how to configure the replay process. Try to put restore_command and recovery_target_time into postgresql.conf:

```
restore_command = 'cp /archive/%f %p'
recovery_target_action = 'promote'
```

After fixing the postgresql.conf file, we can simply start up our server. However, before that, there's one task of key importance:

touch recovery.signal

The data directory you want to use for recovery needs a file called recovery.signal. If this file is missing, PostgreSQL will simply start up without replaying the transaction log – without this file, you'd end up in a *consistent state* (that is, the earliest possible moment). Therefore, it's vital to keep in mind that this file is needed unless you want to risk starting over and over again. If you start the database, the output might look as follows:

```
waiting for server to start....
2024-10-07 19:51:35.600 CEST [14320] LOG:   starting PostgreSQL 17.0
on x86_64-apple-darwin23.4.0, compiled by Apple clang version 15.0.0
(clang-1500.1.0.2.5), 64-bit
2024-10-07 19:51:35.602 CEST [14320] LOG:   listening on IPv6 address
"::1", port 5432
2024-10-07 19:51:35.602 CEST [14320] LOG:   listening on IPv4 address
"127.0.0.1", port 5432
2024-10-07 19:51:35.602 CEST [14320] LOG:   listening on Unix socket "/
tmp/.s.PGSQL.5432"
2024-10-07 19:51:35.610 CEST [14323] LOG:   database system was
interrupted; last known up at 2024-10-07 18:50:41 CEST
cp: /tmp/archive/00000002.history: No such file or directory
2024-10-07 19:51:35.649 CEST [14323] LOG:   starting backup recovery
with redo LSN 0/15000028, checkpoint LSN 0/15000080, on timeline ID 1
2024-10-07 19:51:35.666 CEST [14323] LOG:   restored log file
"000000010000000000000015" from archive
2024-10-07 19:51:35.672 CEST [14323] LOG:   starting archive recovery
2024-10-07 19:51:35.678 CEST [14323] LOG:   redo starts at 0/15000028
2024-10-07 19:51:35.678 CEST [14323] LOG:   completed backup recovery
with redo LSN 0/15000028 and end LSN 0/15000120
2024-10-07 19:51:35.678 CEST [14323] LOG:   consistent recovery state
reached at 0/15000120
2024-10-07 19:51:35.678 CEST [14320] LOG:   database system is ready to
accept read-only connections
2024-10-07 19:51:35.695 CEST [14323] LOG:   restored log file
"000000010000000000000016" from archive
2024-10-07 19:51:35.719 CEST [14323] LOG:   restored log file
```

```
"000000010000000000000017" from archive
2024-10-07 19:51:35.719 CEST [14323] LOG:  contrecord is requested by
0/17000028
2024-10-07 19:51:35.719 CEST [14323] LOG:  redo done at 0/160000A0
system usage: CPU: user: 0.00 s, system: 0.00 s, elapsed: 0.04 s
2024-10-07 19:51:35.731 CEST [14323] LOG:  restored log file
"000000010000000000000016" from archive
cp: /tmp/archive/00000002.history: No such file or directory
2024-10-07 19:51:35.742 CEST [14323] LOG:  selected new timeline ID: 2
cp: /tmp/archive/00000001.history: No such file or directory
2024-10-07 19:51:35.755 CEST [14323] LOG:  archive recovery complete
2024-10-07 19:51:35.756 CEST [14321] LOG:  checkpoint starting: end-
of-recovery immediate wait
2024-10-07 19:51:35.758 CEST [14321] LOG:  checkpoint complete:
wrote 3 buffers (0.0%); 0 WAL file(s) added, 0 removed, 2 recycled;
write=0.001 s, sync=0.001 s, total=0.002 s; sync files=2,
longest=0.001 s, average=0.001 s; distance=32768 kB, estimate=32768
kB; lsn=0/17000028, redo lsn=0/17000028
2024-10-07 19:51:35.765 CEST [14320] LOG:  database system is ready to
accept connections
 done
server started
```

When the server is started, there are a couple of messages to look for to ensure that our recovery works perfectly. The `consistent recovery state reached` message is the most important one to look for. Once you've reached this point, you can be sure that your database is consistent and not corrupted. Given the settings we used, PostgreSQL will consume as much of the transaction log as possible, and once this is done, it will promote the server automatically. The magic trick we can use to define this is the `recovery_target_action` setting, which we've set to `promote`.

Running PITR

For now, we've done what most people want to do: recover as much as possible and use as much of the transaction log as we can find to rescue data. However, this isn't always what we want; often, we want to recover explicitly to a certain point in time. In this case, we need to set the `recovery_target_time` variable. Here's an example.

```
recovery_target_time = '2024-12-29 15:32:12'
```

It simply contains a timestamp that tells PostgreSQL which moment we want to produce. However, two scenarios can occur here:

- We put in a timestamp between the "consistent state" and the end of the WAL

- We put in a timestamp that's in the future

While the first case is usually what we're aiming for, the second case can easily happen. PostgreSQL will report that we tried to recover to an unreachable timestamp by issuing an error message:

```
2024-10-07 19:49:40.727 CEST [14244] FATAL:  recovery ended before
configured recovery target was reached
2024-10-07 19:49:40.728 CEST [14241] LOG:  startup process (PID 14244)
exited with exit code 1
```

But the key question is, how do we know which time we want? This question sounds simple, but it isn't. In everyday life, this is a very common scenario. One of our developers might lose some data in the morning and we're supposed to make things fine again. But at what time in the morning? In reality, this is a really common case and it's often hard to get a handle on the recovery time stamp as the information we receive is often imprecise and not really what the DBA is looking for. What we can do here is play around with the `recovery_target_action` variable.

Doing that is easy. The first thing we have to make sure of is that the `hot_standby` variable is set to on in the `postgresql.conf` file. This will ensure that the database is readable while it's still in recovery mode. Then, we can set the following variable in `postgresql.conf`:

```
recovery_target_action = 'pause'
```

There are various `recovery_target_action` settings. If we use pause, PostgreSQL will pause at the desired time and let us check what's already been replayed. We can adjust the time we want, restart, and try again.

There's also a second way to pause transaction log replay: streaming replication. Here's what can be done during WAL replay:

```
test=# \x
Expanded display is on.
test=#
test=# \df *pause*
List of functions
-[ RECORD 1 ]-------+------------------------------
Schema              | pg_catalog
Name                | pg_get_wal_replay_pause_state
Result data type    | text
Argument data types |
Type                | func
-[ RECORD 2 ]-------+------------------------------
Schema              | pg_catalog
Name                | pg_is_wal_replay_paused
Result data type    | boolean
Argument data types |
Type                | func
```

```
-[ RECORD 3 ]-------+----------------------------
Schema              | pg_catalog
Name                | pg_wal_replay_pause
Result data type    | void
Argument data types |
Type                | func
```

We can call the `SELECT pg_wal_replay_pause();` command to halt `WAL` replay until we call the `SELECT pg_wal_replay_resume();` command.

The idea is to figure out how much `WAL` has already been replayed and to continue as necessary. However, keep in mind that once a server has been promoted, we can't just continue to replay `WAL` without further precautions.

One more function is available in PostgreSQL – `pg_get_wal_replay_pause_state`. It allows you to return whether you're currently pausing or not. Note that this function can only be called if you're in replay mode. Otherwise, it will error out, as shown here:

```
test=# SELECT pg_get_wal_replay_pause_state();
ERROR:   recovery is not in progress
HINT:   Recovery control functions can only be executed during
recovery.
```

This function can return three different text values:

- `not paused`

- `pause requested`

- `paused`

As we've already seen, it can be pretty tricky to figure out how far back we need to recover. Therefore, PostgreSQL provides us with some help. Consider the following real-world example – at midnight, we run a nightly process that ends at a point that's usually unknown. The goal is to recover exactly to the endpoint of the nightly process. The problem is, how do we know when the process has ended? In most cases, this is hard to figure out. So, why not add a marker to the transaction log? The code for this is as follows:

```
postgres=# SELECT pg_create_restore_point('my_daily_process_ended');
 pg_create_restore_point
-----------------------
 1F/E574A7B8
 (1 row)
```

If our process calls this SQL statement as soon as it ends, it will be possible to use this label in the transaction log to recover exactly to a point in time by adding the following directive to the `postgresql.conf` file:

```
recovery_target_name = 'my_daily_process_ended'
```

By using this setting instead of `recovery_target_time`, the replay process will beam us to the end of the nightly process.

Of course, we can also replay up to a certain transaction ID. However, in real life, this has proven to be difficult as the exact transaction ID is rarely ever known to an administrator, so there's not much practical value in this. Keep in mind that setting markers has to be done *before* recovery. This is important.

Cleaning up the transaction log archive

So far, data is being written to the archive all the time and no attention has been paid to cleaning out the archive again to free up space in the filesystem. PostgreSQL can't do this job for us because it has no idea whether we want to use the archive again. Therefore, we're in charge of cleaning up the transaction log. Of course, we can also use a backup tool – however, it's important to know that PostgreSQL has no chance of doing the cleanup for us.

Suppose we want to clean up an old transaction log that isn't needed anymore. Maybe we want to keep several base backups around and clean out all transaction logs that won't be needed anymore to restore one of those backups.

In this case, the `pg_archivecleanup` command-line tool is exactly what we need. We can simply pass the archive directory and the name of the backup file to the `pg_archivecleanup` command, and it will make sure that the files are removed from the disk. Using this tool makes life easier for us because we don't have to figure out which transaction log files to keep. Let's see how it works.

The `pg_archivecleanup` command removes older WAL files from PostgreSQL archives. Here's how we can use it:

```
pg_archivecleanup [OPTION]... ARCHIVELOCATION OLDESTKEPTWALFILE
```

Its options are as follows:

```
  -b, --clean-backup-history  clean up files including backup history
files
  -d, --debug                 generate debug output (verbose mode)
  -n, --dry-run               dry run, show the names of the files
that would be
                              removed
  -V, --version               output version information, then exit
  -x, --strip-extension=EXT   strip this extension before identifying
files for
```

```
                                        clean up
    -?, --help                          show this help, then exit
```

It can be used as `archive_cleanup_command` in `postgresql.conf`:

```
    archive_cleanup_command = 'pg_archivecleanup [OPTION]...
ARCHIVELOCATION %r'
```

Here's an example:

```
    archive_cleanup_command = 'pg_archivecleanup /mnt/server/archiverdir
%r'
```

It can also be used as a standalone archive cleaner, as shown here:

```
    pg_archivecleanup /mnt/server/archiverdir 000000010000000000000010.0
0000020.backup
```

This tool can be used with ease and is available on all platforms.

Now that we've taken a look at transaction log archiving and PITR, we can focus on one of the most widely used features in the PostgreSQL world today – streaming replication.

Making use of incremental backups

PostgreSQL 17 offers a new functionality that's key to handling large database deployment. I'm, of course, talking about incremental backups. Why does this feature matter? Consider the following simple but realistic example:

- Our database size is 10 TB
- We want a daily base backup
- We want to keep it for 7 days

In reality, this means that we have to keep at least 70 TB plus the transaction log for a week. Needless to say, this can be hard to handle or simply expensive to manage. However, if you're dealing with a database of that size, it's quite likely that not too much data will change from day to day. The difference in your database between, say, Monday and Tuesday might just be a couple of gigabytes. So, why not take an initial backup and store the differences between those backups?

This is exactly what PostgreSQL 17 allows you to do. So, let's dive deeper and see how this works. Before we take a look at the command-line output, I'll draft a typical scenario and a workflow to be replicated in code. Consider the following flow:

1. Full backup happens on Sunday.
2. Incremental backups happen from Monday to Saturday.

3. A crash happens on Wednesday.

4. We create a new instance to start Sunday to Tuesday.

5. We perform PITR.

This procedure is important but fortunately relatively easy. Note that these steps are usually not done by hand too often because many backup tools already automate this procedure and it's highly recommended to use such a solution instead of coding up things by hand. However, it makes sense to try the manual procedure to understand what's happening.

Configuring for incremental backups

Configuring PostgreSQL so that it supports incremental backups is simple. What we need is two configuration parameters that can be found in `postgresql.conf` (around line 390). Here they are:

```
# - WAL Summarization -

summarize_wal = on
  # run WAL summarizer process?
#wal_summary_keep_time = '10d'
  # when to remove old summary files, 0 = never
```

The way incremental backups work is as follows: PostgreSQL 17 introduces a new worker process called **summarizer**. What's the idea here? Between two backups, it often happens that a single 8k block in a table, an index, or some other structure changes over and over again. This is quite frequent. In the transaction log, those changes are stored in sequence, which means that 50 changes made to a single block will also result in a high number of WAL changes over and over again. The summarizer will simply keep track of all blocks/pages that have been changed. The next backup will simply pick up those blocks that have changed instead of simply copying the entire data directory over and over again. Of course, the summarizer won't keep those changes forever and has to throw them away. This behavior is controlled by `wal_summary_keep_time` – in our example, we can see that the default value is 10 days.

After enabling the summarizer (a restart is needed), we can look at how the process works.

Running a backup

The following command shows how we can handle those operations:

```
$ pg_basebackup -h localhost -D /path/base_1 --checkpoint=fast
```

This is just a simple base backup that's been taken from the local machine and stored in a directory on the same system. This is nothing new.

Adding incremental backups

However, the next two commands contain a lot of magic:

```
$ pg_basebackup -h localhost -D /path/incremental_1 \
    --checkpoint=fast -i /path/base_1/backup_manifest

$ pg_basebackup -h localhost -D /path/incremental_2 \
    --checkpoint=fast -i /path/incremental_1/backup_manifest
```

What we did here is run two incremental backups that depend on each other. The first incremental backup refers to the initial base backup by pointing to the cluster manifest. The second incremental base backup stores the difference between the first and the second incremental backup.

This is pretty simple. The benefit of the incremental backups can easily be observed. Consider the following listing:

```
[incremental_2]$ du -h | tail -n 1
 23M   .
[incremental_2]$ cd ..
[path]$ du -h base_1 | tail -n1
287M  base_1
```

Simply observe the difference in size between the original base backup and the second incremental one. In this simplistic example, we're talking about a 10x difference in size.

Combining backups again

However, a backup is worth nothing if we can't replay it. The first thing we must do is start the primary instance we've used to fetch the backup (note that this is normally not done by hand but by using systemctl– I'm just using plain metal commands here because it's easier for demonstration purposes):

```
$ pg_ctl -D /path/db17/ stop
```

Then, we can try to launch the incremental backup:

```
$ pg_ctl -D ./incremental_2/ start
waiting for server to start....
2024-10-07 22:45:06.917 CEST [19023] LOG:  starting PostgreSQL 17.0
on x86_64-apple-darwin23.4.0, compiled by Apple clang version 15.0.0
(clang-1500.1.0.2.5), 64-bit
2024-10-07 22:45:06.920 CEST [19023] LOG:  listening on IPv6 address
"::1", port 5432
2024-10-07 22:45:06.920 CEST [19023] LOG:  listening on IPv4 address
"127.0.0.1", port 5432
2024-10-07 22:45:06.920 CEST [19023] LOG:  listening on Unix socket "/
tmp/.s.PGSQL.5432"
```

```
2024-10-07 22:45:06.929 CEST [19026] LOG:  database system was
interrupted; last known up at 2024-10-07 22:36:30 CEST
2024-10-07 22:45:06.956 CEST [19026] FATAL:  this is an incremental
backup, not a data directory
2024-10-07 22:45:06.956 CEST [19026] HINT:  Use pg_combinebackup to
reconstruct a valid data directory.
2024-10-07 22:45:06.957 CEST [19023] LOG:  startup process (PID 19026)
exited with exit code 1
2024-10-07 22:45:06.957 CEST [19023] LOG:  aborting startup due to
startup process failure
2024-10-07 22:45:06.958 CEST [19023] LOG:  database system is shut
down
```

The FATAL error followed by a hint tells us that we can't start this backup directly as it's only an incremental piece of data. Therefore, we have to make use of pg_combinebackup to build a data directory we can fire up and use:

$ pg_combinebackup --help

```
pg_combinebackup reconstructs full backups from incrementals.
```

Here's an example of its usage:

```
pg_combinebackup [OPTION]... DIRECTORY...
```

It has the following options:

```
-d, --debug               generate lots of debugging output
-n, --dry-run             do not actually do anything
-N, --no-sync             do not wait for changes to be written
safely to disk
-o, --output=DIRECTORY    output directory
-T, --tablespace-mapping=OLDDIR=NEWDIR
                          relocate tablespace in OLDDIR to NEWDIR
    --clone               clone (reflink) files instead of copying
    --copy                copy files (default)
    --copy-file-range     copy using copy_file_range() system call
    --manifest-checksums=SHA{224,256,384,512}|CRC32C|NONE
                          use algorithm for manifest checksums
    --no-manifest         suppress generation of backup manifest
    --sync-method=METHOD  set method for syncing files to disk
-V, --version             output version information, then exit
-?, --help                show this help, then exit
```

This command is all we need to put our backup together and use it directly to either start the database or implement PITR, something we've seen in this chapter already (a freshly combined backup serves as a normal base backup and can be used the same way):

```
$ pg_combinebackup -o /path/new_base \
  /path/base_1 \
  /path/incremental_1 \
  /path/incremental_2/
pg_combinebackup: warning: manifest file "/path/incremental_2//backup_
manifest" contains no entry for file "postmaster.opts"
$ cd new_base/
$ du -h | tail -n1
287M
```

The way the command is structured is easy: the first argument as defined by -o is the output directory. This is where the new backup will be stored. Then, we point to the original base backup. Finally, we simply list all incremental backups in order. PostgreSQL will then take all the incremental ones and apply them to the original backup. This way, we end up with a fresh backup in the output directory that's a combination of the full – as well as all the partial – ones.

The freshly created backup is now identical to a full base backup – it just took us a simple intermediate step to make it happen. Of course, this additional step isn't free, but keep in mind that a recovery process shouldn't happen too often and the goal here is to save on space as much as possible. In real life, this is almost always a win as combining those backups doesn't add insane overhead.

Setting up asynchronous replication

The idea behind streaming replication is simple. After an initial base backup, the secondary backup can connect to the primary, fetch a transaction log in real time, and apply it. Transaction log replay isn't a single operation anymore but rather a continuous process that's supposed to keep running for as long as a cluster exists.

Performing a basic setup

In this section, we'll learn how to set up asynchronous replication quickly and easily. The goal is to set up a system that consists of two nodes.

Most of the work has already been done for WAL archiving. However, to make it easy to understand, we'll look at the entire process of setting up streaming because we can't assume that WAL shipping has already been set up as needed.

The first thing we must do is go to the postgresql.conf file and adjust the following parameters:

```
wal_level = replica
max_wal_senders = 10    # or whatever value >= 2
```

```
                              # this is the default value already
                              # in more recent versions
  hot_standby = on            # in already a default setting
```

Just as we did previously, the wal_level variable has to be adjusted to ensure that PostgreSQL produces enough transaction logs to sustain a replica. Then, we have to configure the max_wal_senders variable. When a replica is up and running or when a base backup is created, a WAL sender process will talk to a WAL receiver process on the client side. The max_wal_senders setting allows PostgreSQL to create enough processes to serve those clients.

> **Important note**
>
> Theoretically, it's enough to have just one WAL sender process. However, it's pretty inconvenient. A base backup that uses the --wal-method=stream parameter (default setting) will already need two WAL sender processes. If you want to run a replica and perform a base backup at the same time, there are already three processes in use. So, make sure that you allow PostgreSQL to create enough processes to prevent pointless restarts.

Then, there's the hot_standby variable. A primary ignores the hot_standby variable and doesn't consider it. All it does is make the replica readable during WAL replay. So, why do we care? Keep in mind that the pg_basebackup command will clone the entire server, including its configuration. This means that if we've already set the value on the primary, the replicas will automatically receive it when the data directory is cloned.

After setting the postgresql.conf file, we can turn our attention to the pg_hba.conf file – just allow the replica to perform replication by adding rules. Those rules are the same as those we saw for PITR.

Then, restart the database server, just like you did for PITR.

Now, the pg_basebackup command can be called on the replica. Before we do that, make sure that the /target directory is empty. If you're using RPM packages, ensure that you shut down a potentially running instance and empty the directory (for example, /var/lib/pgsql/data). The following code shows how pg_basebackup can be used:

```
pg_basebackup -D /target
          -h primary.example.com
          --checkpoint=fast
          --wal-method=stream -R
```

Just replace the /target directory with your desired destination directory and replace primary.example.com with the IP or DNS name of your primary. The --checkpoint=fast parameter will trigger an instant checkpoint. Then, there's the --wal-method=stream parameter; it will open two streams. One will copy the data, while the other will fetch the WAL data that's created while the backup is running.

Finally, there's the -R flag:

```
-R, --write-recovery-conf    # write configuration
                             # for replication
```

The -R flag is a really good feature. The pg_basebackup command can automatically create the replica configuration.

After running the pg_basebackup command, the services can be started. The first thing we should check is whether the primary shows wal sender process:

```
$ ps ax | grep sender
17873 ? Ss 0:00 postgres: wal sender process
                          hs ::1(57596) streaming 1F/E9000060
```

If it does, the replica will also show wal receiver process:

```
17872 ? Ss 0:00 postgres: wal receiver process
                           streaming 1F/E9000060
```

If those processes are there, we're already on the right track, and the replication process is working as expected. Both sides are now talking to each other, and WAL flows from the primary to the replica.

Improving security

So far, we've seen that data is streamed as a superuser. However, it isn't a good idea to allow superuser access from a remote site. Fortunately, PostgreSQL allows us to create a user that's only allowed to consume the transaction log stream and not anything else.

Creating a user just for streaming is easy. Here's how it works:

```
test=# CREATE USER repl LOGIN REPLICATION;
CREATE ROLE
```

By assigning replication to the user, it's possible to use it just for streaming – everything else is forbidden.

It's highly recommended to not use your superuser account to set up streaming. Simply change the configuration file to the newly created user. Not exposing superuser accounts will dramatically improve security, just like giving the replication user a password.

Halting and resuming replication

Once streaming replication has been set up, it works flawlessly without too much administrator intervention. However, in some cases, it might make sense to halt replication and resume it at a later point. But why would anybody want to do that?

Consider the following use case – you're in charge of a primary/replica setup, which is running an inept **content management system** (**CMS**) or some dubious forum software. Suppose you want to update your application from the awful CMS 1.0 to the dreadful CMS 2.0. Some changes will be executed in your database, which will instantly be replicated in the replica database. What if the upgrade process does something wrong? The error will be instantly replicated to both nodes due to streaming.

To avoid instant replication, we can halt replication and resume as needed. In the case of our CMS update, we could simply do the following things:

1. Halt replication.

2. Perform the application update on the primary.

3. Check that our application still works. If so, we resume replication. If not, we fail over to the replica, which still contains the old data.

With this mechanism, we can protect our data because we can fall back to the data as it was before the problem. Later in this chapter, we'll learn how to promote a replica so that it becomes the new primary server.

The main question now is, how can we halt replication? Let's see how it works. Execute the following line on the standby:

```
test=# SELECT pg_wal_replay_pause();
```

This line will halt replication. Note that the transaction log will still flow from the primary to the replica – only the replay process is halted. Your data is still protected as it persists on the replica. In the case of a server crash, no data will be lost.

Keep in mind that the replay process has to be halted on the replica. Otherwise, an error will be thrown by PostgreSQL:

```
ERROR: recovery is not in progress
HINT: Recovery control functions can only be executed during recovery.
```

Once replication is to be resumed, the following line will be needed on the replica:

```
SELECT pg_wal_replay_resume();
```

PostgreSQL will start to replay WAL again.

Checking replication to ensure availability

One of the core jobs of every administrator is to ensure that replication stays up and running at all times. If replication is down, data could be lost if the primary crashes. Therefore, keeping an eye on replication is necessary.

Fortunately, PostgreSQL provides system views that allow us to take a deep look at what's going on. One of those views is `pg_stat_replication`:

```
test=# \d pg_stat_replication
                    View "pg_catalog.pg_stat_replication"
        Column        |             Type   ...
----------------------+------------... 
 pid                  | integer ...
 usesysid             | oid ...
 usename              | name ...
 application_name     | text ...
 client_addr          | inet ...
 client_hostname      | text ...
 client_port          | integer ...
 backend_start        | timestamp with time zone ...
 backend_xmin         | xid ...
 state                | text ...
 sent_lsn             | pg_lsn ...
 write_lsn            | pg_lsn ...
 flush_lsn            | pg_lsn ...
 replay_lsn           | pg_lsn ...
 write_lag            | interval ...
 flush_lag            | interval ...
 replay_lag           | interval ...
 sync_priority        | integer ...
 sync_state           | text ...
 reply_time           | timestamp with time zone ...
```

The `pg_stat_replication` view will contain information about the sender. I don't want to use the word *primary* here because replicas can be connected to some other replica. It's possible to build a tree of servers. In the case of a tree of servers, the primary will only have information about the replicas it's directly connected to.

The first thing we'll see in this view is the process ID of the WAL sender process. It helps us to identify the process if something goes wrong. This is usually not the case. Then, we'll see the username that's being used by the replica to connect to its sending server. The `client_*` fields will indicate where the replicas are. We'll be able to extract network information from those fields. The `backend_start` field shows when the replicas started to stream from our server.

Then, there's the magical `backend_xmin` field. Suppose you're running a primary/replica setup. It's possible to tell the replica to report its transaction ID to the primary. The idea behind this is to delay cleanup on the primary so that data isn't taken from a transaction running on the replica.

The `state` field informs us about the state of the server. If our system is fine, the field will contain streaming. Otherwise, a closer inspection is needed.

The next four fields are really important. The `sent_lsn` field, formerly the `sent_location` field, indicates how much WAL has already reached the other side, which implies that the fields have been accepted by the WAL receiver. We can use it to figure out how much data has already made it to the replica. Then, there's the `write_lsn` field, formerly the `write_location` field. Once WAL has been accepted, it's passed on to the OS. The `write_lsn` field will tell us that the WAL position has safely made it to the OS already. The `flush_lsn` field, formerly the `flush_location` field, will know how much WAL the database has already flushed to disk.

Finally, there's `replay_lsn`, formerly the `replay_location` field. The fact that WAL has made it to the disk on standby doesn't mean that PostgreSQL has already replayed or been made visible to the end user. Suppose that replication is paused. Data will still flow to the standby disk. However, it will be applied later. The `replay_lsn` field will tell us how much data is already visible.

Finally, PostgreSQL tells us whether replication is synchronous or asynchronous.

When running this on the primary, the `pg_current_wal_lsn()` function returns the current transaction log position. PostgreSQL has a special datatype for transaction log positions called `pg_lsn`. It features a couple of operators, which are used here to subtract the replica's WAL position from the primary's WAL position. So, the view outlined here returns the difference between the two servers in bytes (the replication delay).

While the `pg_stat_replication` system view contains information on the sending side, the `pg_stat_wal_receiver` system view will provide us with similar information on the receiving side:

```
test=# \d pg_stat_wal_receiver
                    View "pg_catalog.pg_stat_wal_receiver"
        Column           |              Type      ...
-------------------------+--------------------- ...
 pid                     | integer   ...
 status                  | text   ...
 receive_start_lsn       | pg_lsn   ...
 receive_start_tli       | integer …
 written_lsn             | pg_lsn   ...
 flushed_lsn             | pg_lsn   ...
 received_tli            | integer    ...
 last_msg_send_time      | timestamp with time zone ...
 last_msg_receipt_time   | timestamp with time zone ...
 latest_end_lsn          | pg_lsn   ...
 latest_end_time         | timestamp with time zone ...
 slot_name               | text   ...
 sender_host             | text   ...
 sender_port             | integer   ...
 conninfo                | text   ...
```

After the process ID of the WAL receiver process, PostgreSQL will provide you with the status of the process. Then, the `receive_start_lsn` field will tell you about the transaction log position the WAL receiver started at, while the `receive_start_tli` field will inform you about the timeline that was used when the WAL receiver was started.

The `written_lsn` and `flushed_lsn` fields contain information about the WAL position, which was already written and flushed to disk. Then, we've got some information about the time, as well as about slots and connections.

In general, many people find it easier to read the `pg_stat_replication` system view than the `pg_stat_wal_receiver` view, and most tools are built around the `pg_stat_replication` view.

Performing failovers and understanding timelines

Once a primary/replica setup has been created, it usually works flawlessly for a very long time. However, everything can fail, so it's important to understand how a failed server can be replaced with a backup system.

PostgreSQL makes failovers and promotion easy. All we have to do is use the `pg_ctl` parameter to tell a replica to promote itself:

```
pg_ctl -D data_dir promote
```

The server will disconnect itself from the primary and perform the promotion instantly. Remember, the replica may already support thousands of read-only connections while being promoted. One nice feature of PostgreSQL is that all open connections will be turned into read/write connections during promotion – there isn't even any need to reconnect.

Note that PostgreSQL 12 and beyond are also able to promote the database from replica to primary using plain SQL. Just use `SELECT pg_promote();`. It's even possible to delay the promotion for a couple of seconds:

```
test=# \df *promote*
List of functions
-[ RECORD 1 ]-------+----------------------------------------------------
--
Schema              | pg_catalog
Name                | pg_promote
Result data type    | boolean
Argument data types | wait boolean DEFAULT true, wait_seconds integer
DEFAULT 60
Type                | func
```

When promoting a server, PostgreSQL will increment the timeline; if you set up a brand-new server, it will be in timeline 1. If a replica is cloned from that server, it will be in the same timeline as its primary. So, both boxes will be in timeline 1. If the replica is promoted to an independent primary, it will move on to timeline 2.

Timelines are especially important to PITR. Suppose we create a base backup around midnight. At midnight, the replica is promoted. At 3:00 P.M., something crashes, and we want to recover to 2:00 P.M. We'll replay the transaction log that was created after the base backup and follow the WAL stream of our desired server, as those two nodes started to diverge at midnight.

The timeline change will also be visible in the name of the transaction log files. Here's an example of a WAL file in timeline 1:

```
000000010000000000000F5
```

If the timeline switches to 2, the new filename will be as follows:

```
000000020000000000000F5
```

As you can see, WAL files from different timelines could theoretically exist in the same archive directory.

Managing conflicts

So far, we've learned a lot about replication. However, it's important to take a look at replication conflicts. The main question that arises is, how can a conflict ever happen in the first place?

Consider the following example:

Primary	Replica
	BEGIN;
	SELECT … FROM tab WHERE ...
	… running ...
DROP TABLE tab;	… conflict happens ...
	... transaction is allowed to continue for 30 seconds ...
	... conflict is resolved or ends before timeout ...

Table 10.1 – Primary and replica comparison

The problem here is that the primary doesn't know that there's a transaction happening on the replica. Therefore, the DROP TABLE command doesn't block until the reading transaction is gone. If those two transactions happened on the same node, this would, of course, be the case. However, we're looking at two servers here. The DROP TABLE command will execute normally, and a request to kill those data files on disk will reach the replica through the transaction log. The replica isn't in trouble – if the table is removed from disk, the SELECT clause has to die; if the replica waits for the SELECT clause to complete before applying WAL, it might fall hopelessly behind.

The ideal solution is a compromise that can be controlled using a configuration variable:

```
max_standby_streaming_delay = 30s
    # max delay before canceling queries
    # when reading streaming WAL;
```

The idea is to wait for 30 seconds before resolving the conflict by killing the query on the replica. Depending on our application, we might want to change this variable to a more or less aggressive setting. Note that 30 seconds is for the entire replication stream, not for a single query. It might be that a single query is killed a lot earlier because some other query has already waited for some time.

While the DROP TABLE command is a conflict, some operations are less obvious. Here's an example:

```
BEGIN;
...
DELETE FROM tab WHERE id < 10000;
COMMIT;
...
VACUUM tab;
```

Once again, let's assume that there's a long-running SELECT clause happening on the replica. The DELETE clause isn't the problem here as it only flags the row as deleted – it doesn't remove it. The commit isn't a problem either because it simply marks the transaction as done. Physically, the row is still there.

The problem starts when an operation such as VACUUM kicks in. It will destroy the row on disk. Of course, these changes will make it to WAL and eventually reach the replica, which will then be in trouble.

To prevent typical problems caused by standard OLTP workloads, the PostgreSQL development team has introduced a config variable:

```
hot_standby_feedback = off
        # send info from standby to prevent
        # query conflicts
```

If this setting is on, the replica will send the oldest transaction ID to the primary periodically. In this case, VACUUM will know that there's an older transaction going on somewhere in the system and defer the cleanup age to a later point, when it's safe to clean out the rows. The hot_standby_feedback parameter causes the same effect as a long transaction on the primary.

As we can see, the hot_standby_feedback parameter is off by default. Why is that the case? Well, there's a good reason for this – if it's off, a replica doesn't have a real impact on the primary. Transaction log streaming doesn't consume a lot of CPU power, making streaming replication cheap and efficient. However, if a replica (which might not even be under our control) keeps transactions open for too long, our primary might suffer from table bloat due to late cleanup. In a default setup, this is less desirable than reduced conflicts.

Having `hot_standby_feedback = on` will usually avoid 99% of all OLTP-related conflicts, which is especially important if your transactions take longer than just a couple of milliseconds.

Making replication more reliable

In this chapter, we've seen that setting up replication is easy and doesn't require a lot of effort. However, there are always some corner cases that can cause operational challenges. One of those corner cases concerns transaction log retention.

Consider the following scenario:

1. A base backup is fetched.

2. After the backup, nothing happens for 1 hour.

3. The replica is started.

Keep in mind that the primary doesn't care too much about the existence of the replica. Therefore, the transaction log needed for the replica to start up might not exist on the primary anymore as it might have been removed by checkpoints already. The problem is that a resync is needed to be able to fire up the replica. In the case of a multi-TB database, this is a problem.

A potential solution to this problem is to use the `wal_keep_segments` setting:

```
#wal_keep_size = 0
  # in megabytes; 0 disables
```

By default, PostgreSQL keeps enough transaction logs around to survive an unexpected crash, but not much more. With the `wal_keep_size` setting, we can tell the server to preserve more data so that a replica can catch up, even if it falls behind.

It's important to keep in mind that servers not only fall behind because they're too slow or too busy – in many cases, a delay happens because a network is too slow. Suppose you're creating an index on a 1 TB table – PostgreSQL will sort the data, and when the index is built, it's also sent to the transaction log. Just imagine what happens when hundreds of megabytes of `WAL` are sent over a wire that can maybe only handle 1 GB or so. The loss of many gigabytes of data might be the consequence of this and will happen within seconds. Therefore, when adjusting the `wal_keep_size` setting, you shouldn't focus on the typical delay but on the highest delay tolerable to an administrator (maybe with some margin of safety).

Investing in a reasonably high setting for the `wal_keep_size` setting makes a lot of sense, and I recommend ensuring that there's always enough data around.

An alternative and more practical solution to the problem of running out of transaction logs is replication slots, which will be covered later in this chapter.

Upgrading to synchronous replication

So far, asynchronous replication has been covered in reasonable detail. However, asynchronous replication means that a commit on a replica is allowed to happen after the commit on a primary. If the primary crashes, data that hasn't made it to the replica might be lost, even if replication is occurring.

Synchronous replication is here to solve the problem – if PostgreSQL replicates synchronously, a commit has to be flushed to disk by at least one replica to go through on the primary. Therefore, synchronous replication reduces the odds of data loss substantially.

In PostgreSQL, configuring synchronous replication is easy. Only two things have to be done (in any order):

- Adjust the `synchronous_standby_names` setting in the `postgresql.conf` file on the primary

- Add an `application_name` setting to the `primary_conninfo` parameter in the `config` file in the replica

Let's get started with the `postgresql.conf` file on the primary:

```
synchronous_standby_names = ''
        # standby servers that provide sync rep
        # number of sync standbys and comma-separated
        # list of application_name
        # from standby(s); <*> = all
```

If we add `'*'`, all nodes will be considered synchronous candidates. However, in real-life scenarios, it's more likely that only a couple of nodes will be listed. Here's an example:

```
synchronous_standby_names = 'replica1, replica2, replica3'
```

In the preceding case, we got three synchronous candidates. Now, we have to change the `config` file and add `application_name`:

```
primary_conninfo = '... application_name=replica2'
```

The replica will now connect to the primary as `replica2`. The primary will check its configuration and figure out that `replica2` is the first one on the list that constitutes a viable replica. Therefore, PostgreSQL will ensure that a commit on the primary will only be successful if the replica confirms that the transaction is there.

Now, let's assume that `replica2` goes down for some reason – PostgreSQL will try to turn one of the other two nodes into a synchronous standby. But what if there's no other server?

In this case, PostgreSQL will wait on commit forever if a transaction is supposed to be synchronous. PostgreSQL won't continue to commit unless there are at least two viable nodes available. Remember, we've asked PostgreSQL to store data on at least two nodes – if we can't provide enough hosts at any given point in time, it's our fault. In reality, this means that synchronous replication is best achieved with at least three nodes – one primary and two replicas – as there's always a chance that one host will be lost.

Talking about host failures, there's an important thing to note at this point – if a synchronous partner dies while a commit is happening, PostgreSQL will wait for it to return. Alternatively, the synchronous commit can happen with some other potential synchronous partner. The end user might not even notice that the synchronous partners have changed.

In some cases, storing data on just two nodes might not be enough; maybe we want to improve safety even more and store the data on even more nodes. To achieve that, we can make use of the following syntax:

```
synchronous_standby_names =
"4(replica1, replica2, replica3, replica4, replica5, replica6)"
```

Of course, this comes at a price – keep in mind that speed will go down if we add more and more synchronous replicas. There's no such thing as a free lunch. PostgreSQL provides a couple of ways to keep the performance overhead under control, which we'll discuss in the following section.

But there's more. Let's take a look at the relevant parts of the protocol:

```
[FIRST] num_sync ( standby_name [, ...] )
ANY num_sync ( standby_name [, ...] )
standby_name [, ...]
```

Here, the `ANY` and `FIRST` keywords have been introduced. The `FIRST` keyword allows you to set the priorities of your servers, while the `ANY` keyword gives PostgreSQL a bit more flexibility when it commits a synchronous transaction.

Adjusting durability

In this chapter, we've seen that data is either replicated synchronously or asynchronously. However, this isn't a global thing. To ensure good performance, PostgreSQL allows us to configure things in a very flexible way. It's possible to replicate everything synchronously or asynchronously, but in many cases, we might want to do things in a more fine-grained way. This is exactly when the `synchronous_commit` setting is needed.

Assuming that synchronous replication, the `application_name` setting, and the `synchronous_standby_names` setting in the `postgresql.conf` file have been configured, the `synchronous_commit` setting will offer the following options:

- `off`: This is an asynchronous replication. So, WAL won't be flushed to disk on the primary instantly, and the primary won't wait for the replica to write everything to disk. If the primary fails, some data might be lost (up to three times – `wal_writer_delay`).

- `local`: The transaction log is flushed to disk on a commit by the primary. However, the primary doesn't wait for the replica (asynchronous replication).

- `remote_write`: The `remote_write` setting already makes PostgreSQL replicate synchronously. However, only the primary saves data to disk. For the replica, it's enough to send the data to the OS. The idea is to not wait for the second disk flush to speed things up. It's very unlikely that both storage systems will crash at the same time. Therefore, the risk of data loss is close to zero.

- `on`: In this case, a transaction is OK if the primary and the replicas have successfully flushed the transaction to disk. The application won't receive a commit unless data is safely stored on two servers (or more, depending on the configuration).

- `remote_apply`: While on ensures that data is safely stored on two nodes, it doesn't guarantee that we can simply load-balance right away. The fact that data is flushed on disk doesn't ensure that the user can already see the data. For example, if there's a conflict, a replica will halt transaction replay; however, a transaction log is still sent to the replica during a conflict and flushed to disk. In short, data may be flushed on the replica, even if it isn't visible to the end user yet. The `remote_apply` option fixes this problem. It ensures that data must be visible on the replica so that the next read request can be safely executed on the replica, which can already see the changes that have been made to the primary and expose them to the end user. The `remote_apply` option is, of course, the slowest way to replicate data because it requires the replica to already expose the data to the end user.

In PostgreSQL, the `synchronous_commit` parameter isn't a global value. It can be adjusted on various levels, just like many other settings. We might want to do something such as the following:

```
test=# ALTER DATABASE test SET synchronous_commit TO off;
ALTER DATABASE
```

Sometimes, only a single database should replicate in a certain way. It's also possible to just synchronously replicate if we're connected as a specific user. Last, but not least, it's also possible to tell a single transaction how to commit. By adjusting the `synchronous_commit` parameter on the fly, it's even possible to control things on a per-transaction level.

For example, consider the following two scenarios:

- Writing to a log table, where we might want to use an asynchronous commit because we want to be quick

- Storing a credit card payment where we want to be safe, so a synchronous transaction might be the desired thing

As we can see, the very same database might have different requirements, depending on which data is modified. Therefore, changing data at the transaction level is very useful and helps to improve speed.

Making use of replication slots

Now that I've introduced synchronous replication and dynamically adjustable durability, I want to focus on a feature called **replication slots**.

What's the purpose of a replication slot? Let's consider the following example – there's a primary and a replica. On the primary, a large transaction is executed, and the network connection isn't fast enough to ship all the data in time. At some point, the primary removes its transaction log (checkpoint). If the replica is too far behind, a resync is needed. As we've already seen, the wal_keep_size setting can be used to reduce the risk of failing replication. The question is, what's the best value for the wal_keep_size setting? Sure, more is better, but how much is best?

Replication slots will solve this problem for us – if we're using a replication slot, a primary can only recycle the transaction log once it's been consumed by all replicas. The advantage here is that a replica can never fall behind so much that a resync is needed.

The trouble is, what if we shut down a replica without telling the primary about it? The primary would keep a transaction log forever and the disk on the primary server would eventually fill up, causing unnecessary downtime.

There are two things to keep in mind to reduce the risk. First of all, proper monitoring is needed to make sure that nothing fails. The second option is to control a replication slot through a runtime variable:

```
#max_slot_wal_keep_size = -1     # in megabytes; -1 disables
```

Normally, a replication slot keeps data until it's consumed. However, this has caused countless outages. Things just failed because of disks becoming full and so on. Starting with PostgreSQL 14, we can now limit the amount of WAL a slot is allowed to accumulate. By default, it's still "unlimited." However, we recommend limiting this amount to a reasonable number. Ideally, you should set this to a value that ensures that the filesystem can't fill up entirely but to a large enough number to still make full use of replication slots.

To reduce this risk for the primary, replication slots should only be used in conjunction with proper monitoring and alerting (regardless of storage limitations imposed by max_slot_wal_keep_size). It's simply necessary to keep an eye on open replication slots that could potentially cause issues or might not be in use anymore.

In PostgreSQL, there are two types of replication slots:

- Physical replication slots
- Logical replication slots

Physical replication slots can be used for standard streaming replication. They will ensure that data isn't recycled too early. Logical replication slots do the same thing. However, they're used for logical decoding. The idea behind logical decoding is to give users a chance to attach to the transaction log and decode it with a plugin. Therefore, a logical replication slot is some sort of -f tail for database instances. It allows the user to extract changes that have been made to the database – and, therefore, to the transaction log – in any format and for any purpose.

In many cases, a logical replication slot is used for logical replication.

Handling physical replication slots

To make use of replication slots, changes have to be made to the postgresql.conf file, as follows:

```
wal_level = logical
max_replication_slots = 10     # or whatever number is needed
```

With physical slots, logical isn't necessary – a replica is enough. However, for logical slots, we need a higher wal_level setting. Then, the max_replication_slots setting has to be checked (the default value is 10). Here, we just put in a number that serves our purpose. My recommendation is to add some spare slots so that we can easily attach more consumers without restarting the server along the way.

After a restart, the slot can be created:

```
test=# \x
Expanded display is on.
test=# \df *create*physical*slot
List of functions
-[ RECORD 1 ]-------+---------------------------
Schema              | pg_catalog
Name                | pg_create_physical_replication_slot
Result data type    | record
Argument data types | slot_name name, immediately_reserve boolean
DEFAULT false, temporary boolean DEFAULT false, OUT slot_name name,
OUT lsn pg_lsn
Type                | func
```

The pg_create_physical_replication_slot function is here to help us to create the slot. It can be called with one of two parameters. If only a slot name is passed, the slot will be active when it's used for the first time. If `true` is passed as the second parameter, the slot will start immediately to conserve the transaction log:

```
test=# SELECT *
FROM pg_create_physical_replication_slot('some_slot_name', true);
 slot_name       | lsn
-----------------+---------------
 some_slot_name  | 0/EF8AD1D8
 (1 row)
```

To see which slots are active on the primary, consider running the following SQL statement:

```
test=# \x
Expanded display is on.
test=# SELECT * FROM pg_replication_slots;
-[ RECORD 1 ]-------+------------------------------
slot_name           | some_slot_name
plugin              |
slot_type           | physical
datoid              |
database            |
temporary           | f
active              | f
active_pid          |
xmin                |
catalog_xmin        |
restart_lsn         | 0/18000DE8
confirmed_flush_lsn |
wal_status          | reserved
safe_wal_size       |
two_phase           | f
inactive_since      | 2024-10-07 21:23:32.531121+02
conflicting         |
invalidation_reason |
failover            | f
synced              | f
```

The view tells us a lot about the slot. It contains information about the type of slot in use, the transaction log positions, and more.

To make use of the slot, all we have to do is add it to the configuration file, as follows:

```
primary_slot_name = 'some_slot_name'
```

Once streaming is restarted, the slot will be used directly and protect replication. If we don't want our slot anymore, we can drop it easily:

```
test=# \df *drop*slot*
List of functions
-[ RECORD 1 ]-------+-------------------------
Schema              | pg_catalog
Name                | pg_drop_replication_slot
Result data type    | void
Argument data types | name
Type                | normal
```

When a slot is dropped, there's no distinction between a logical and a physical slot anymore. Just pass the name of the slot to the function and execute it.

> **Important note**
> Nobody is allowed to use the slot when it's dropped. Otherwise, PostgreSQL will error out with good reason.

Handling logical replication slots

Logical replication slots are essential for logical replication. Due to space limitations in this chapter, it isn't possible to cover all aspects of logical replication. However, I want to outline some of the basic concepts that are essential for logical decoding and, therefore, also for logical replication.

If we want to create a replication slot, here's how it works. The function that's needed here takes two parameters – the first one will define the name of the replication slot, while the second one will carry the plugin that will be used to decode the transaction log. It will determine the format PostgreSQL is going to use to return the data. Let's take a look at how a replication slot can be made:

```
test=# SELECT *
FROM pg_create_logical_replication_slot(
    'logical_slot', 'test_decoding');
 slot_name      | lsn
---------------+---------------
 logical_slot  | 0/EF8AD4B0
 (1 row)
```

We can check for the existence of the slot using the same command that we used earlier. To check what a slot does, a small test can be created:

```
test=# CREATE TABLE t_demo
(
```

```
    id    int,
    name    text,
    payload text
);
CREATE TABLE
test=#BEGIN;
BEGIN
test=# INSERT INTO t_demo
VALUES (1, 'hans', 'some data');
INSERT 0 1
test=# INSERT INTO t_demo VALUES (2, 'paul', 'some more data');
INSERT 0 1
test=# COMMIT;
COMMIT
test=# INSERT INTO t_demo VALUES (3, 'joe', 'less data');
INSERT 0 1
```

Note that two transactions were executed. The changes that have been made to those transactions can now be extracted from the slot:

```
test=# SELECT pg_logical_slot_get_changes(
    'logical_slot', NULL, NULL);
                    pg_logical_slot_get_changes
------------------------------------------------------------ (0/
EF8AF5B0,606546,"BEGIN 606546")
 (0/EF8CCCA0,606546,"COMMIT 606546")
 (0/EF8CCCD8,606547,"BEGIN 606547")
 (0/EF8CCCD8,606547,"table public.t_demo: INSERT: id[integer]:1
    name[text]:'hans' payload[text]:'some data'")
 (0/EF8CCD60,606547,"table public.t_demo: INSERT: id[integer]:2
    name[text]:'paul' payload[text]:'some more data'")
 (0/EF8CCDE0,606547,"COMMIT 606547")
 (0/EF8CCE18,606548,"BEGIN 606548")
 (0/EF8CCE18,606548,"table public.t_demo: INSERT: id[integer]:3
   name[text]:›joe› payload[text]:›less data›")
 (0/EF8CCE98,606548,"COMMIT 606548")
(9 rows)
```

The format that's used here depends on the output plugin we chose previously. There are various output plugins for PostgreSQL, such as wal2json..

Important note

If default values are used, the logical stream will contain real values, not just functions. The logical stream contains the data that ended up in the underlying tables.

Also, keep in mind that the slot doesn't return data anymore once it's consumed:

```
test=# SELECT pg_logical_slot_get_changes('logical_slot', NULL, NULL);
 pg_logical_slot_get_changes
-----------------------------
(0 rows)
```

Therefore, the result set on the second call is empty. If we want to fetch data repeatedly, PostgreSQL offers the pg_logical_slot_peek_changes function. It works just like the pg_logical_slot_get_changes function but ensures that the data will still be available in the slot.

Using plain SQL is, of course, not the only way to consume a transaction log. There's also a command-line tool called pg_recvlogical. It can be compared to using the -f tail on an entire database instance and receives a flow of data in real time.

Let's start the pg_recvlogical tool with the following command:

```
$ pg_recvlogical -S logical_slot -P test_decoding
                 -d test -U postgres --start -f -
```

In this case, the tool connects to the test database and consumes data from logical_slot. The -f tail means that the stream will be sent to stdout. Let's kill some data:

```
test=# DELETE FROM t_demo WHERE id < random()*10;
DELETE 3
```

The changes will make it into the transaction log. However, by default, the database only cares about what the table will look like after the deletion. It knows which blocks have to be touched and so on, but it doesn't know what the table was previously:

```
BEGIN 606549
table public.t_demo: DELETE: (no-tuple-data)
table public.t_demo: DELETE: (no-tuple-data)
table public.t_demo: DELETE: (no-tuple-data)
COMMIT 606549
```

Therefore, the output is pretty pointless. To fix that, the following line comes to the rescue:

```
test=# ALTER TABLE t_demo REPLICA IDENTITY FULL;
ALTER TABLE
```

If the table is repopulated with data and deleted again, the transaction log stream will look something like this:

```
BEGIN 606558
table public.t_demo: DELETE: id[integer]:1 name[text]:'hans'
    payload[text]:'some data'
```

```
table public.t_demo: DELETE: id[integer]:2 name[text]:'paul'
    payload[text]:'some more data'
table public.t_demo: DELETE: id[integer]:3 name[text]:'joe'
    payload[text]:'less data'
COMMIT 606558
```

Now that all of the changes are in, let's take a look at logical replication slots.

There are various use cases for logical replication slots. The most simplistic use case is the one shown in the following section. Data can be fetched from the server in the desired format and used to audit, debug, or simply monitor a database instance.

In this section, you learned about logical decoding and some other basic techniques. Now, let's take a look at the CREATE PUBLICATION and CREATE SUBSCRIPTION commands.

Making use of the CREATE PUBLICATION and CREATE SUBSCRIPTION commands

The PostgreSQL community provides two increasingly important commands: CREATE PUBLICATION and CREATE SUBSCRIPTION. These can be used for logical replication, which means that you can now selectively replicate data and achieve close-to-zero downtime upgrades. So far, binary replication and transaction log replication have been fully covered. However, sometimes, we might not want to replicate an entire database instance – replicating a table or two might be enough. This is exactly when logical replication is the right thing to use.

Before getting started, the first thing we must do is change wal_level to logical in postgresql. conf, and then restart:

```
wal_level = logical
```

Then, we can create a simple table:

```
test=# CREATE TABLE t_test (a int, b int);
CREATE TABLE
```

The same table layout has to exist in the second database to make this work. PostgreSQL won't automatically create those tables for us:

```
test=# CREATE DATABASE repl;
CREATE DATABASE
```

After creating the database, an identical table can be added. Reconnect to the repl database and then execute the following command:

```
repl=# CREATE TABLE t_test (a int, b int);
CREATE TABLE
```

The goal here is to publish the contents of the `t_test` table in the test database somewhere else. In this case, they'll simply be replicated in a database on the same instance. To publish those changes, PostgreSQL offers the `CREATE PUBLICATION` command:

```
test=# \h CREATE PUBLICATION
Command:     CREATE PUBLICATION
Description: define a new publication
Syntax:
CREATE PUBLICATION name
    [ FOR ALL TABLES
      | FOR publication_object [, ... ] ]
    [ WITH ( publication_parameter [= value] [, ... ] ) ]

where publication_object is one of:

  TABLE [ ONLY ] table_name [ * ] [ ( column_name [, ... ] ) ]        [
WHERE ( expression ) ] [, ... ]
    TABLES IN SCHEMA { schema_name | CURRENT_SCHEMA } [, ... ]

URL: https://www.postgresql.org/docs/17/sql-createpublication.html
```

The syntax is pretty easy. All we need is a name and a list of all the tables that the system is supposed to replicate:

```
test=# CREATE PUBLICATION pub1 FOR TABLE t_test;
CREATE PUBLICATION
```

Now, the subscription can be created. The syntax is, again, pretty straightforward:

```
test=# \h CREATE SUBSCRIPTION
Command:     CREATE SUBSCRIPTION
Description: define a new subscription
Syntax:
CREATE SUBSCRIPTION subscription_name
    CONNECTION 'conninfo'
    PUBLICATION publication_name [, ...]
    [ WITH ( subscription_parameter [= value] [, ... ] ) ]

URL: https://www.postgresql.org/docs/17/sql-createsubscription.html
```

Creating a subscription directly is no problem. However, if we play this game inside the same instance from the test database to the `repl` database, it's necessary to create the replication slot in use manually. Otherwise, `CREATE SUBSCRIPTION` will never finish. This is important – many people have reported issues by not following up on this requirement. However, in general, publications and subscriptions aren't used within the same instance. The feature isn't meant to be used that way but, instead, across multiple hosts and instances. Here's an example of how the slot can be created:

```
test=# SELECT pg_create_logical_replication_slot('sub1', 'pgoutput');
 pg_create_logical_replication_slot
------------------------------------
 (sub1,0/27E2B2D0)
(1 row)
```

In this case, the name of the slot that's created on the primary database is sub1. Then, we need to connect to the target database and run the following command:

```
repl=# CREATE SUBSCRIPTION sub1
CONNECTION 'host=localhost dbname=test user=postgres'
PUBLICATION pub1
WITH (create_slot = false);
CREATE SUBSCRIPTION
```

Of course, we have to adjust our database's CONNECTION parameters. Then, PostgreSQL will sync the data, and we're done.

> **Important note**
>
> Note that `create_slot = false` is only used because the test is running inside the same database server instance. If we happen to use different databases, there's no need to manually create the slot and no need for `create_slot = false`.

Summary

In this chapter, we learned about the most important features of PostgreSQL replication, such as streaming replication and replication conflicts. Then, we learned about PITR, as well as replication slots. A book on replication is never complete unless it spans around 400 pages thereabouts, but we've learned the key points that every administrator should know. You also learned how to set up replication and now understand the most important aspects.

The next chapter, Chapter 11, *Deciding on Useful Extensions*, is about useful extensions for PostgreSQL. We'll learn about extensions that provide even more functionality and have been widely adopted by the industry.

Deciding on Useful Extensions

In *Chapter 10, Making Sense of Backups and Replication*, our focus was on replication, transaction log shipping, and logical decoding. After looking at mostly administration-related topics, the goal now is to look at a broader topic. In the PostgreSQL world, many things are done using extensions. Extensibility is one of the core design goals of PostgreSQL itself, and there are countless places in a server that allow developers to add code and functionality. One such concept that plays on the idea of extensibility is the idea of adding "extensions" to your server. The advantage of extensions is that features can be added without bloating the PostgreSQL core. Not bloating the database engine itself is important. Writing a database server is a long-term project, and therefore, the community has to ensure that the code base can be understood, maintained, and developed over a very long period of time. By allowing users to choose their preferred tools, we can keep the database server slim and even allow for different development cycles.

In this chapter, we will discuss some of the most commonly used extensions for PostgreSQL. However, before digging deeper into this issue, I want to state that it is totally impossible to explain all the extensions out there. Even explaining all the widely used extensions is wildly beyond the scope of this chapter, as there are literally hundreds of modules. New information is published every day, and it is sometimes even hard for a database professional to be aware of all the cool stuff out there. New extensions are being published as we speak, so it may be a good idea to take a look at the **PostgreSQL Extension Network (PGXN)** (https://pgxn.org/), which contains a large variety of extensions for PostgreSQL.

In this chapter, we will cover the following topics:

- Understanding how extensions work
- Making use of `contrib` modules
- Other useful extensions

Note that only the most important extensions will be covered.

Understanding how extensions work

Before digging into the available extensions, it is a good idea to take a look at how extensions work in the first place. Understanding the inner workings of the extension machinery can be quite beneficial.

Let's take a look at the syntax first:

```
test=# \h CREATE EXTENSION
Command: CREATE EXTENSION
Description: install an extension
Syntax:
CREATE EXTENSION [ IF NOT EXISTS ] extension_name
    [ WITH ] [ SCHEMA schema_name ]
             [ VERSION version ]
             [ CASCADE ]
 URL: https://www.postgresql.org/docs/17/sql-createextension.html
```

When you want to deploy an extension, simply call the CREATE EXTENSION command. It will check for the extension and load it into your database. Note that the extension will be loaded into a database and not into the entire instance.

If we load an extension, we can decide on the schema that we want to use. Many extensions can be relocated so that the user can choose which schema to use. Then, it is possible to decide on a specific version of the extension. Often, we don't want to deploy the latest version of an extension because a client may be running outdated software. In these cases, it may be handy to be able to deploy any version that's available on the system.

Make sure that the SCHEMA clause specifies the schema containing these pre-existing objects. Only use it when you have old modules around.

Finally, we have the CASCADE clause. Some extensions depend on other extensions. The CASCADE option will automatically deploy those software packages, too. The following is an example:

```
test=# CREATE EXTENSION earthdistance;
ERROR: required extension "cube" is not installed
HINT: Use CREATE EXTENSION ... CASCADE to install required extensions
too.
```

The earthdistance module implements great-circle distance calculations. As you may already know, the shortest distance between two points on Earth cannot be followed in a straight line; instead, a pilot has to adjust their course constantly to find the fastest route when flying from one point to the other. The earthdistance extension depends on the cube extension, which allows you to perform operations on a sphere.

To automatically deploy this dependency, the CASCADE clause can be used, as we described previously:

```
test=# CREATE EXTENSION earthdistance CASCADE;
NOTICE: installing required extension "cube"
CREATE EXTENSION
```

In this case, both extensions will be deployed, as shown by the NOTICE message. In the next section, we will figure out which extensions the system provides.

Checking for available extensions

PostgreSQL offers various views so that we can figure out which extensions are on the system and which ones are actually deployed. One of those views is pg_available_extensions:

```
test=# \d pg_available_extensions
        View "pg_catalog.pg_available_extensions"
     Column         | Type | Collation | Nullable | Default
--------------------+------+-----------+----------+---------
 name               | name |           |          |
 default_version    | text |           |          |
 installed_version  | text | C         |          |
 comment            | text |           |          |
```

This contains a list of all of the available extensions, including their names, their default versions, and the versions that are currently installed. To make this easier for the end user, there is also a description available that tells us more about the extension.

The following listing contains two lines (RECORD 1 and RECORD 2 are two lines in an expanded format) that have been taken from pg_available_extensions:

```
test=# \x
Expanded display is on.
test=# SELECT *
FROM   pg_available_extensions
ORDER BY 1
LIMIT 2;
-[ RECORD 1 ]-----+----------------------------------------
name              | amcheck
default_version   | 1.4
installed_version |
comment           | functions for verifying relation integrity
-[ RECORD 2 ]-----+----------------------------------------
```

```
name             | autoinc
default_version  | 1.0
installed_version |
comment          | functions for autoincrementing fields
```

The `CREATE EXTENSION earthdistance CASCADE` command ensures that both `earthdistance` and `cube` extensions are enabled in my database. The `plpgsql` extension is there by default, and `earthdistance` was added along with `cube` immediately before. The beauty of this view is that you can quickly get an overview of what is installed and what can be installed.

However, in some cases, extensions are available in more than just one version. To find out more about versioning, check out the following view:

```
test=# \d pg_available_extension_versions
View "pg_catalog.pg_available_extension_versions"
  Column      | Type    | Modifiers
--------------+---------+-----------
 name         | name    |
 version      | text    |
 installed    | boolean |
 superuser    | boolean |
 trusted      | boolean |
 relocatable  | boolean |
 schema       | name    |
 requires     | name[]  |
 comment      | text    |
```

The system views show everything you need to know about an extension.

Some more detailed information is available here, as shown in the following listing:

```
test=# SELECT *
FROM   pg_available_extension_versions
WHERE name = 'isn';
-[ RECORD 1 ]---------------------------------------------
name         | isn
version      | 1.1
installed    | f
superuser    | t
trusted      | t
relocatable  | t
schema       |
requires     |
comment      | data types for international product
               numbering standards
```

```
-[ RECORD 2 ]-----------------------------------------
name        | isn
version     | 1.2
installed   | f
superuser   | t
trusted     | t
relocatable | t
schema      |
requires    |
comment     | data types for international product
              numbering standards
```

PostgreSQL will also tell you whether an extension can be relocated, which schema it has been deployed in, and what other extensions are needed. Then, there is the comment describing the extension, which was shown previously.

You may be wondering where PostgreSQL finds all of this information about extensions on the system. Assuming that you have deployed PostgreSQL 17.0 from the official PostgreSQL RPM repository, the `/usr/pgsql-17/share/extension` directory will contain a couple of files. The next listing shows all the files associated with another important extension, `citext`. It introduces a data type that handles case-insensitive text for a more efficient search:

```
...
-bash-4.3$ ls -l citext*
-rw-r--r-- 1 hs  staff   1028 Apr  2 16:00 citext--1.0--1.1.sql
-rw-r--r-- 1 hs  staff   3424 Apr  2 16:00 citext--1.1--1.2.sql
-rw-r--r-- 1 hs  staff    850 Apr  2 16:00 citext--1.2--1.3.sql
-rw-r--r-- 1 hs  staff    668 Apr  2 16:00 citext--1.3--1.4.sql
-rw-r--r-- 1 hs  staff   2284 Apr  2 16:00 citext--1.4--1.5.sql
-rw-r--r-- 1 hs  staff  13466 Apr  2 16:00 citext--1.4.sql
-rw-r--r-- 1 hs  staff    427 Apr  2 16:00 citext--1.5--1.6.sql
-rw-r--r-- 1 hs  staff    173 Apr  2 16:00 citext.control
...
```

The default version of the `citext` (**case-insensitive text**) extension is 1.6, so there's a file called `citext--1.4.sql`. In addition to that, certain files are used to move from one version to the next (1.0 → 1.1, 1.1 → 1.2, and so on).

Then, there is the `.control` file:

```
-bash-4.3$ cat citext.control
# citext extension
comment = 'data type for case-insensitive character strings'
default_version = '1.6'
module_pathname = '$libdir/citext'
```

```
relocatable = true
trusted = true
```

This file contains all of the metadata related to the extension; the first entry contains the comment. Note that this content is what will be shown in the system views we just discussed. When you access those views, PostgreSQL will go to this directory and read all of the `.control` files. Then, there is the default version and the path to the binaries.

If you are installing a typical extension from RPM, the directory is going to be `$libdir`, which is inside your PostgreSQL binary directory. However, if you have written your own commercial extension, it may very well reside somewhere else.

The last setting will tell PostgreSQL whether the extension can reside in any schema or whether it has to be in a fixed, predefined schema.

Finally, there is the unpackaged file. The following is an extract from it:

```
. . .
ALTER EXTENSION citext ADD type citext;
ALTER EXTENSION citext ADD function citextin(cstring);
ALTER EXTENSION citext ADD function citextout(citext);
ALTER EXTENSION citext ADD function citextrecv(internal);
. . .
```

The unpackaged file will turn any existing code into an extension. Therefore, it is important to consolidate existing code in your database. Following this basic introduction to extensions in general, we will now examine several additional extensions.

Making use of contrib modules

Now that we have had a look at a theoretical introduction to extensions, it is time to take a look at some of the most important extensions. In this section, you will learn about modules that are provided to you as part of the PostgreSQL `contrib` module. When you install PostgreSQL, I recommend that you always install these `contrib` modules, as they contain vital extensions that can really make your life easier.

In the upcoming section, we will walk you through some extensions that I find the most interesting and the most useful for a variety of reasons (for debugging, performance tuning, and so on).

Applying bloom filters

Since PostgreSQL 9.6, it has been possible to add index types on the fly using extensions. The new `CREATE ACCESS METHOD` command, along with some additional features, has made it possible for us to create fully functional and transaction-logged index types on the fly.

The `bloom` extension provides PostgreSQL users with `bloom` filters, which are pre-filters that help us efficiently reduce the amount of data as soon as possible. The idea behind a `bloom` filter is that we can calculate a bitmask and compare the bitmask with the query. The `bloom` filter may produce some false positives, but it will still reduce the amount of data dramatically.

This is especially useful when a table consists of hundreds of columns and millions of rows. It isn't possible to index hundreds of columns with B-trees, so a `bloom` filter is a good alternative because it allows us to index everything at once.

To understand how things work, we will install the extension:

```
test=# CREATE EXTENSION bloom;
CREATE EXTENSION
```

Now, we need to create a table containing various columns:

```
test=# CREATE TABLE t_bloom
(
    id    serial,
    col1  int4 DEFAULT random() * 1000,
    col2  int4 DEFAULT random() * 1000,
    col3  int4 DEFAULT random() * 1000,
    col4  int4 DEFAULT random() * 1000,
    col5  int4 DEFAULT random() * 1000,
    col6  int4 DEFAULT random() * 1000,
    col7  int4 DEFAULT random() * 1000,
    col8  int4 DEFAULT random() * 1000,
    col9  int4 DEFAULT random() * 1000
);
CREATE TABLE
```

To make this easier, these columns have a default value so that data can easily be added, using a simple SELECT clause:

```
test=# INSERT INTO t_bloom
    SELECT * FROM generate_series(1, 1000000);

INSERT 0 1000000
```

The preceding query adds 1 million rows to the table. Now, the table can be indexed:

```
test=# CREATE INDEX idx_bloom ON t_bloom
    USING bloom(col1, col2, col3, col4,
                col5,col6, col7,col8, col9);
CREATE INDEX
```

Note that the index contains nine columns at a time. In contrast to a B-tree, the order of those columns doesn't really make a difference.

> **Note**
>
> The table we just created is around 65 MB without indexes.

The index adds another 15 MB to the storage footprint:

```
test=# \di+ idx_bloom
```

We will see the following result:

```
                              List of relations
 Schema |    Name    | Type  | Owner |  Table   | Persistence | Access method | Size  | Description
--------+------------+-------+-------+----------+-------------+---------------+-------+-----------+--
 public | idx_bloom  | index | hs    | t_bloom  | permanent   | bloom         | 15 MB |
```

Figure 11.1 – The result showing a list of relations

The beauty of the `bloom` filter is that it is possible to look for any combination of columns:

```
test=# SET max_parallel_workers_per_gather TO 0;
SET
test=# explain SELECT count(*)
FROM   t_bloom
WHERE col4 = 454 AND col3 = 354 AND col9 = 423;

                    QUERY PLAN
----------------------------------------------------------------
Aggregate  (cost=20352.02..20352.03 rows=1 width=8)
    -> Bitmap Heap Scan on t_bloom
          (cost=20348.00..20352.02 rows=1 width=0)
          Recheck Cond: ((col3 = 354) AND (col4 = 454)
             AND (col9 = 423))
          -> Bitmap Index Scan on idx_bloom
                (cost=0.00..20348.00 rows=1 width=0)
                Index Cond: ((col3 = 354)
                    AND (col4 = 454) AND (col9 = 423))
 (5 rows)
```

What you have seen so far feels unusual. A natural question that might arise is, why not always use a `bloom` filter? The reason is simple – the database has to read the entire `bloom` filter in order to use it. In the case of, say, a B-tree, this is not necessary.

In the future, more index types will likely be added to ensure that even more use cases can be covered with PostgreSQL.

> **Note**
>
> If you want to read more about `bloom` filters, consider reading our blog post at `https://www.cybertec-postgresql.com/en/trying-out-postgres-bloom-indexes/`.

Deploying btree_gist and btree_gin

There are even more indexing-related features that can be added. In PostgreSQL, we have the concept of operator classes, which we discussed in *Chapter 3, Making Use of Indexes*.

The `contrib` module offers two extensions (namely, `btree_gist` and `btree_gin`) so that we can add B-tree functionality to the GiST and GIN indexes, respectively. Why is this so useful? GiST indexes offer various features that are not supported by B-trees. One of those features is the ability to perform a **k-nearest neighbor** (**KNN**) search.

Why is this relevant? Imagine that somebody is looking for data that was added yesterday, around noon. So, where was that? In some cases, it may be hard to come up with boundaries – for example, if somebody is looking for a product that costs around 70 euros. KNN can come to the rescue here. Here is an example:

```
test=# CREATE TABLE t_test (id int);
CREATE TABLE
```

Some simple data needs to be added:

```
test=# INSERT INTO t_test SELECT * FROM generate_series(1, 100000);
INSERT 0 100000
```

Now, the extension can be added:

```
test=# CREATE EXTENSION btree_gist;

CREATE EXTENSION
```

Adding a `gist` index to the column is easy; just use the `USING gist` clause. Note that adding a `gist` index to an integer column only works if the extension is present. Otherwise, PostgreSQL will report that there is no suitable operator class:

```
test=# CREATE INDEX idx_id ON t_test USING gist(id);
CREATE INDEX
```

Once the index has been deployed, it is possible to order by distance:

```
test=# SELECT *
FROM    t_test
ORDER BY id <-> 70
LIMIT 6;
 id
----
 70
 71
 69
 68
 72
 73
(6 rows)
```

As you can see, the first row is an exact match. The matches that follow are already less precise and get worse. The query will always return a fixed number of rows.

The important thing here is the execution plan:

```
test=# explain SELECT *
FROM    t_test
ORDER BY id <-> 70
LIMIT 6;
                            QUERY PLAN
-----------------------------------------------------------
-  Limit  (cost=0.28..0.53 rows=6 width=8)
    ->  Index Only Scan using idx_id on t_test
        (cost=0.28..4196.28 rows=100000 width=8)
          Order By: (id <-> 70)
(3 rows)
```

As you can see, PostgreSQL goes straight for an index scan, which speeds up the query significantly. However, speed is only one benefit; a KNN search also opens the door to producing more useful, end-user-friendly output, as it covers a common use case found in many applications.

dblink – make sure it is outphased

The desire to use database links has been around for many years. However, at the turn of the century, PostgreSQL foreign data wrappers weren't even on the horizon, and a traditional database link implementation was definitely not in sight either. Around this time, a PostgreSQL developer from California (**Joe Conway**) pioneered work on database connectivity by introducing the concept of dblink to PostgreSQL. While dblink served people well over the years, it is no longer state-of-the-art. Sure, there are still use cases in which `dblink` can serve us well. However, in general, we recommend considering other, more transparent approaches.

It is recommended that we move away from `dblink` to the more modern SQL/MED implementation (which is a specification that defines the way external data can be integrated with a relational database). The `postgres_fdw` extension has been built on top of SQL/MED and offers more than just database connectivity, as it allows you to connect to basically any data source.

Fetching files with file_fdw

In some cases, it can make sense to read a file from disk and expose it to PostgreSQL as a table. This is exactly what you can achieve with the `file_fdw` extension. The idea is to have a module that allows you to read data from a disk and query it using SQL.

Installing the module works as expected:

```
CREATE EXTENSION file_fdw;
```

Now, we need to create a virtual server:

```
CREATE SERVER file_server
    FOREIGN DATA WRAPPER file_fdw;
```

`file_server` is based on the `file_fdw` extension foreign data wrapper, which tells PostgreSQL how to access a file.

To expose a file as a table, use the following command:

```
CREATE FOREIGN TABLE t_passwd
(
    username    text,
    passwd      text,
    uid         int,
    gid         int,
    gecos       text,
    dir         text,
    shell       text
) SERVER file_server
OPTIONS (format 'text', filename '/etc/passwd',
        header 'false', delimiter ':');
```

In this example, the `/etc/passwd` file will be exposed. All the fields have to be listed, and the data types have to be mapped accordingly. All of the additional important information is passed to the module using `OPTIONS`. In this example, PostgreSQL has to know the type of the file (text), the name and path of the file, as well as the delimiter. It is also possible to tell PostgreSQL whether there is a header. If the setting is `true`, the first line will be skipped and deemed unimportant. Skipping headers is especially important if you happen to load a CSV file.

Once the table has been created, it is possible to read data:

```
SELECT * FROM t_passwd;
```

Unsurprisingly, PostgreSQL returns the content of /etc/passwd:

```
test=# \x
Expanded display is on.
test=# SELECT * FROM t_passwd LIMIT 1;
 -[ RECORD 1 ]-------
username | root
passwd   | x
uid      | 0
gid      | 0
gecos    | root
dir      | /root
shell    | /bin/bash
```

When looking at the execution plan, you will see that PostgreSQL uses what is known as a **foreign scan** to fetch the data from the file:

```
test=# explain (verbose true, analyze true)
SELECT * FROM t_passwd;
                          QUERY PLAN
------------------------------------------------------------
Foreign Scan on public.t_passwd
(cost=0.00..2.70 rows=17 width=168)
     (actual time=0.018..0.090 rows=58 loops=1)
   Output: username, passwd, uid, gid, gecos, dir, shell
   Foreign File: /etc/passwd
   Foreign File Size: 3194 b
 Planning Time: 0.066 ms
 Execution Time: 0.142 ms
(6 rows)
```

The execution plan also tells us about the file's size, and so on. Since we're talking about the planner, there is a side note that is worth mentioning – PostgreSQL will even fetch statistics for the file. The planner checks the file size and assigns the same costs to the file, just like it would to a normal PostgreSQL table of the same size.

Inspecting storage using pageinspect

If you are facing storage corruption or some other storage-related problem that may be related to bad blocks in a table, the pageinspect extension may be the module you are looking for. We will begin by creating the extension, as shown in the following example:

```
test=# CREATE EXTENSION pageinspect;
CREATE EXTENSION
```

The idea behind pageinspect is to provide you with a module that allows you to inspect a table at the binary level.

When using this module, the most important thing to do is fetch a block:

```
test=# SELECT * FROM get_raw_page('pg_class', 0);
...
```

This function will return a single block. In the preceding example, it is the first block in the pg_class parameter, which is a system table. Of course, it is up to the user to pick any other table.

Next, you can extract the page header:

```
test=# \x
Expanded display is on.
test=# SELECT *
FROM    page_header(get_raw_page('pg_class', 0));
-[ RECORD 1 ]--------
lsn        | 0/8A8E310
checksum   | 0
flags      | 1
lower      | 212
upper      | 6880
special    | 8192
pagesize   | 8192
version    | 4
prune_xid  | 0
```

The page header already contains a lot of information about the page. If you want to find out more, you can call the heap_page_items function, which dissects the page and returns one row per tuple:

```
test=# SELECT *
FROM    heap_page_items(get_raw_page('pg_class', 0))
LIMIT 1;
-[ RECORD 1 ]---
lp         | 1
lp_off     | 49
```

```
lp_flags    | 2
lp_len      | 0
t_xmin      |
t_xmax      |
t_field3    |
t_ctid      |
t_infomask2 |
t_infomask  |
t_hoff      |
t_bits      |
t_oid       |
t_data      | ...
```

You can also split the data into various tuples:

```
test=# SELECT tuple_data_split('pg_class'::regclass,
                    t_data, t_infomask,
                    t_infomask2, t_bits)
FROM  heap_page_items(get_raw_page('pg_class', 0))
LIMIT 2;
-[ RECORD 1 ]----+---------------------------------
tuple_data_split |
-[ RECORD 2 ]----+---------------------------------
tuple_data_split | {"\\x6100000000000000000000000000000000000000
00000000000000000000000000000000000000000000000000000000000000000000
0000000000000000000","\\x98080000","\\x50ac0c00","\\x00000000","\\
x01400000","\\x00000000","\\x4eac0c00","\\x00000000","\\xbb010000","\\
x0050c347","\\x00000000","\\x00000000","\\x01","\\x00","\\x70","\\
x72","\\x0100","\\x0000","\\x00","\\x00","\\x00","\\x00","\\x00","\\
x00","\\x00","\\x01","\\x64","\\xc3400900","\\x01000000",NULL,NULL}
```

To read the data, we have to familiarize ourselves with the on-disk format of PostgreSQL. Otherwise, the data may appear to be pretty obscure.

pageinspect provides functions for all possible access methods (tables, indexes, and so on) and allows us to dissect storage so that more details can be provided.

Investigating caching with pg_buffercache

After this brief introduction to the pageinspect extension, we will turn our attention to the pg_buffercache extension, which allows you to take a detailed look at the contents of your I/O cache:

```
test=# CREATE EXTENSION pg_buffercache;

CREATE EXTENSION
```

The `pg_buffercache` extension provides you with a view containing the following fields:

```
test=# \d pg_buffercache
```

```
View "public.pg_buffercache"
      Column        |   Type   | Collation | Nullable | ...
------------------+----------+-----------+----------+------
 bufferid         | integer  |           |          |
 relfilenode      | oid      |           |          |
 reltablespace    | oid      |           |          |
 reldatabase      | oid      |           |          |
 relforknumber    | smallint |           |          |
 relblocknumber   | bigint   |           |          |
 isdirty          | boolean  |           |          |
 usagecount       | smallint |           |          |
 pinning_backends | integer  |           |          |
```

The `bufferid` field is just a number; it identifies the buffer. Then, there's the `relfilenode` field, which points to the file on disk. If we want to look up which table a file belongs to, we can check out the `pg_class` module, which also contains a field called `relfilenode`. Then, we have the `reldatabase` and `reltablespace` fields. Note that all the fields are defined as being the `oid` type, so to extract data in a more useful way, it is necessary to join system tables together.

The `relforknumber` field tells us which part of a table is cached. It could be the heap, the free space map, or some other component, such as the visibility map. In the future, we can expect to see more types of relation forks.

The next field, `relblocknumber`, tells us which block has been cached. Finally, there is the `isdirty` flag, which tells us that a block has been modified, as well as telling us about the usage counter (`usagecount`) and the number of backends pinning the block (`pinning_backends`).

If you want to make sense of the `pg_buffercache` extension, it is important to add additional information. To figure out which database uses caching the most, the following query may help:

```
test=# SELECT datname,
       count(*),
       count(*) FILTER (WHERE isdirty = true) AS dirty
FROM   pg_buffercache AS b, pg_database AS d
WHER   d.oid = b.reldatabase
GROUP  BY ROLLUP (1);
 datname  | count | dirty
----------+-------+-------
 abc      | 132   | 1
 postgres | 30    | 0
 test     | 11975 | 53
```

```
                |  12137  |  54
  (4 rows)
```

In this case, the pg_database extension has to be joined. As we can see, oid is the join criterion, which may not be obvious to people who are new to PostgreSQL.

Sometimes, we may want to know which blocks in the database that are connected to us are cached. Here is how it works:

```
test=# SELECT  relname,
        relkind,
        count(*),
        count(*) FILTER (WHERE isdirty = true) AS dirty
  FROM    pg_buffercache AS b,
        pg_database AS d, pg_class AS c
  WHERE   d.oid = b.reldatabase
        AND c.relfilenode = b.relfilenode
        AND datname = 'test'
  GROUP  BY 1, 2
  ORDER  BY 3 DESC
  LIMIT  7;
   relname                      | relkind| count| dirty
  ----------------------------+--------+-------+-------
   t_bloom                      | r      | 8338  | 0
   idx_bloom                    | i      | 1962  | 0
   idx_id                       | i      | 549   | 0
   t_test                       | r      | 445   | 0
   pg_statistic                 | r      | 90    | 0
   pg_depend                    | r      | 60    | 0
   pg_depend_reference_index  | i      | 34    | 0
  (7 rows)
```

In this case, we filtered the current database and joined it with the pg_class module, which contains the list of objects. The relkind column is especially noteworthy – r refers to the table (relation) and i refers to the index. This tells us which object we are looking at.

Encrypting data with pgcrypto

One of the most powerful modules in the entire contrib module section is pgcrypto. It was originally written by one of the Skype sysadmins and offers countless functions so that we can encrypt and decrypt data.

It offers functions for symmetric as well as asymmetric encryption. Due to the large number of available functions, it is definitely recommended to check out the documentation page at https://www.postgresql.org/docs/current/static/pgcrypto.html.

Due to the limited scope of this chapter, it is impossible to dig into all of the details of the pgcrypto module.

Prewarming caches with pg_prewarm

When PostgreSQL operates normally, it tries to cache important data. The shared_buffers variable is important, as it defines the size of the cache that's managed by PostgreSQL. The problem now is this – if you restart the database server, the cache managed by PostgreSQL will be lost. Maybe the operating system still has some data to reduce the impact on the disk wait time, but in many cases, this won't be enough. The solution to this problem is called the pg_prewarm extension. Let's now install pg_prewarm and see what we can do with it:

```
test=# CREATE EXTENSION pg_prewarm;
CREATE EXTENSION
```

This extension deploys a function that allows us to explicitly prewarm the cache whenever this is needed. The listing shows the functions associated with this extension:

```
test=# \x
Expanded display is on.
test=# \df *prewa*
List of functions
-[ RECORD 1 ]
 Schema              | public
 Name                | autoprewarm_dump_now
 Result data type    | bigint
 Argument data types |
 Type                | func
-[ RECORD 2 ]
 Schema              | public
 Name                | autoprewarm_start_worker
 Result data type    | void
 Argument data types |
 Type                | func
-[ RECORD 3 ]
 Schema              | public
 Name                | pg_prewarm
 Result data type    | bigint
 Argument data types | regclass, mode text
                            DEFAULT 'buffer'::text,
                        fork text DEFAULT 'main'::text,
                        first_block bigint
                            DEFAULT NULL::bigint,
```

```
                              last_block bigint
                                 DEFAULT NULL::bigint
        Type                | func
```

The easiest and most common way to call the `pg_prewarm` extension is to ask it to cache an entire object:

```
test=# SELECT pg_prewarm('t_test');
```

```
pg_prewarm
------------
       443
(1 row)
```

> **Note**
>
> If a table is so large that it doesn't fit into the cache, only parts of the table will stay in the cache, which is fine in most cases.

The function returns the number of 8-KB blocks that were processed by the function call.

If you don't want to cache all of an object's blocks, you can also select a specific range inside the table. In the following example, we can see that blocks `10` to `30` are cached in the main fork:

```
test=# SELECT pg_prewarm('t_test','buffer', 'main', 10, 30);
pg_prewarm
------------
        21
(1 row)
```

Here, it's clear that `21` blocks were cached.

Inspecting performance with pg_stat_statements

`pg_stat_statements` is the most important `contrib` module that's available. It should always be enabled and is there to provide superior performance data. Without the `pg_stat_statements` module, it is really difficult to track down performance problems. The overhead is minimal, and it should just always be there. Without it, performance tuning can be really hard because the relevant data is simply missing.

Inspecting storage with pgstattuple

Sometimes, it may be the case that tables in PostgreSQL grow out of proportion. The technical term for tables that have grown too much is **table bloat**. The questions that arise now are, which tables have bloated, and how much bloat is there? The pgstattuple extension will help us to answer those questions:

```
test=# CREATE EXTENSION pgstattuple;
CREATE EXTENSION
```

As we stated previously, the pgstattuple module deploys a couple of functions. In the case of the pgstattuple extension, these functions return a row consisting of a composite type. Therefore, the function has to be called in the FROM clause to ensure a readable result:

```
test=# \x
Expanded display is on.
test=# SELECT * FROM pgstattuple('t_test');
 -[ RECORD 1 ]
 --------------------+--------------
  table_len          | 3629056
  tuple_count        | 100000
  tuple_len          | 2800000
  tuple_percent      | 77.16
  dead_tuple_count   | 0
  dead_tuple_len     | 0
  dead_tuple_percent | 0
  free_space         | 16652
  free_percent       | 0.46
```

In this example, the table that was used for testing seems to be in a pretty good state – the table is 3.6 MB in size and doesn't contain any dead rows. Free space is also limited. If access to your table is slowed down by table bloat, then this means that the number of dead rows and the amount of free space will have grown out of proportion. Some free space and a handful of dead rows are normal; however, if the table has grown so much that it mostly consists of dead rows and free space, decisive action is needed to bring the situation under control again.

The pgstattuple extension also provides a function that we can use to inspect indexes:

```
test=# DROP INDEX IF EXISTS idx_id;
DROP INDEX
test=# CREATE INDEX idx_id ON t_test (id);
CREATE INDEX
```

The pgstattindex function returns a lot of information about the index we want to inspect:

```
test=# SELECT * FROM pgstatindex('idx_id');
 -[ RECORD 1 ]
 --------------------+--------------
  version            | 4
```

```
tree_level              | 1
index_size              | 2260992
root_block_no           | 3
internal_pages          | 1
leaf_pages              | 274
empty_pages             | 0
deleted_pages           | 0
avg_leaf_density        | 89.83
leaf_fragmentation      | 0
```

Our index is pretty dense (89%). This is a good sign. The default FILLFACTOR setting for an index is 90%, so a value close to 90% indicates that the index is very good.

Sometimes, you don't want to check a single table; instead, you want to check all of the tables, or just all of those in a schema. How can this be achieved? Normally, the list of objects you want to process is in the FROM clause. However, in my example, the function is already in the FROM clause, so how can we make PostgreSQL loop over a list of tables? The answer is to use a LATERAL join.

Keep in mind that pgstattuple has to read the entire object. If our database is large, it can take quite a long time to process. Therefore, it can be a good idea to store the results of the query we have just seen so that we can inspect them thoroughly, without having to rerun the query again and again.

Fuzzy searching with pg_trgm

The pg_trgm module allows you to perform fuzzy searching. This module was discussed in *Chapter 3, Making Use of Indexes*.

Connecting to remote servers using postgres_fdw

Data is not always available in just one location. More often than not, data is spread all over the infrastructure, and it may be that data residing in various places has to be integrated.

The solution to this problem is a foreign data wrapper, as defined by the SQL/MED standard.

In this section, we will discuss the postgres_fdw extension. It is a module that allows us to dynamically fetch data from a PostgreSQL data source. The first thing we need to do is deploy the foreign data wrapper:

```
test=# \h CREATE FOREIGN DATA WRAPPER
Command: CREATE FOREIGN DATA WRAPPER
Description: define a new foreign-data wrapper
Syntax:
 CREATE FOREIGN DATA WRAPPER name
    [ HANDLER handler_function | NO HANDLER ]
    [ VALIDATOR validator_function | NO VALIDATOR ]
```

```
        [ OPTIONS ( option 'value' [, ... ] ) ]
  URL: https://www.postgresql.org/docs/17/sql-createforeigndatawrapper.
html
```

Fortunately, the CREATE FOREIGN DATA WRAPPER command is hidden inside an extension. It can easily be installed using the normal process, as follows:

```
test=# CREATE EXTENSION postgres_fdw;
CREATE EXTENSION
```

Now, a virtual server has to be defined. It will point to the other host and tell PostgreSQL where to get the data. At the end of the data, PostgreSQL has to build a complete connect string – the server data is the first thing PostgreSQL has to know about. User information will be added later on. The server will only contain the host, port, and so on. The syntax of CREATE SERVER is as follows:

```
test=# \h CREATE SERVER
Command: CREATE SERVER
Description: define a new foreign server
Syntax:
 CREATE SERVER [ IF NOT EXISTS ] server_name
        [ TYPE 'server_type' ] [ VERSION 'server_version' ]
    FOREIGN DATA WRAPPER fdw_name
    [ OPTIONS ( option 'value' [, ... ] ) ]
 URL: https://www.postgresql.org/docs/17/sql-createserver.html
```

To understand how this works, we will create a second database on the same host and create a server:

```
[hs@zenbook~]$ createdb customer
[hs@zenbook~]$ psql customer
customer=# CREATE TABLE t_customer (id int, name text);
CREATE TABLE
customer=# CREATE TABLE t_company (
    country     text,
    name        text,
    active      text
);
CREATE TABLE
customer=# \d
List of relations
 Schema    | Name        | Type    | Owner
-----------+-------------+---------+-------
 public    | t_company   | table   | hs
 public    | t_customer  | table   | hs
 (2 rows)
```

Now, the server should be added to the standard test database:

```
test=# CREATE SERVER customer_server
FOREIGN DATA WRAPPER postgres_fdw
OPTIONS (host 'localhost', dbname 'customer', port '5432');
CREATE SERVER
```

Note that all the important information is stored as an OPTIONS clause. This is somewhat important because it gives users a lot of flexibility. There are many different foreign data wrappers, and each of them will need different options.

Once the server has been defined, it is time to map users. If we connect from one server to the other, we may not have the same user in both locations. Therefore, foreign data wrappers require users to define the actual user mapping, as follows:

```
test=# \h CREATE USER MAPPING
Command:     CREATE USER MAPPING
Description: define a new mapping of a user to a foreign server
Syntax:
CREATE USER MAPPING [ IF NOT EXISTS ]
FOR { user_name | USER | CURRENT_ROLE | CURRENT_USER | PUBLIC }
    SERVER server_name
    [ OPTIONS ( option 'value' [ , ... ] ) ]
URL: https://www.postgresql.org/docs/17/sql-createusermapping.html
```

The syntax is pretty simple and can be used easily:

```
test=# CREATE USER MAPPING
FOR CURRENT_USER SERVER customer_server
OPTIONS (user 'hs', password 'abc');
CREATE USER MAPPING
```

Again, all of the important information is hidden in the OPTIONS clause. Depending on the type of foreign data wrapper, the list of options will differ. Note that we have to use proper user data here, which will work for our setup. In this case, we will simply use local users.

Once the infrastructure is in place, we can create foreign tables. The syntax to create a foreign table is pretty similar to how we would create a normal local table. All of the columns have to be listed, including their data types:

```
test=# CREATE FOREIGN TABLE f_customer (id int, name text)
SERVER customer_server
OPTIONS (schema_name 'public', table_name 't_customer');
CREATE FOREIGN TABLE
```

All of the columns are listed, just like in the case of a normal CREATE TABLE clause. The unique thing here is that the foreign table points to a table on the remote side. The name of the schema and the name of the table have to be specified in the OPTIONS clause. Once the table has been created, it can be used:

```
test=# SELECT * FROM f_customer ;
 id | name
----+------
(0 rows)
```

To check what PostgreSQL does internally, it is a good idea to run the EXPLAIN clause with the analyze parameter. This will reveal some information about what's really going on in the server:

```
test=# EXPLAIN (analyze true, verbose true)
SELECT * FROM f_customer ;
                           QUERY PLAN
-------------------------------------------------------------
Foreign Scan on public.f_customer
     (cost=100.00..150.95 rows=1365 width=36)
     (actual time=0.221..0.221 rows=0 loops=1)
   Output: id, name
   Remote SQL: SELECT id, name FROM public.t_customer
 Planning time: 0.067 ms
 Execution time: 0.451 ms
(5 rows)
```

The important part here is remote SQL. The foreign data wrapper will send a query to the other side and fetch as little data as possible, since as many restrictions as possible are executed on the remote side to ensure that not much data is processed locally. Filter conditions, joins, and even aggregates can be performed remotely (as of PostgreSQL 10.0).

While the CREATE FOREIGN TABLE clause is surely a nice thing to use, it can be quite cumbersome to list all of those columns over and over again.

The solution to this problem is the IMPORT clause. This allows us to quickly and easily import entire schemas into a local database, as well as create foreign tables:

```
test=# \h IMPORT
Command: IMPORT FOREIGN SCHEMA
Description: import table definitions from a foreign server
Syntax:
 IMPORT FOREIGN SCHEMA remote_schema
    [ { LIMIT TO | EXCEPT } ( table_name [, ...] ) ]
    FROM SERVER server_name
```

```
        INTO local_schema
        [ OPTIONS ( option 'value' [, ... ] ) ]
    URL: https://www.postgresql.org/docs/17/sql-importforeignschema.html
```

IMPORT allows us to link large sets of tables easily. It also reduces the chances of typos and mistakes, since all of the information is fetched directly from the remote data source.

Here is how it works:

```
test=# IMPORT FOREIGN SCHEMA public
FROM SERVER customer_server INTO public;
IMPORT FOREIGN SCHEMA
```

In this case, all of the tables that were created previously in the public schema are linked directly. As we can see, all of the remote tables are now available:

```
test=# \det
List of foreign tables
 Schema  |   Table     |    Server
---------+-------------+------------------
 public  | f_customer  | customer_server
 public  | t_company   | customer_server
 public  | t_customer  | customer_server
 (3 rows)
```

\det lists all the foreign tables, as shown in the previous code.

However, sometimes things go wrong when wiring up a foreign table. What can we do if there is a typo in the configuration? Let's find out.

Handling mistakes and typos

Creating foreign tables isn't hard; however, it sometimes happens that people make mistakes, or maybe the passwords that have been used simply change. To handle such issues, PostgreSQL offers two commands – ALTER SERVER and ALTER USER MAPPING.

ALTER SERVER allows you to modify a server. Here is its syntax:

```
test=# \h ALTER SERVER
Command:     ALTER SERVER
Description: change the definition of a foreign server
Syntax:
ALTER SERVER name [ VERSION 'new_version' ]
    [ OPTIONS ( [ ADD | SET | DROP ] option ['value'] [, ... ] ) ]
ALTER SERVER name OWNER TO { new_owner | CURRENT_ROLE |
    CURRENT_USER | SESSION_USER }
```

```
ALTER SERVER name RENAME TO new_name
URL: https://www.postgresql.org/docs/17/sql-alterserver.html
```

We can use this command to add and remove options for a specific server, which is a good thing if we have forgotten something.

To modify user information, we can alter the user mapping as well:

```
test=# \h ALTER USER MAPPING
Command:     ALTER USER MAPPING
Description: change the definition of a user mapping
Syntax:
ALTER USER MAPPING FOR { user_name | USER | CURRENT_ROLE | CURRENT_
USER | SESSION_USER | PUBLIC }
    SERVER server_name
    OPTIONS ( [ ADD | SET | DROP ] option ['value'] [, ... ] )
URL: https://www.postgresql.org/docs/17/sql-alterusermapping.html
```

The SQL/MED interface is continually being improved, and at the time of writing, features are being added. In the future, even more optimizations will make it to the core, making the SQL/MED interface a good choice for improving scalability.

So far, you have learned how to use foreign data wrappers. Let's now take a look at some more useful extensions.

Other useful extensions

The extensions that we have described so far are all part of the PostgreSQL contrib package, which is shipped as part of the PostgreSQL source code. However, the packages that we've looked at here aren't the only ones that are available in the PostgreSQL community. Many more packages allow us to do all kinds of things.

The number of modules is growing daily, and it is impossible to cover them all. Therefore, I only want to point out the ones I find the most important.

PostGIS (http://postgis.net/) is the **geographical information system** (**GIS**) database interface in the open source world. It has been adopted around the globe and is the de facto standard in the relational open source database world. It is a professional and extremely powerful solution.

If you are looking for geospatial routing, pgRouting may be just the thing. It offers various algorithms that you can use to find the best connections between locations, and it works on top of PostgreSQL.

In this chapter, we have already learned about the postgres_fdw extension, which allows us to connect to some other PostgreSQL databases. There are many more foreign data wrappers available. One of the most famous and professional ones is the oracle_fdw extension. It allows you to integrate with Oracle and fetch data over the wire, which can be done with the postgres_fdw extension.

In some cases, you may also be interested in testing the stability of your infrastructure with `pg_crash` (`https://github.com/cybertec-postgresql/pg_crash`). The idea is to have a module that constantly crashes your database. The `pg_crash` module is an excellent choice for testing and debugging connection pools, and it allows you to reconnect to a failing database. The `pg_crash` module will periodically wreak havoc and kill database sessions or corrupt memory. It is ideal for long-term testing.

Summary

In this chapter, we learned about some of the most promising modules that are shipped with the PostgreSQL standard distribution. These modules are pretty diverse and offer everything, from database connectivity to case-insensitive text and modules, so that we can inspect the server. However, in this chapter, you learned about the most important modules available. This will help you to deploy even greater database setups.

Now that we have dealt with extensions, in the next chapter, we will shift our attention to migration. There, we will learn how we can move to PostgreSQL most simplistically.

12
Troubleshooting PostgreSQL

In *Chapter 11, Deciding on Useful Extensions*, we learned about some useful extensions that are widely adopted and can give your deployment a real boost. By way of a follow-up, you will now be introduced to PostgreSQL troubleshooting. The idea is to give you a systematic approach to inspecting and fixing your system to improve its performance and avoid common pitfalls. Having a systematic approach definitely pays off. Many users face similar issues, so it makes sense to take a look at the most common problems haunting people all over the world. Keep in mind that such a chapter can never cover all cases but is able to give you insights into what might happen in real life.

In this chapter, the following topics will be covered:

- Approaching an unknown database
- Inspecting `pg_stat_activity`
- Checking for slow queries
- Inspecting the log
- Checking for missing indexes
- Checking for memory and I/O
- Understanding noteworthy error scenarios
- Classical cloud and Kubernetes problems

Many things can go wrong in the database, so it is important to comprehensively monitor it and get a handle on potential pitfalls. To figure out what is wrong with your database setup, you have to look into the system professionally.

Approaching an unknown database

If you happen to administer a large-scale system, you might not know what the system is actually doing. Managing hundreds of systems implies that you won't know what is going on with each of them to have any chance of finding relevant problems.

The most important thing when it comes to troubleshooting boils down to a single word: **data**. If there is not enough data, there is no way to fix things. Therefore, the first step to troubleshooting is to always set up a monitoring tool, such as pgwatch2 (available at `https://www.cybertec-postgresql.com/en/products/pgwatch2/`), which gives you some insights into your database server. Without proper data collection, troubleshooting is basically impossible. Always keep in mind that without data, you will be clueless. Of course, there are many more monitoring tools out there, and you can decide on which one you like best.

Once a reporting tool informs you about a situation that is worth checking, this means it has been proven useful for approaching the system in an organized way.

Inspecting pg_stat_activity

Firstly, let's check the content of `pg_stat_activity` and answer the following questions:

- How many concurrent queries are currently being executed on your system?
- Do you see similar types of queries showing up in the query column all the time?
- Do you see queries that have been running for a long time?
- Are there any locks that have not been granted?
- Do you see suspicious wait events?
- Do you see connections from suspicious hosts?

The `pg_stat_activity` view should always be checked first because it will give us an idea of what is happening in the system. Of course, graphical monitoring is supposed to give you a first impression of the system. However, at the end of the day, it really boils down to the queries that actually run on the server. Therefore, a good overview of the system, as provided by `pg_stat_activity`, is more than vital for tracking down issues.

To make it easier for you, I have compiled a couple of queries that I find useful for spotting various types of problems as quickly as possible.

Querying pg_stat_activity

The following query shows you how many queries are currently being executed on your database:

```
test=# SELECT datname,
count(*) AS open,
count(*) FILTER (WHERE state = 'active') AS active,
count(*) FILTER (WHERE state = 'idle') AS idle,
count(*) FILTER (WHERE state = 'idle_in_transaction')
AS idle_in_trans
FROM  pg_stat_activity
```

```
WHERE backend_type = 'client backend'
GROUP BY ROLLUP(1);
 datname | open | active | idle | idle_in_trans
---------+------+--------+------+---------------
 test    | 2    | 1      | 0    | 1
         | 2    | 1      | 0    | 1
 (2 rows)
```

To show as much information as possible on the same screen, partial aggregates are used. We can see **active**, **idle**, and **idle-in-transaction** queries. If we can see a high number of idle-in-transaction queries, it is definitely important to dig deeper in order to figure out how long those transactions have been kept open. The following listing shows how long transactions can be found:

```
test=# SELECT pid, xact_start, now() - xact_start AS duration
FROM pg_stat_activity
WHERE state LIKE '%transaction%'
ORDER BY 3 DESC;
 pid   | xact_start                     | duration
-------+--------------------------------+-----------------
 19758 | 2024-06-21 10:33:09.058342+02  | 22:12:10.194363
 (1 row)
```

The transaction in the preceding listing has been open for more than 22 hours. The main question now is: How can a transaction be open for that long? In most applications, a transaction that takes so long is highly suspicious and potentially highly dangerous. Where does the danger come from? The VACUUM command can only clean up dead rows if no transaction can see them anymore. Now, if a transaction stays open for hours or even days, the VACUUM command cannot produce useful results, which will lead to table bloat, and table bloat will naturally lead to incredibly bad performance. Therefore, we have to keep an eye on the output of this query. The pgwatch2 tool has a metric built into it to help you monitor these things. The same is true for other high-quality monitoring tools.

It is therefore highly recommended to ensure that long transactions are monitored or killed in case they become *too* long. From version 9.6 onward, PostgreSQL has a feature called **snapshot too old**, which allows us to terminate long transactions if snapshots are alive for too long. However, this setting is not available anymore in the latest releases, so we recommend using a different method such as **cron** to kill long transactions in case this is needed.

It is also a good idea to check whether any long-running queries are going on:

```
test=# SELECT now() - query_start AS duration, datname, query
FROM  pg_stat_activity
WHERE state = 'active'
ORDER BY 1 DESC;
 duration          | datname | query
-------------------+---------+----------------------------
```

```
00:00:38.814526  | dev   | SELECT pg_sleep(10000);
00:00:00          | test  | SELECT now() - query_start AS duration,
                                   datname, query
                           FROM  pg_stat_activity
                           WHERE state = 'active'
                           ORDER BY 1 DESC;
(2 rows)
```

In this case, all active queries are inspected, and the statements calculate how long each query has already been active. Often, we see similar queries coming out on top, which can give us some valuable clues about what is happening in our system. If you want to terminate a query that has been alive on your system, we recommend taking a look at the pg_terminate_backend function, which can do exactly that.

Treating Hibernate statements

Many **object-relational mappers** (**ORMs**), such as Hibernate, generate insanely long SQL statements. The trouble is this—pg_stat_activity will only store the first 1,024 bytes of the query in the system view. The rest is truncated. In the case of a long query generated by an ORM such as Hibernate, the query is cut off before the interesting parts (such as the FROM clause, among others) actually start.

The solution to this problem is to set a config parameter in the postgresql.conf file as follows:

```
test=# SHOW track_activity_query_size;
 track_activity_query_size
---------------------------
 1kB
(1 row)
```

If we increase this parameter to a reasonably high value (maybe 32,768) and restart PostgreSQL, we will then be able to see much longer queries and be able to detect issues more easily.

Figuring out where queries come from

When inspecting pg_stat_activity, certain fields will tell us where a query comes from:

```
client_addr     | inet    |
client_hostname | text    |
client_port     | integer |
```

These fields will contain IP addresses and hostnames (if configured), but what happens if every application sends its requests from the very same IP because, for example, all of the applications reside on the same application server? It will be very hard for us to see which application generated which query.

The solution to this problem is to ask the developers to set an `application_name` variable, as shown in the following block:

```
test=# SHOW application_name ;
 application_name
------------------
 psql
(1 row)

test=# SET application_name TO 'some_name';
SET

test=# SHOW application_name;
 application_name
------------------
 some_name
(1 row)
```

If users and developers are cooperative, the `application_name` variable will show up in the system view and make it a lot easier to see where a query comes from. The `application_name` variable can also be set as part of the `connect` string. In the next section, we will try to figure out everything relating to slow queries.

Checking for slow queries

After inspecting `pg_stat_activity`, it makes sense to take a look at slow, time-consuming queries. Basically, there are two ways to approach this problem:

- Look for individual slow queries in the log
- Look for types of queries that take too much time

Finding single, slow queries is the classic approach to performance tuning. By setting the `log_min_duration_statement` variable to a desired threshold, PostgreSQL will start to write a log line for each query that exceeds this threshold. By default, the slow query log is off, as follows:

```
test=# SHOW log_min_duration_statement;
 log_min_duration_statement
----------------------------
                         -1
(1 row)
```

However, setting this variable to a reasonably good value makes perfect sense. Depending on your workload, the desired time may, of course, vary.

In many cases, the desired value might differ from database to database. Therefore, it is also possible to use the variable in a more fine-grained way, as shown here:

```
test=# ALTER DATABASE test
SET log_min_duration_statement TO 10000;
ALTER DATABASE
```

Setting the parameter only for a certain database makes perfect sense if your databases face different workloads.

When using the slow query log, it is important to consider one important factor—many smaller queries may result in a greater load than just a handful of slow-running queries. Of course, it always makes sense to be aware of individual slow queries, but sometimes, those queries are not the problem.

Consider the following example: On your system, 1 million queries, each taking 500 milliseconds, are executed, along with some analytical queries that run for a couple of milliseconds each. Clearly, the real problem will never show up in the slow query log, while every data export, every index creation, and every bulk load (which cannot be avoided in most cases anyway) will spam the log and point us in the wrong direction.

Therefore, my personal recommendation is to use a slow query log but use it carefully and with caution. Most importantly, though, be aware of what we are really measuring.

The better approach, in my opinion, is to work more intensively with the `pg_stat_statements` view. It will offer aggregated information, and not just information about single queries. The `pg_stat_statements` view was discussed already. However, its importance cannot be stressed enough.

Inspecting individual queries

Sometimes, slow queries are identified, but we still don't have a clue about what is really going on. The next step is, of course, to inspect the execution plan of the query and see what happens. Identifying those key operations in the plan that are responsible for bad runtime is fairly simple. Try to use the following checklist:

- Try to see where it is in the plan that the time starts to skyrocket.
- Check for missing indexes (one of the main reasons for bad performance).
- Use the `EXPLAIN` clause (buffers `true`, analyze `true`, and so on) to see whether your query uses too many buffers.
- Turn on the `track_io_timing` parameter to figure out whether there is an I/O problem or a CPU problem (explicitly check whether there is random I/O going on).
- Look for incorrect estimates and try to fix them.

- Look for stored procedures that are executed too frequently.

- Try to figure out whether some of them can be marked as STABLE or IMMUTABLE, provided this is possible.

Note that pg_stat_statements does not account for parse time, so if your queries are very long (such as query strings), then pg_stat_statements may be slightly misleading.

Digging deeper with perf

In most cases, working through this tiny checklist will help you track down the majority of problems in a pretty fast and efficient way. However, even the information that's been extracted from the database engine is sometimes not enough.

The perf tool is an analysis tool for Linux that allows you to directly see which C functions are causing problems on your system. Usually, perf is not installed by default, so it is recommended that you install it. To use perf on your server, just log in to a root and run the following command:

```
perf top
```

The screen will refresh itself every couple of seconds, and you will have the chance to see what is going on live. The following listing shows you what a standard, read-only benchmark might look like:

```
Samples: 164K of event 'cycles:ppp', Event count (approx.):
109789128766
Overhead  Shared Object      Symbol
   3.10%  postgres          [.] AllocSetAlloc
   1.99%  postgres          [.] SearchCatCache
   1.51%  postgres          [.] base_yyparse
   1.42%  postgres          [.] hash_search_with_hash_value
   1.27%  libc-2.22.so      [.] vfprintf
   1.13%  libc-2.22.so      [.] _int_malloc
   0.87%  postgres          [.] palloc
   0.74%  postgres          [.] MemoryContextAllocZeroAligned
   0.66%  libc-2.22.so      [.] __strcmp_sse2_unaligned
   0.66%  [kernel]          [k] _raw_spin_lock_irqsave
   0.66%  postgres          [.] _bt_compare
   0.63%  [kernel]          [k] __fget_light
   0.62%  libc-2.22.so      [.] strlen
```

You can see that no single function takes too much CPU time in our sample, which tells us that the system is just fine.

However, this may not always be the case. There is a problem called **spinlock contention** that is quite common. Spinlocks are used by the PostgreSQL core to synchronize things such as buffer access. A spinlock is a feature provided by modern CPUs to avoid operating system interactions for small operations (such as incrementing a number). If you get the feeling that you might be facing spinlock contention, the symptoms are as follows:

- A really high CPU load
- Incredibly low throughput (queries that usually take milliseconds suddenly take seconds)
- I/O is unusually low because the CPU is busy trading locks

In many cases, spinlock contention happens suddenly. Your system is just fine when, all of a sudden, the load goes up and the throughput drops like a stone. The `perf top` command will reveal that most of this time is spent on a C function called `s_lock`. If this is the case, you should try to do the following:

```
huge_pages = try                  # on, off, or try
```

Change huge_pages from `try` to `off`. It can be a good idea to turn off huge_pages altogether at the operating system level. In general, it seems that some kernels are more prone to producing these kinds of problems than others. In recent years, this problem seems to have gone away in most cases. However, I decided to keep this information in the book to help people running PostgreSQL in older deployments.

The `perf` tool is also interesting if you use PostGIS. If the top functions in the list are all GIS-related (as in, from some underlying library), you know that the problem is most likely not coming from bad PostgreSQL tuning but is simply related to expensive operations that take time to complete.

Inspecting the log

If your system is in trouble, it makes sense to inspect the log to see what is going on. The important point is this: not all log entries are created equally. PostgreSQL has a hierarchy of log entries that range from DEBUG to PANIC.

For the administrator, the following three error levels are of great importance:

- ERROR
- FATAL
- PANIC

The ERROR error level is used for problems such as syntax errors, permission-related problems, and more. Your log will always contain error messages. The critical factor is this—how often does a certain type of error show up? Producing millions of syntax errors is certainly not an ideal strategy for running a database server.

The FATAL error level is scarier than ERROR; you will see messages such as could not allocate memory for shared memory name or unexpected walreceiver state. In other words, these error messages are already really scary and will tell you that things are going wrong.

Finally, there is PANIC. If you come across this kind of message, you know that something is really, really wrong. Classic examples of PANIC are lock tables being corrupted or too many semaphores being created. Another example would be "out of memory." This will result in a shutdown of the database server.

In the next section, you will learn about missing indexes.

Checking for missing indexes

Once we are done with the first three steps, it is important to take a look at performance in general. As I have continually stated throughout this book, missing indexes are fully responsible for super-bad database performance, so whenever we face a slow system, it is recommended that we check for missing indexes and deploy whatever is needed.

Usually, customers ask us to optimize the RAID level, tune the kernel, or do some other fancy stuff. In reality, these complicated requests often boil down to a handful of missing indexes. In my opinion, it always makes sense to spend some extra time just checking whether all of the desired indexes are there. Checking for missing indexes is neither hard nor time-consuming, so it should be done all the time, regardless of the kind of performance problem that you face.

Here is my favorite query to get an impression of where an index may be missing:

```
SELECT schemaname, relname, seq_scan, seq_tup_read,
        idx_scan, seq_tup_read / seq_scan AS avg
FROM   pg_stat_user_tables
WHERE  seq_scan > 0
ORDER BY seq_tup_read DESC
LIMIT 20;
```

Try to find large tables (with a high avg value) that are scanned frequently. These tables will typically come out at the top.

Checking for memory and I/O

Once we have found missing indexes, we can inspect the memory and I/O. To figure out what is going on, it makes sense to activate track_io_timing. If it is on, PostgreSQL will collect information about the disk wait time and present it to you.

Often, the main question asked by a customer is: If we add more disks, will it be faster? It is possible to guess what will happen, but in general, measuring is the better and more useful strategy. Enabling track_io_timing will help you gather the data to really figure this out.

PostgreSQL exposes the disk wait time in various ways. One way to inspect things is to take a look at pg_stat_database:

```
test=# \d pg_stat_database
View "pg_catalog.pg_stat_database"
  Column          | Type                     | Modifiers
------------------+--------------------------+-----------
  datid           | oid                      |
  datname         | name                     |
  ...
  conflicts       | bigint                   |
  temp_files      | bigint                   |
  temp_bytes      | bigint                   |
  ...
  blk_read_time   | double precision         |
  blk_write_time  | double precision         |
```

Note that there are two fields toward the end of the preceding block—blk_read_time and blk_write_time. They will tell us about the amount of time PostgreSQL has spent waiting for the operating system to respond. Note that we are not really measuring the disk wait time here but rather the time the operating system takes to return data.

If the operating system produces cache hits, this time will be fairly low. If the operating system has to handle really nasty random I/O, we will see that a single block can even take a couple of milliseconds.

In many cases, high blk_read_time and blk_write_time values occur when temp_files and temp_bytes show high numbers. Also, in many cases, this points to a bad work_mem setting or a bad maintenance_work_mem setting. Remember this: if PostgreSQL cannot do things in memory, it has to spill to the disk. You can use the temp_files operation to detect this. Whenever there are temp_files operations, there is the chance of a nasty disk wait time.

While a global view on a per-database level makes sense, it does not yield in-depth information about the real source of trouble. Often, only a few queries are to blame for bad performance. The way to spot these is to use pg_stat_statements, as shown in the following block:

```
test=# \d pg_stat_statements
View "public.pg_stat_statements"
  Column          | Type             | Modifiers
------------------+------------------+-----------
  ...
  query           | text             |
  calls           | bigint           |
  ...
  total_exec_time | double precision |
  ...
```

```
temp_blks_read          | bigint           |
temp_blks_written       | bigint           |
blk_read_time           | double precision |
blk_write_time          | double precision |
```

You will be able to see, on a per-query basis, whether there is a disk wait. The important part is the `blk_time` value in combination with `total_time`. The ratio is what counts. In general, a query representing more than 30% of the disk wait can be seen as heavily I/O-bound.

Once we have checked the PostgreSQL system tables, it makes sense to inspect what the `vmstat` command on Linux tells us. Alternatively, we can use the `iostat` command:

```
[hs@computer ~]$ vmstat 2
^lprocs -----------memory---------- ---swap-- -----io---- -system--
------cpu-----
 r b swpd free buff cache si so bi bo in cs us sy id wa st
 0 0 367088 199488 96 2320388 0 2 83 96 106 156 16 6 78 0 0
 0 0 367088 198140 96 2320504 0 0 0 10 595 2624 3 1 96 0 0
 0 0 367088 191448 96 2320964 0 0 0 8 920 2957 8 2 90 0 0
```

When working on databases, we should focus our attention on three fields: `bi`, `bo`, and `wa`. The `bi` field tells us about the number of blocks read; 1,000 is equivalent to 1 Mbps. The `bo` field refers to blockouts. It tells us about the amount of data written on the disk. In a way, `bi` and `bo` are the raw throughput. I would not consider a number to be harmful. What if a problem has a high `wa` value? Low values for the `bi` and `bo` fields, combined with a high `wa` value, tell us about a potential disk bottleneck, which is most likely related to a lot of random I/O taking place on your system. The higher the `wa` value, the slower your queries because you must wait on the disk to respond.

> **Important note**
>
> Good raw throughput is a good thing, but sometimes, it can also point to a problem. If high throughput is needed on an **online transaction processing** (**OLTP**) system, it can tell you that there is not enough RAM to cache things or that indexes are missing and PostgreSQL has to read too much data. Keep in mind that things are interconnected, and data should not be viewed in isolation.

Understanding noteworthy error scenarios

After going through the basic guidelines to hunt down the most common issues that you will face in your database, the upcoming sections will discuss some of the most common error scenarios that occur in the PostgreSQL world.

Facing clog corruption

PostgreSQL has a thing called the commit log (now called `pg_xact`; it was formally known as `pg_clog`). This tracks the state of every transaction on the system and helps PostgreSQL determine whether a row can be seen. In general, a transaction can be in four states:

```
#define TRANSACTION_STATUS_IN_PROGRESS    0x00
#define TRANSACTION_STATUS_COMMITTED      0x01
#define TRANSACTION_STATUS_ABORTED        0x02
#define TRANSACTION_STATUS_SUB_COMMITTED  0x03
```

The clog has a separate directory in the PostgreSQL database instance (`pg_xact`).

In the past, people have reported something called **clog corruption**, which can be caused by faulty disks or bugs in PostgreSQL that have been fixed over the years. A corrupted commit log is a pretty nasty thing to have because all of our data is there, but PostgreSQL does not know whether things are still valid. Corruption in this area is nothing short of a total disaster.

How does the administrator figure out that the commit log is broken? Here is what we normally see:

```
ERROR: could not access status of transaction 118831
```

If PostgreSQL cannot access the status of a transaction, various issues will occur. The main question is: How can this be fixed? To put it to you straight, there is no way to really fix the problem—we can only try to rescue as much data as possible.

As we've stated already, the commit log keeps 2 bits per transaction. This means that we have 4 transactions per byte, leaving us with 32,768 transactions per block. Once we have figured out which block it is, we can fake the transaction log:

```
dd if=/dev/zero of=<data directory location>/pg_xact/0001
    bs=256K count=1
```

We can use `dd` (an old Unix command for low-level I/O) to fake the transaction log and set the `commit` status to the desired value. The core question is really: Which transaction state should be used? The answer is that any state is actually wrong because we really don't know how those transactions ended.

However, usually, it is a good idea to just set them to committed so that we lose less data. It really depends on our workload and our data when deciding what is less disruptive.

When we have to use this technique, we should fake as little clog as is necessary. Remember—we are essentially faking the commit status, which is not a nice thing to do to a database engine.

Once we have faked the clog, we should create a backup as fast as we can and recreate the database instance from scratch. The system we are working with is no longer very trustworthy, so we should try to extract the data as fast as we can.

> **Note**
> Keep in mind that the data we are about to extract could be contradictory and wrong, so we will make sure that some quality checks are imposed on whatever we can rescue from our database server.

Understanding checkpoint messages

Checkpoints are essential to data integrity, as well as performance. The further checkpoints are apart, the better the performance usually is. In PostgreSQL, the default configuration is usually fairly conservative, and checkpoints are therefore comparatively fast. If a lot of data is changed in the database core at the same time, PostgreSQL may tell us that it considers checkpoints to be too frequent. The LOG file will show the following entries:

```
LOG: checkpoints are occurring too frequently (2 seconds apart)
LOG: checkpoints are occurring too frequently (3 seconds apart)
```

During heavy writing due to dumping, restoration, or some other large operation, PostgreSQL might notice that the configuration parameters are too low. A message is sent to the LOG file to tell us exactly that.

If we see this kind of message, it is strongly recommended, for performance reasons, that we increase the checkpoint distances by increasing the `max_wal_size` parameter dramatically (in older versions, the setting was called `checkpoint_segments`). In recent versions of PostgreSQL, the default configuration is already a lot better than it used to be. However, writing data too frequently can still happen easily.

When we see a message about checkpoints, there is one thing that we have to keep in mind. Checkpointing too frequently is not dangerous at all—it just happens to lead to bad performance. Writing is simply a lot slower than it could be, but our data is not in danger. Increasing the distance between two checkpoints sufficiently will make the error go away, and it will speed up our database instance at the same time.

Managing corrupted data pages

PostgreSQL is a very stable database system. It protects data as much as possible, and it has proven its worth over the years. However, PostgreSQL relies on solid hardware and a filesystem that is working properly. If the storage breaks, so will PostgreSQL—there isn't much that we can do about it, apart from adding replicas to make things more fail-safe.

Once in a while, it happens that the filesystem or the disk fails. In many cases, however, the entire thing will not go south; just a couple of blocks become corrupted for whatever reason. Recently, we have seen this happening in virtual environments. Some virtual machines don't flush to the disk by default, which means that PostgreSQL cannot rely on things being written to the disk. This kind of behavior can lead to random problems that are hard to predict.

When a block can no longer be read, you may encounter an error message such as the following:

```
"could not read block %u in file "%s": %m"
```

The query that you are about to run will error out and stop working. Fortunately, PostgreSQL has a means of dealing with these things:

```
test=# SET zero_damaged_pages TO on;
SET
test=# SHOW zero_damaged_pages;
 zero_damaged_pages
--------------------
 on
(1 row)
```

The `zero_damaged_pages` variable is a config variable that allows us to deal with broken pages. Instead of throwing an error, PostgreSQL will take the block and simply fill it with zeros.

Note that this will definitely lead to data loss, but remember—the data was broken or lost before anyway, so this is simply a way to deal with the corruption that is caused by bad things happening in our storage system.

> **Important note**
>
> I would advise everybody to handle the `zero_damaged_pages` variable with care—be aware of what you are doing when you call it.

Careless connection management

In PostgreSQL, every database connection is a separate process. All of those processes are synchronized using shared memory (technically, in most cases, it is mapped memory, but for this example, this makes no difference). This shared memory contains the I/O cache and a list of active database connections, locks, and other vital things that allow the system to function properly.

When a connection is closed, it will remove all relevant entries from the shared memory and leave the system in a sane state. However, what happens when a database connection simply crashes for whatever reason?

The postmaster (the main process) will detect that one of the child processes is missing. Then, all of the other connections will be terminated, and a roll-forward process will be initialized. Why is this necessary? When a process crashes, the shared memory area may be edited by the process. In other words, a crashing process can corrupt the shared memory. Therefore, the postmaster reacts and kicks every user out before the corruption can spread through the system. All the memory is cleaned, and everybody has to reconnect.

From an end user's point of view, this feels like PostgreSQL has crashed and restarted, which is not the case. Since a process cannot react to its own crash (segmentation fault) or some other signal, cleaning out everything is absolutely essential in order to protect your data.

The same happens if you use the `kill -9` command on a database connection. The connection cannot catch the signal (`-9` cannot be caught by definition), and therefore the postmaster has to react again.

Fighting table bloat

Table bloat is one of the most important issues when dealing with PostgreSQL. When we face bad performance, it is always a good idea to figure out whether there are objects that require a lot more space than they are supposed to have.

How can we figure out where table bloat is happening? Check out the `pg_stat_user_tables` view:

```
test=# \d pg_stat_user_tables
View "pg_catalog.pg_stat_user_tables"
 Column            | Type             | Modifiers
-------------------+------------------+-----------
 relid             | oid              |
 schemaname        | name             |
 relname           | name             |
 ...
 n_live_tup        | bigint           |
 n_dead_tup        | bigint           |
```

The `n_live_tup` and `n_dead_tup` fields give us an impression of what is going on, and we can also use `pgstattuple`.

What can we do if there is serious table bloat? The first option is to run the `VACUUM FULL` command. The trouble is that the `VACUUM FULL` clause needs a table lock. On a large table, this can be a real problem because users cannot write to the table while it is being rewritten.

> **Important note**
>
> If you are using at least PostgreSQL 9.6, you can use a tool called `pg_squeeze`. This organizes a table behind the scenes without blocking (`https://www.cybertec-postgresql.com/en/products/pg_squeeze/`). This is especially useful if you are reorganizing a very large table.

Classical cloud and Kubernetes problems

In recent years, many people have moved to the cloud or to Kubernetes deployments, which have in many cases greatly simplified deployments and operations. However, every new technology comes with certain challenges and things one has to take into consideration.

CPU throttling – capacity control unleashed

In a cloud environment, what one essentially buys or deploys is a certain amount of CPU and I/O power. What does that mean? The host operating system therefore has to ensure that you don't exceed what you have paid for. When the load is low, this is usually not a problem. However, when you are getting closer and closer to your limits, the system tends to use more and more capacity to keep you within your limits. Controlling deployments eventually becomes the overarching task on the host. The net effect is that your performance can seriously suffer as soon as you are approaching the limit of your deployment.

The problem can show itself in two forms:

- Horrible CPU performance
- Very bad disk throughput

While the first part is obvious, the second part often comes as a surprise. The reason is that to control and limit I/O throughput, the OS and thus the CPU have to do some scheduling work. The more the CPU is limited by throttling, the higher your I/O latency will become, which leads to a performance-death spiral.

In the past, we have seen systems that showed more than 20 milliseconds I/O latency providing us with 4 MB/second (which is less than a stone-old USB stick can deliver). The logical action taken by most users when they see bad I/O is to throw more money at I/O capacity. However, this is not the solution here – the right solution is to ensure that your CPU usage in a cloud deployment always presents a solid margin of safety. In case your overall CPU usage is over 80%, you might face I/O issues as well as all kinds of other issues.

Informing yourself about CPU consumption can easily be done using the cloud provider's dashboards.

Summary

In this chapter, we learned how to systematically approach a database system and detect the most common issues that people face with PostgreSQL. We learned about some important system tables, as well as some other important factors that can determine whether we will succeed or fail. It is especially important to keep an eye on table bloat and dangerous error messages. Note that depending on the type of workload, you might face different challenges. The most important ones have been covered in this chapter.

In the final chapter of this book, we will focus our attention on migrating to PostgreSQL. If you are using Oracle or some other database system, you might want to check out PostgreSQL. In *Chapter 13, Migrating to PostgreSQL*, we'll discuss everything involved in this.

Migrating to PostgreSQL

In *Chapter 12, Troubleshooting PostgreSQL*, we learned how to approach the most common issues related to PostgreSQL troubleshooting. The important thing is to have a systematic approach to tracking down problems, which is exactly what is provided here. Technology is constantly evolving and therefore, it is good to have a playbook that helps you to keep things under control at all times.

The final chapter of this book is about moving from other databases to PostgreSQL. Many of you may still be suffering from the pain caused by commercial database license costs. I want to give all of you out there a way out and show you how data can be moved from a proprietary system to PostgreSQL. Moving to PostgreSQL makes sense not only from a financial point of view but also if you are looking for more advanced features and flexibility. PostgreSQL has so much to offer, and, at the time of writing, new features are being added daily. The same applies to the number of tools that are available to help you migrate to PostgreSQL. Things are getting better and better, and developers are publishing more, and better, tools all the time.

The following topics will be covered in this chapter:

- Migrating SQL statements to PostgreSQL
- Moving from Oracle to PostgreSQL

By the end of this chapter, you should be able to move a basic database from another system to PostgreSQL.

Migrating SQL statements to PostgreSQL

When moving from a database to PostgreSQL, it makes sense to take a look and figure out which database engine provides which kind of functionality. Moving the data and the structure itself is usually fairly easy. However, rewriting SQL might not be. Therefore, I decided to include a section that explicitly focuses on various advanced features of SQL and their availability in today's database engines.

Using LATERAL joins

In SQL, a LATERAL join can basically be seen as some sort of loop. This allows us to parameterize a join and execute everything inside the LATERAL clause more than once. Here is a simple example of this:

```
test=# SELECT *
FROM generate_series(1, 4) AS x,
     LATERAL (
         SELECT array_agg(y) FROM generate_series(1, x) AS y
     ) AS z;
 x  | array_agg
----+-----------
 1  | {1}
 2  | {1,2}
 3  | {1,2,3}
 4  | {1,2,3,4}
(4 rows)
```

The LATERAL clause will be called for each instance of x. To the end user, it is basically some sort of loop.

Supporting LATERAL joins

One important SQL feature is LATERAL joins. The following list shows which engines support LATERAL joins and which don't:

- **PostgreSQL**: Supported since PostgreSQL 9.3

- **SQLite**: Not supported (a master thesis about this topic has recently been published: https://db.cs.uni-tuebingen.de/theses/2021/jonatan-braun/thesis-braun-2021.pdf)

- **Db2 LUW**: Supported since version 9.1 (2005)

- **Oracle**: Supported since 12c

- **Microsoft SQL Server**: Supported since 2005 but using a different syntax

LATERAL joins are important. Unfortunately, this type of join is often underappreciated or simply not known about. It is therefore highly recommended to dive into this topic in more detail.

Using grouping sets

Grouping sets are very useful if we want to run more than one aggregate at the same time. Using grouping sets can speed up aggregation because we don't have to process the data more than once.

Here is an example of this:

```
test=# SELECT x % 2, array_agg(x)
FROM generate_series(1, 4) AS x
GROUP BY ROLLUP (1);
 ?column? | array_agg
----------+-----------
        0 | {2,4}
        1 | {1,3}
          | {2,4,1,3}
(3 rows)
```

PostgreSQL offers more than just the ROLLUP clause. The CUBE and GROUPING SETS clauses are also supported.

Supporting grouping sets

Grouping sets are essential for generating more than just one aggregation in a single query. The following list shows which engines support grouping sets and which don't:

- **PostgreSQL**: Supported since PostgreSQL 9.5
- **SQLite**: Not supported
- **Db2 LUW**: Supported since at least 1999
- **Oracle**: Supported since 9iR1 (around 2000)
- **Microsoft SQL Server**: Supported since 2008

Grouping sets are really useful if you are dealing with all kinds of analytical workloads.

Using the WITH clause – common table expressions

Common table expressions are a nice way to execute things inside a SQL statement, but only once. PostgreSQL will execute all the WITH clauses and allow us to use the results throughout the query.

Here is a simplified example of this:

```
test=# WITH x AS (
    SELECT avg(id) FROM generate_series(1, 10) AS id
)
SELECT *, y - (SELECT avg FROM x) AS diff
FROM   generate_series(1, 10) AS y
WHERE  y > (SELECT avg FROM x);
 y | diff
---+--------------------
```

```
 6 | 0.5000000000000000
 7 | 1.5000000000000000
 8 | 2.5000000000000000
 9 | 3.5000000000000000
10 | 4.5000000000000000
(5 rows)
```

In this example, the WITH clause's **common table expressions (CTEs)** calculate the average value of the time series generated by the generate_series function. The resulting x can be used just like a table all over the query. In my example, x is used twice.

Supporting the WITH clause

The following list shows which engines support the WITH clause and which don't:

- **PostgreSQL**: Supported since PostgreSQL 8.4
- **SQLite**: Supported since 3.8.3
- **Db2 LUW**: Supported since 8 (2000)
- **Oracle**: Supported since 9iR2
- **Microsoft SQL Server**: Supported since 2005

> **Important note**
> Note that, in PostgreSQL, a CTE can even support writes (the INSERT, UPDATE, and DELETE clauses).

Using the WITH RECURSIVE clause

The WITH clause comes in two forms:

- Standard CTEs, as shown in the previous section (using the WITH clause)
- A method to run recursions in SQL

The simple form of a CTE was covered in the previous section. In the next section, the recursive version will be covered.

Supporting the WITH RECURSIVE clause

The following list shows which engines support the WITH RECURSIVE clause and which don't:

- **PostgreSQL**: Supported since PostgreSQL 8.4
- **SQLite**: Supported since 3.8.3

- **Db2 LUW**: Supported since 7 (2000)

- **Oracle**: Supported since 11gR2 (in Oracle, it is usually more common to use the CONNECT BY clause instead of the WITH RECURSIVE clause)

- **Microsoft SQL Server**: Supported since 2005

Using the FILTER clause

When looking at the SQL standard itself, you will notice that the FILTER clause has been around since SQL (2003). However, not many systems actually support this highly useful syntax element.

Here's an example of this:

```
test=# SELECT count(*),
       count(*) FILTER (WHERE id < 5),
       count(*) FILTER (WHERE id > 2)
FROM generate_series(1, 10) AS id;
 count | count | count
-------+-------+-------
    10 |     4 |     8
(1 row)
```

The FILTER clause is useful if a condition cannot be used inside a normal WHERE clause because some other aggregate needs the data.

Before the introduction of the FILTER clause, the same could be achieved using a more cumbersome form of syntax:

```
SELECT sum(CASE WHEN .. THEN 1 ELSE 0 END) AS whatever
FROM some_table;
```

Supporting the FILTER clause

The following list shows which engines support the FILTER clause and which don't:

- **PostgreSQL**: Supported since PostgreSQL 9.4

- **SQLite**: Not supported

- **Db2 LUW**: Not supported (a CASE/WHEN workaround is needed)

- **Oracle**: Not supported (a CASE/WHEN workaround is needed)

- **Microsoft SQL Server**: Not supported

Using windowing functions

Windowing and analytics have already been discussed extensively in this book in *Chapter 4, Handling Advanced SQL*. Therefore, we can jump straight into SQL compliance.

Supporting windowing and analytics

The following list shows which engines support Windows functions and which don't:

- **PostgreSQL**: Supported since PostgreSQL 8.4

- **SQLite**: Supported since version 3.25.0 (2018-09-15)

- **Db2 LUW**: Supported since version 7

- **Oracle**: Supported since version 8i

- **Microsoft SQL Server**: Supported since 2005

> **Important note**
> Some other databases, such as Hive, Impala, Spark, and NuoDB, also support analytics.

Using ordered sets – the WITHIN GROUP clause

Ordered sets are fairly new to PostgreSQL. The difference between an ordered set and a normal aggregate is that, in the case of an ordered set, the way data is fed to the aggregate *does* make a difference. Suppose you want to find a trend in your data – the order of the data is relevant.

Here is a simple example of calculating a median value:

```
test=# SELECT
    id % 2, percentile_disc(0.5) WITHIN GROUP (ORDER BY id)
FROM  generate_series(1, 123) AS id
GROUP BY 1;
 ?column? | percentile_disc
----------+-----------------
        0 | 62
        1 | 61
(2 rows)
```

The median can only be determined if there is a sorted input.

Supporting the WITHIN GROUP clause

The following list shows which engines support Windows functions and which don't:

- **PostgreSQL**: Supported since PostgreSQL 9.4

- **SQLite**: Not supported

- **Db2 LUW**: Supported

- **Oracle**: Supported since version 9iR1

- **Microsoft SQL Server**: Supported, but the query has to be remodeled using the windowing function

Using the TABLESAMPLE clause

Table sampling has long been the real strength of commercial database vendors. Traditional database systems have provided sampling for many years. However, the monopoly has been broken. Since PostgreSQL 9.5, we have also had a solution to the problem of sampling.

Here's how it works:

```
test=# CREATE TABLE t_test (id int);
CREATE TABLE

test=# INSERT INTO t_test
SELECT * FROM generate_series(1, 1000000);
INSERT 0 1000000
```

First, a table containing 1 million rows is created. Then, tests can be executed:

```
test=# SELECT count(*), avg(id)
FROM    t_test TABLESAMPLE BERNOULLI (1);
 count  |        avg
--------+--------------------
 9802   |    502453.220873291165
(1 row)
test=# SELECT count(*), avg(id)
FROM    t_test TABLESAMPLE BERNOULLI (1);
 count  |        avg
--------+--------------------
 10082  |    497514.321959928586
(1 row)
```

In this example, the same test is executed twice. A 1% random sample is used in each case. Both average values are pretty close to 5 million, so the result is pretty good from a statistical point of view.

Supporting the TABLESAMPLE clause

The following list shows which engines support the TABLESAMPLE clause and which don't:

- **PostgreSQL**: Supported since PostgreSQL 9.5
- **SQLite**: Not supported
- **Db2 LUW**: Supported since version 8.2
- **Oracle**: Supported since version 8
- **Microsoft SQL Server**: Supported since 2005

Using the FETCH FIRST clause

Limiting a result in SQL is a somewhat sad story. In short, every database does things differently. Although there is actually a SQL standard on limiting results, not everybody fully supports the way things are supposed to be. The correct way to limit data is to use the following syntax:

```
test=# SELECT * FROM t_test FETCH FIRST 3 ROWS ONLY;
  id
  ----
   1
   2
   3
(3 rows)
```

If you have never seen this syntax before, don't worry. You are definitely not alone.

Supporting the FETCH FIRST clause

The following list shows which engines support the FETCH FIRST clause and which don't:

- **PostgreSQL**: Supported since PostgreSQL 8.4 (usually, limit/offset is used)
- **SQLite**: Supported since version 2.1.0
- **Db2 LUW**: Supported since version 7
- **Oracle**: Supported since version 12c (uses subselects with the row_num function)
- **Microsoft SQL Server**: Supported since 2012 (traditionally, top *n* is used)

Using the OFFSET clause

The OFFSET clause is similar to the FETCH FIRST clause. It is easy to use, but it hasn't been widely adopted. It isn't as bad as it is in the FETCH FIRST clause, but it still tends to be an issue.

Supporting the OFFSET clause

The following list shows which engines support the `OFFSET` clause and which don't:

- **PostgreSQL**: Supported since PostgreSQL 6.5

- **SQLite**: Supported since version 2.1.0

- **Db2 LUW**: Supported since version 11.1

- **Oracle**: Supported since version 12c

- **Microsoft SQL Server**: Supported since 2012

Using temporal tables

Temporal tables are provided by some database engines to handle versioning. Unfortunately, there is no such thing as out-of-the-box versioning in PostgreSQL. So, if you are moving from Db2 or Oracle, there's some work ahead of you to port the desired functionality to PostgreSQL. Basically, changing the code a bit on the PostgreSQL side isn't too hard. However, it does require some manual intervention – it is no longer a straight copy-and-paste job.

Supporting temporal tables

The following list shows which engines support temporal tables and which don't:

- **PostgreSQL**: Not supported

- **SQLite**: Not supported

- **Db2 LUW**: Supported since version 10.1

- **Oracle**: Supported since version 12cR1

- **Microsoft SQL Server**: Supported since 2016

Matching patterns in time series

At the time of writing, the most recent SQL standard (SQL 2016) provides a feature that's designed to find matches in time series. So far, only Oracle has implemented this functionality in its latest version of the product.

At this point, no other database vendor has followed it and added similar functionality. If you want to model this state-of-the-art technology in PostgreSQL, you have to work with the `window` function and subselects. Matching time series patterns in Oracle is pretty powerful; there isn't just one type of query to achieve this in PostgreSQL.

Moving from Oracle to PostgreSQL

So far, we have seen how the most important advanced SQL features can be ported or used in PostgreSQL. Given this introduction, it is time to take a look at migrating Oracle database systems in particular.

These days, migrating from Oracle to PostgreSQL has become really popular due to Oracle's new license and business policy. What is stunning to see is that back in the old days, costs were pretty much the main driver – these days, more and more people are moving away from Oracle for technical reasons. In particular, those moving to a Kubernetes-based stack favor PostgreSQL over Oracle as it is more flexible and a lot easier to handle.

Using the oracle_fdw extension to move data

One of my preferred methods to move users from Oracle to PostgreSQL is Laurenz Albe's `oracle_fdw` extension (`https://github.com/laurenz/oracle_fdw`). It is a **foreign data wrapper** (**FDW**) that allows you to represent a table in Oracle as a table in PostgreSQL. The `oracle_fdw` extension is one of the most sophisticated FDWs and is rock-solid, well-documented, free, and open source.

Installing the `oracle_fdw` extension requires you to install the Oracle client library. Fortunately, there are already RPM packages that can be used out of the box (`http://www.oracle.com/technetwork/topics/linuxx86-64soft-092277.html`). The `oracle_fdw` extension needs the OCI driver to talk to Oracle. In addition to ready-made Oracle client drivers, there is also an RPM package for the `oracle_fdw` extension itself, which is provided by the community. If you aren't using an RPM-based system, you might have to compile things on your own, which is clearly possible but a bit more labor-intensive.

Once the software has been installed, it can be enabled easily:

```
test=# CREATE EXTENSION oracle_fdw;
```

The `CREATE EXTENSION` clause loads the extension into your desired database. Now, a server can be created, and users can be mapped to their counterparts on the Oracle side, as follows:

```
test=# CREATE SERVER oraserver
FOREIGN DATA WRAPPER oracle_fdw
OPTIONS (dbserver '//dbserver.example.com/ORADB');

test=# CREATE USER MAPPING FOR postgres
SERVER oradb
OPTIONS (user 'orauser', password 'orapass');
```

Now, it's time to fetch some data. My preferred way is to use the `IMPORT FOREIGN SCHEMA` clause to import the data definitions. The `IMPORT FOREIGN SCHEMA` clause will create a foreign table for each table in a remote schema and expose the data on the Oracle side, which can then be read easily.

The easiest way to make use of the schema import is to create separate schemas on PostgreSQL that just hold the database schema. Then, data can be sucked into PostgreSQL easily using the FDW. This applies to pretty much every FDW that supports the `IMPORT FOREIGN SCHEMA` clause. If you want to learn how the Oracle Foreign Data Mapper is handling data type conversions, consider checking out the GitHub page at `https://github.com/laurenz/oracle_fdw?tab=readme-ov-file#data-types`.

If you want to use geometries, make sure that PostGIS is installed on your database server.

The downside of the `oracle_fdw` extension is that it cannot migrate procedures out of the box. Stored procedures are somewhat special and require some manual intervention.

CYBERTEC Migrator – large-scale migrations

If you are looking for a more comprehensive commercial solution that comes with 24/7 support and a lot more, we can recommend taking a look at **CYBERTEC Migrator**, which is available on my website (`https://www.cybertec-postgresql.com/en/products/cybertec-migrator/`). It comes with built-in parallelism, advanced data type prediction, zero downtime migration, automatic code rewrites, and a lot more.

During our tests, we have seen transfer speeds of up to 1.5 GB/second, which is the fastest implementation I am currently aware of. Check out my website to find out more.

Using Ora2Pg to migrate from Oracle

People migrated from Oracle to PostgreSQL long before FDWs existed. High license costs have plagued users for a long time, so moving to PostgreSQL has been a natural thing to do for many years.

The alternative to the `oracle_fdw` extension is something called **Ora2Pg**, which has been around for many years and can be downloaded for free from `https://github.com/darold/Ora2Pg`. Ora2Pg is written in Perl and has a long tradition of new releases.

The features that are provided by Ora2Pg are stunning:

- Migration of the full database schema, including tables, views, sequences, and indexes (unique, primary, foreign key, and check constraints).
- Migration of privileges for users and groups.
- Migration of partitioned tables.
- Ability to export predefined functions, triggers, procedures, packages, and package bodies.
- Migration of full or partial data (using a `WHERE` clause).
- Full support of Oracle BLOB objects as PostgreSQL `bytea`.
- Ability to export Oracle views as PostgreSQL tables.

- Ability to export Oracle user-defined types.

- Basic automatic conversion of PL/SQL code to PL/pgSQL code. Note that a fully automated conversion of everything isn't possible. However, a lot of stuff can be transformed automatically.

- Ability to export Oracle tables as FDW tables.

- Ability to export materialized views.

- Ability to display detailed reports regarding Oracle database content.

- Assessment of the complexity of the migration process of an Oracle database.

- Migration cost assessment of PL/SQL code from a file.

- Ability to generate XML files to be used with the Pentaho Data Integrator (Kettle).

- Ability to export Oracle locator and spatial geometries into PostGIS.

- Ability to export database links as Oracle FDWs.

- Ability to export synonyms as views.

- Ability to export a directory as an external table or a directory for the `external_file` extension.

- Ability to dispatch a list of SQL orders over multiple PostgreSQL connections.

- Ability to perform a `diff` function between Oracle and PostgreSQL databases for test purposes.

Using Ora2Pg looks hard at first glance. However, it is actually a lot easier than it seems. The basic concept is as follows:

```
/usr/local/bin/Ora2Pg -c /some_path/new_Ora2Pg.conf
```

Ora2Pg needs a config file to run. The config file contains all the information that's needed to handle the process. The default config file is already really nice and is a good starting point for most migrations. In the Ora2Pg language, a migration is a project.

The configuration will drive the entire project. When you run it, Ora2Pg will create a couple of directories with all the data that's been extracted from Oracle:

```
Ora2Pg --project_base /app/migration/ --init_project test_project
Creating project test_project.
/app/migration/test_project/
                    schema/
                            dblinks/
                            directories/
                            functions/
                            grants/
                            mviews/
                            packages/
                            partitions/
```

```
                              procedures/
                              sequences/
                              synonyms/
                              tables/
                              tablespaces/
                              triggers/
                              types/
                              views/
                    sources/
                              functions/
                              mviews/
                              packages/
                              partitions/
                              procedures/
                              triggers/
                              types/
                              views/
                    data/
                    config/
                    reports/
    Generating generic configuration file
    Creating script export_schema.sh to automate all exports.
    Creating script import_all.sh to automate all imports.
```

As you can see, scripts that can just be executed are generated. The resulting data can then be imported into PostgreSQL easily. Be prepared to change procedures here and there. Not everything can be migrated automatically, so manual intervention is necessary.

Common pitfalls

There are some very basic syntax elements that work in Oracle that might not work in PostgreSQL. This section lists some of the most important pitfalls to take into consideration. Of course, this list is not complete by any means, but it should point you in the right direction.

In Oracle, you may have come across the following statement:

```
DELETE mytable;
```

In PostgreSQL, this statement is wrong, since PostgreSQL requires that you use a FROM clause in the DELETE statement. The good news is that this kind of statement is easy to fix.

The next thing you might find is the following:

```
SELECT sysdate FROM dual;
```

PostgreSQL has neither a `sysdate` function nor a `dual` function. The `dual` function part is easy to fix as you can simply create a `VIEW` function returning one line. In Oracle, the `dual` function works as follows:

```
SQL> desc dual
Name      Null?    Type
---------------------------
DUMMY              VARCHAR2(1)
SQL> select * from dual;
D
-
X
```

In PostgreSQL, the same can be achieved by creating the following `VIEW` function:

```
CREATE VIEW dual AS SELECT 'X' AS dummy;
```

The `sysdate` function is also easy to fix. In PostgreSQL, if `SYSDATE` is being used in SQL, then we have to use `statement_timestamp()`, and if `SYSDATE` is used in PL/PGSQL, then we have to use `clock_timestamp()`.

That is, `SYSDATE` behaves like PostgreSQL's `STABLE` function when we use this in an SQL statement.

Another common problem is the lack of data types, such as `VARCHAR2`, as well as the lack of special functions that are only supported by Oracle. A good way to get around these issues is to install the `orafce` extension, which provides most of the information that's typically needed, including the most commonly used functions. It certainly makes sense to check out `https://github.com/orafce/orafce` to learn more about the `orafce` extension. It has been around for many years and is a solid piece of software.

A recent study has shown that the `orafce` extension helps ensure that 73% of all Oracle SQLs can be executed on PostgreSQL without modifications if the `orafce` extension is available (done by NTT).

One of the most common pitfalls is the way Oracle handles outer joins. Consider the following example:

```
SELECT employee_id, manager_id
FROM   employees
WHERE  employees.manager_id(+) = employees.employee_id;
```

This kind of syntax is not provided by PostgreSQL and never will be. Therefore, the join has to be rewritten as a proper outer join. The + sign is highly Oracle-specific and has to be removed.

In this chapter, you have already learned some valuable lessons about how to move from databases such as Oracle to PostgreSQL. The reason they are valuable is that Oracle might be expensive and a bit cumbersome from time to time. The same applies to Informix. However, both Informix and Oracle have one important thing in common: the CHECK constraints are honored properly, and data types are handled properly. In general, we can safely assume that the data in those commercial systems is largely correct and doesn't violate the most basic rules of data integrity and common sense.

Summary

In this chapter, we understood how to migrate SQL statements to PostgreSQL and learned how to move a basic database from another system to PostgreSQL. Migration is an important topic, and more and more people are adopting PostgreSQL every day.

PostgreSQL 17 has many new features, such as incremental base backups and a lot more. In the future, we will see many more developments in all the areas of PostgreSQL, especially ones that allow users to scale out more and run queries even faster. We are yet to see what the future has in store for us. The technology is constantly evolving and we will enjoy many more features as well as performance improvements in the next releases.

Index

H

hash indexes 78
hash joins 187
hash partitioning 226, 227
Hibernate statements
  treating 410
host-based access control 293
hypothetical aggregates 112
  writing 138, 139

I

idle-in-transaction queries 409
idle queries 409
incremental backups
  adding 356
  backup, running 355
  backups, combining 356-358
  configuring for 355
  using 354, 355
incremental base backups
  handling 15, 16
indexes 50, 163
  additional indexes, adding 85, 86
  Block Range Indexes (BRINs) 84, 85
  combined indexes 66, 67
  de-duplication 61
  deploying 55, 56
  functional indexes 68
  Generalized Inverted (GIN) indexes 81, 82
  GiST indexes 78-81
  hash indexes 78
  multiple indexes, using 57, 58
  space consumption, reducing 68, 69
  SP-GiST indexes 83
  using 59-61

index-only scans
  using 65, 66
inherited structures
  modifying 220
inherited tables
  creating 216, 217
instance-level permissions 293
instance-level security
  handling 304, 305
Internet Protocol (IP) addresses 294
I/O
  checking for 415-417
  statistics, inspecting 164-166

J

join_collapse_limit variable 210
join pruning 197, 198
joins 187, 207
  hash joins 187
  merge joins 188
  nested loops 187
  outer joins, processing 209
  working 207-209
JSON 143
JSONB 143
JSON documents
  accessing 146-149
  creating 144
  displaying 144, 145
  turning, into rows 145, 146
JSONPath 149, 150
just-in-time (JIT) compilation 240
  configuration options 241
  queries, running 242-244

packtpub.com

Subscribe to our online digital library for full access to over 7,000 books and videos, as well as industry leading tools to help you plan your personal development and advance your career. For more information, please visit our website.

Why subscribe?

- Spend less time learning and more time coding with practical eBooks and Videos from over 4,000 industry professionals

- Improve your learning with Skill Plans built especially for you

- Get a free eBook or video every month

- Fully searchable for easy access to vital information

- Copy and paste, print, and bookmark content

Did you know that Packt offers eBook versions of every book published, with PDF and ePub files available? You can upgrade to the eBook version at packtpub.com and as a print book customer, you are entitled to a discount on the eBook copy. Get in touch with us at customercare@packtpub.com for more details.

At www.packtpub.com, you can also read a collection of free technical articles, sign up for a range of free newsletters, and receive exclusive discounts and offers on Packt books and eBooks.

Other Books You May Enjoy

If you enjoyed this book, you may be interested in these other books by Packt:

Database Design and Modeling with PostgreSQL and MySQL

Alkin Tezuysal, Ibrar Ahmed

ISBN: 978-1-80323-347-5

- Design a schema, create ERDs, and apply normalization techniques
- Gain knowledge of installing, configuring, and managing MySQL and PostgreSQL
- Explore topics such as denormalization, index optimization, transaction management, and concurrency control
- Scale databases with sharding, replication, and load balancing, as well as implement backup and recovery strategies
- Integrate databases with web apps, use SQL, and implement best practices
- Explore emerging trends, including NoSQL databases and cloud databases, while understanding the impact of AI and ML

Learn T-SQL Querying - Second Edition

Pedro Lopes, Pam Lahoud

ISBN: 978-1-83763-899-4

- Identify opportunities to write well-formed T-SQL statements

- Familiarize yourself with the Cardinality Estimator for query optimization

- Create efficient indexes for your existing workloads

- Implement best practices for T-SQL querying

- Explore Query Execution Dynamic Management Views

- Utilize the latest performance optimization features in SQL Server 2017, 2019, and 2022

- Safeguard query performance during upgrades to newer versions of SQL Server

Packt is searching for authors like you

If you're interested in becoming an author for Packt, please visit `authors.packtpub.com` and apply today. We have worked with thousands of developers and tech professionals, just like you, to help them share their insight with the global tech community. You can make a general application, apply for a specific hot topic that we are recruiting an author for, or submit your own idea.

Share Your Thoughts

Now you've finished *Mastering PostgreSQL 17 – Sixth Edition*, we'd love to hear your thoughts! Scan the QR code below to go straight to the Amazon review page for this book and share your feedback or leave a review on the site that you purchased it from.

`https://packt.link/r/1-836-20597-X`

Your review is important to us and the tech community and will help us make sure we're delivering excellent quality content.

Download a free PDF copy of this book

Thanks for purchasing this book!

Do you like to read on the go but are unable to carry your print books everywhere?

Is your eBook purchase not compatible with the device of your choice?

Don't worry, now with every Packt book you get a DRM-free PDF version of that book at no cost.

Read anywhere, any place, on any device. Search, copy, and paste code from your favorite technical books directly into your application.

The perks don't stop there, you can get exclusive access to discounts, newsletters, and great free content in your inbox daily

Follow these simple steps to get the benefits:

1. Scan the QR code or visit the link below

https://packt.link/free-ebook/978-1-83620-597-5

2. Submit your proof of purchase
3. That's it! We'll send your free PDF and other benefits to your email directly

www.ingramcontent.com/pod-product-compliance
Lightning Source LLC
LaVergne TN
LVHW080110070326
832902LV00015B/2508